Yozakura Quartet

3

Suzuhito Yasuda

Translated by Satsuki Yamashita
Adapted by Nunzio DeFilippis and Christina Weir
Lettered by North Market Street Graphics

Ballantine Books · New York

A Del Rey Manga/Kodansha Trade Paperback Original

Yozakura Quartet volume 3 copyright © 2007 by Suzuhito Yasuda
English translation copyright © 2008 by Suzuhito Yasuda

Published in the United States by Del Rey, an imprint of The Random House Publishing Group, a division of Random House, Inc., New York.

DEL REY is a registered trademark and the Del Rey colophon is a trademark of Random House, Inc.

Publication rights arranged through Kodansha Ltd.

First published in Japan in 2007 by Kodansha Ltd., Tokyo.

ISBN 978-0-345-50679-5

Printed in the United States of America

www.delreymanga.com

9 8 7 6 5 4 3 2 1

Translator: Satsuki Yamashita
Adapters: Nunzio DeFilippis and Christina Weir
Lettering and retouch: North Market Street Graphics

Contents

A Note from the Author

I usually try to include an eating or sleeping scene in each chapter.
This is so I'll remember that these kids are still growing…
Actually, I just like seeing people eat and sleep.

Suzuhito Yasuda

Honorifics Explained

Throughout the Del Rey Manga books, you will find Japanese honorifics left intact in the translations. For those not familiar with how the Japanese use honorifics and, more important, how they differ from American honorifics, we present this brief overview.

Politeness has always been a critical facet of Japanese culture. Ever since the feudal era, when Japan was a highly stratified society, use of honorifics—which can be defined as polite speech that indicates relationship or status—has played an essential role in the Japanese language. When addressing someone in Japanese, an honorific usually takes the form of a suffix attached to one's name (example: "Asuna-san"), is used as a title at the end of one's name, or appears in place of the name itself (example: "Negi-sensei," or simply "Sensei!").

Honorifics can be expressions of respect or endearment. In the context of manga and anime, honorifics give insight into the nature of the relationship between characters. Many English translations leave out these important honorifics and therefore distort the feel of the original Japanese. Because Japanese honorifics contain nuances that English honorifics lack, it is our policy at Del Rey not to translate them. Here, instead, is a guide to some of the honorifics you may encounter in Del Rey Manga.

-san: This is the most common honorific and is equivalent to Mr., Miss, Ms., or Mrs. It is the all-purpose honorific and can be used in any situation where politeness is required.

-sama: This is one level higher than "-san" and is used to confer great respect.

-dono: This comes from the word "tono," which means "lord." It is an even higher level than "-sama" and confers utmost respect.

-kun: This suffix is used at the end of boys' names to express familiarity or endearment. It is also sometimes used by men among friends, or when addressing someone younger or of a lower station.

-chan: This is used to express endearment, mostly toward girls. It is also used for little boys, pets, and even among lovers. It gives a sense of childish cuteness.

Bozu: This is an informal way to refer to a boy, similar to the English terms "kid" and "squirt."

Sempai/
Senpai: This title suggests that the addressee is one's senior in a group or organization. It is most often used in a school setting, where underclassmen refer to their upperclassmen as "sempai." It can also be used in the workplace, such as when a newer employee addresses an employee who has seniority in the company.

Kohai: This is the opposite of "sempai" and is used toward underclassmen in school or newcomers in the workplace. It connotes that the addressee is of a lower station.

Sensei: Literally meaning "one who has come before," this title is used for teachers, doctors, or masters of any profession or art.

-[blank]:   This is usually forgotten in these lists, but it is perhaps the most significant difference between Japanese and English. The lack of honorific means that the speaker has permission to address the person in a very intimate way. Usually, only family, spouses, or very close friends have this kind of permission. Known as *yobisute*, it can be gratifying when someone who has earned the intimacy starts to call one by one's name without an honorific. But when that intimacy hasn't been earned, it can be very insulting.

Yozakura
Quartet 3

Suzuhito Yasuda

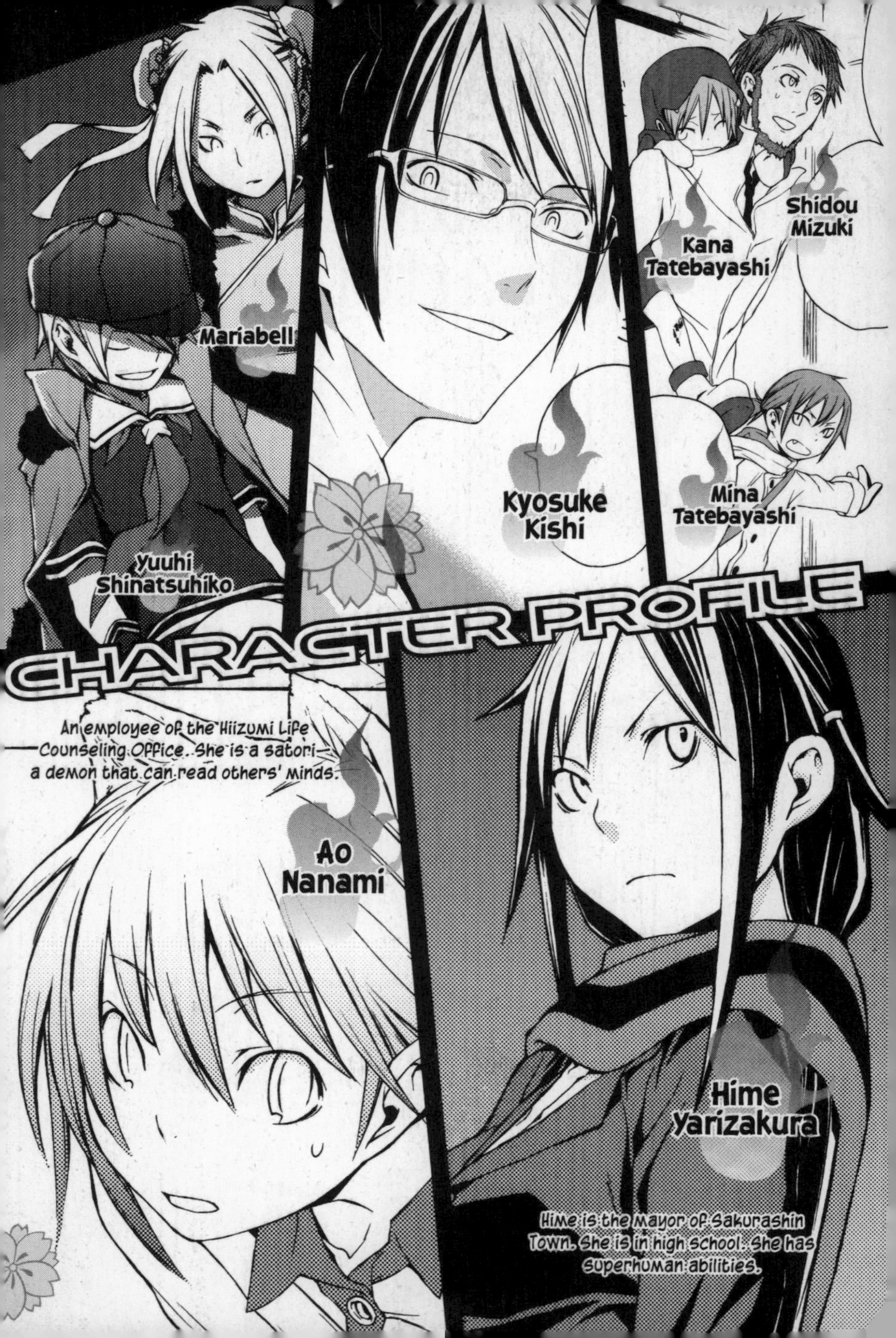
Shidou Mizuki
Kana Tatebayashi
Mina Tatebayashi
Kyosuke Kishi
Mariabell
Yuuhi Shinatsuhiko
CHARACTER PROFILE
Hime Yarizakura
Hime is the mayor of Sakurashin Town. She is in high school. She has superhuman abilities.
Ao Nanami
An employee of the Hiizumi Life Counseling Office. She is a satori—a demon that can read others' minds.

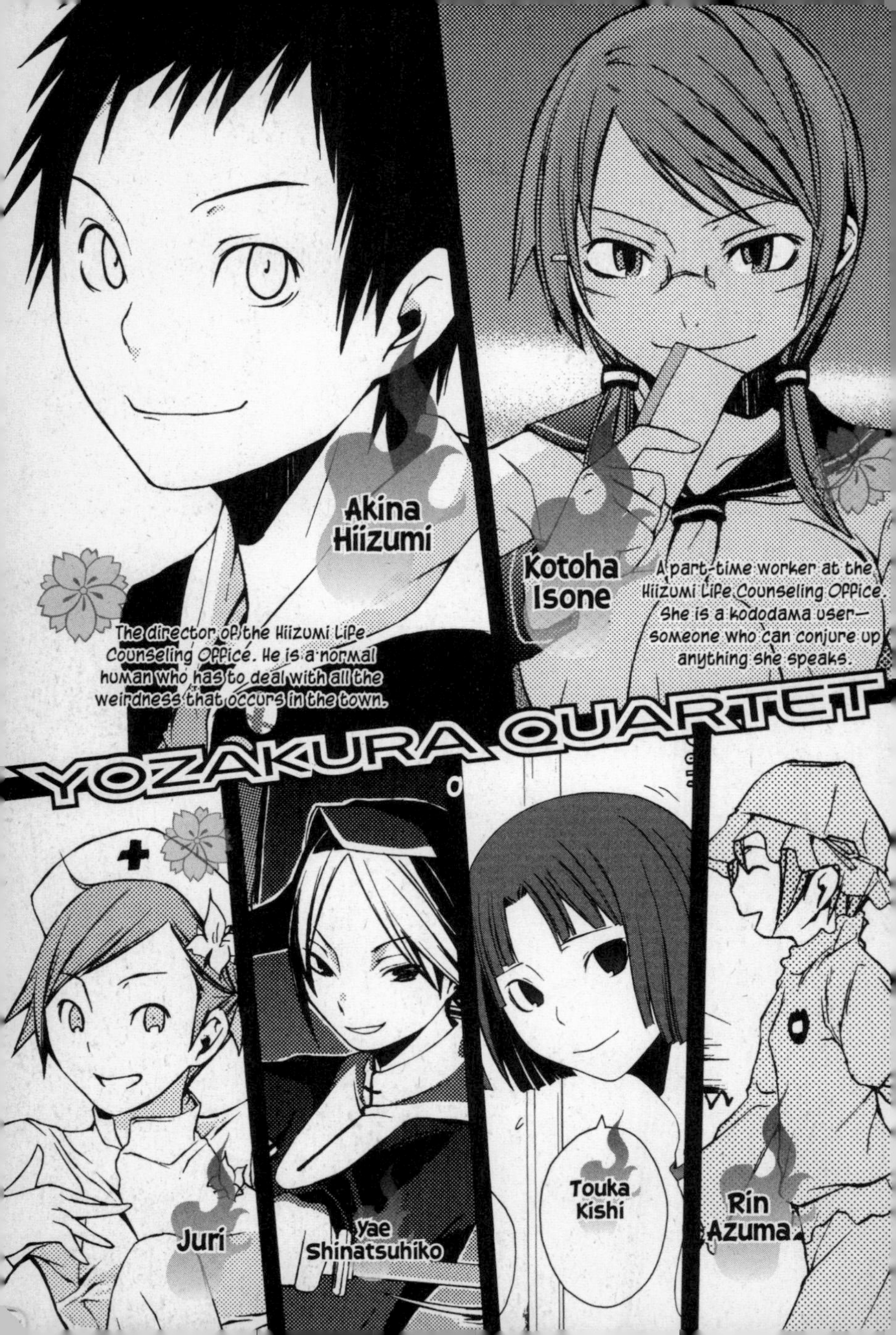
Kotoha
Isone
A part-time worker at the Hiizumi Life Counseling Office. She is a kododama user—someone who can conjure up anything she speaks.
Akina
Hiizumi
The director of the Hiizumi Life Counseling Office. He is a normal human who has to deal with all the weirdness that occurs in the town.
YOZAKURA QUARTET
Rin
Azuma
Touka
Kishi
Yae
Shinatsuhiko
Juri

Yozakura Quartet Contents

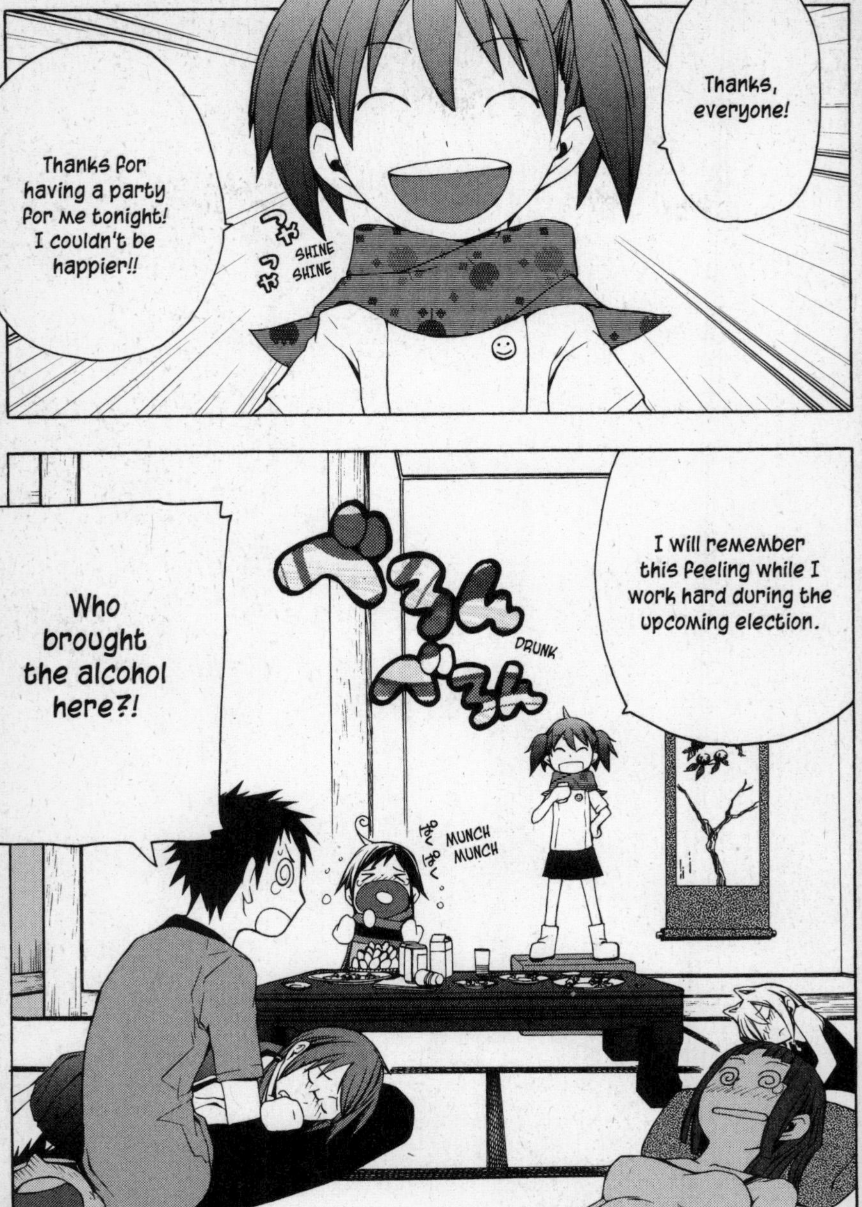

Thanks, everyone!
Thanks for having a party for me tonight! I couldn't be happier!!
SHINE SHINE
I will remember this feeling while I work hard during the upcoming election.
DRUNK
MUNCH MUNCH
Who brought the alcohol here?!

12th Night: Thorny Road (Part 2)

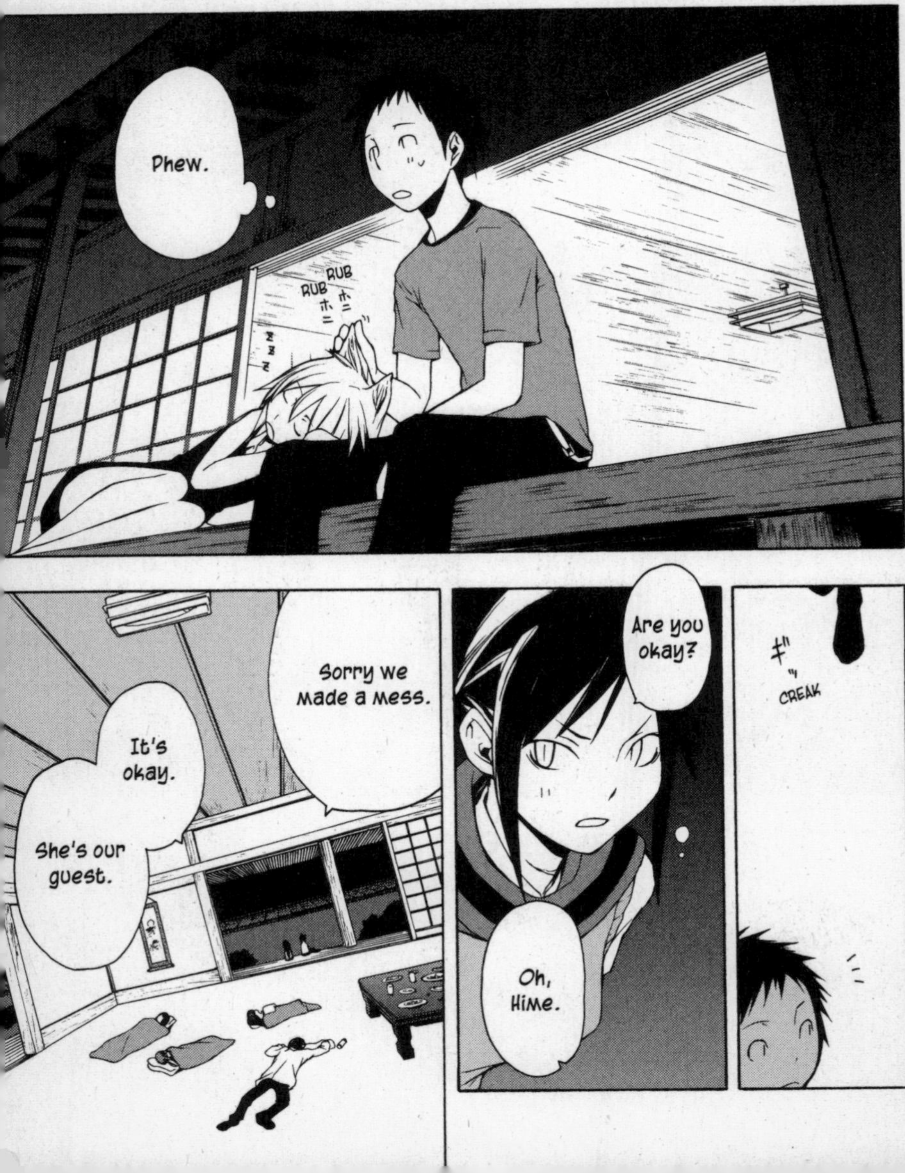
Phew.
RUB
RUB
ホニ
ホニ
Z Z Z
ギ
CREAK
Are you okay?
Oh, Hime.
Sorry we made a mess.
It's okay.
She's our guest.

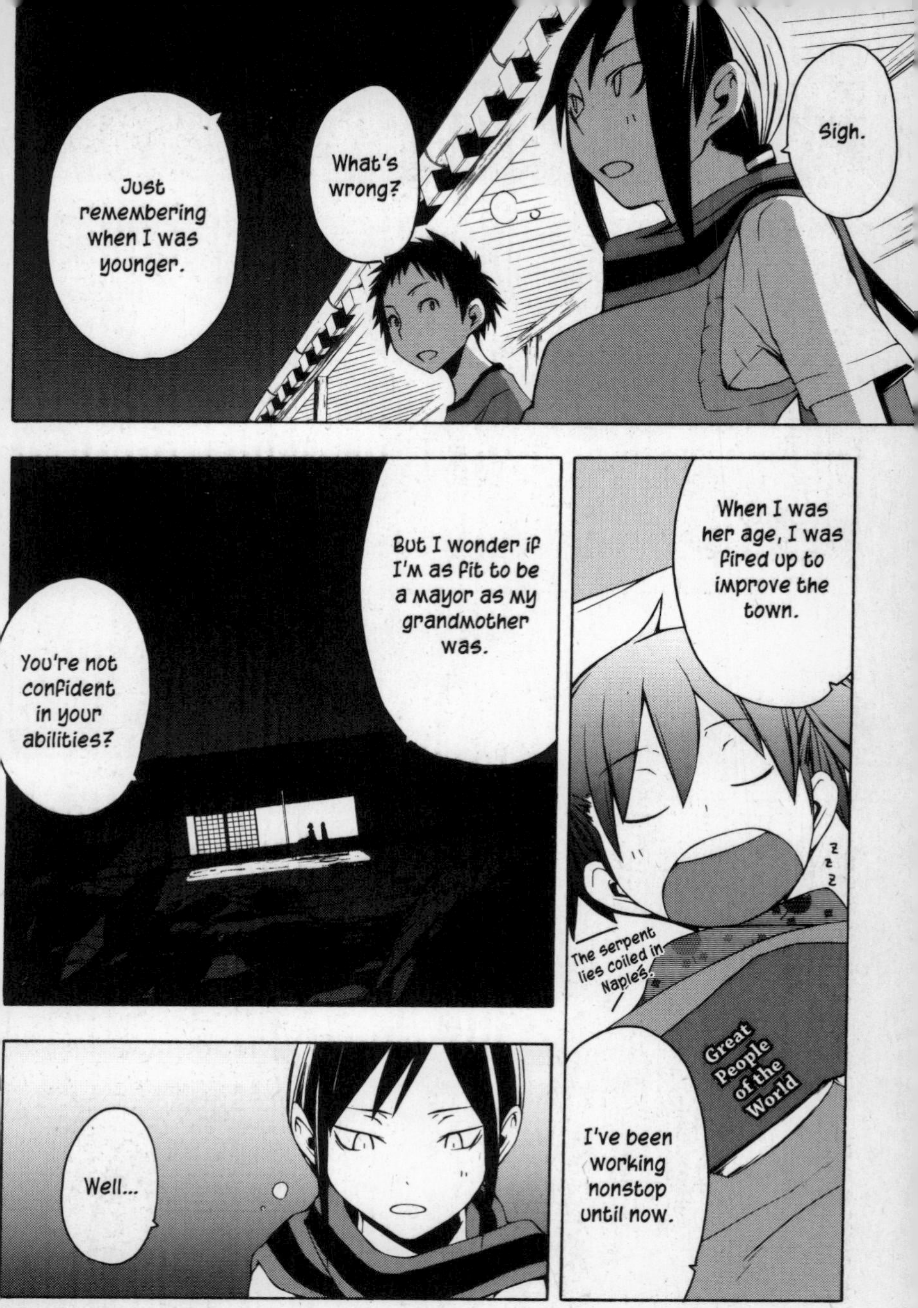
Sigh.
What's wrong?
Just remembering when I was younger.
When I was her age, I was fired up to improve the town.
z z z
The serpent lies coiled in Naples.
Great People of the World
I've been working nonstop until now.
But I wonder if I'm as fit to be a mayor as my grandmother was.
You're not confident in your abilities?
Well...

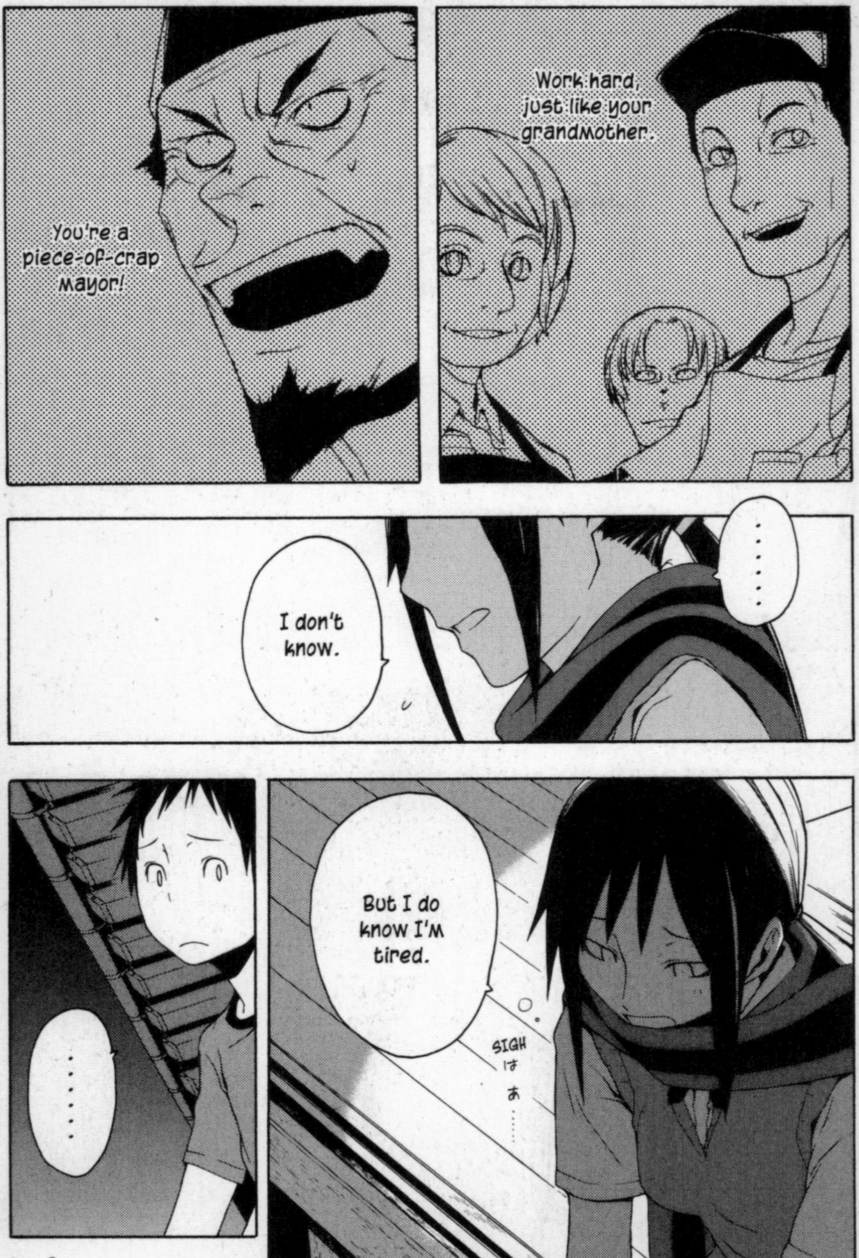
Work hard, just like your grandmother.
You're a piece-of-crap mayor!
......
I don't know.
But I do know I'm tired.
SIGH はあ……
......

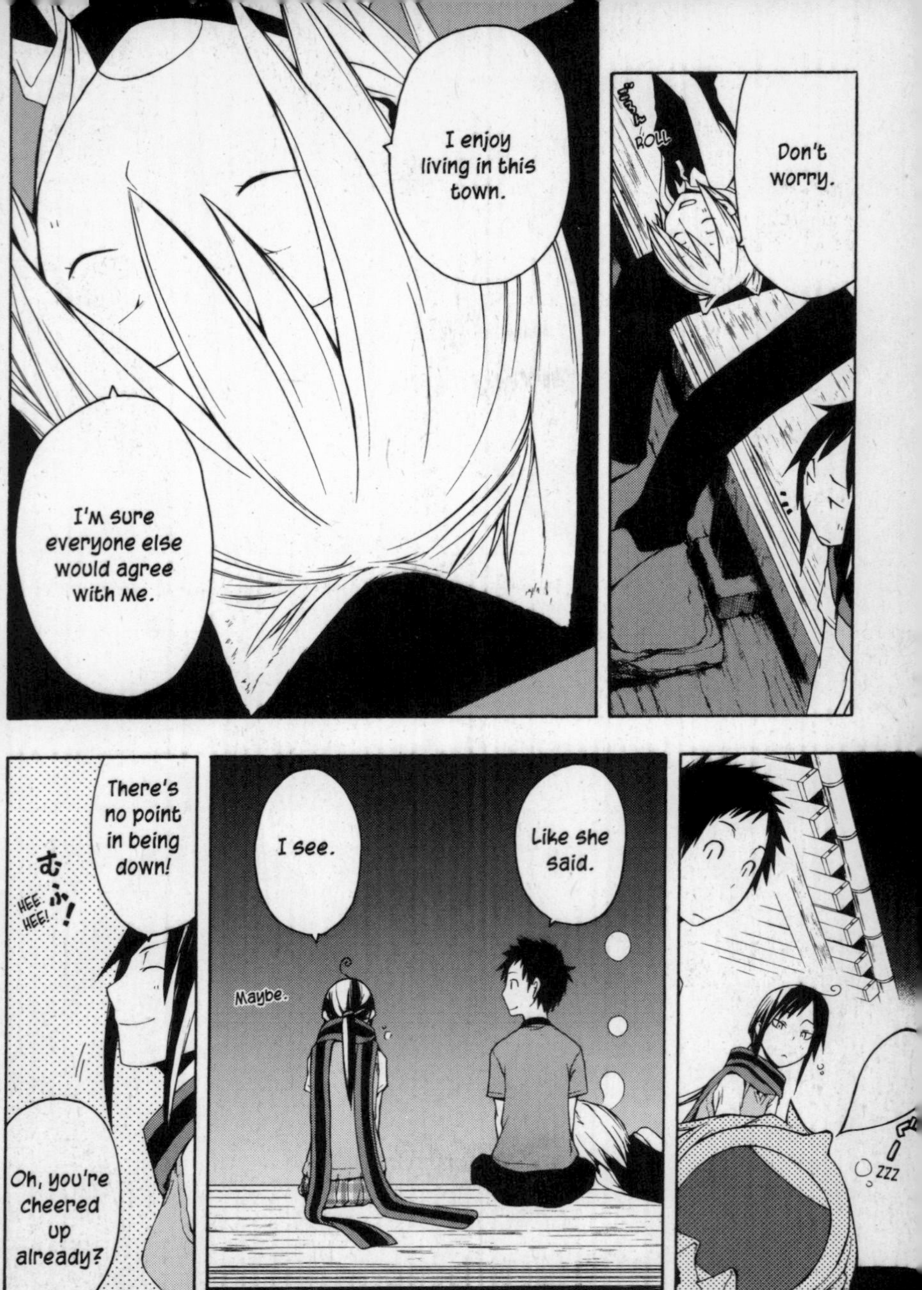

Don't worry.
ROLL
I enjoy living in this town.
I'm sure everyone else would agree with me.
ZZZ
Like she said.
I see.
Maybe.
There's no point in being down!
むふ!
HEE HEE!
Oh, you're cheered up already?

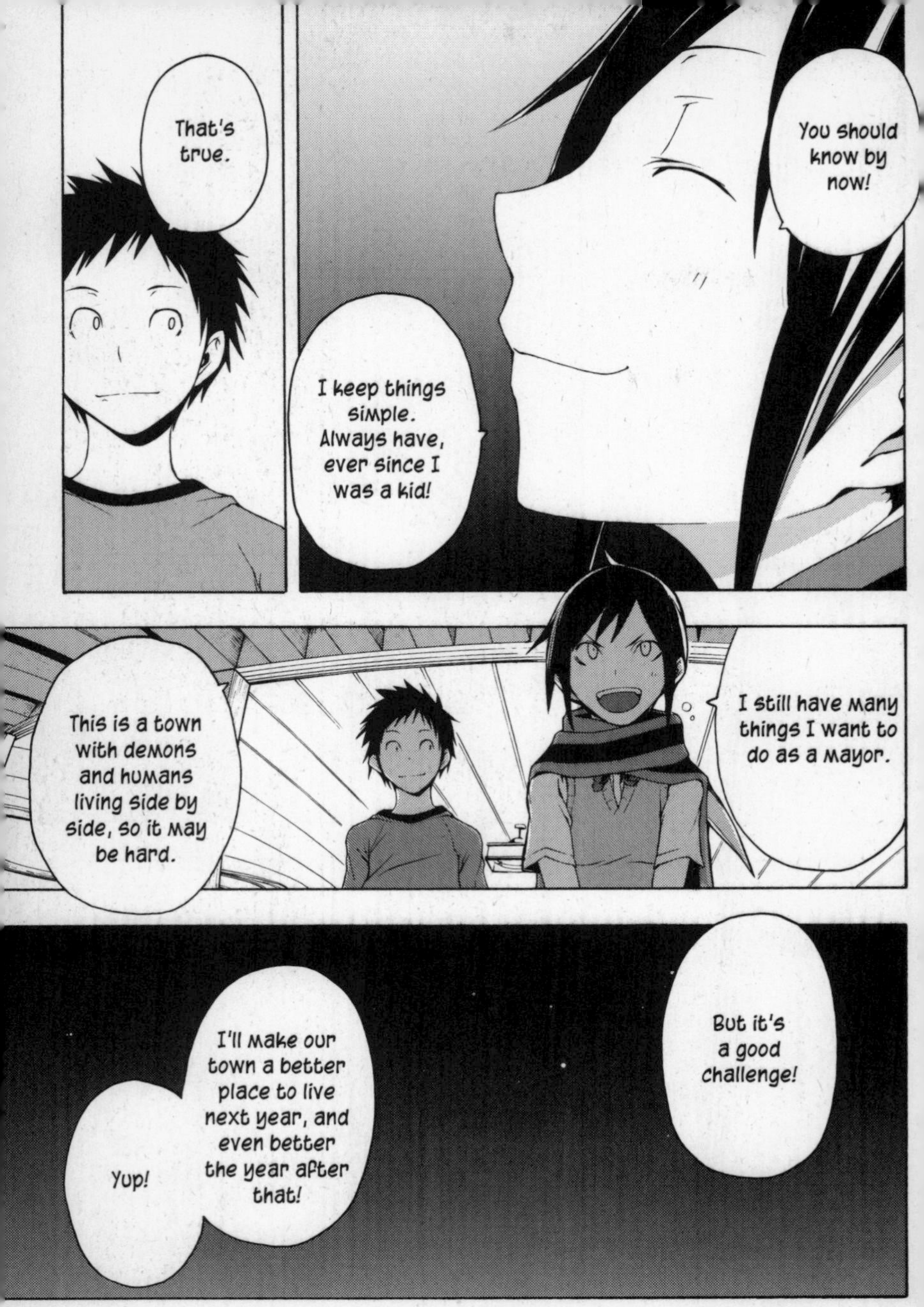
You should know by now!
I keep things simple. Always have, ever since I was a kid!
That's true.
I still have many things I want to do as a mayor.
This is a town with demons and humans living side by side, so it may be hard.
But it's a good challenge!
I'll make our town a better place to live next year, and even better the year after that!
Yup!

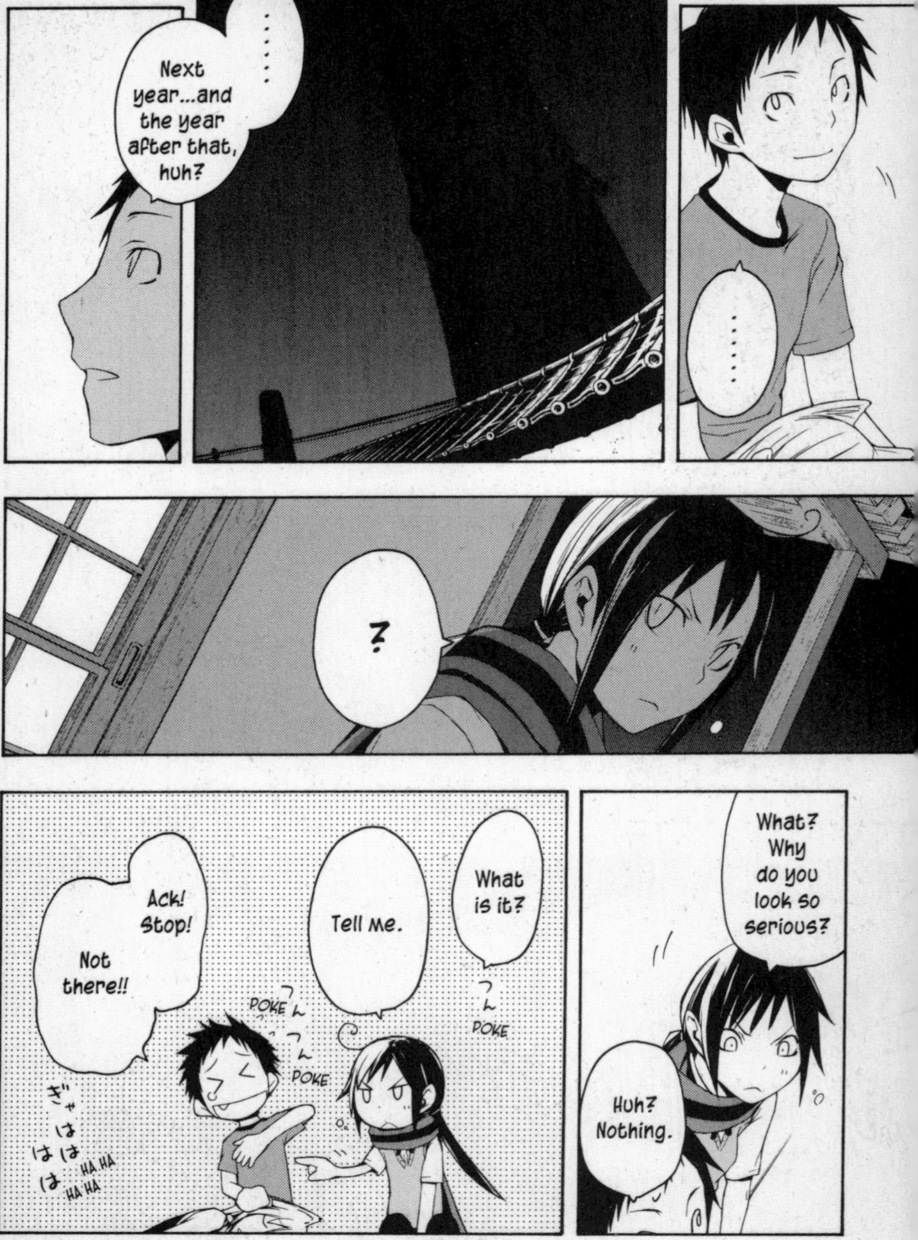
......
......
Next year...and the year after that, huh?
?
What? Why do you look so serious?
Huh? Nothing.
What is it?
POKE
Tell me.
POKE
POKE
Ack! Stop!
Not there!!
ぎゃははははは
HA HA HA HA

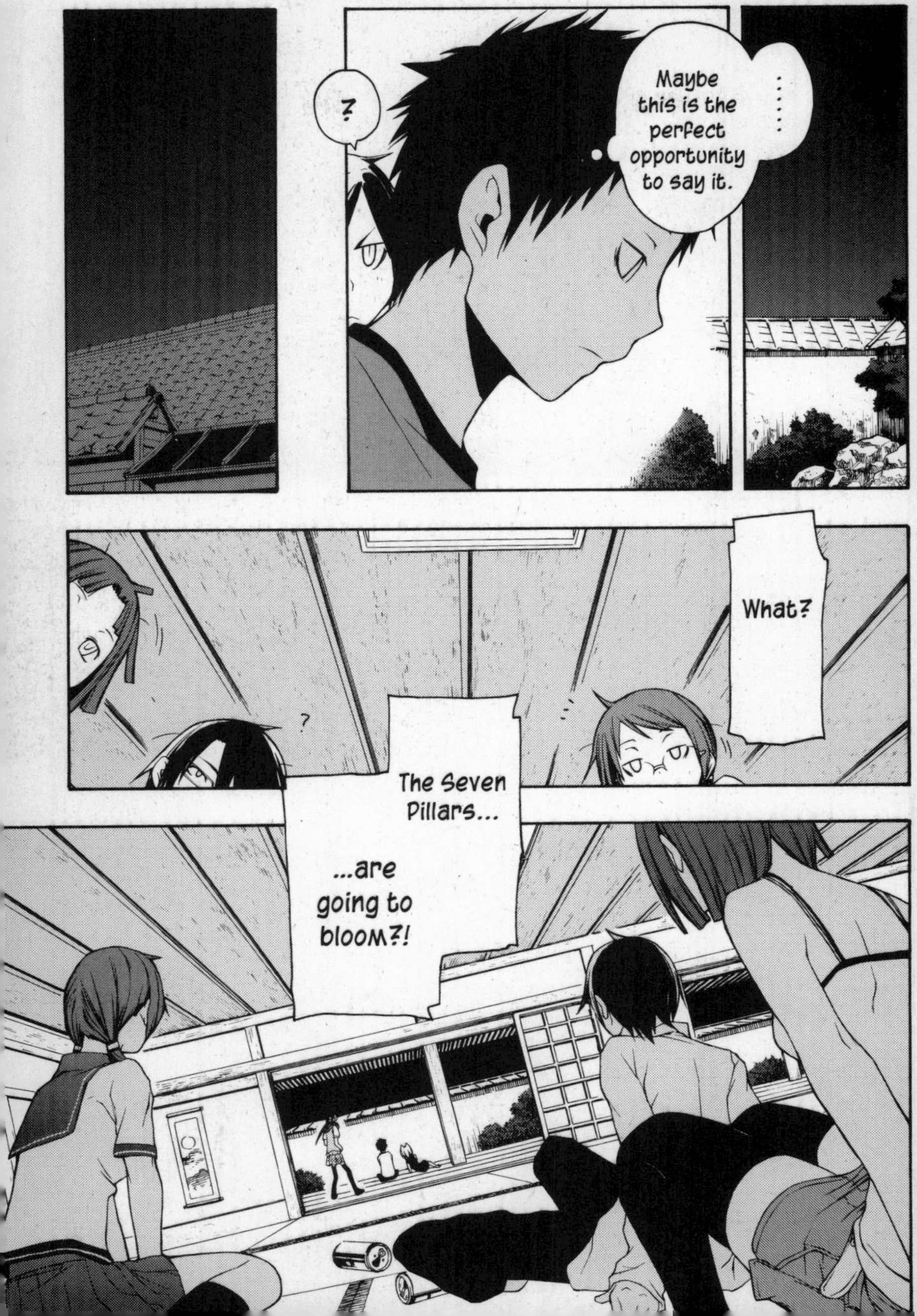
......
Maybe this is the perfect opportunity to say it.
?
What?!
?
The Seven Pillars...
...are going to bloom?!

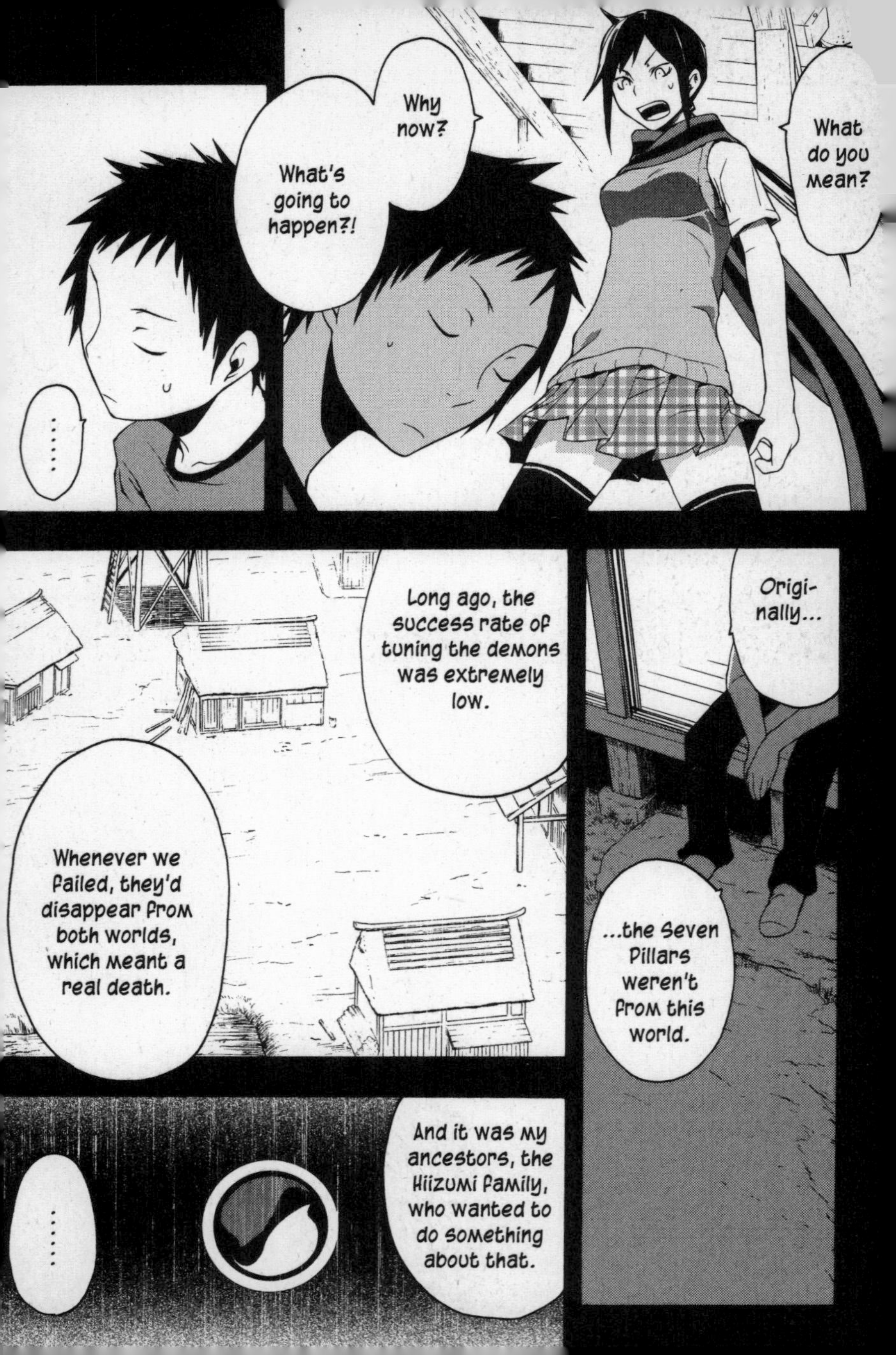
What do you mean?
Why now?
What's going to happen?!
......
Origi-nally...
...the Seven Pillars weren't from this world.
Long ago, the success rate of tuning the demons was extremely low.
Whenever we failed, they'd disappear from both worlds, which meant a real death.
And it was my ancestors, the Hiizumi family, who wanted to do something about that.
......

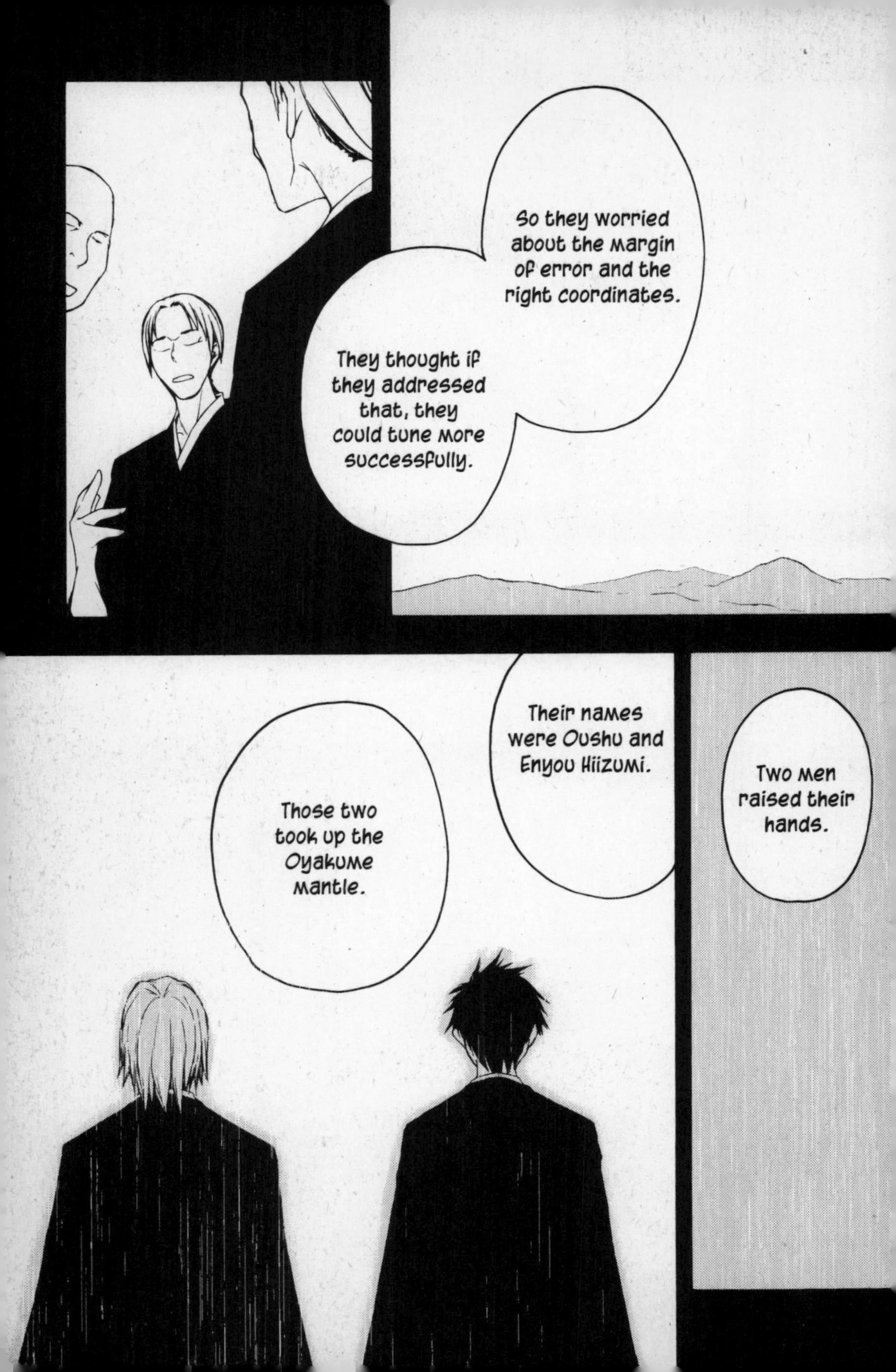
So they worried about the margin of error and the right coordinates.
They thought if they addressed that, they could tune more successfully.
Two men raised their hands.
Their names were Oushu and Enyou Hiizumi.
Those two took up the Oyakume mantle.

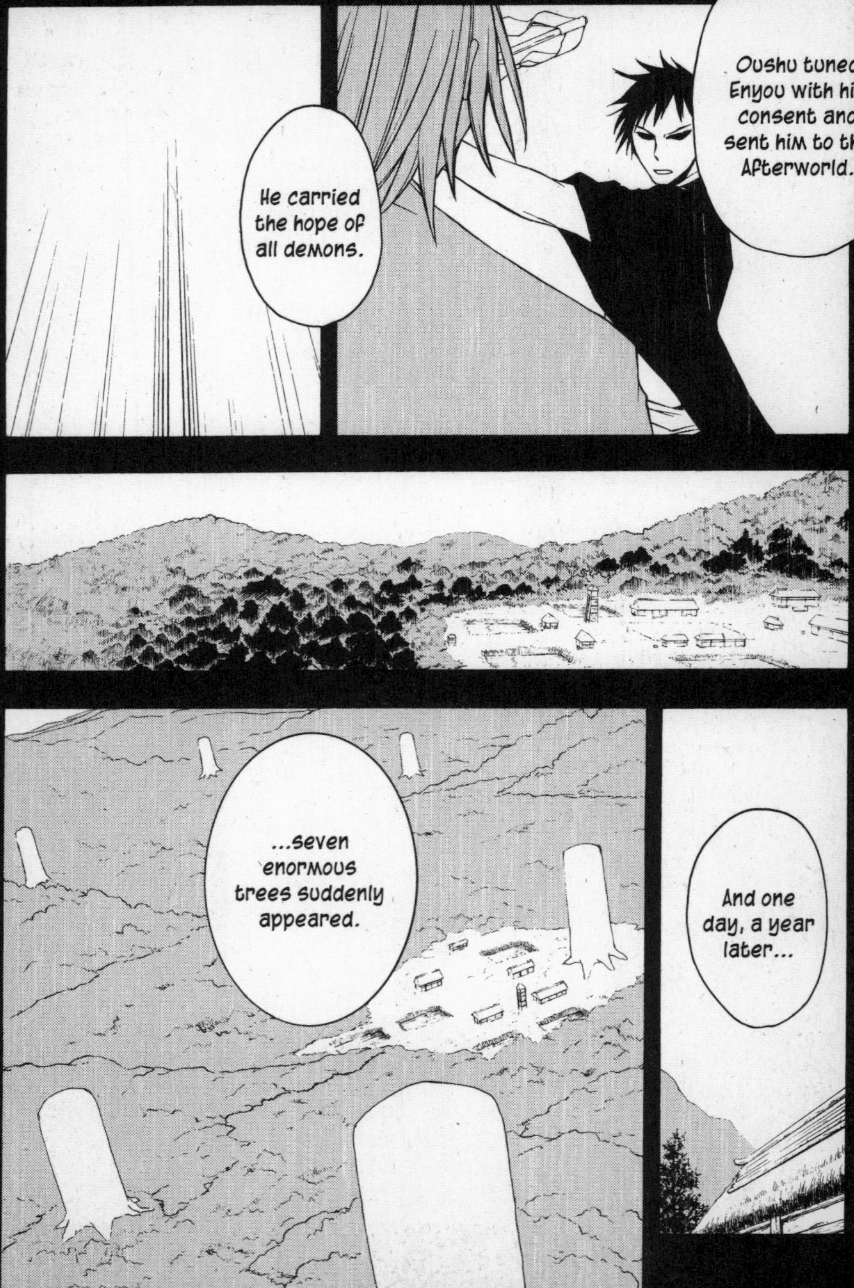
Oushu tuned Enyou with his consent and sent him to the Afterworld.
He carried the hope of all demons.
And one day, a year later...
...seven enormous trees suddenly appeared.

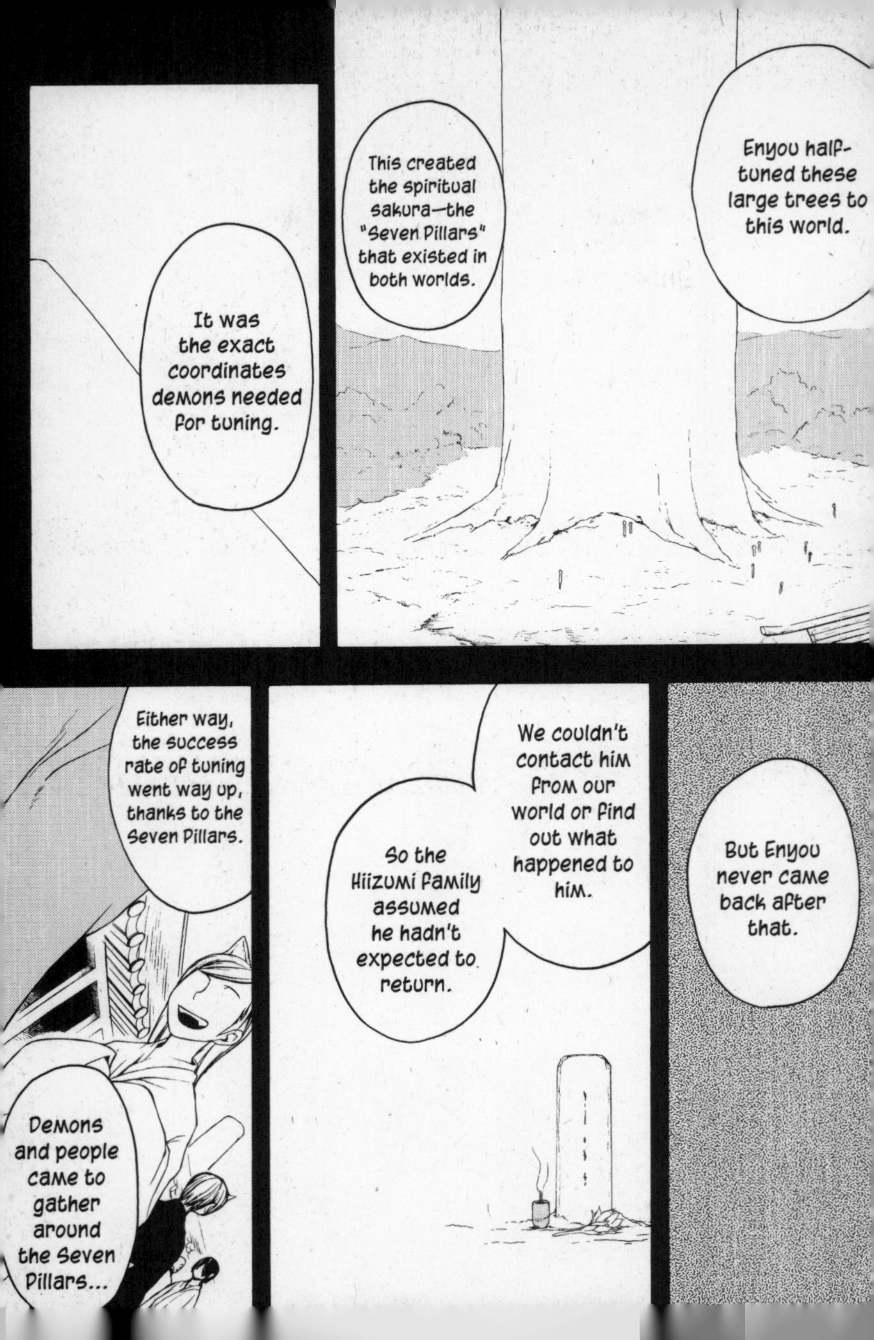
Enyou half-tuned these large trees to this world.
This created the spiritual sakura—the "Seven Pillars" that existed in both worlds.
It was the exact coordinates demons needed for tuning.
But Enyou never came back after that.
We couldn't contact him from our world or find out what happened to him.
So the Hiizumi family assumed he hadn't expected to return.
Either way, the success rate of tuning went way up, thanks to the Seven Pillars.
Demons and people came to gather around the Seven Pillars...

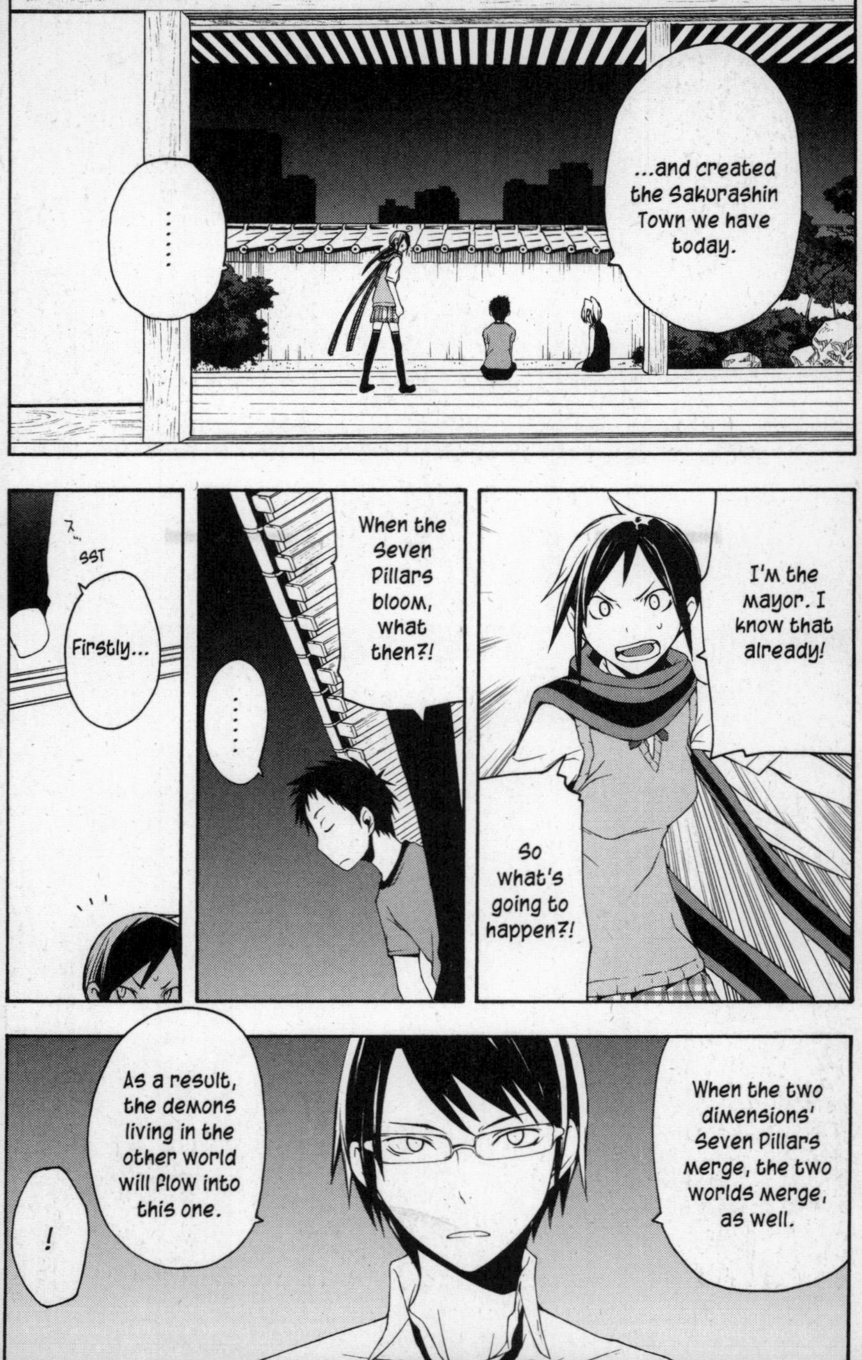
...and created the Sakurashin Town we have today.
......
I'm the mayor. I know that already!
So what's going to happen?!
When the Seven Pillars bloom, what then?!
......
SST
Firstly...
When the two dimensions' Seven Pillars merge, the two worlds merge, as well.
As a result, the demons living in the other world will flow into this one.
!

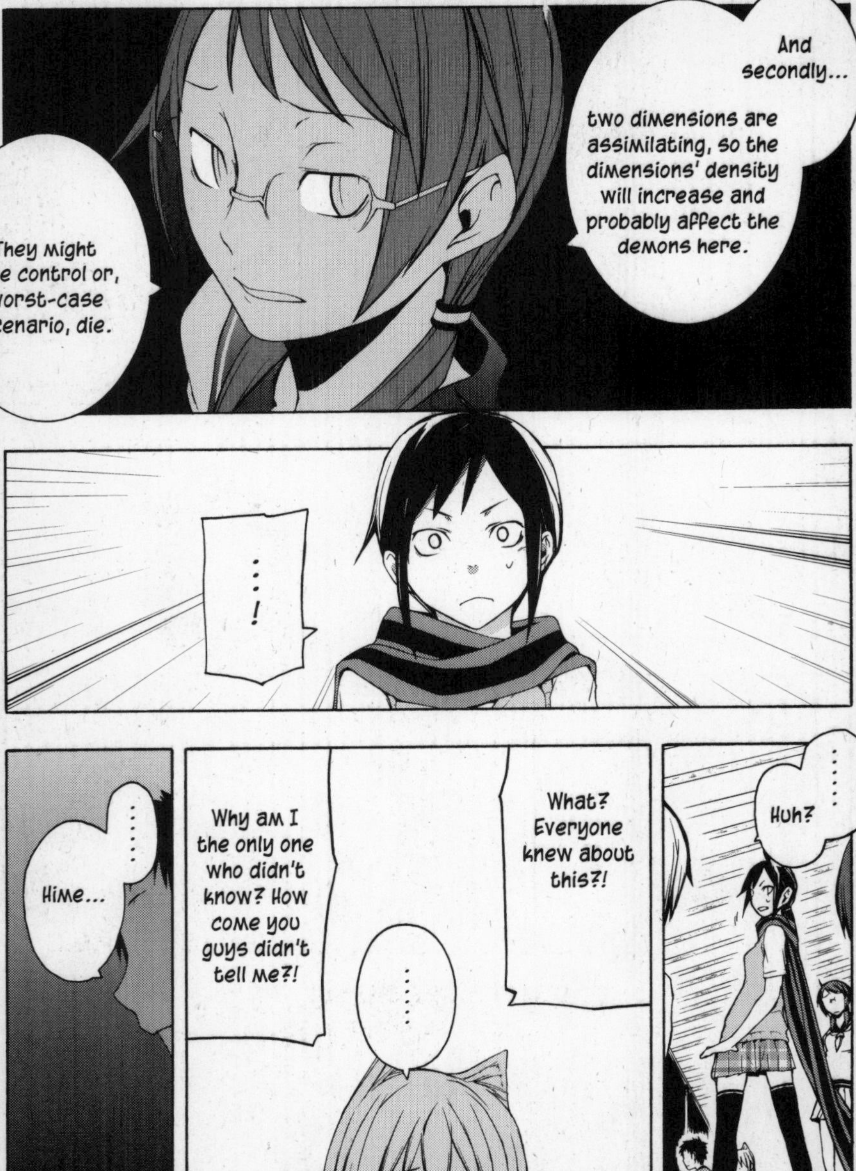

And secondly...
two dimensions are assimilating, so the dimensions' density will increase and probably affect the demons here.
They might lose control or, worst-case scenario, die.
...!
......
Huh?
What? Everyone knew about this?!
Why am I the only one who didn't know? How come you guys didn't tell me?!
......
......
Hime...

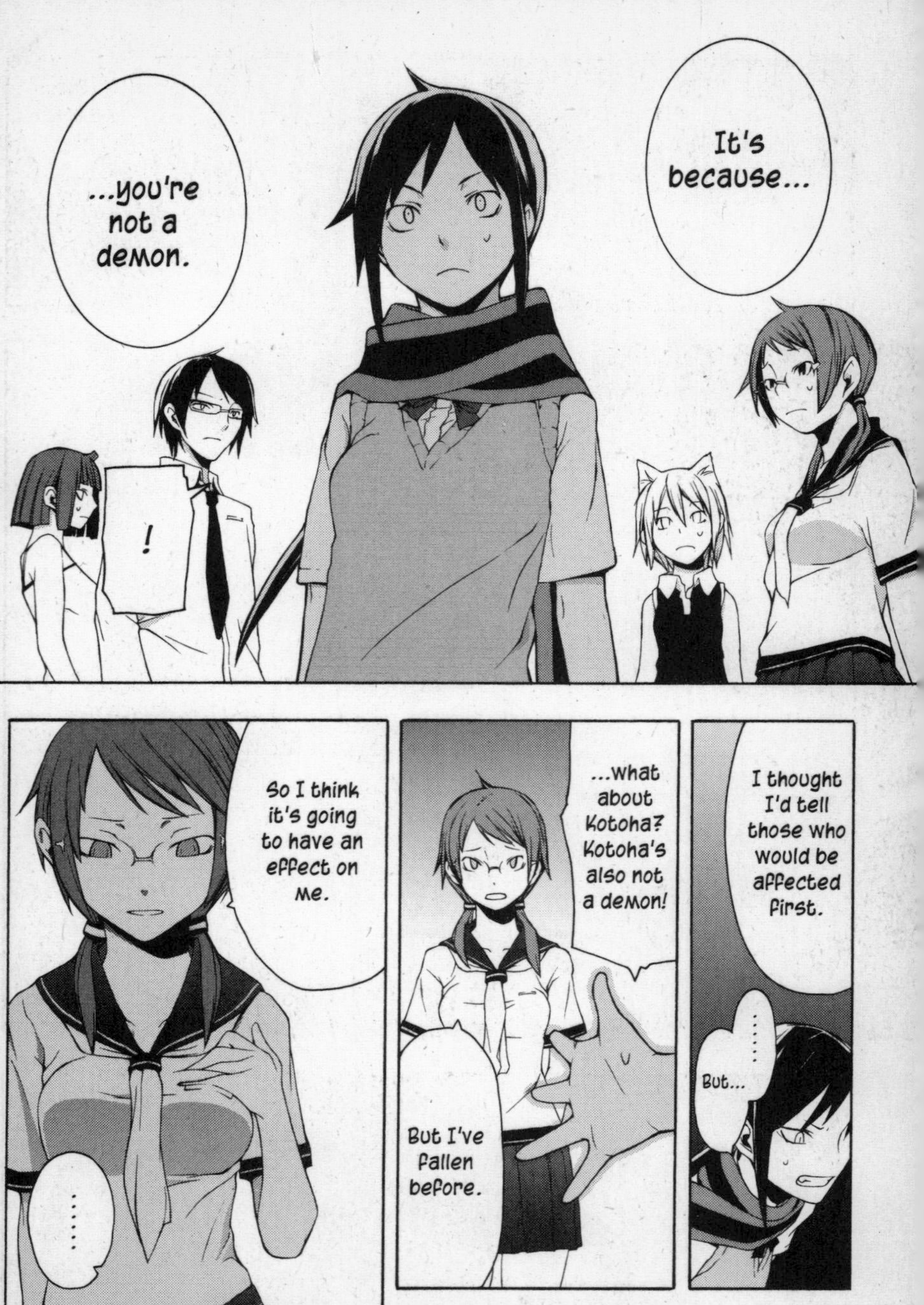
It's because...
...you're not a demon.
!
I thought I'd tell those who would be affected first.
......
But...
...what about Kotoha? Kotoha's also not a demon!
But I've fallen before.
So I think it's going to have an effect on me.
......

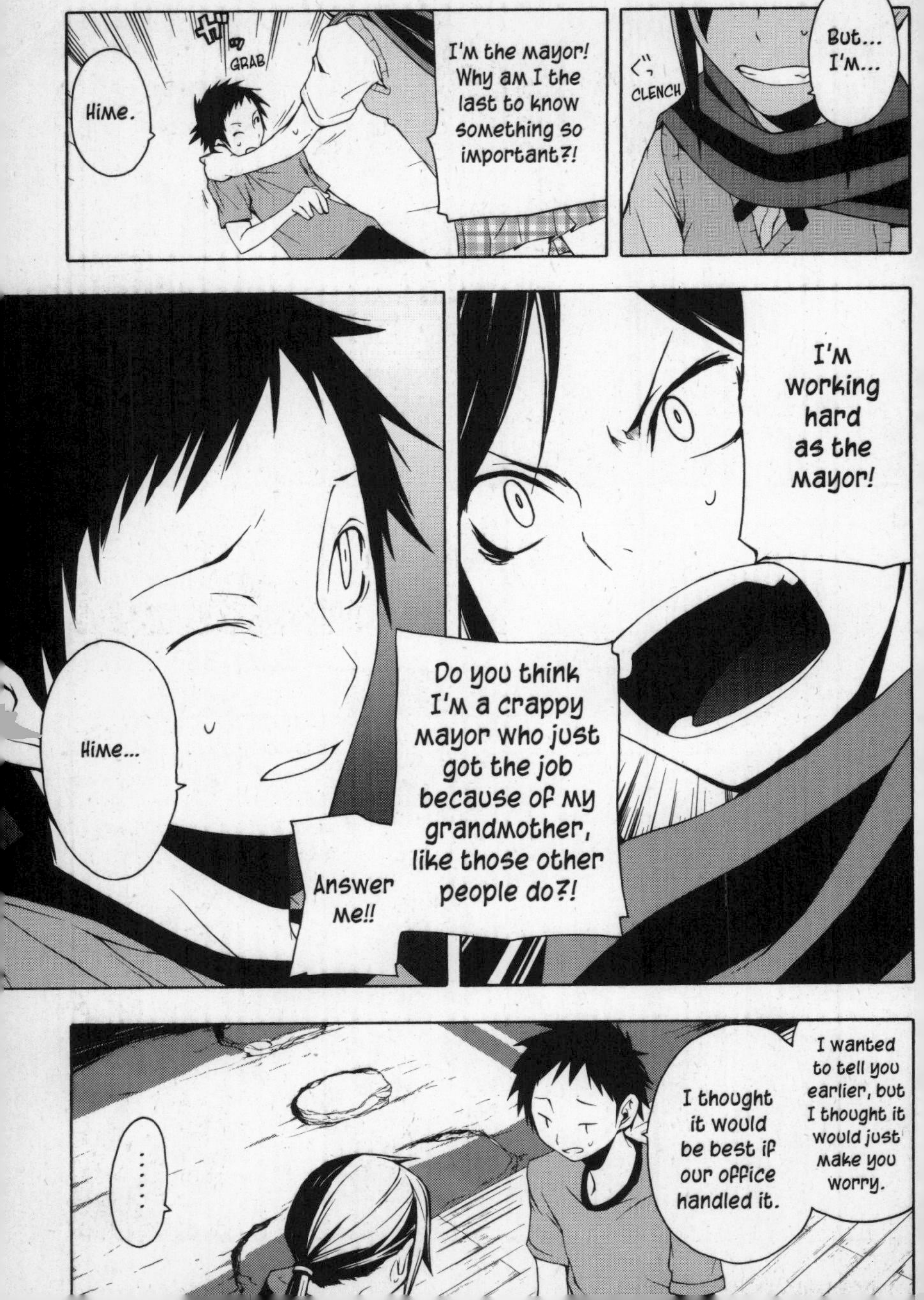
But... I'm...
CLENCH
I'm the mayor! Why am I the last to know something so important?!
GRAB
Hime.
I'm working hard as the mayor!
Do you think I'm a crappy mayor who just got the job because of my grandmother, like those other people do?!
Answer me!!
Hime...
I wanted to tell you earlier, but I thought it would just make you worry.
I thought it would be best if our office handled it.
......

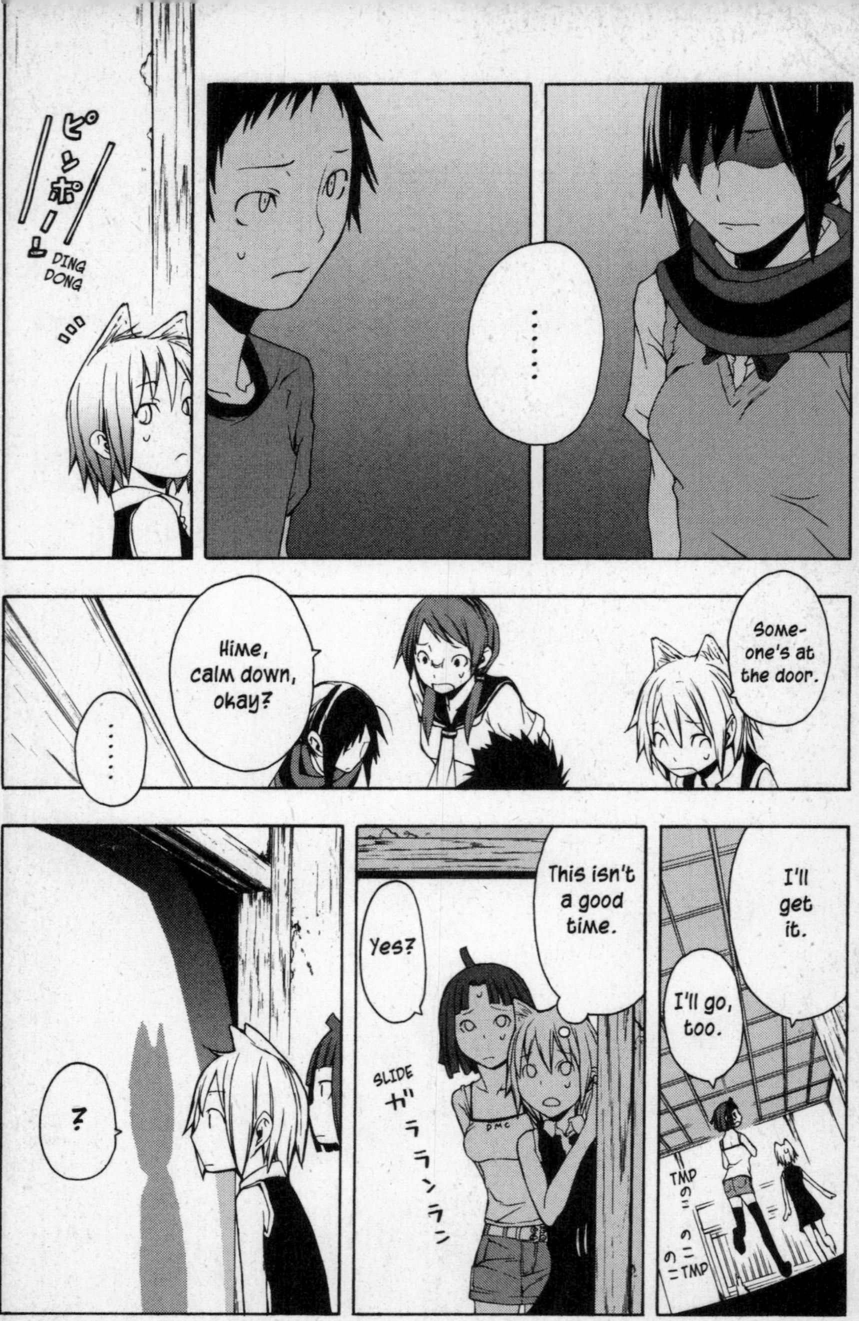
......
ピンポーン
DING DONG
...
Some-one's at the door.
Hime, calm down, okay?
......
I'll get it.
I'll go, too.
TMP
のニ
のニ
TMP
This isn't a good time.
Yes?
SLIDE
ガラランラン
?

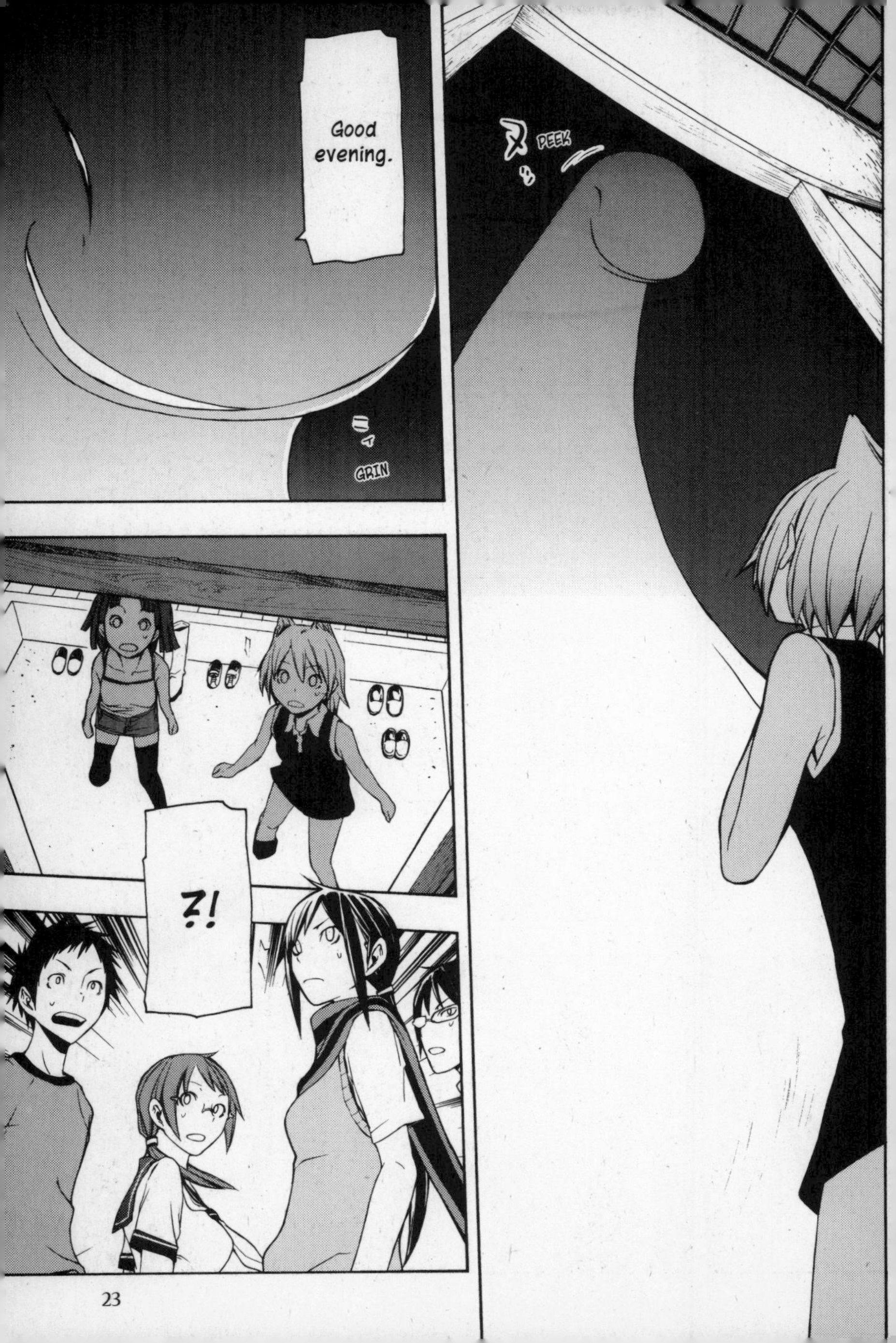
PEEK
Good evening.
GRIN
?!

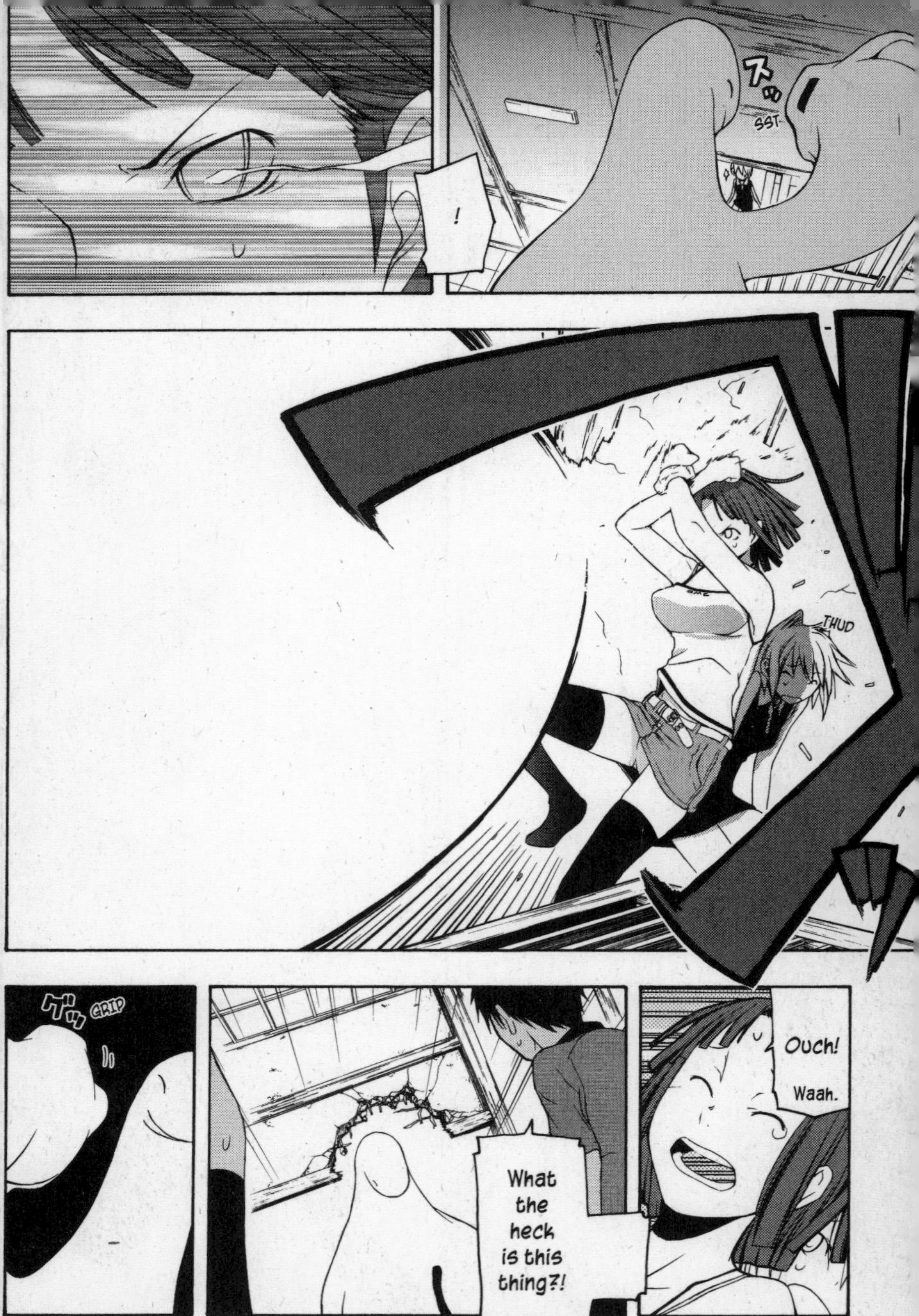
SST
!
THUD
Ouch!
Waah.
What the heck is this thing?!
GRIP

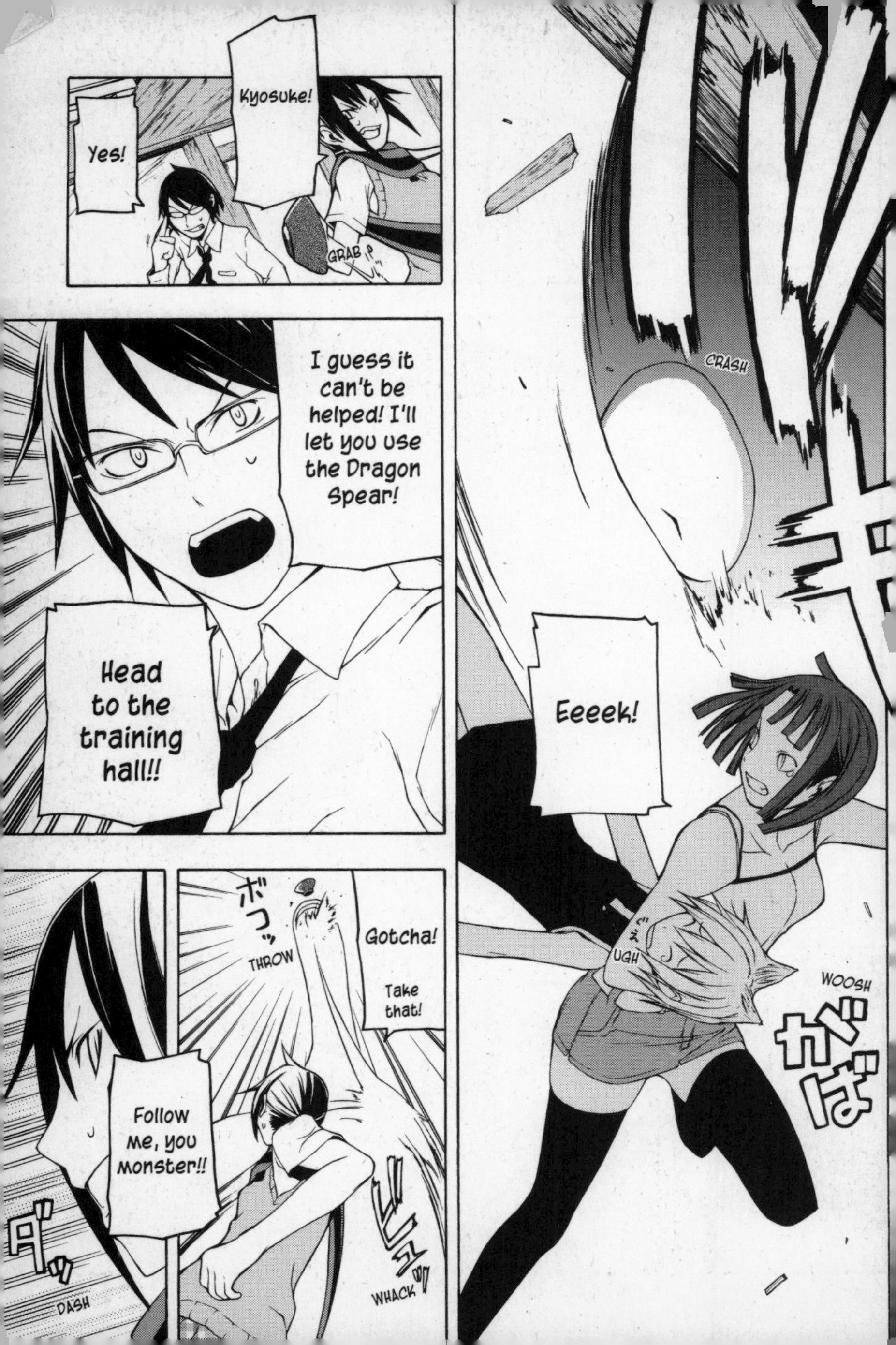
CRASH
Eeeek!
ぐえ
UGH
WOOSH
がば
Kyosuke!
Yes!
GRAB
I guess it can't be helped! I'll let you use the Dragon Spear!
Head to the training hall!!
ボコッ
THROW
Gotcha!
Take that!
WHACK
Follow me, you monster!!
ダッ
DASH

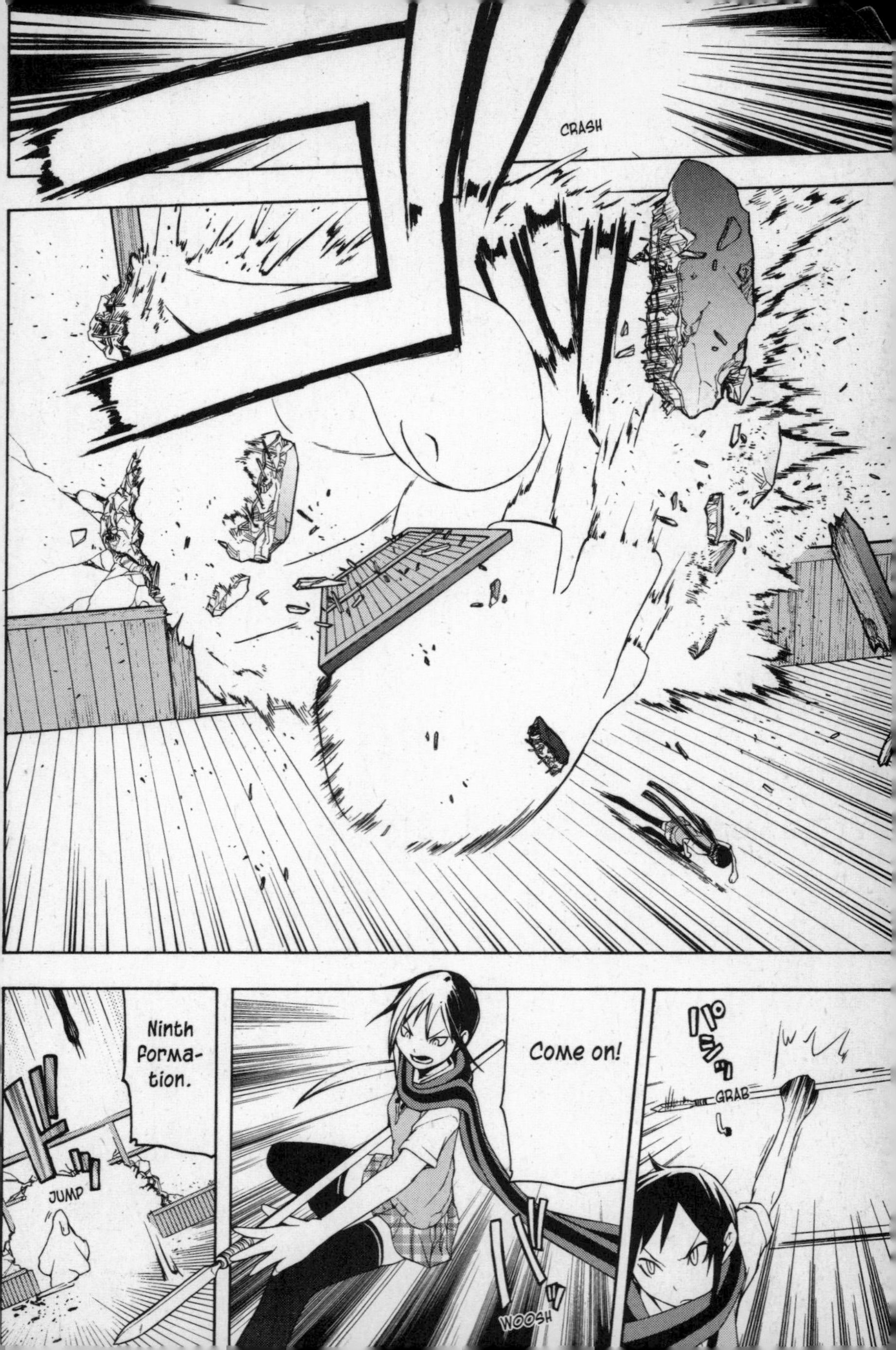
CRASH
GRAB
Come on!
WOOSH
Ninth formation.
JUMP

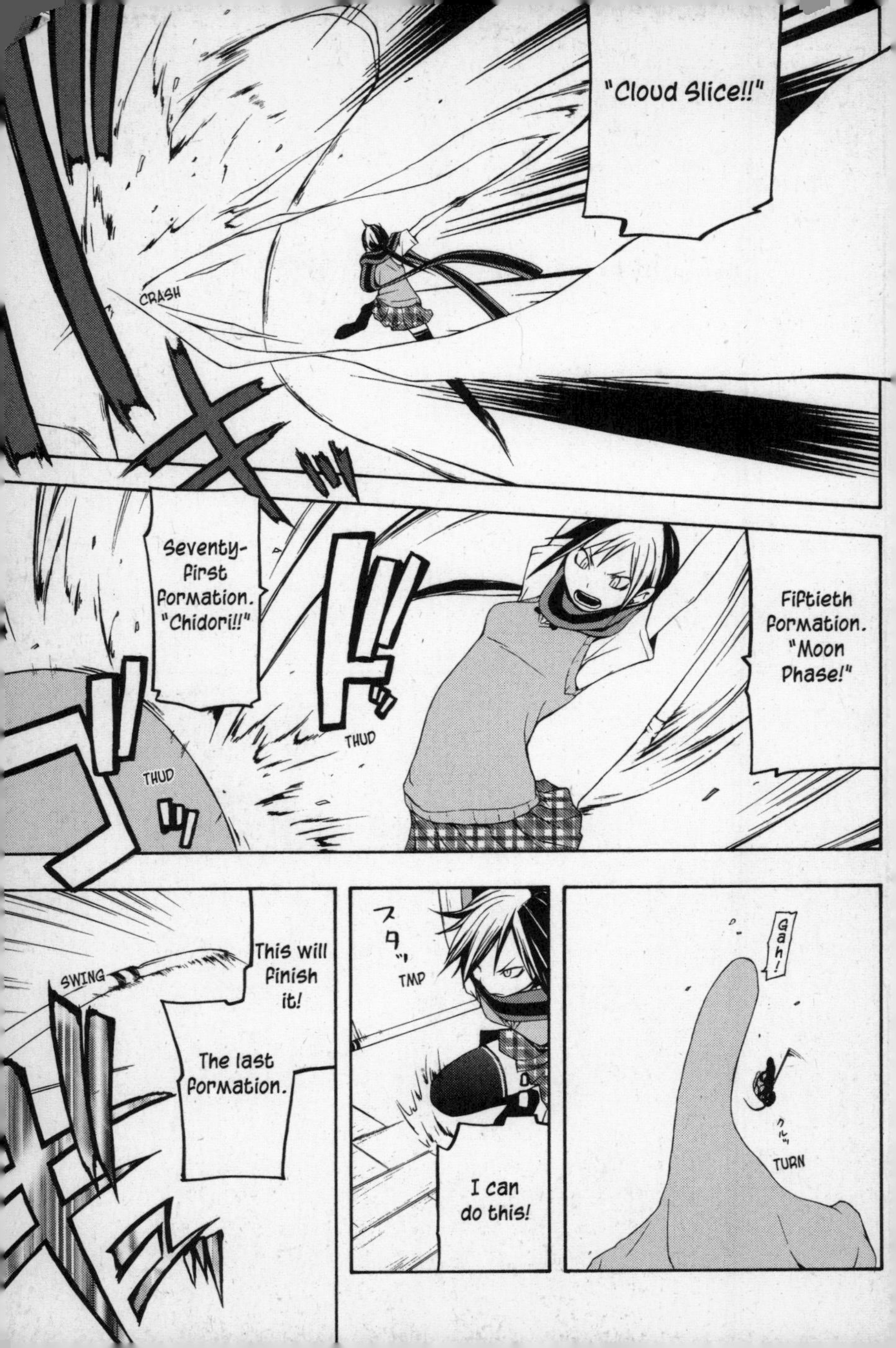
"Cloud Slice!!"
CRASH
Fiftieth formation. "Moon Phase!"
Seventy-first formation. "Chidori!!"
THUD
THUD
Gah!
クルッ
TURN
スタッ
TMP
I can do this!
This will finish it!
The last formation.
SWING

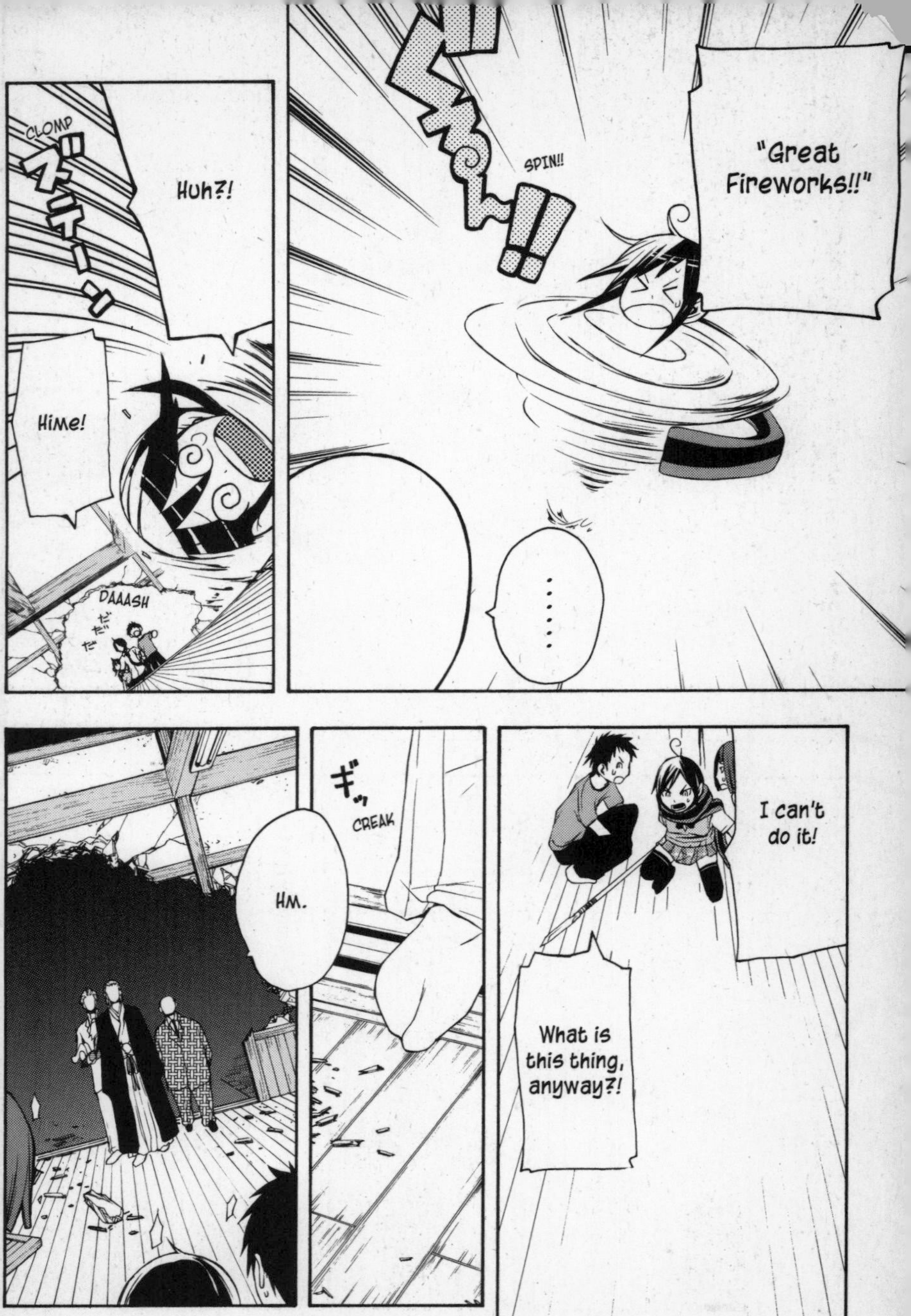
"Great Fireworks!!"
SPIN!!
……
CLOMP
Huh?!
Hime!
DAAASH
I can't do it!
What is this thing, anyway?!
ギッ
CREAK
Hm.

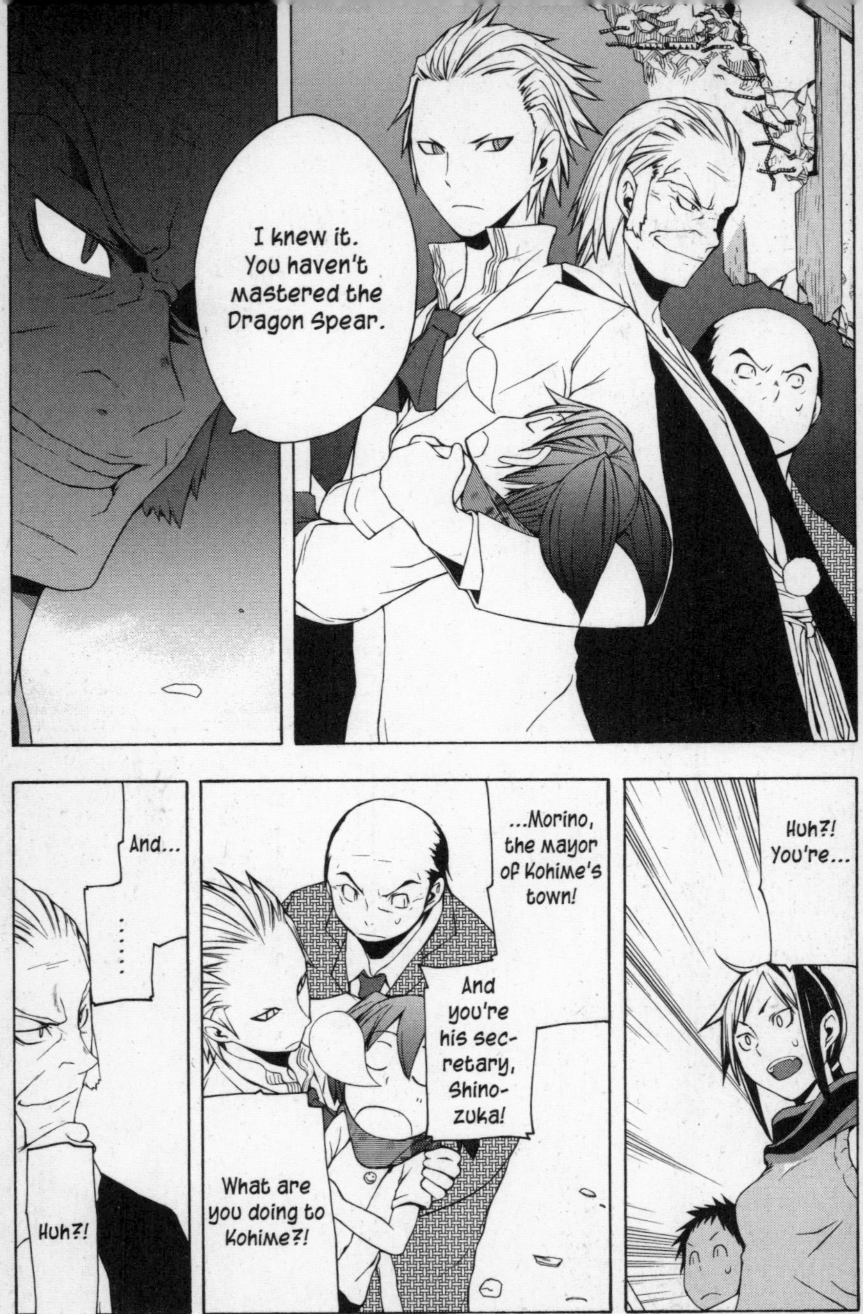
I knew it. You haven't mastered the Dragon Spear.
Huh?! You're...
...Morino, the mayor of Kohime's town!
And you're his secretary, Shinozuka!
What are you doing to Kohime?!
And...
......
Huh?!

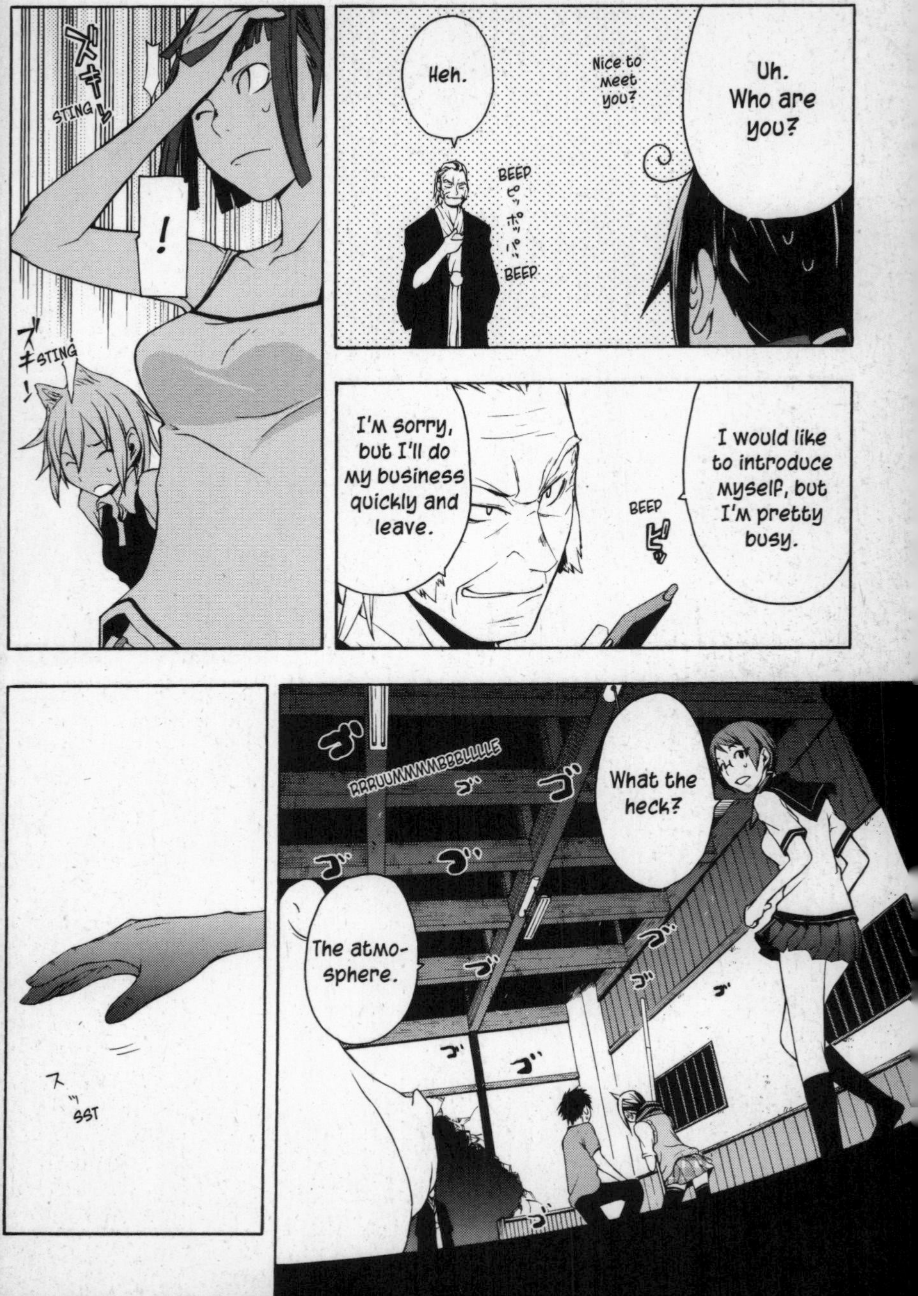
Uh. Who are you?
Nice to Meet you?
Heh.
BEEP
ピッ ポッ パッ
BEEP
I would like to introduce Myself, but I'M pretty busy.
BEEP
ピ
I'M sorry, but I'll do My business quickly and leave.
ズキッ
STING
!
ズキ!
STING
What the heck?
ゴ
RRRUUMMMMBBBLLLE
The atmo-sphere.
スッ
SST

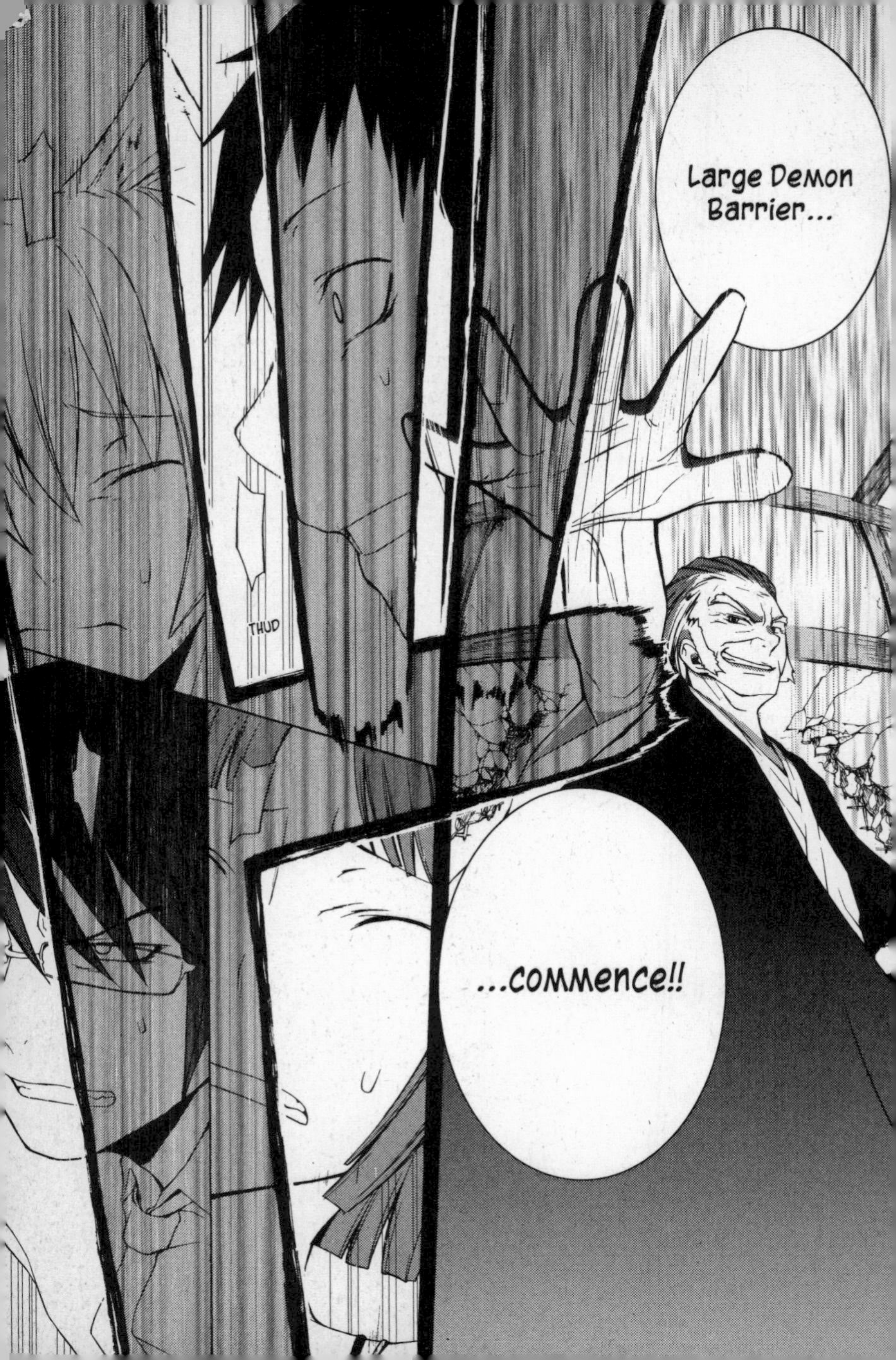
Large Demon Barrier...
THUD
...COMMENCE!!

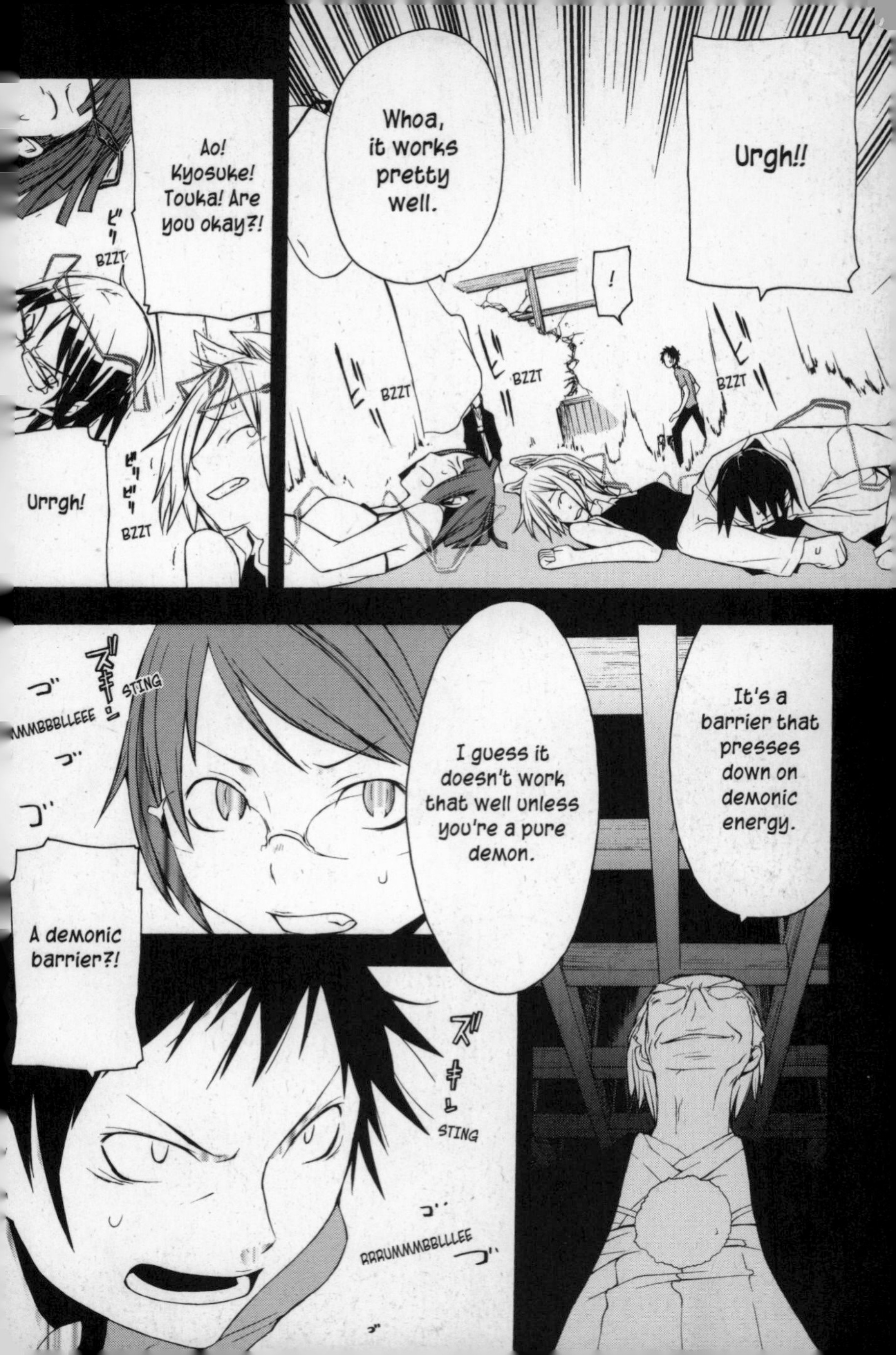
Urgh!!
Whoa, it works pretty well.
!
BZZT
BZZT
BZZT
Ao! Kyosuke! Touka! Are you okay?!
BZZT
Urrgh!
BZZT
It's a barrier that presses down on demonic energy.
I guess it doesn't work that well unless you're a pure demon.
STING
MMMBBBLLEEE
A demonic barrier?!
STING
RRRUMMMBBLLLEE

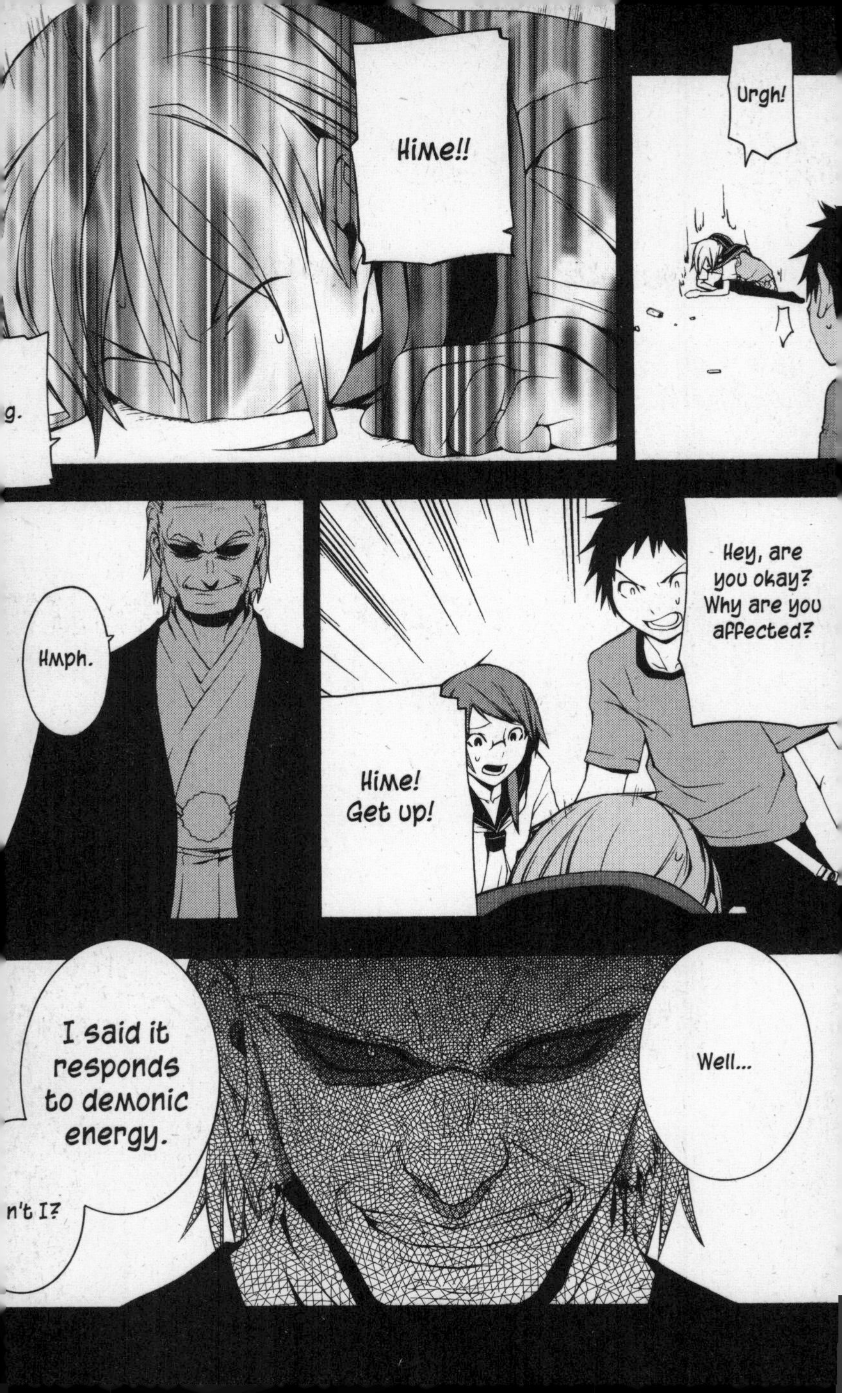
Urgh!
Hime!!
g.
Hey, are you okay? Why are you affected?
Hime! Get up!
Hmph.
Well...
I said it responds to demonic energy.
n't I?

12th Night: Thorny Road (Part 2) END

Yozakura Quartet 3

Primary Stages of Yozakura Quartet

Age: 24

Hobbies:
Cruising with Yae

Favorites

Food:
Spicy food

Music Group:
ACIDMAN

Comedian:
Kirin

Uchi-P Member:
Azu-chan

Little-Known Fact:
She sleeps ten hours a day.

Juri-san

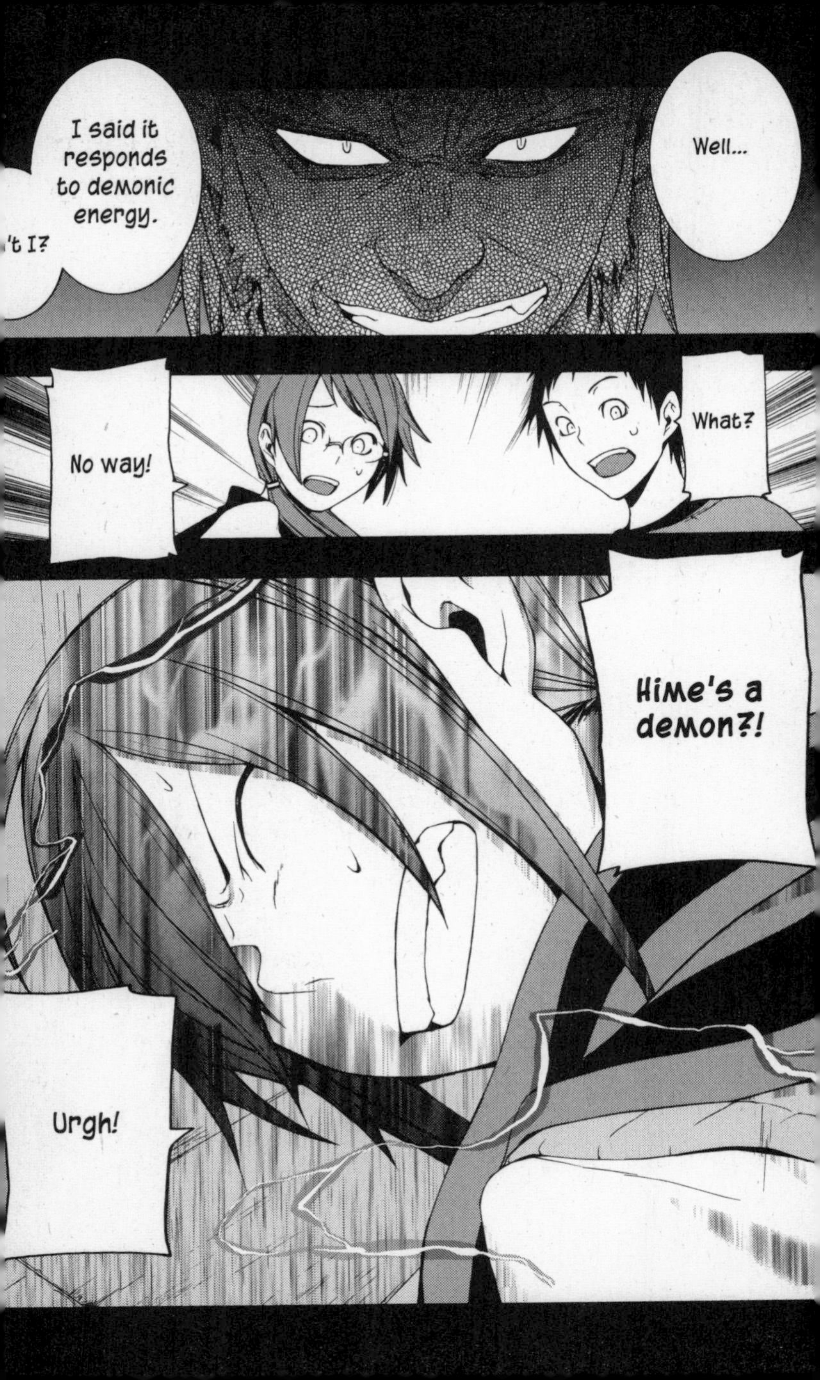
Well...
I said it responds to demonic energy.
't I?
What?
No way!
Hime's a demon?!
Urgh!

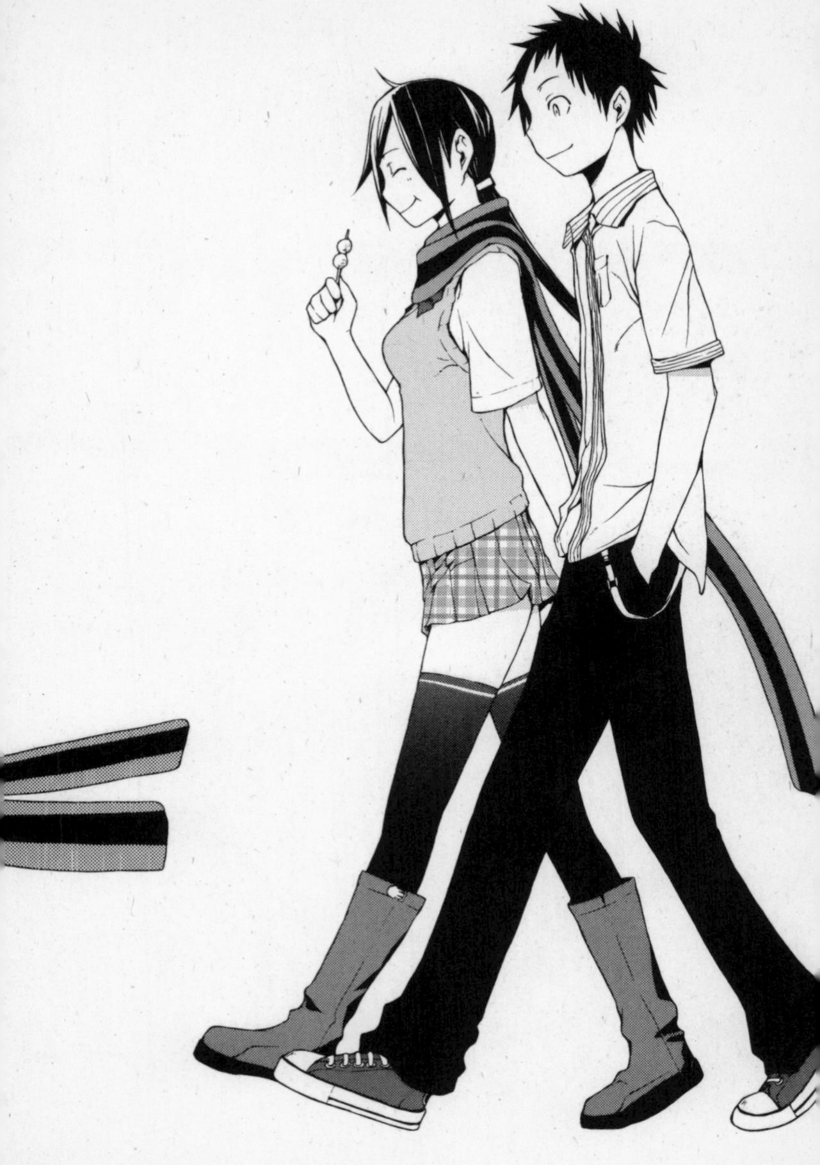

13th Night: Thorny Road (Part 3)

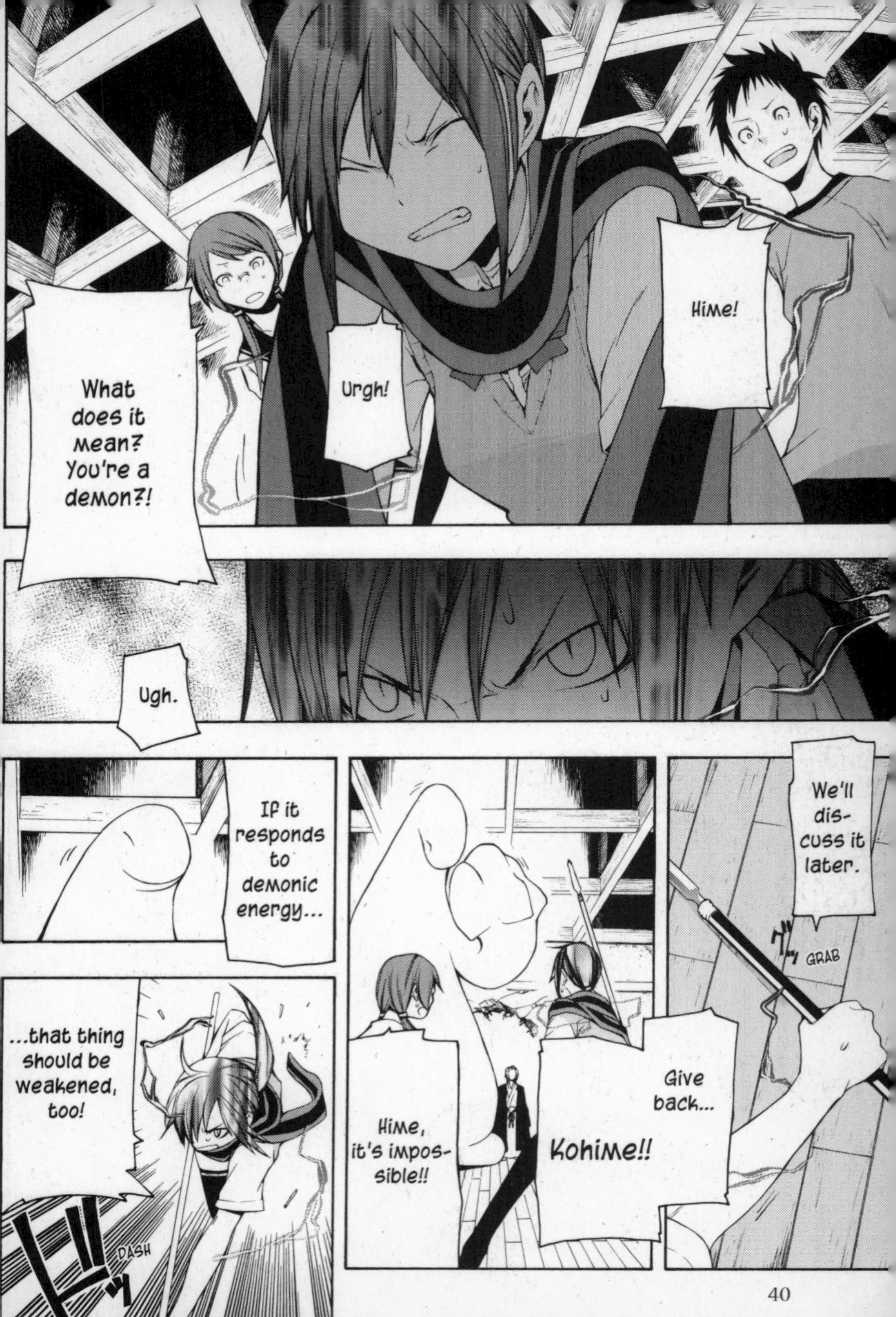
Hime!
Urgh!
What does it mean? You're a demon?!
Ugh.
We'll dis-cuss it later.
GRAB
Give back...
Kohime!!
Hime, it's impos-sible!!
If it responds to demonic energy...
...that thing should be weakened, too!
DASH

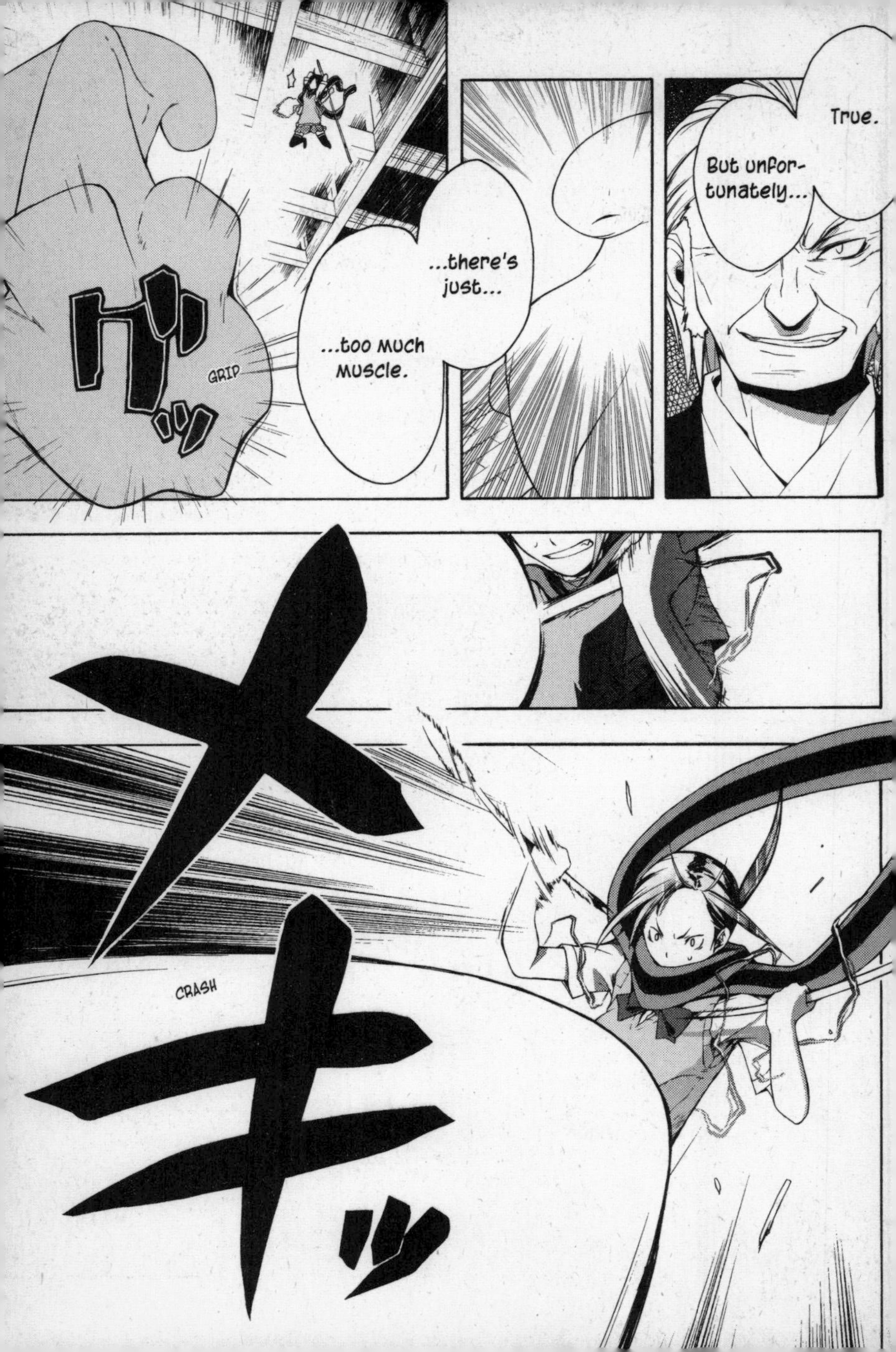
True.
But unfor-tunately...
...there's just...
...too much muscle.
GRIP
CRASH

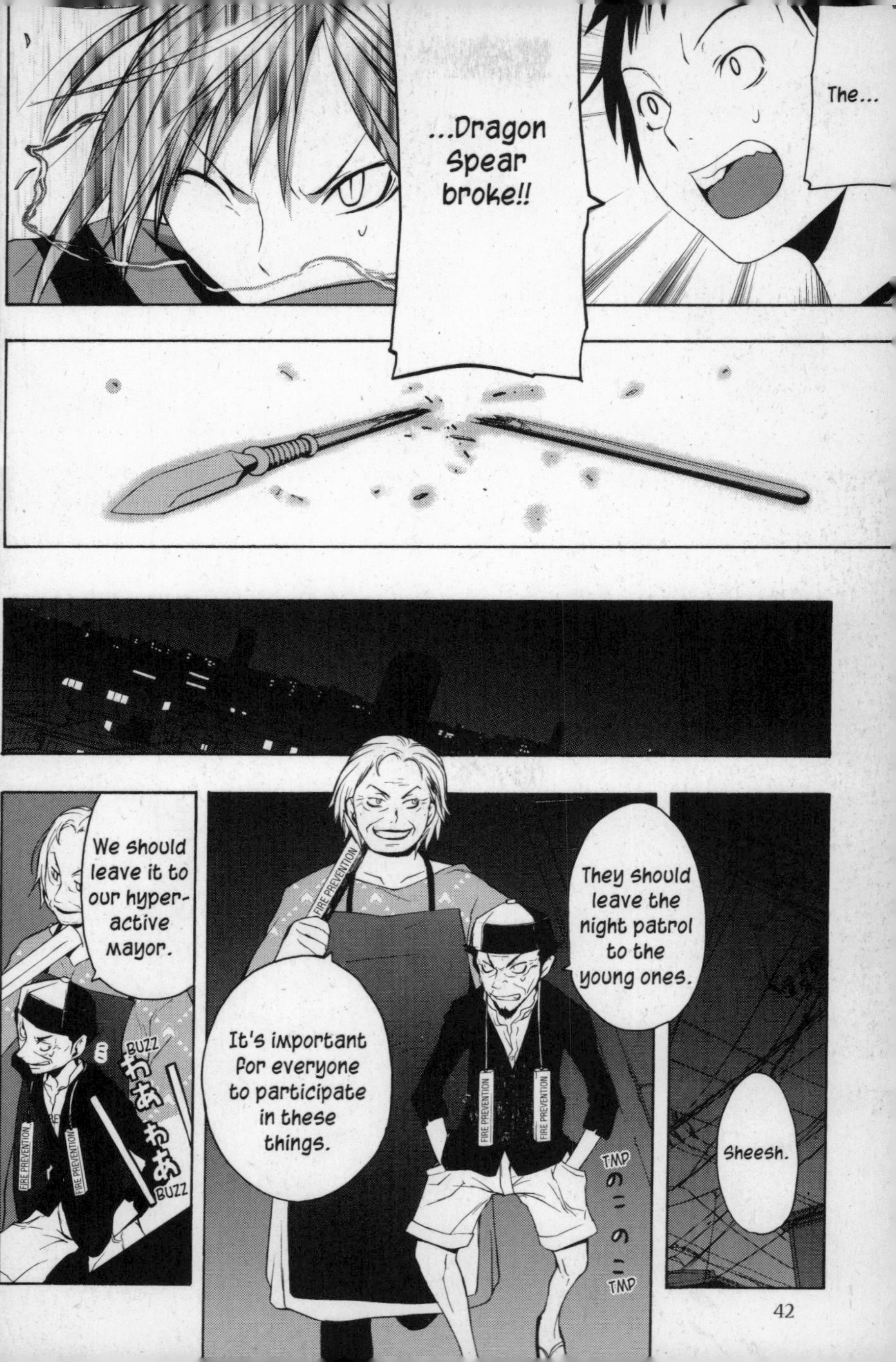
The...
...Dragon Spear broke!!
Sheesh.
They should leave the night patrol to the young ones.
It's important for everyone to participate in these things.
FIRE PREVENTION
FIRE PREVENTION
FIRE PREVENTION
TMP のこのこ TMP
We should leave it to our hyper-active mayor.
BUZZ わあわあ BUZZ
FIRE PREVENTION
FIRE PREVENTION

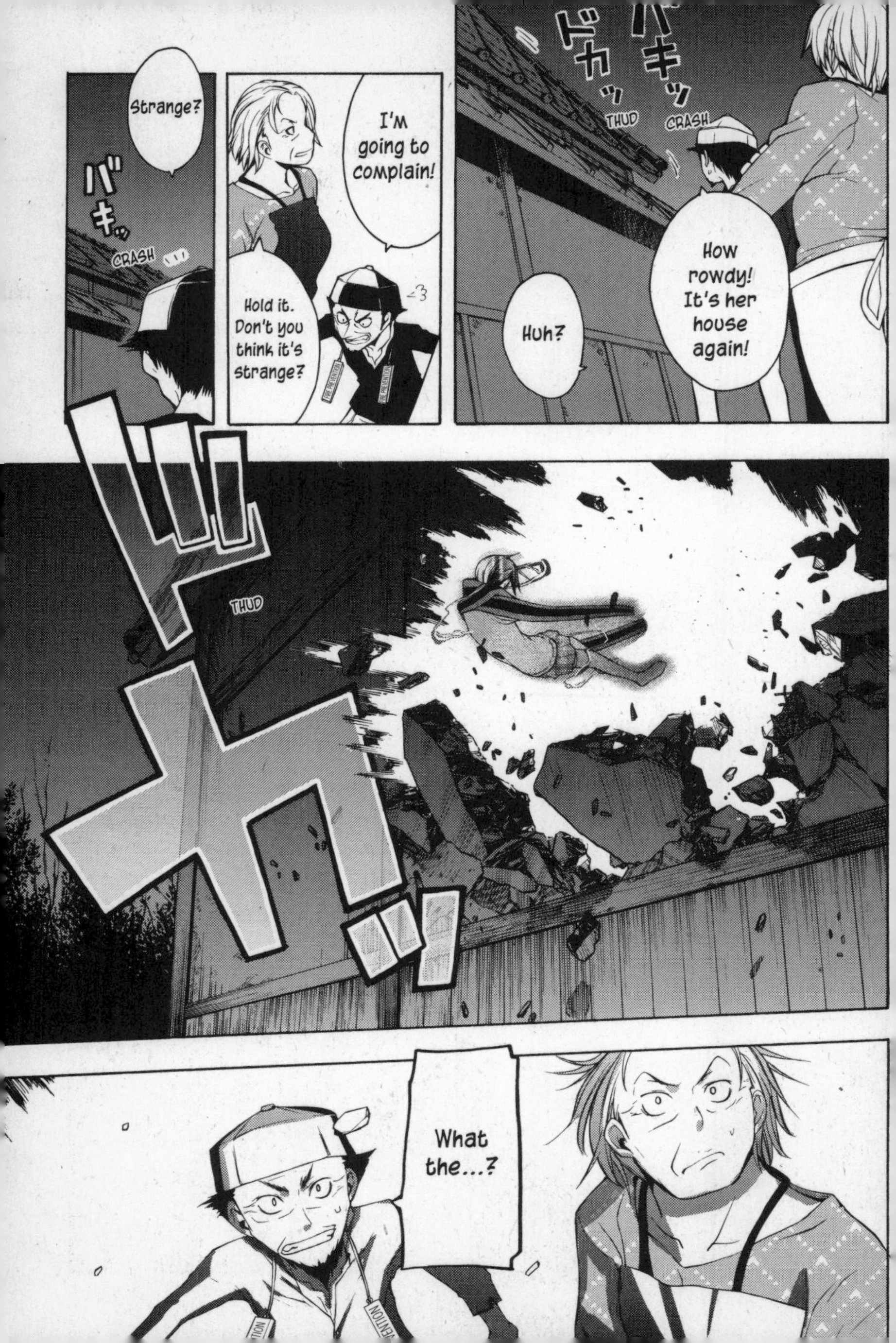

バキッ
CRASH
ドカッ
THUD
How rowdy! It's her house again!
Huh?
I'm going to complain!
Hold it. Don't you think it's strange?
Strange?
バキッ
CRASH
THUD
What the...?

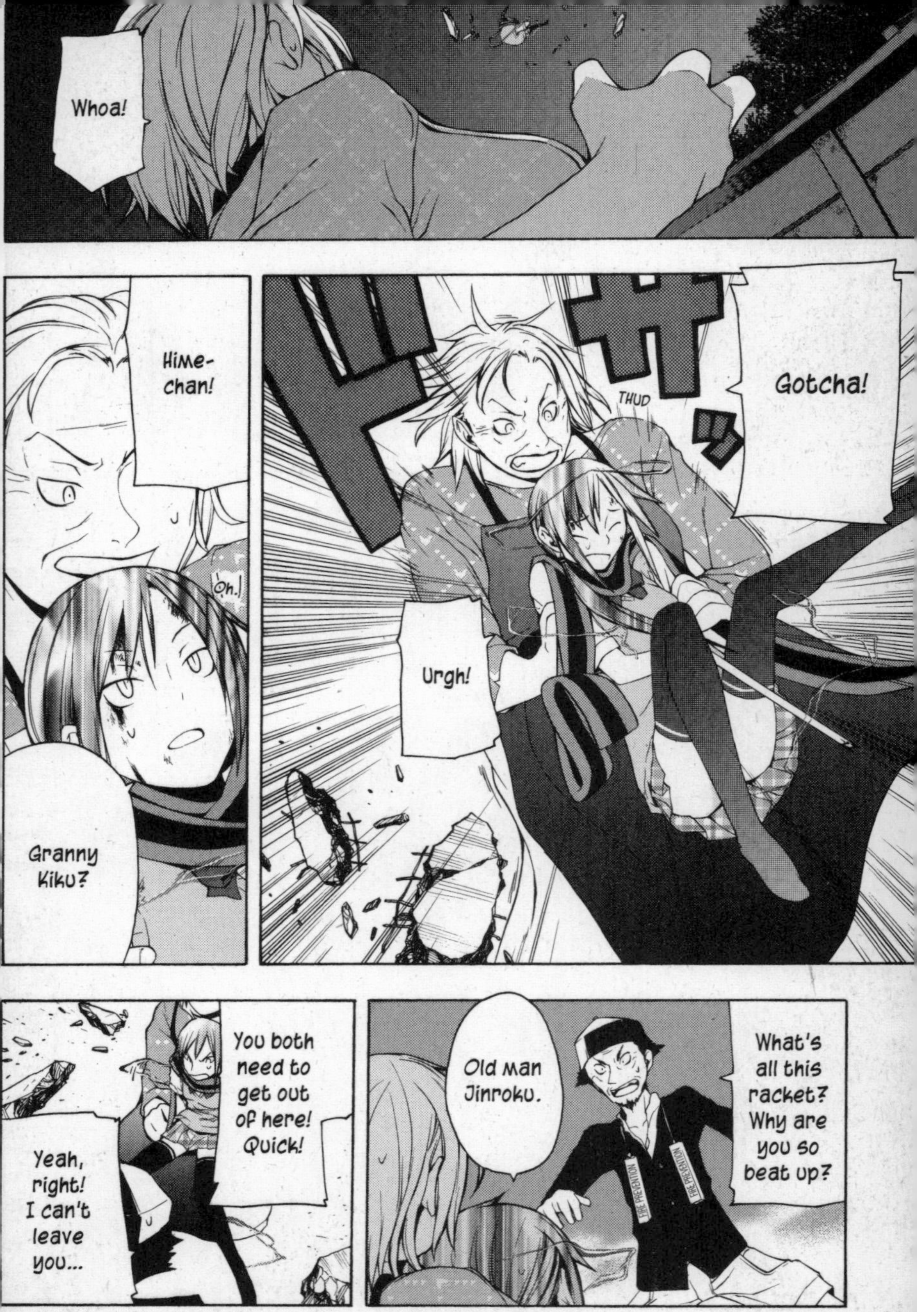
Whoa!
Gotcha!
THUD
Urgh!
Hime-chan!
Oh.
Granny Kiku?
What's all this racket? Why are you so beat up?
FIRE PREVENTION
FIRE PREVENTION
Old man Jinroku.
You both need to get out of here! Quick!
Yeah, right! I can't leave you...

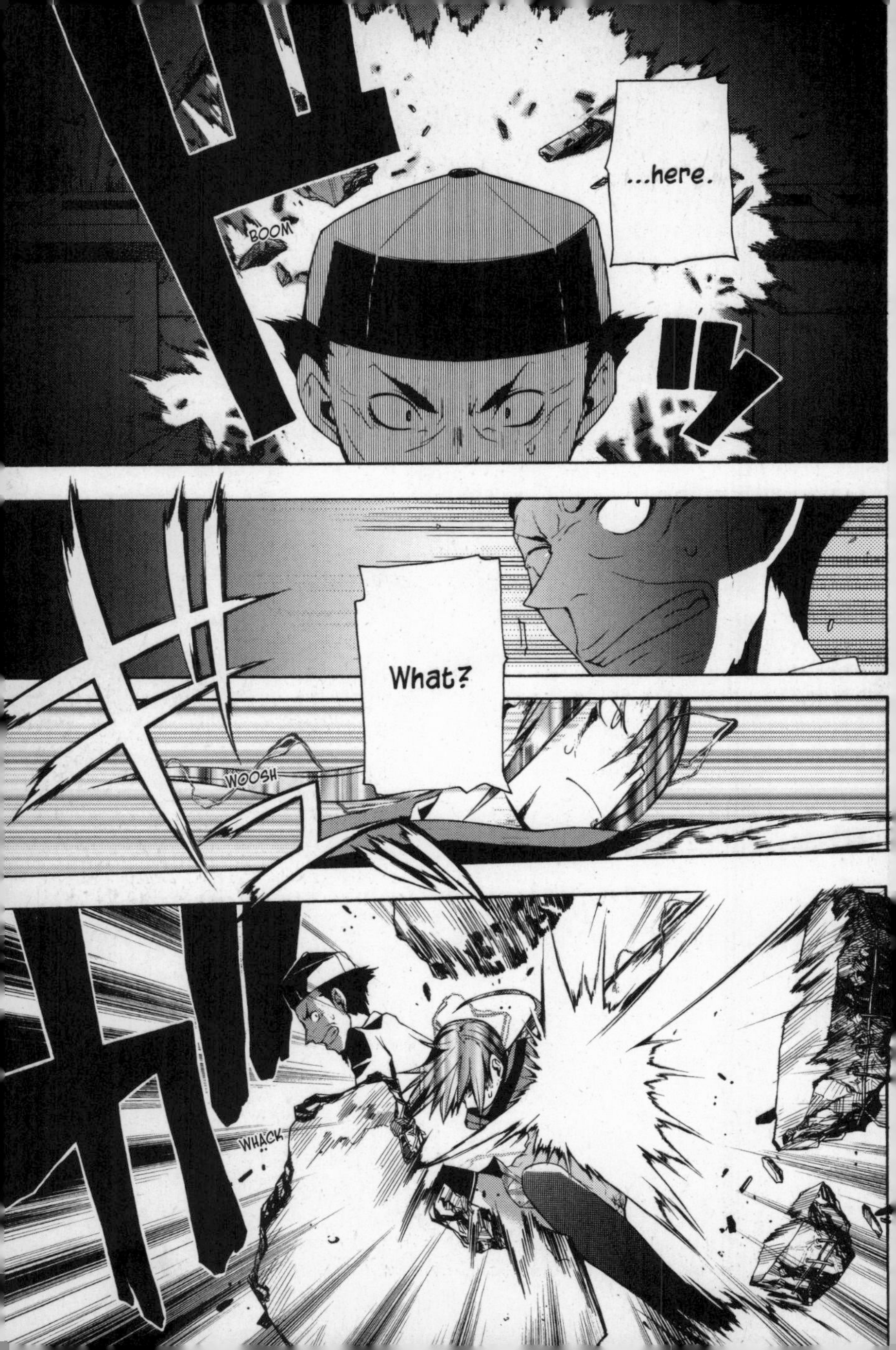
...here.
BOOM
What?
WOOSH
WHACK

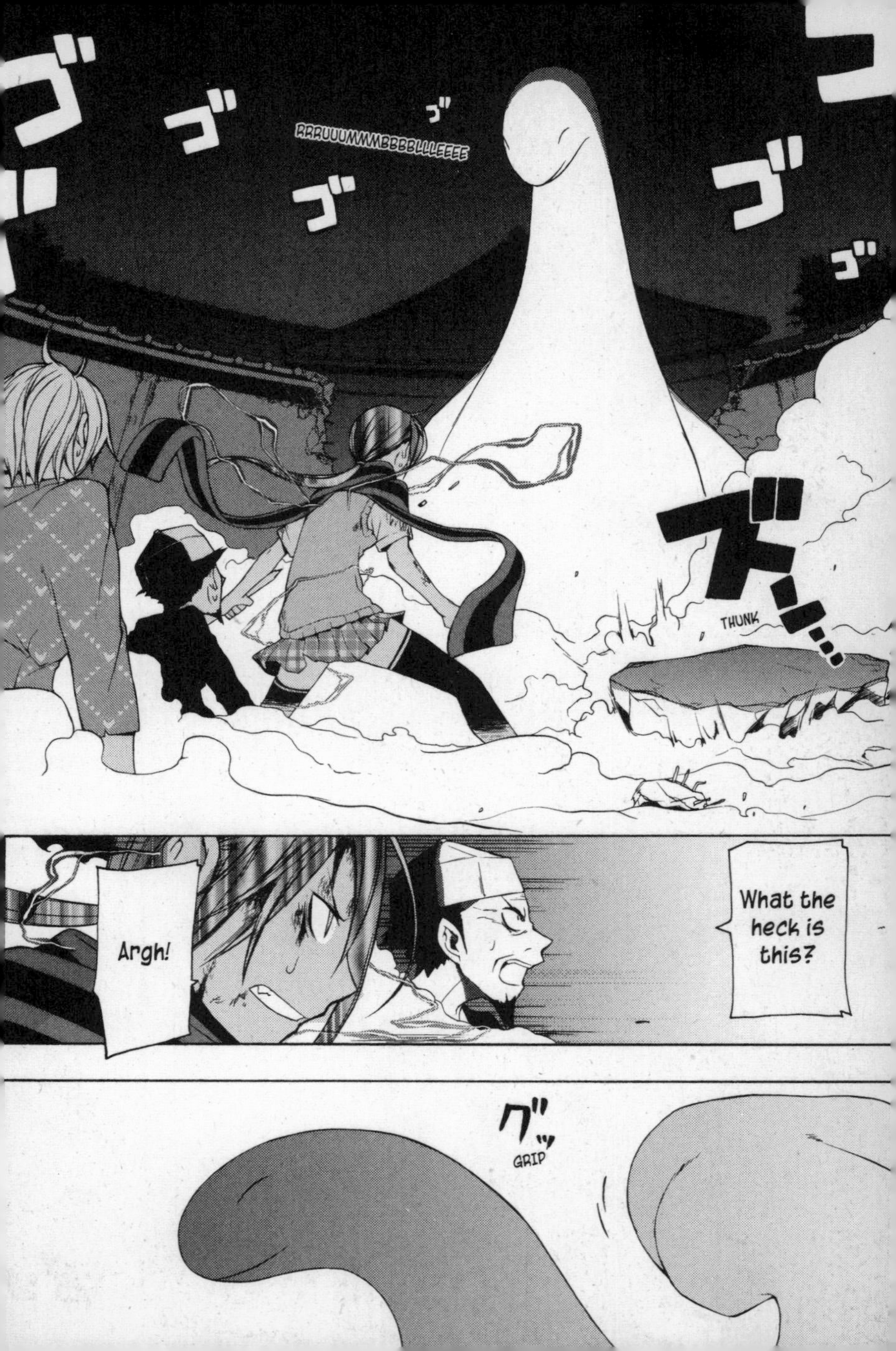
RRRUUUMMMBBBBLLLEEEE
THUNK
What the heck is this?
Argh!
グッ
GRIP

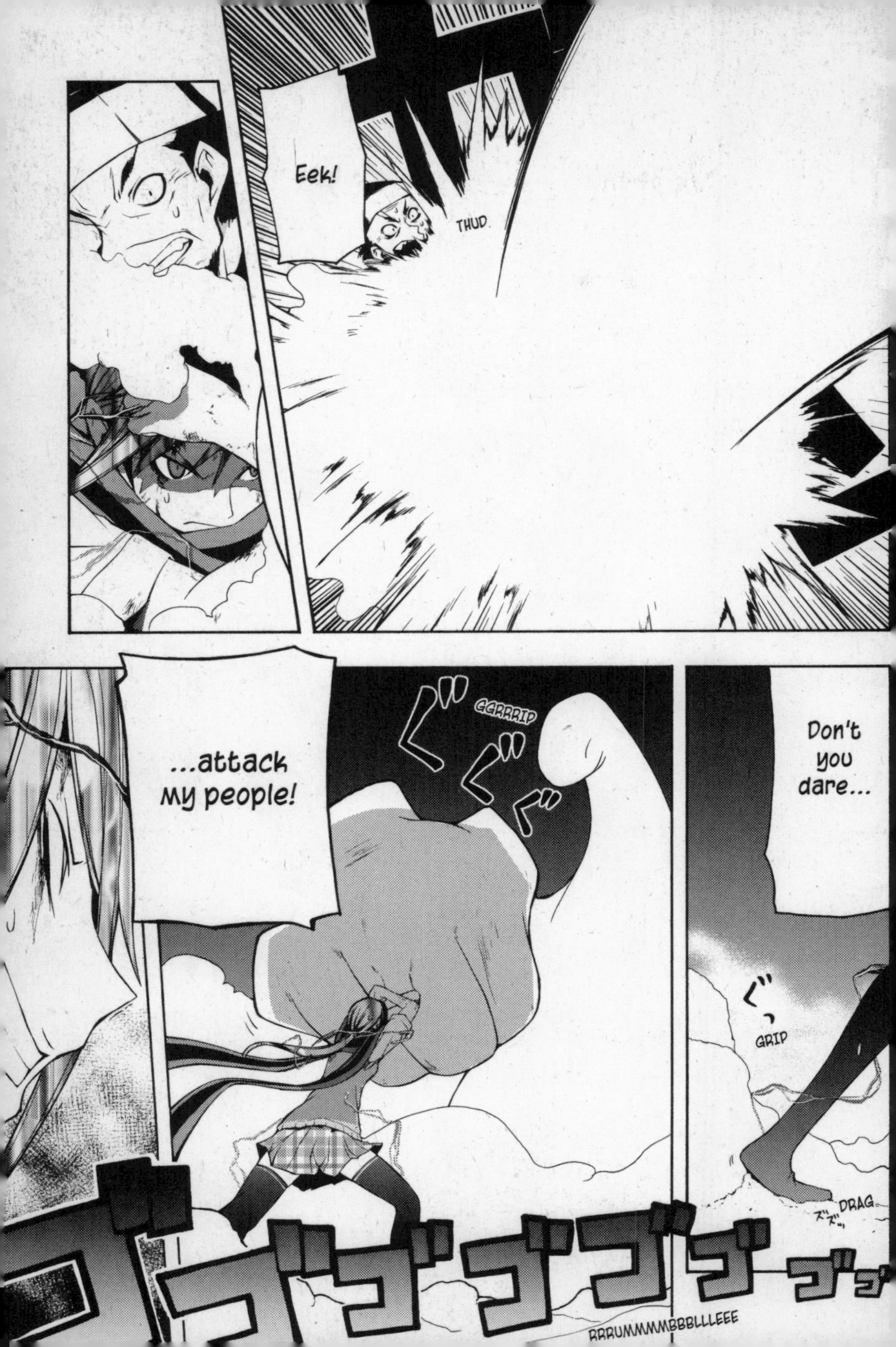

Eek!
THUD
Don't you dare...
GRIP
DRAG
...attack my people!
GGRRRIP
BRRUMMMMBBBLLLEEE

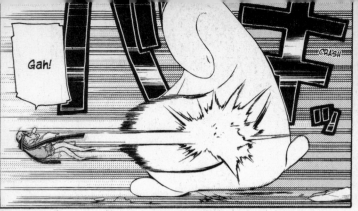

Gah!

CRASH!

GRIP

Hime-chan!

STOMP

STOMP

Grrgh.

THUD

Urgh.

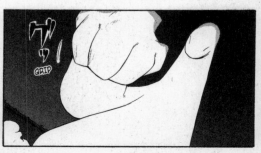

GRIP

48

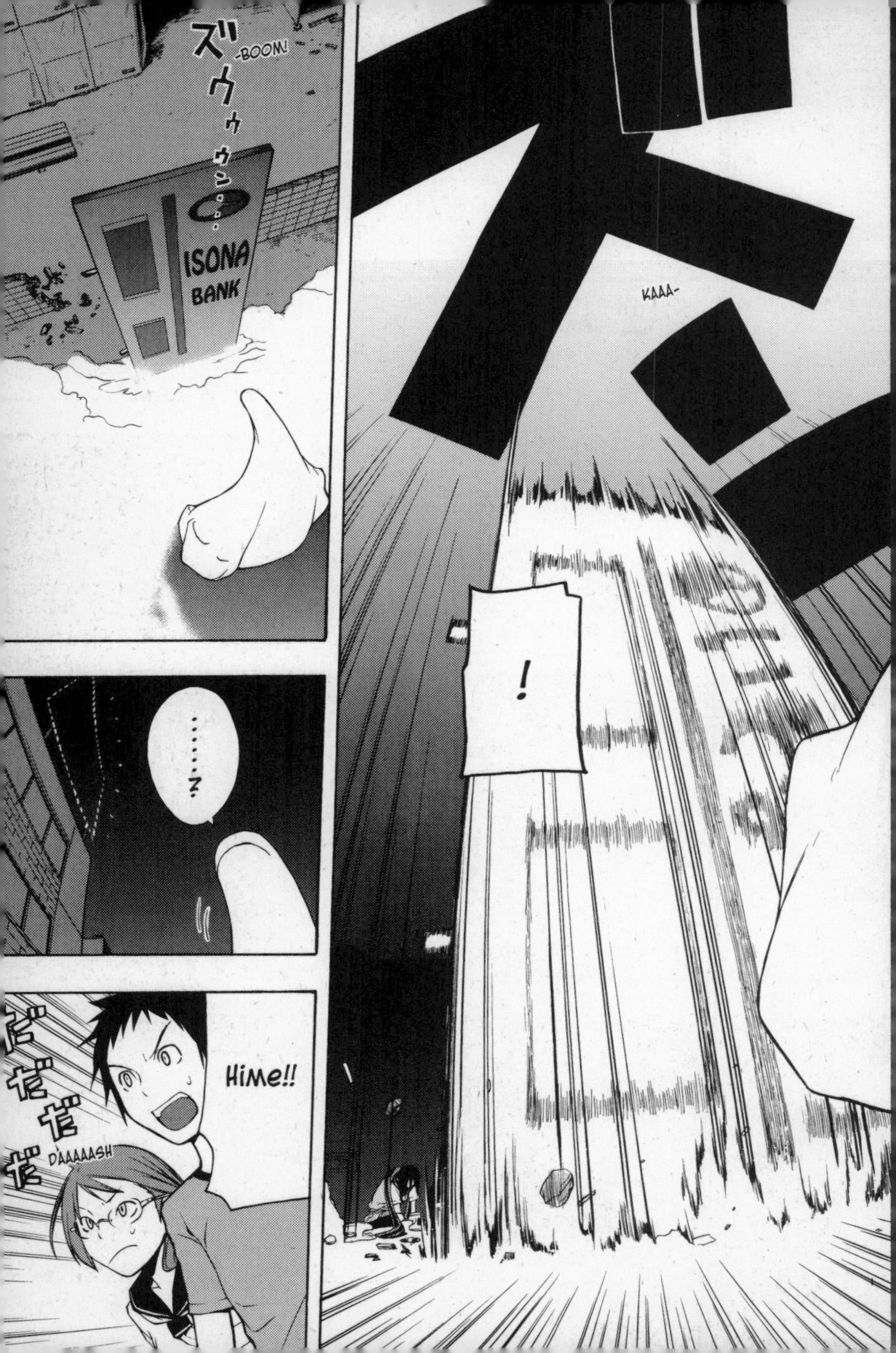
KAAA-
!
-BOOM!
ISONA BANK
......?
だだだだ
D'AAAAASH
Hime!!

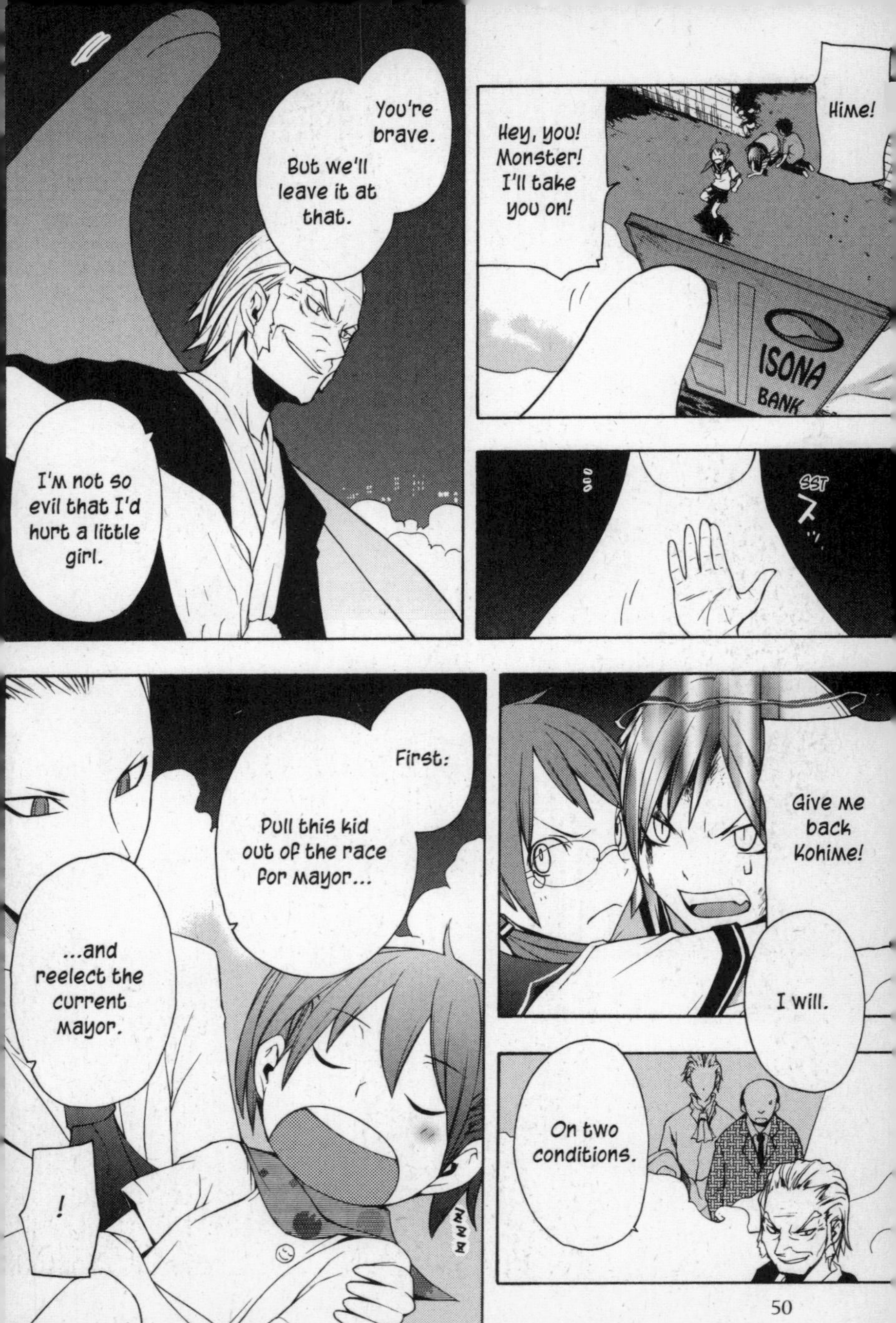
Hime!
Hey, you! Monster! I'll take you on!
ISONA BANK
SST
You're brave.
But we'll leave it at that.
I'm not so evil that I'd hurt a little girl.
Give me back Kohime!
I will.
On two conditions.
First:
Pull this kid out of the race for mayor...
...and reelect the current mayor.
!

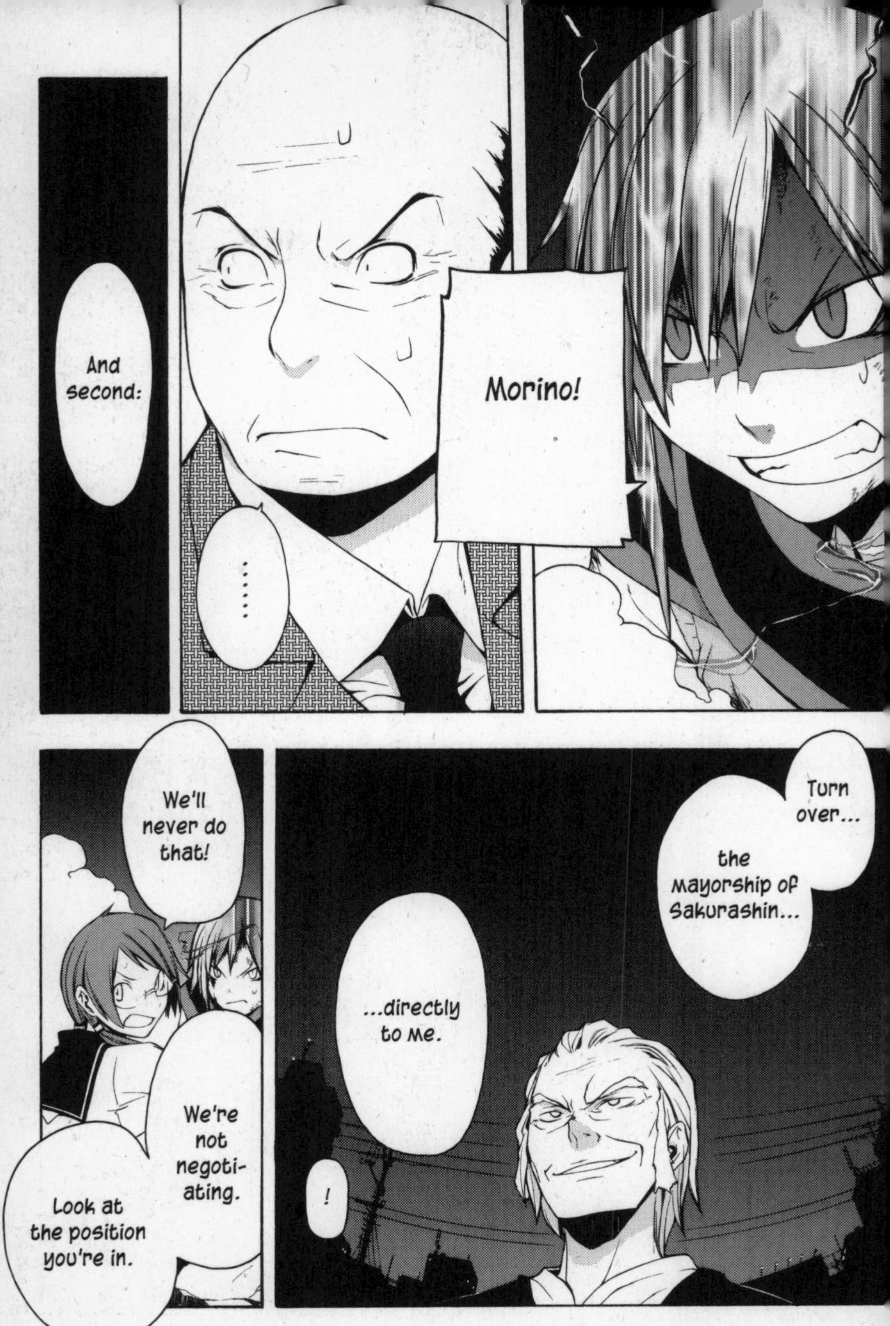
Morino!
……
And second:
Turn over...
the mayorship of Sakurashin...
...directly to me.
!
We'll never do that!
We're not negotiating.
Look at the position you're in.

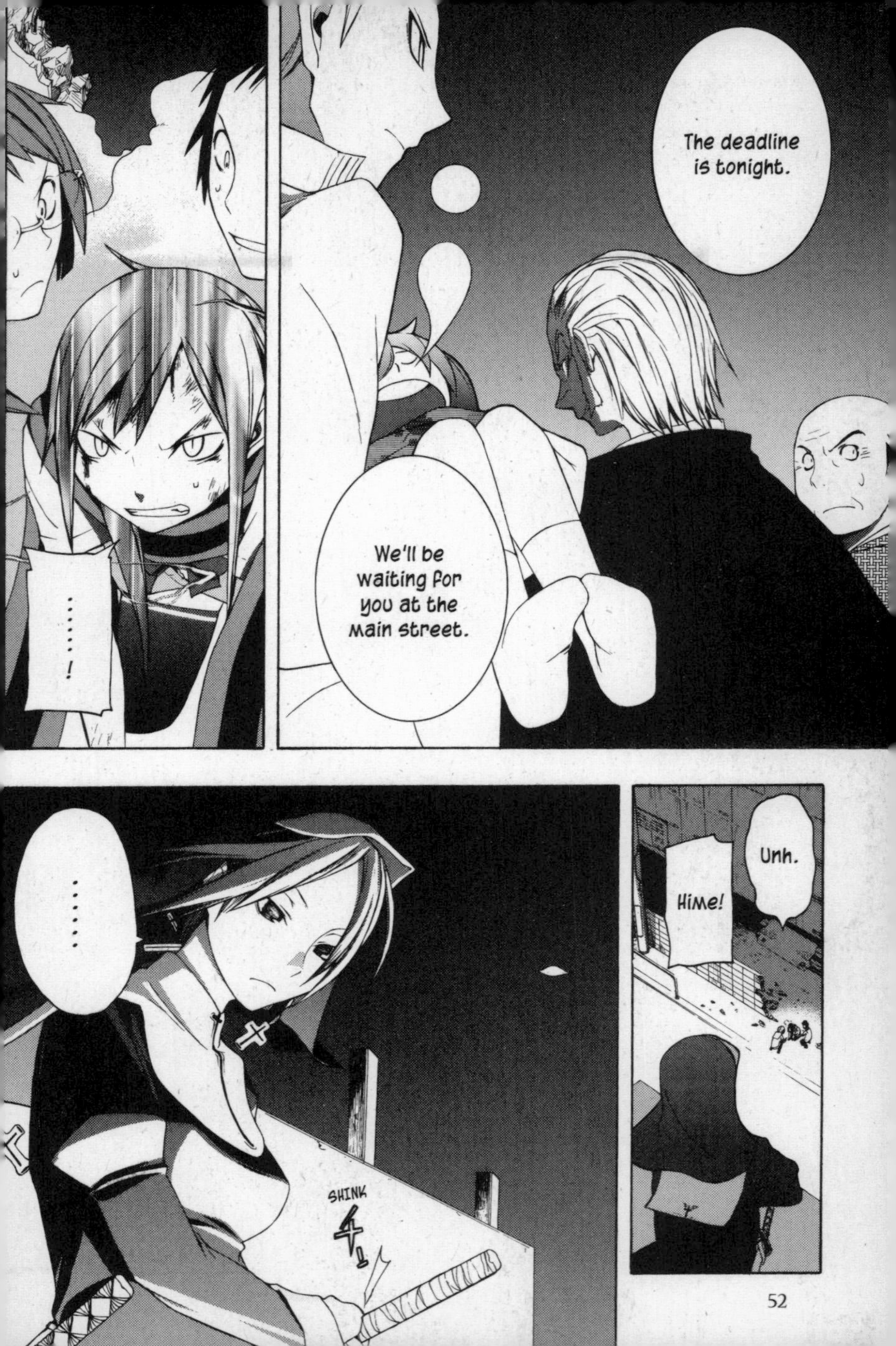
The deadline is tonight.
We'll be waiting for you at the main street.
......!
Unh.
Hime!
......
SHINK

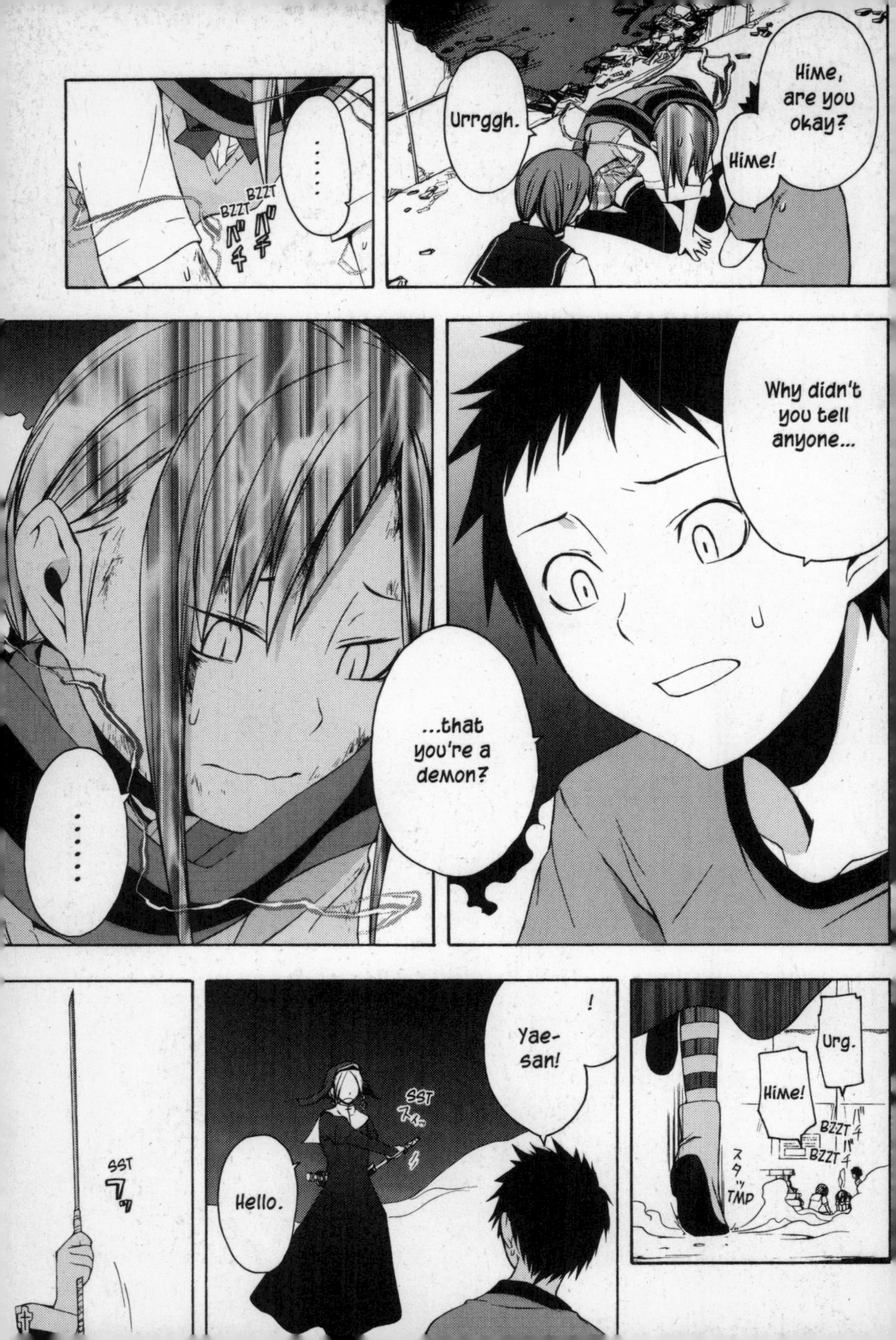
Hime, are you okay?
Hime!
Urrggh.
......
BZZT
BZZT
Why didn't you tell anyone...
...that you're a demon?
......
Urg.
Hime!
BZZT
BZZT
TMP
!
Yae-san!
SST
Hello.
SST

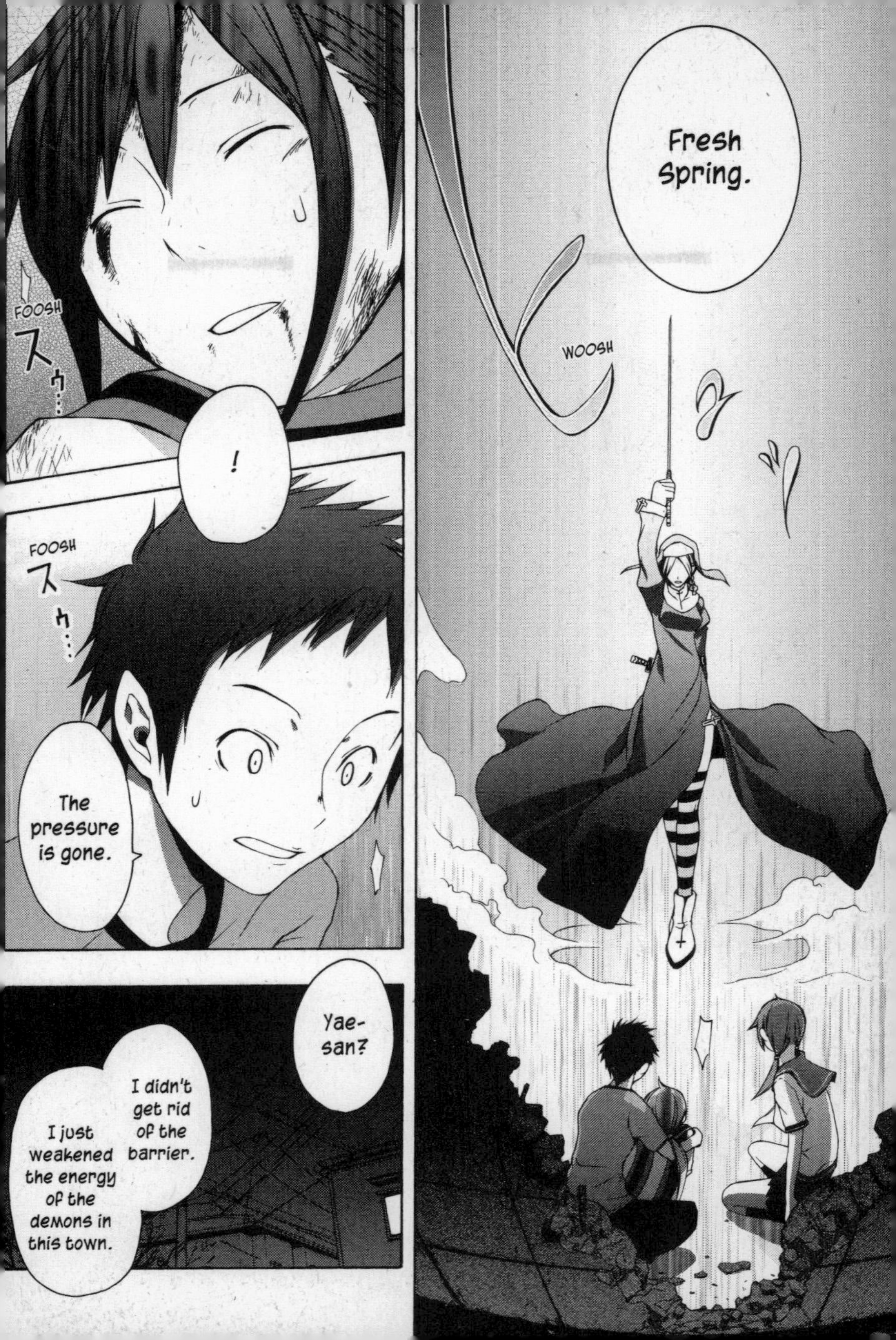
Fresh Spring.
WOOSH
FOOSH
スゥ…
!
FOOSH
スゥ…
The pressure is gone.
Yae-san?
I didn't get rid of the barrier.
I just weakened the energy of the demons in this town.

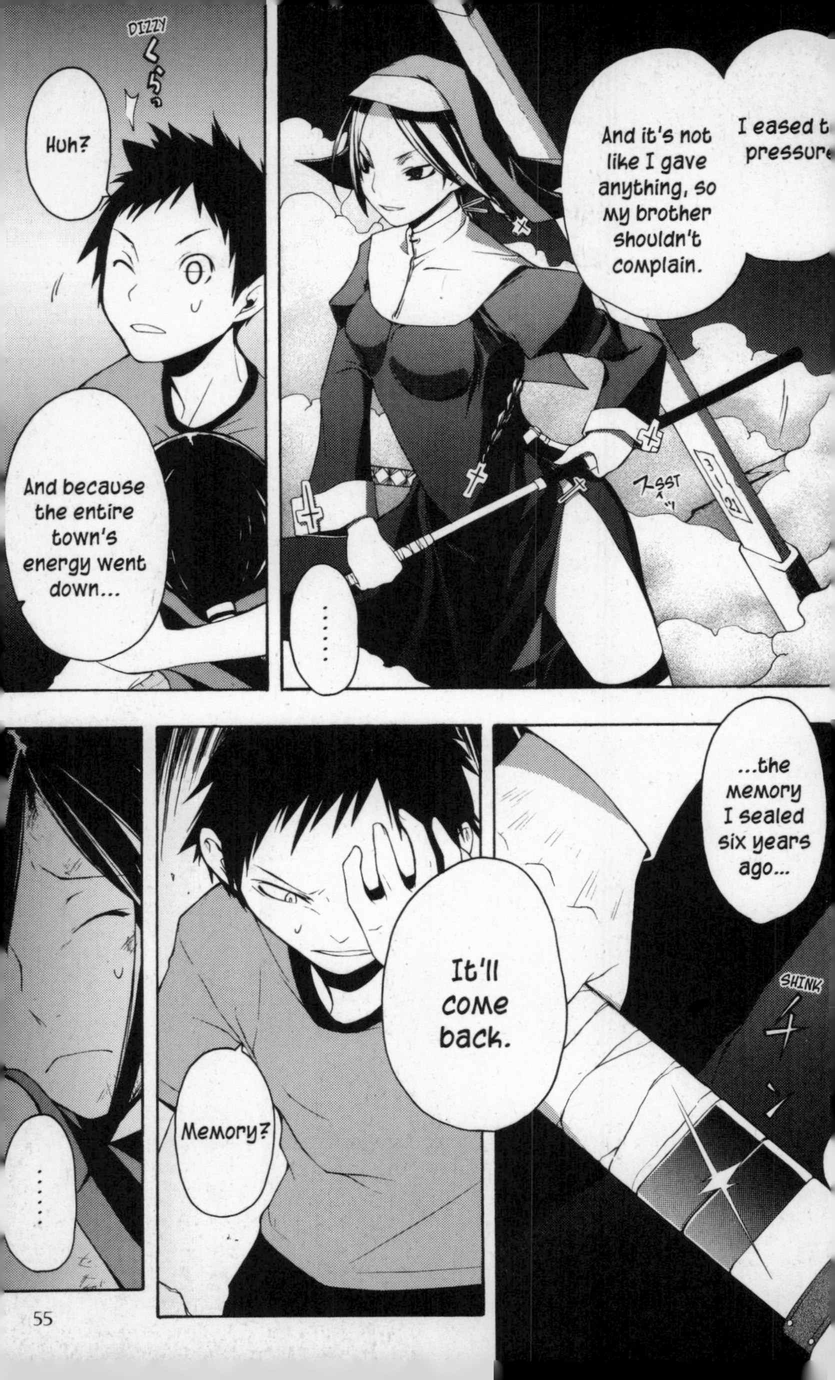
I eased t pressure
And it's not like I gave anything, so my brother shouldn't complain.
SST
......
DIZZY
Huh?
And because the entire town's energy went down...
...the memory I sealed six years ago...
SHINK
It'll come back.
Memory?
......

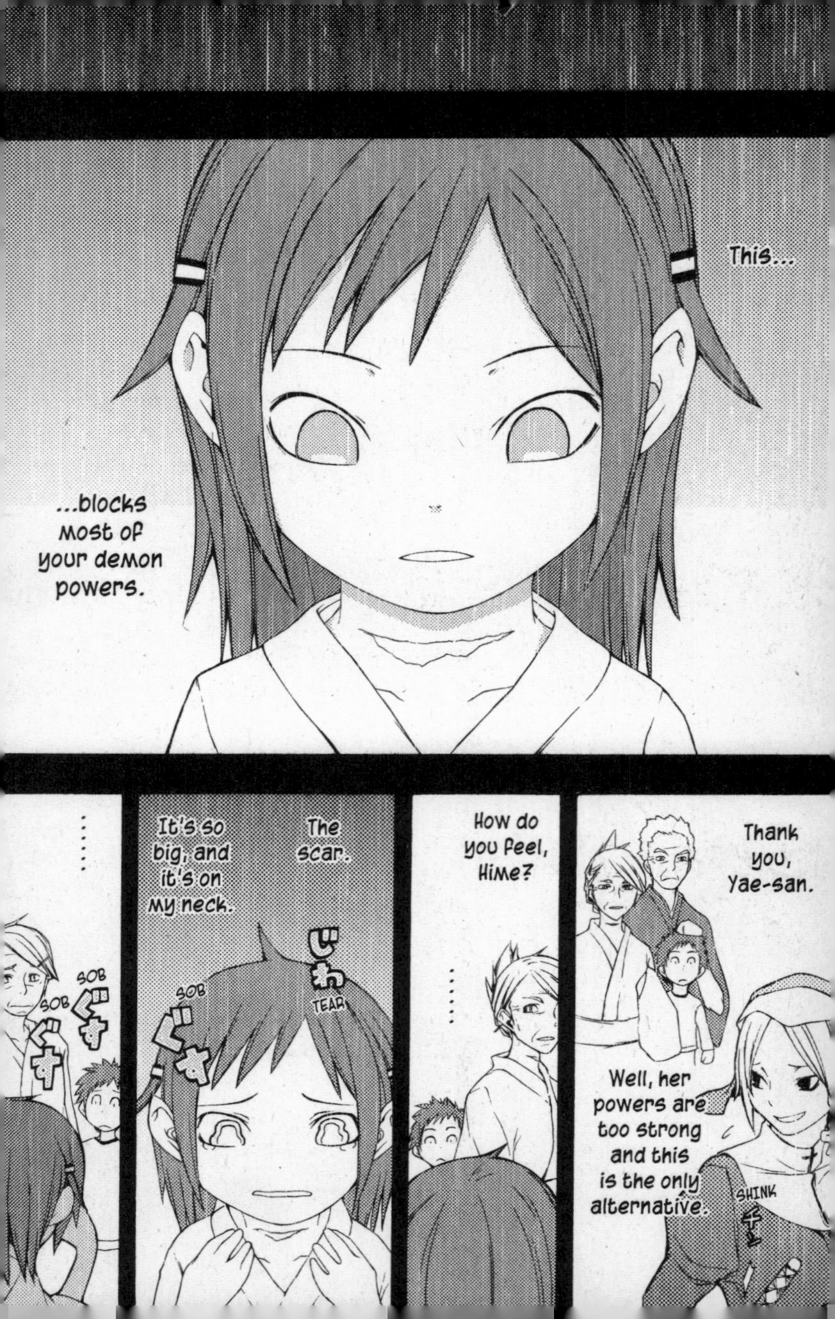
This...
...blocks most of your demon powers.
Thank you, Yae-san.
Well, her powers are too strong and this is the only alternative.
SHINK
How do you feel, Hime?
......
The scar.
It's so big, and it's on my neck.
じわ
TEAR
ぐす
SOB
......
ぐす
SOB
ぐす
SOB

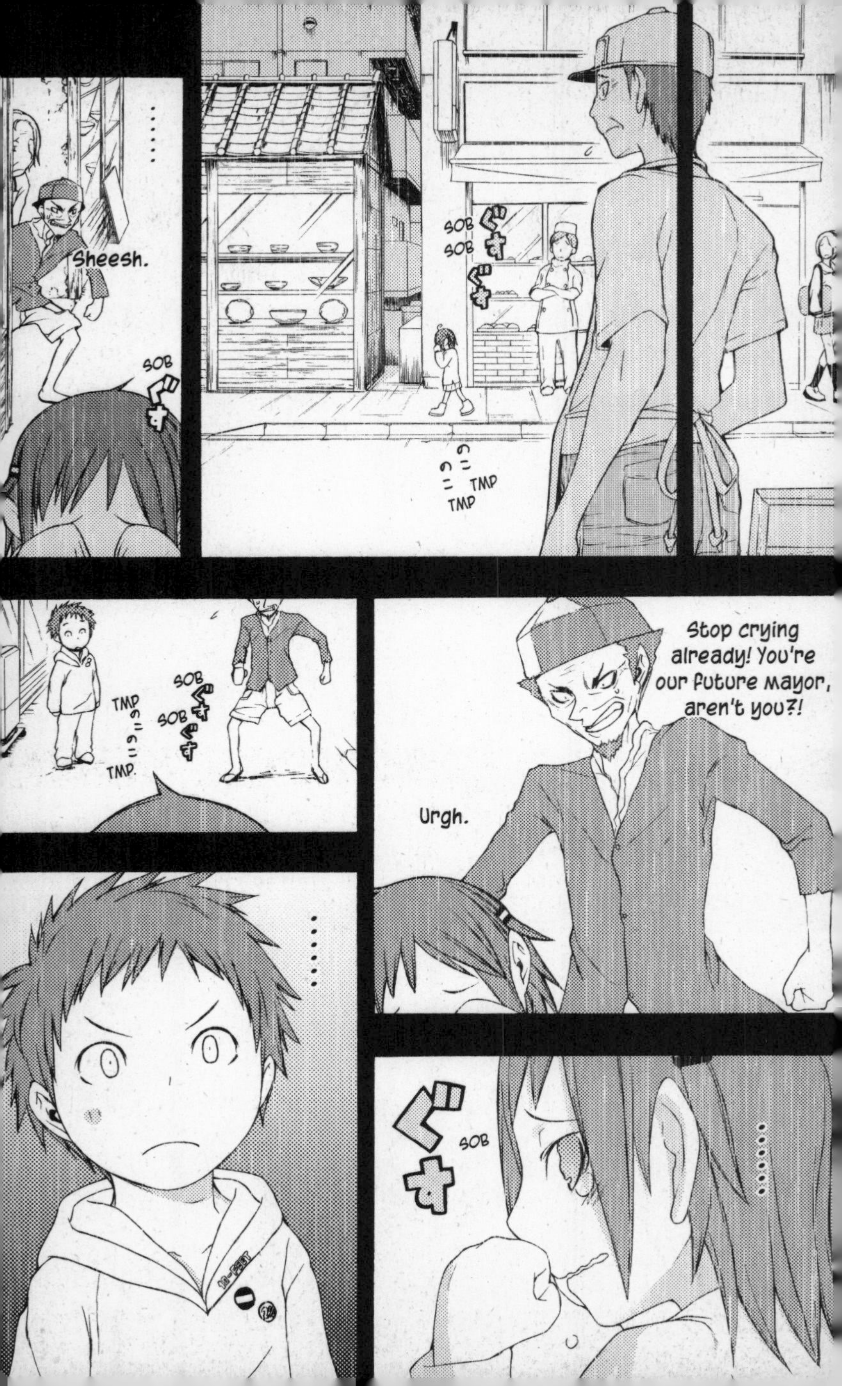
SOB
SOB
TMP
TMP
......
Sheesh.
SOB
Stop crying already! You're our future mayor, aren't you?!
Urgh.
SOB
SOB
TMP
TMP.
SOB
......
......

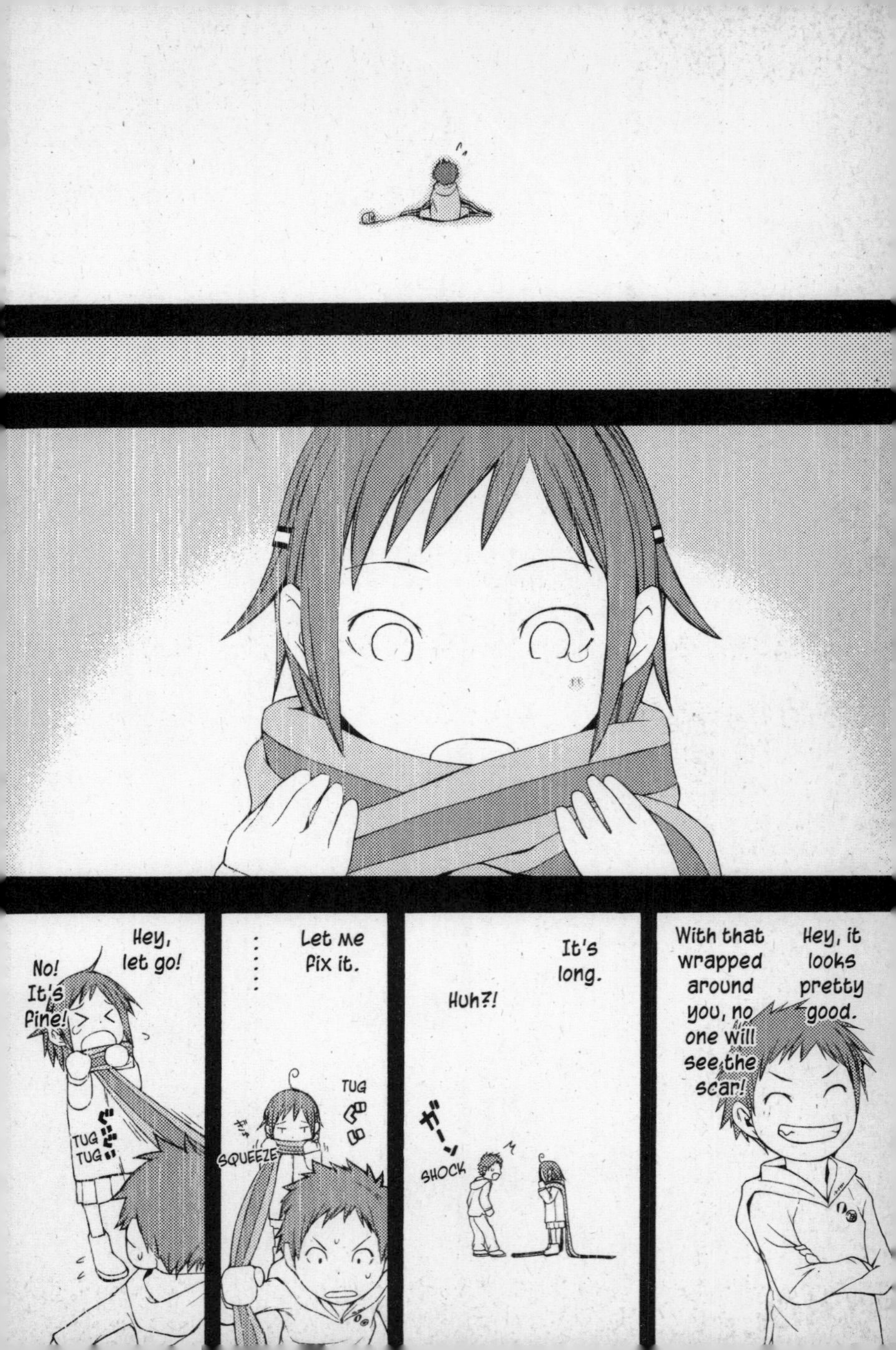
Hey, it looks pretty good.
With that wrapped around you, no one will see the scar!
It's long.
Huh?!
SHOCK
Let me fix it.
......
TUG
SQUEEZE
Hey, let go!
No! It's fine!
TUG TUG

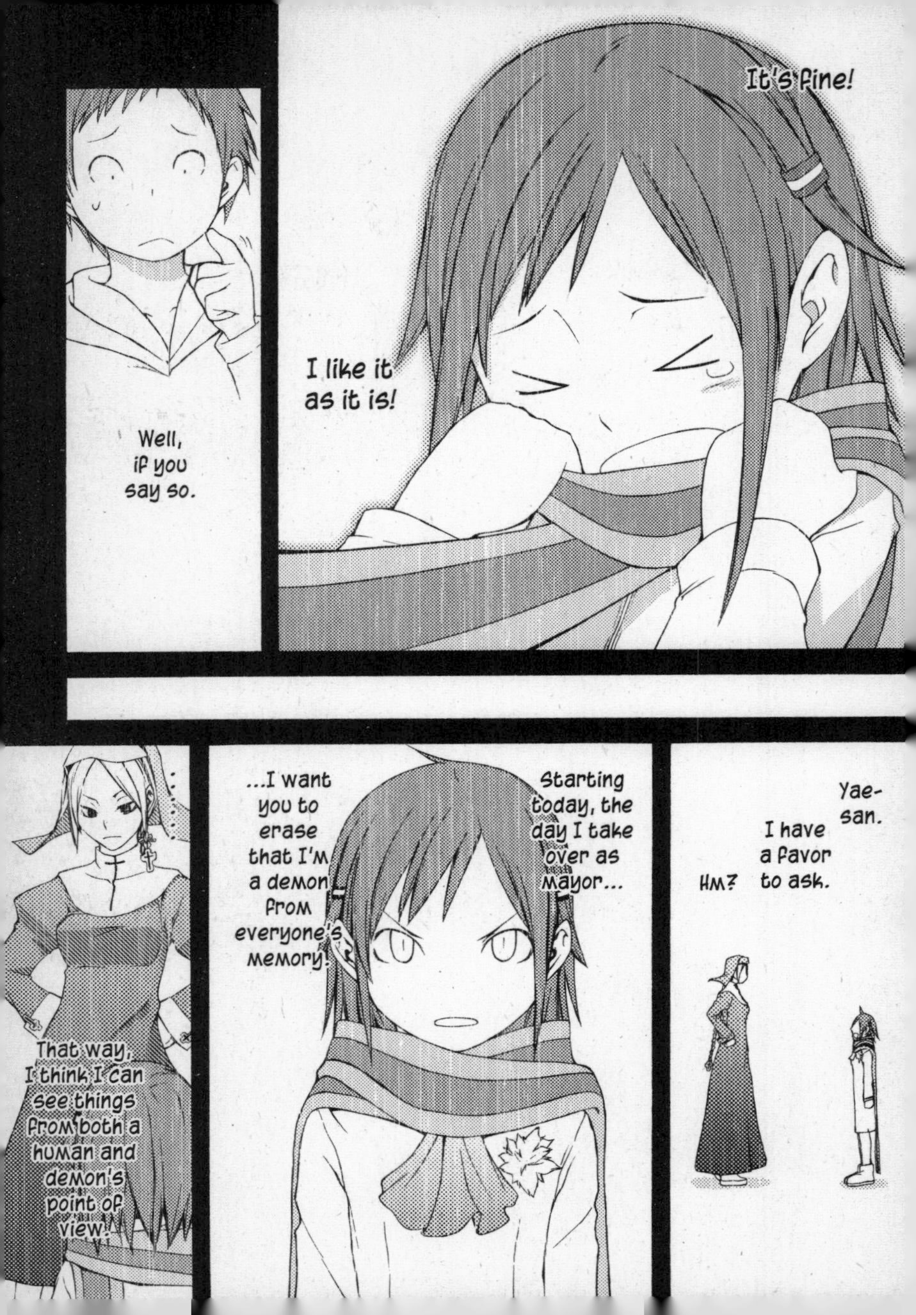
It's fine!
I like it as it is!
Well, if you say so.
Yae-san.
I have a favor to ask.
Hm?
Starting today, the day I take over as mayor...
...I want you to erase that I'm a demon from everyone's memory!
...
That way, I think I can see things from both a human and demon's point of view!

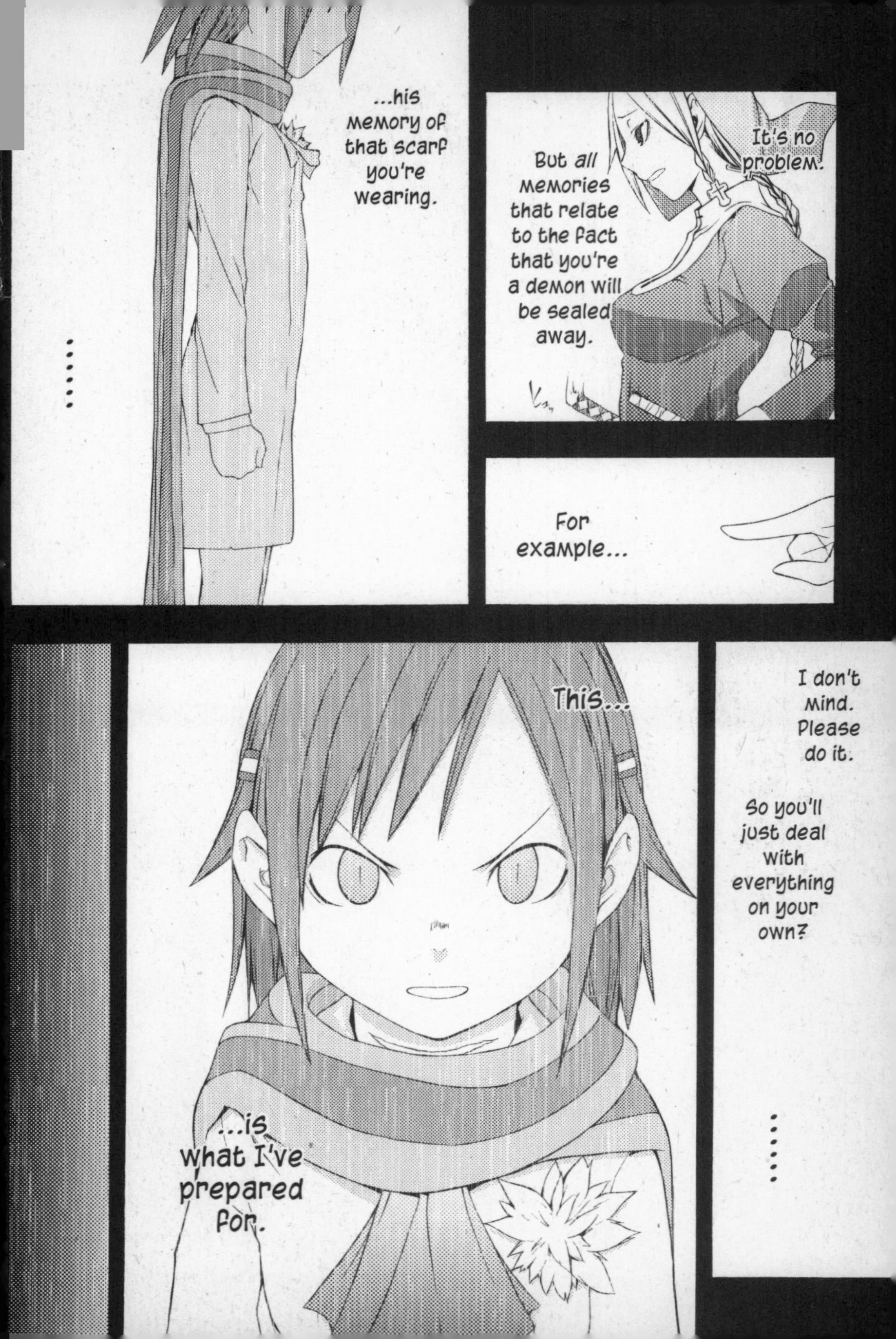
It's no problem.
But all memories that relate to the fact that you're a demon will be sealed away.
For example...
...his memory of that scarf you're wearing.
......
I don't mind. Please do it.
So you'll just deal with everything on your own?
......
This...
...is what I've prepared for.

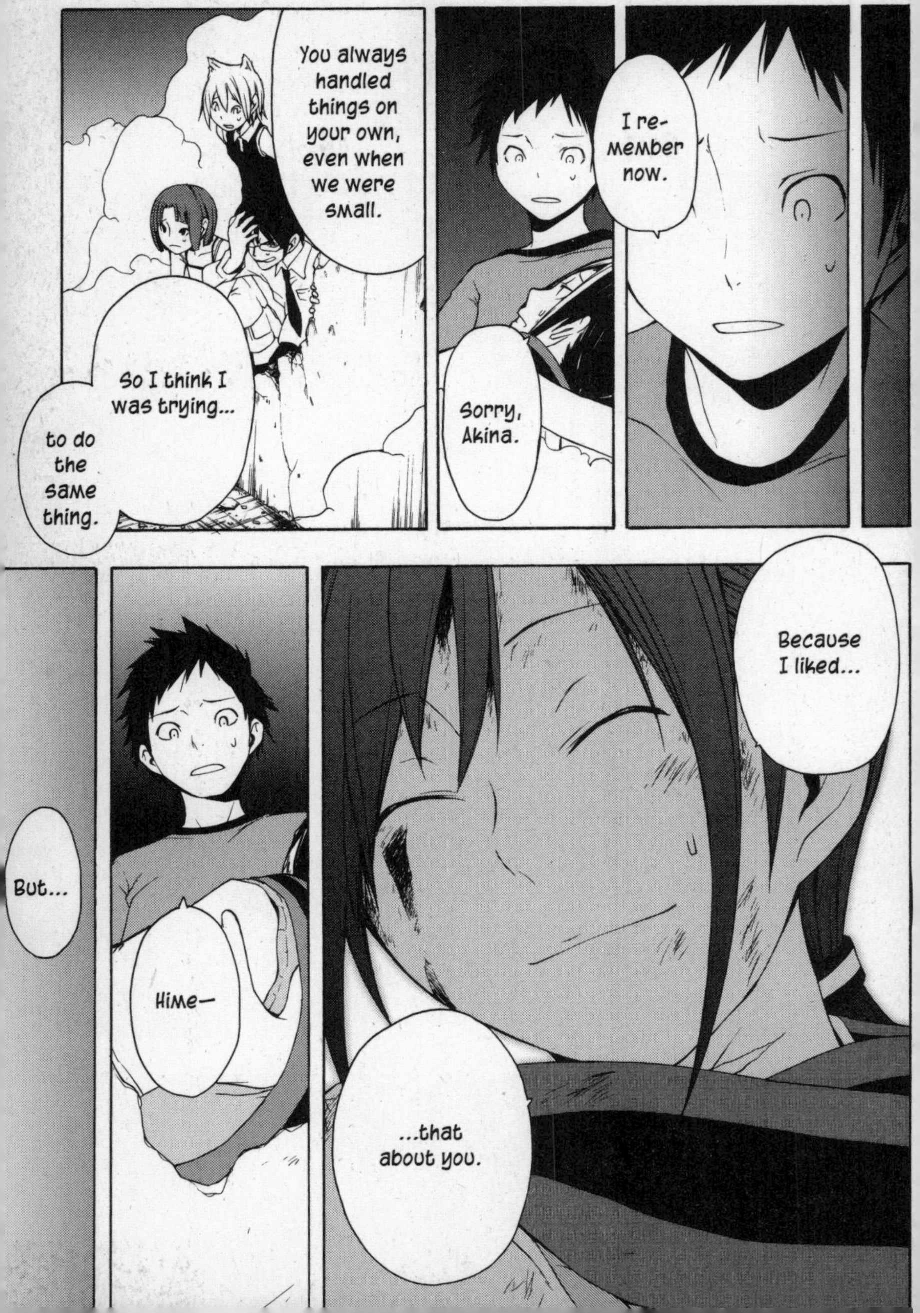
I re-member now.
Sorry, Akina.
You always handled things on your own, even when we were small.
So I think I was trying...
to do the same thing.
Because I liked...
...that about you.
Hime—
But...

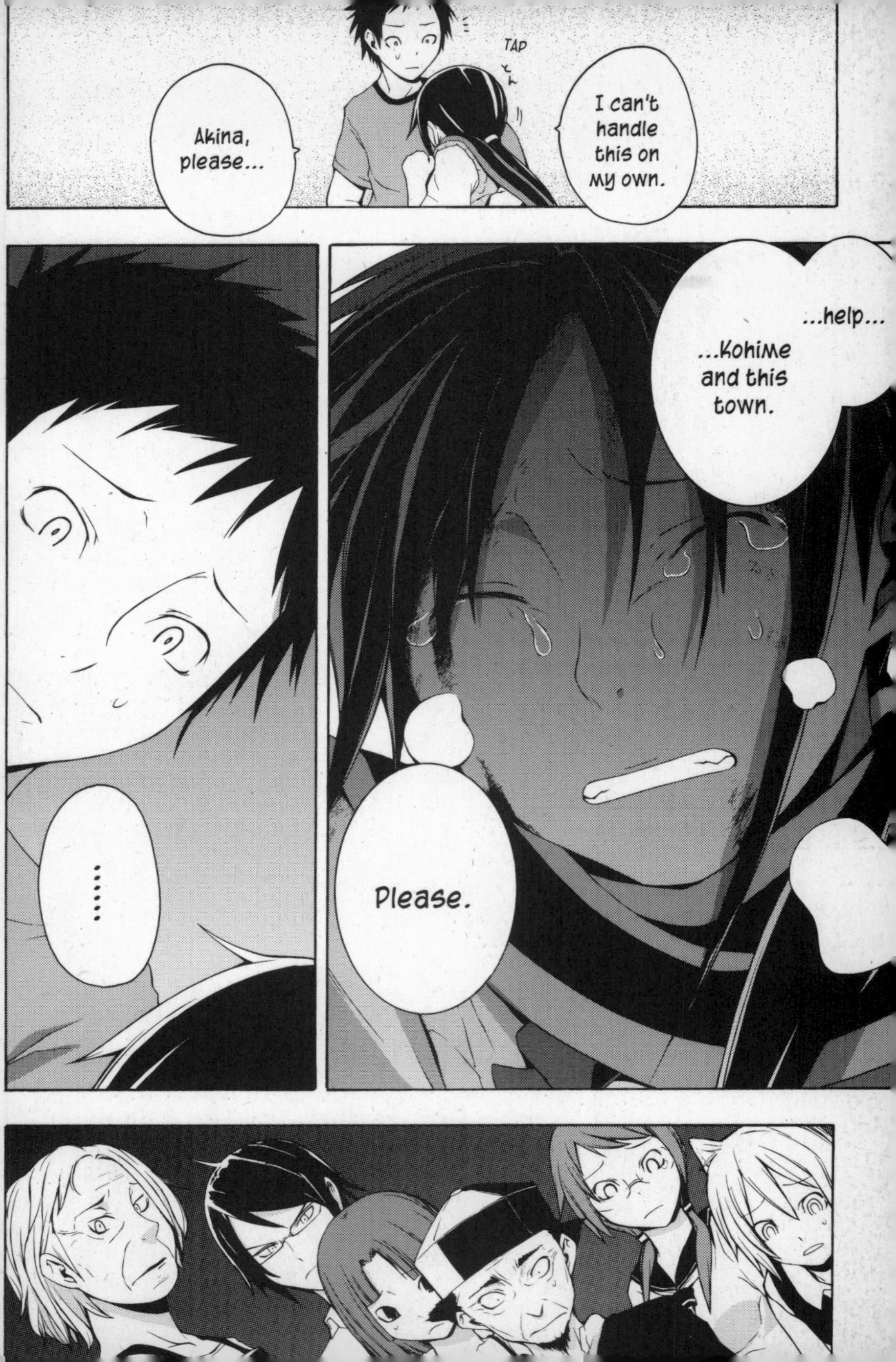
I can't handle this on my own.
TAP
Akina, please...
...help...
...Kohime and this town.
Please.
......

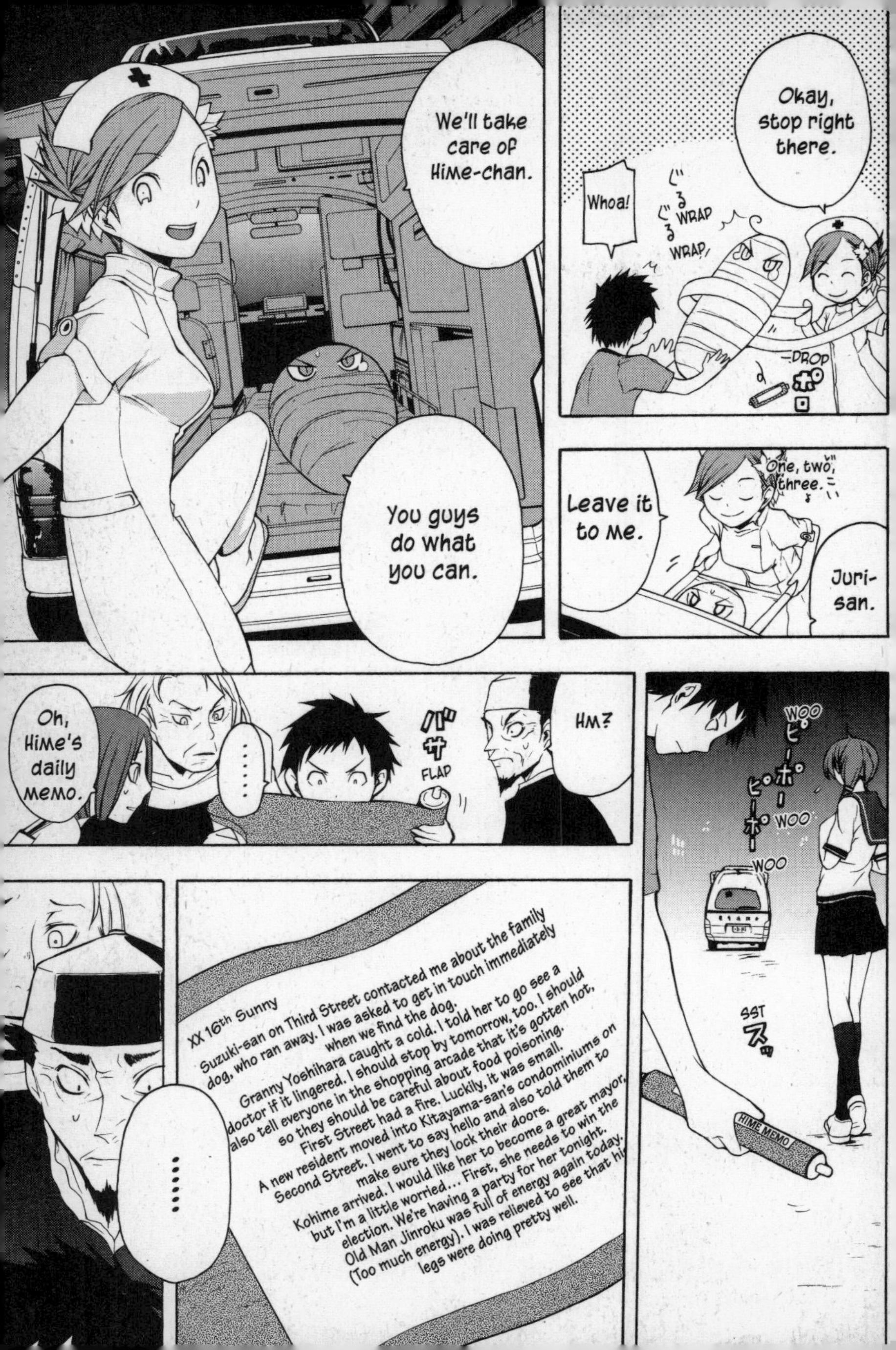
Okay, stop right there.
Whoa!
WRAP
WRAP
DROP
One, two, three.
Juri-san.
Leave it to me.
We'll take care of Hime-chan.
You guys do what you can.
WOO
WOO
WOO
SST
HIME MEMO
Hm?
FLAP
......
Oh, Hime's daily memo.
XX 16th Sunny
Suzuki-san on Third Street contacted me about the family dog, who ran away. I was asked to get in touch immediately when we find the dog.
Granny Yoshihara caught a cold. I told her to go see a doctor if it lingered. I should stop by tomorrow, too. I should also tell everyone in the shopping arcade that it's gotten hot, so they should be careful about food poisoning.
First Street had a fire. Luckily, it was small.
A new resident moved into Kitayama-san's condominiums on Second Street. I went to say hello and also told them to make sure they lock their doors.
Kohime arrived. I would like her to become a great mayor, but I'm a little worried... First, she needs to win the election. We're having a party for her tonight.
Old Man Jinroku was full of energy again today. (Too much energy). I was relieved to see that his legs were doing pretty well.
......

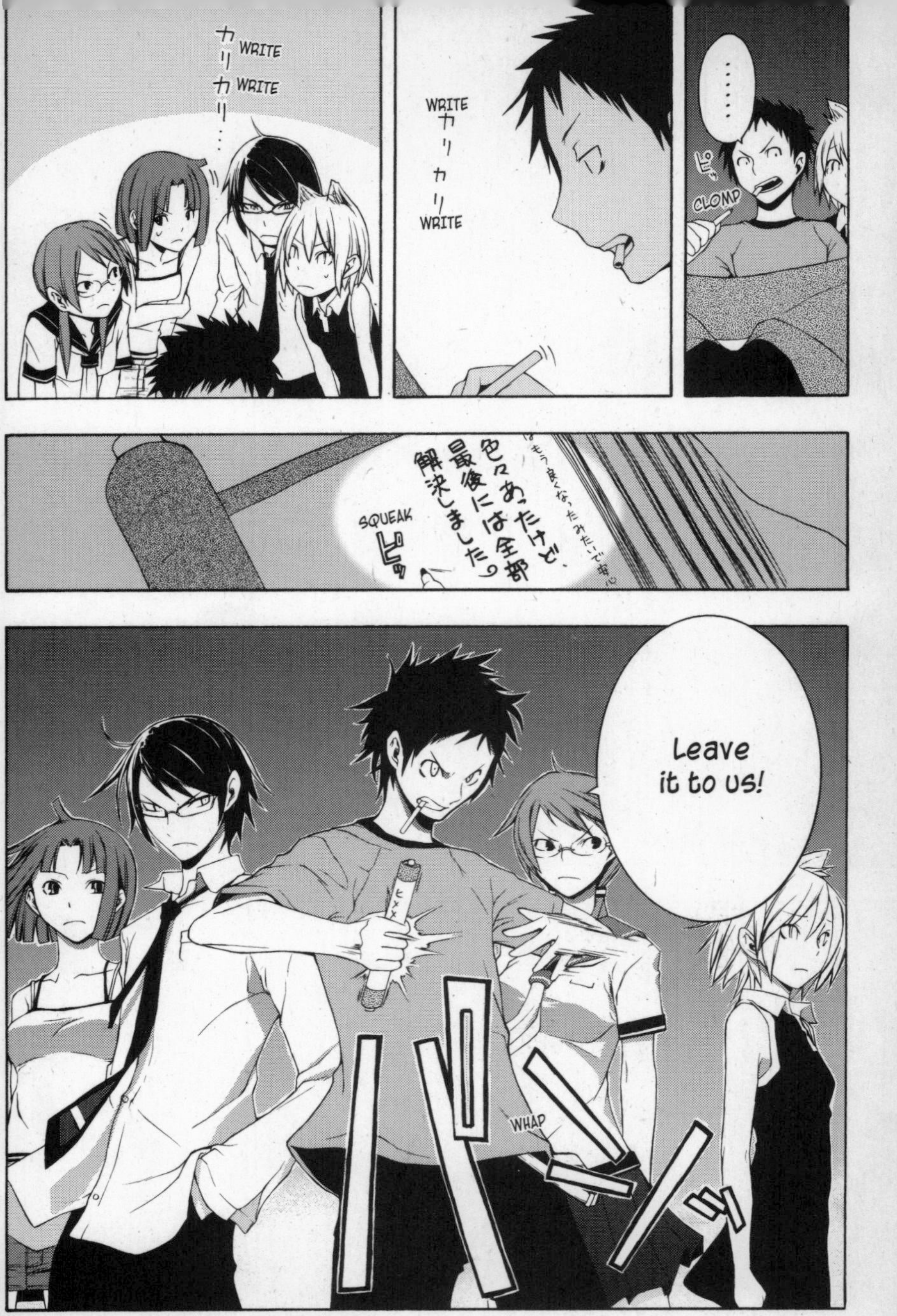
……
ピッ
CLOMP
WRITE
カリカリ
WRITE
カリカリ…
WRITE
WRITE
はもう良くなったみたいで安心
色々あったけど、
最後には全部
解決しました。
SQUEAK
ピッ
Leave it to us!
WHAP

Yozakura Quartet 3

Primary Stages of Yozakura Quartet

Yuuhi Shinatsuhiko

Age: Unknown

Hobbies:
Making Mariabell cosplay

Favorites

Food:
Anything made with flour

Music Group:
Akiyuki Nosaka

Comedian:
Nasu Nakanishi

Uchi-P Member:
Tet-chan

Little-Known Fact:
He is weak against sunlight.

At first,
he was this
cute.

13th Night: Thorny Road (Part 3) END

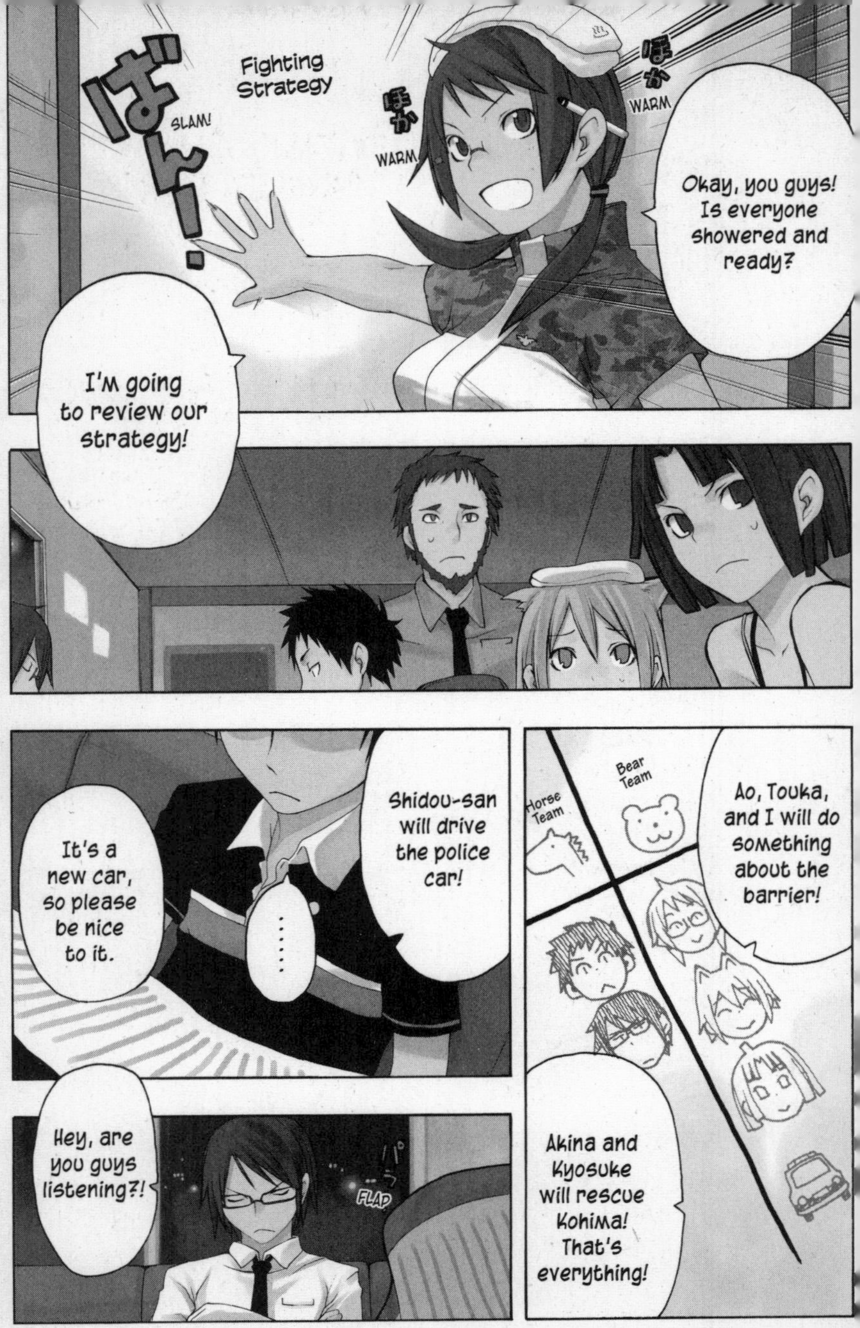
Fighting Strategy
ばん!
SLAM!
ほか
WARM
ほか
WARM
Okay, you guys! Is everyone showered and ready?
I'm going to review our strategy!
Ao, Touka, and I will do something about the barrier!
Bear Team
Horse Team
Akina and Kyosuke will rescue Kohima! That's everything!
Shidou-san will drive the police car!
......
It's a new car, so please be nice to it.
Hey, are you guys listening?!
パ
FLAP

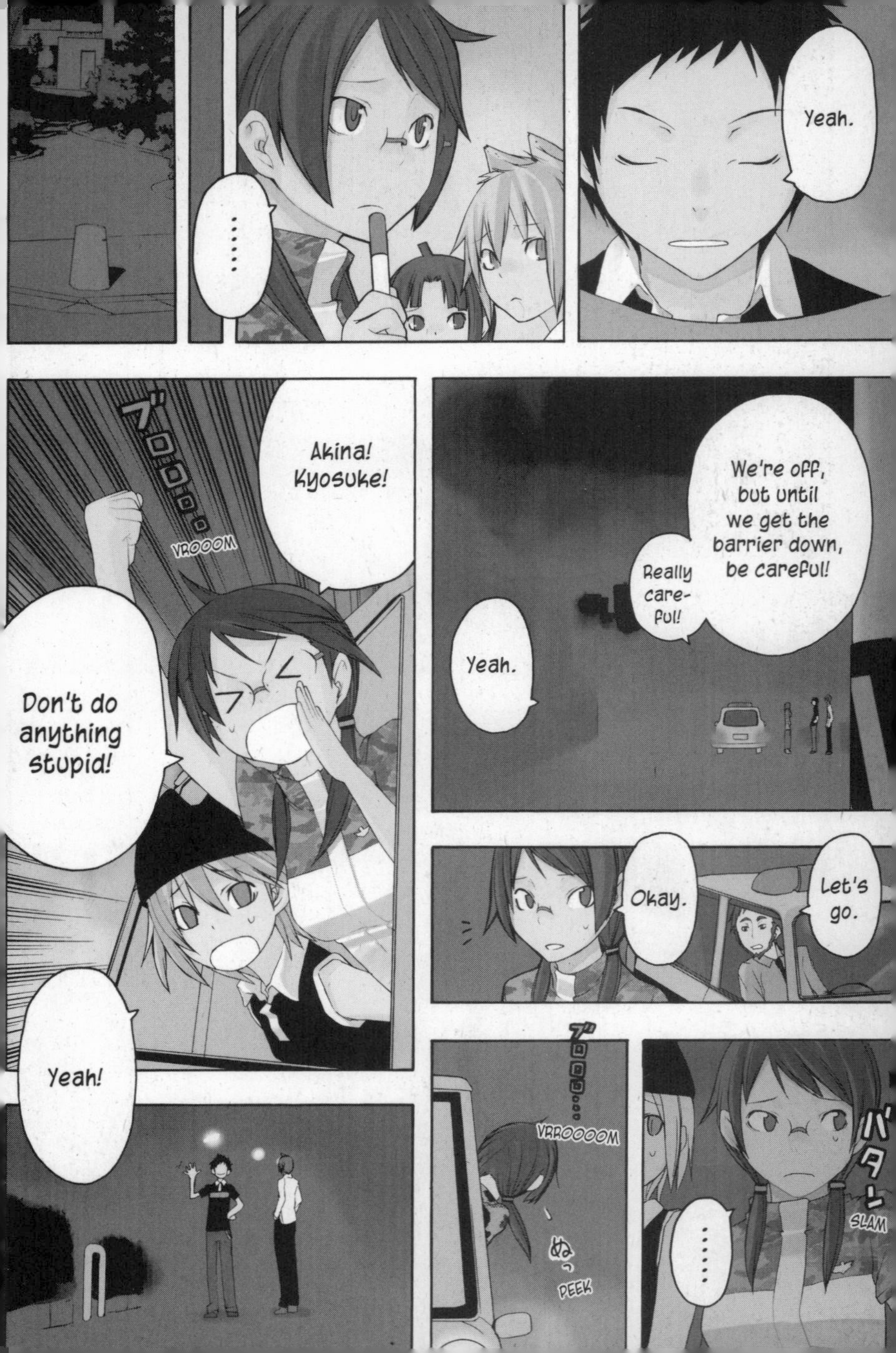
Yeah.
......
We're off, but until we get the barrier down, be careful!
Really care-ful!
Yeah.
Let's go.
Okay.
ブロロロ...
VROOOM
Akina! Kyosuke!
Don't do anything stupid!
Yeah!
バタン
SLAM
......
ブロロロ...
VRROOOOM
ぬっ
PEEK

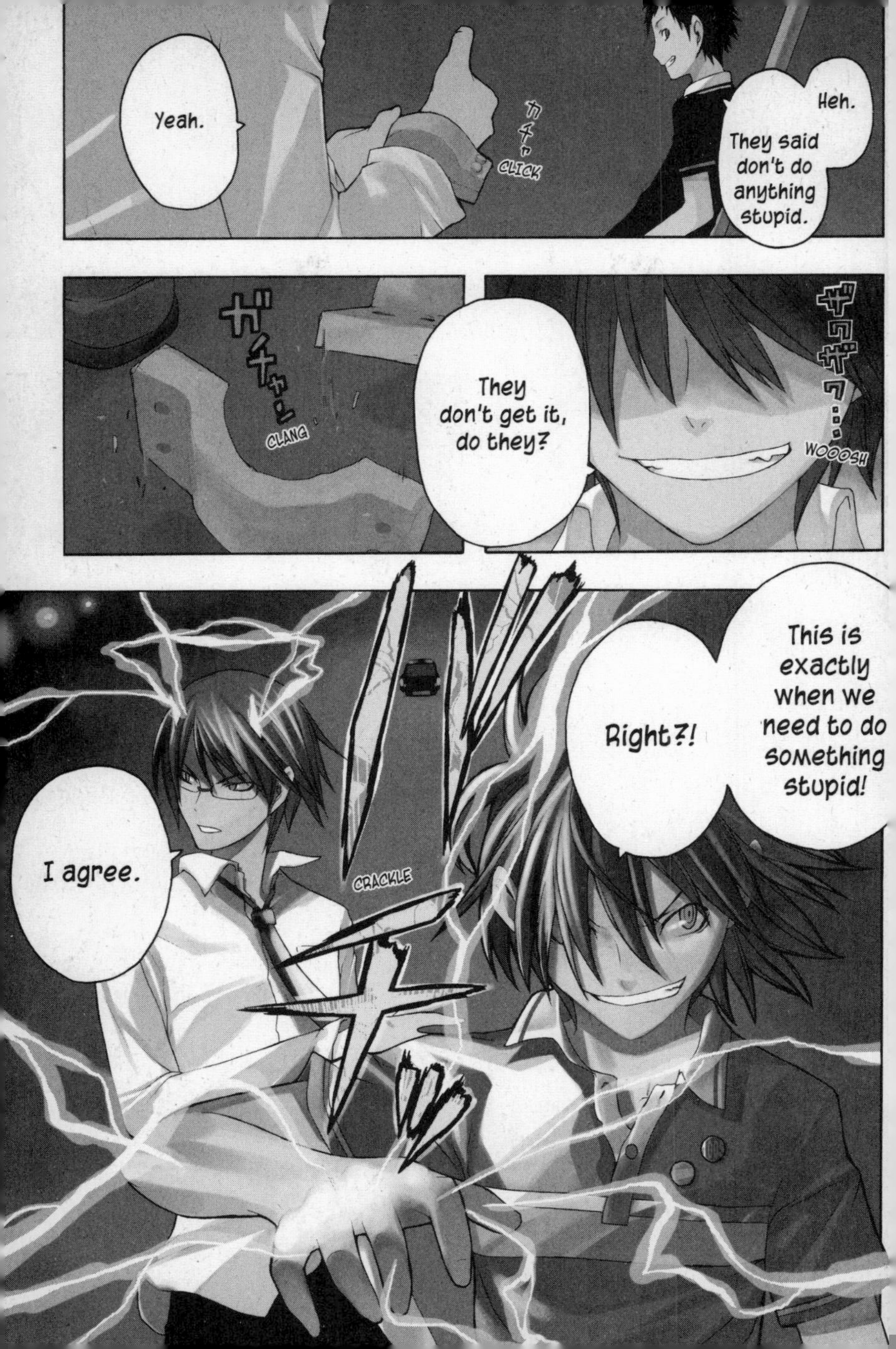
Heh.
They said don't do anything stupid.
CLICK
Yeah.
WOOOSH
They don't get it, do they?
CLANG
This is exactly when we need to do something stupid!
Right?!
CRACKLE
I agree.

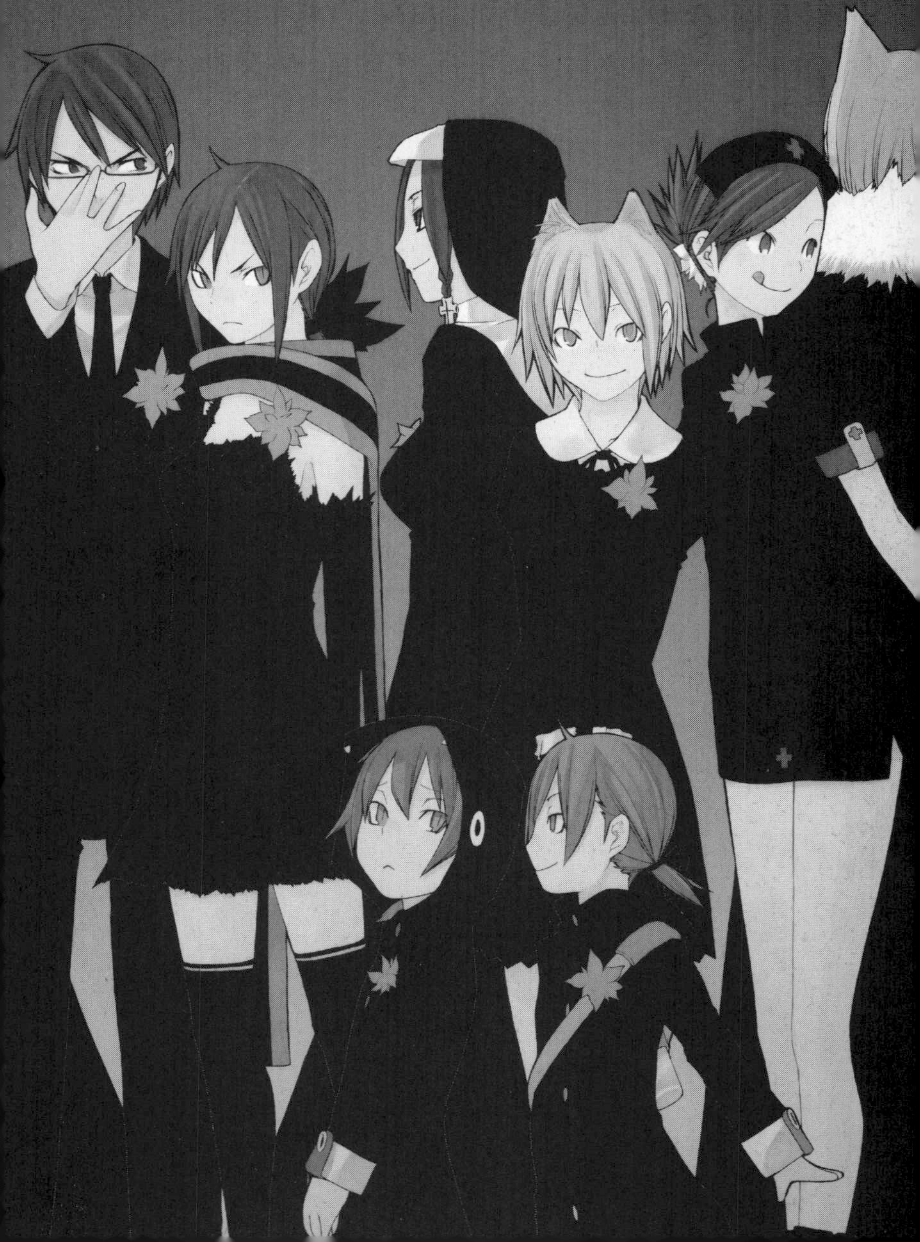

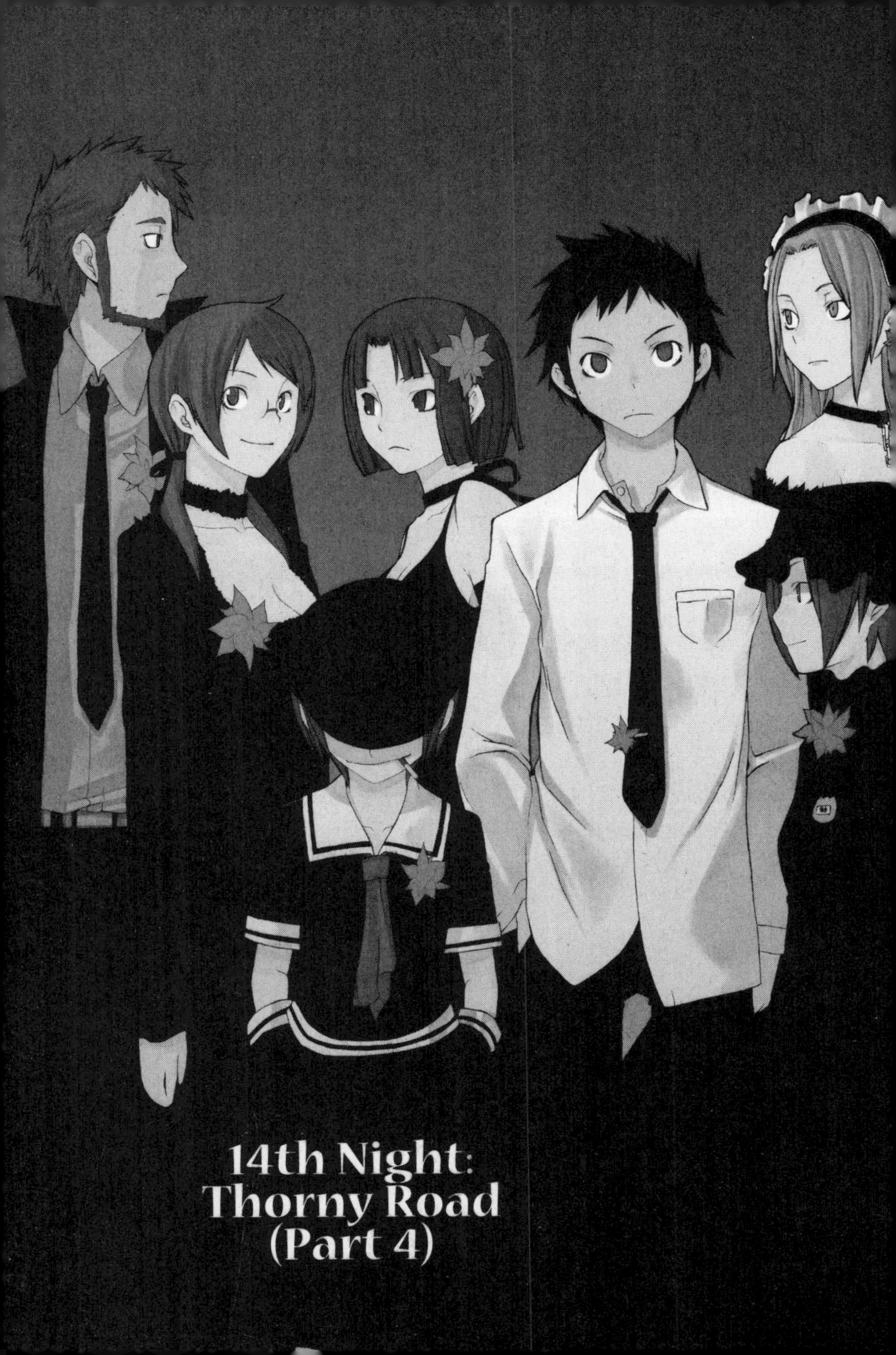

14th Night: Thorny Road (Part 4)

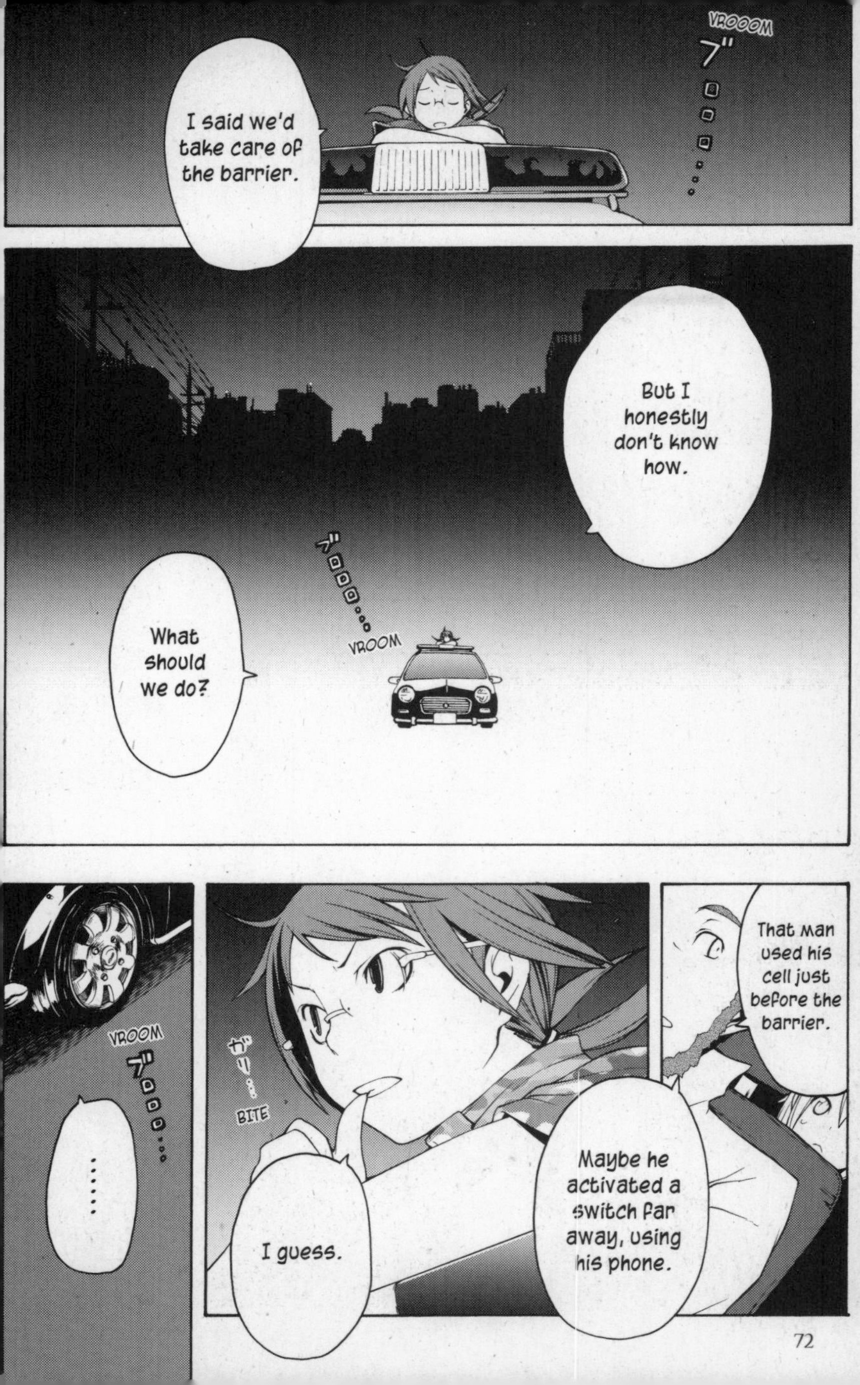
VROOOM
ブロロロ…
I said we'd take care of the barrier.
But I honestly don't know how.
ブロロロ…
VROOM
What should we do?
That man used his cell just before the barrier.
Maybe he activated a switch far away, using his phone.
ガリ…
BITE
I guess.
VROOM
ブロロロ…
……

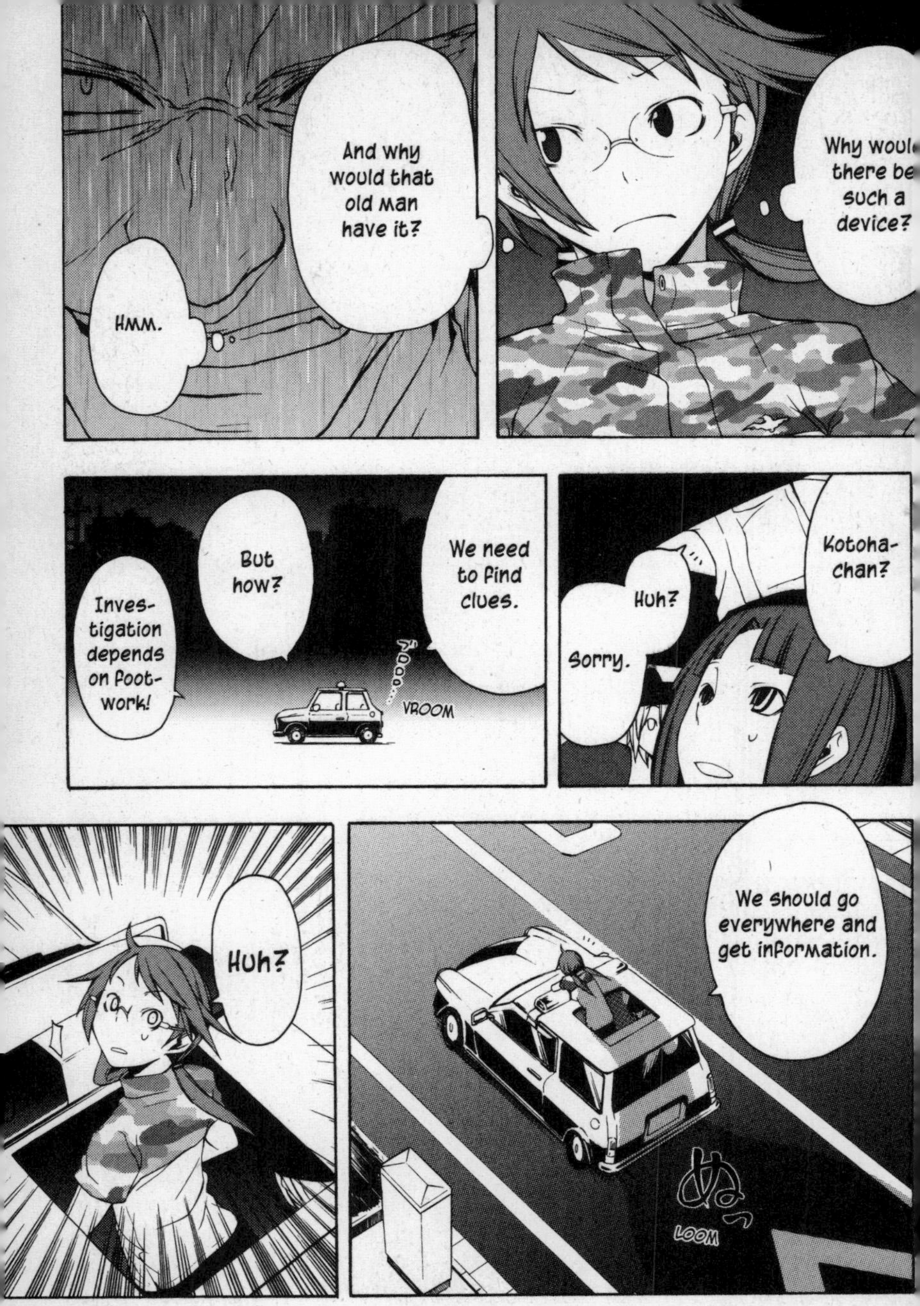
Why woul
there be
such a
device?
And why would that old man have it?
Hmm.
Kotoha-chan?
Huh?
Sorry.
We need to find clues.
But how?
Investigation depends on foot-work!
VROOM
We should go everywhere and get information.
ぬっ
LOOM
Huh?

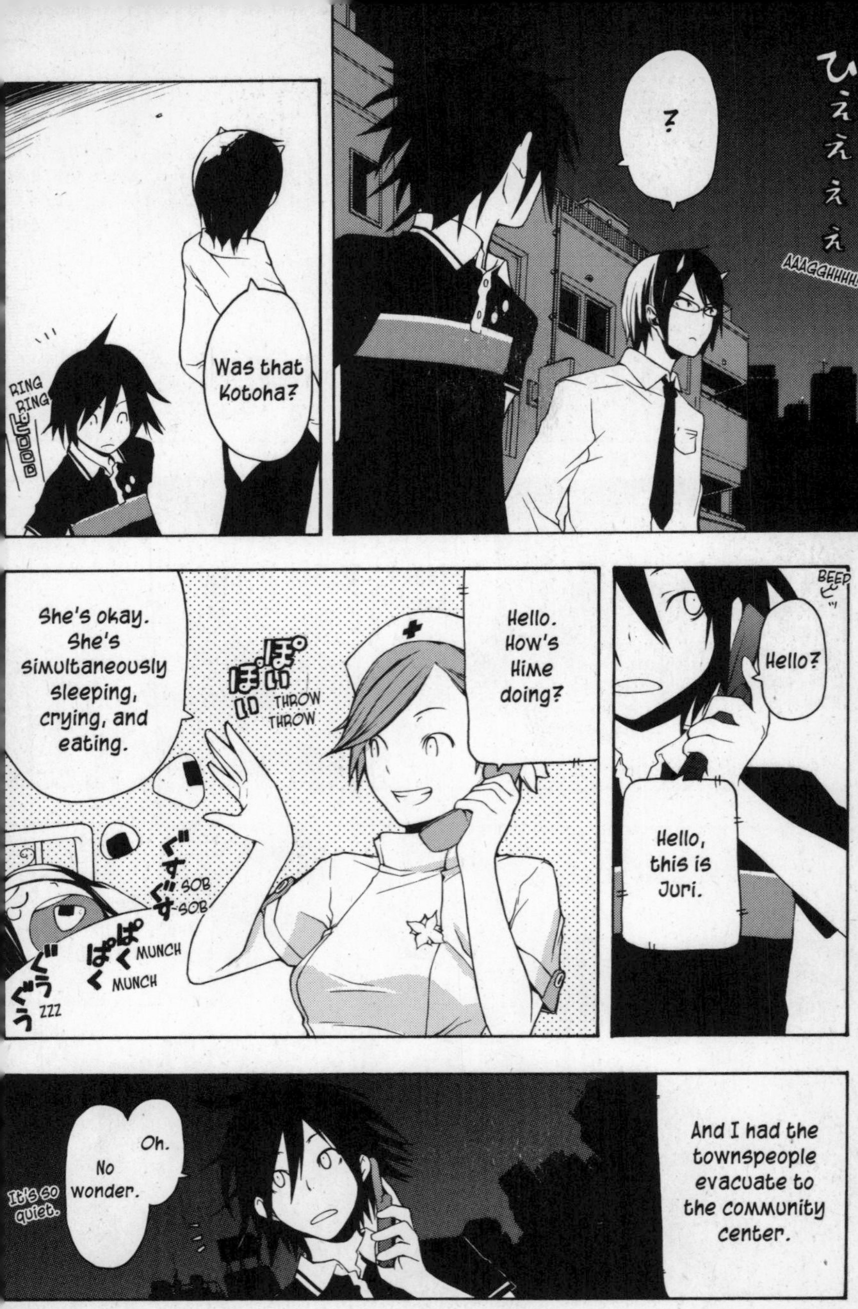
ひえええええ
AAAGGHHHH!
?
Was that Kotoha?
RING RING
BEEP
ピッ
Hello?
Hello, this is Juri.
Hello. How's Hime doing?
She's okay. She's simultaneously sleeping, crying, and eating.
ぽいぽい
THROW THROW
ぐすぐす
SOB SOB
ぱくぱく
MUNCH MUNCH
ぐうぐう
ZZZ
And I had the townspeople evacuate to the community center.
Oh.
No wonder.
It's so quiet.

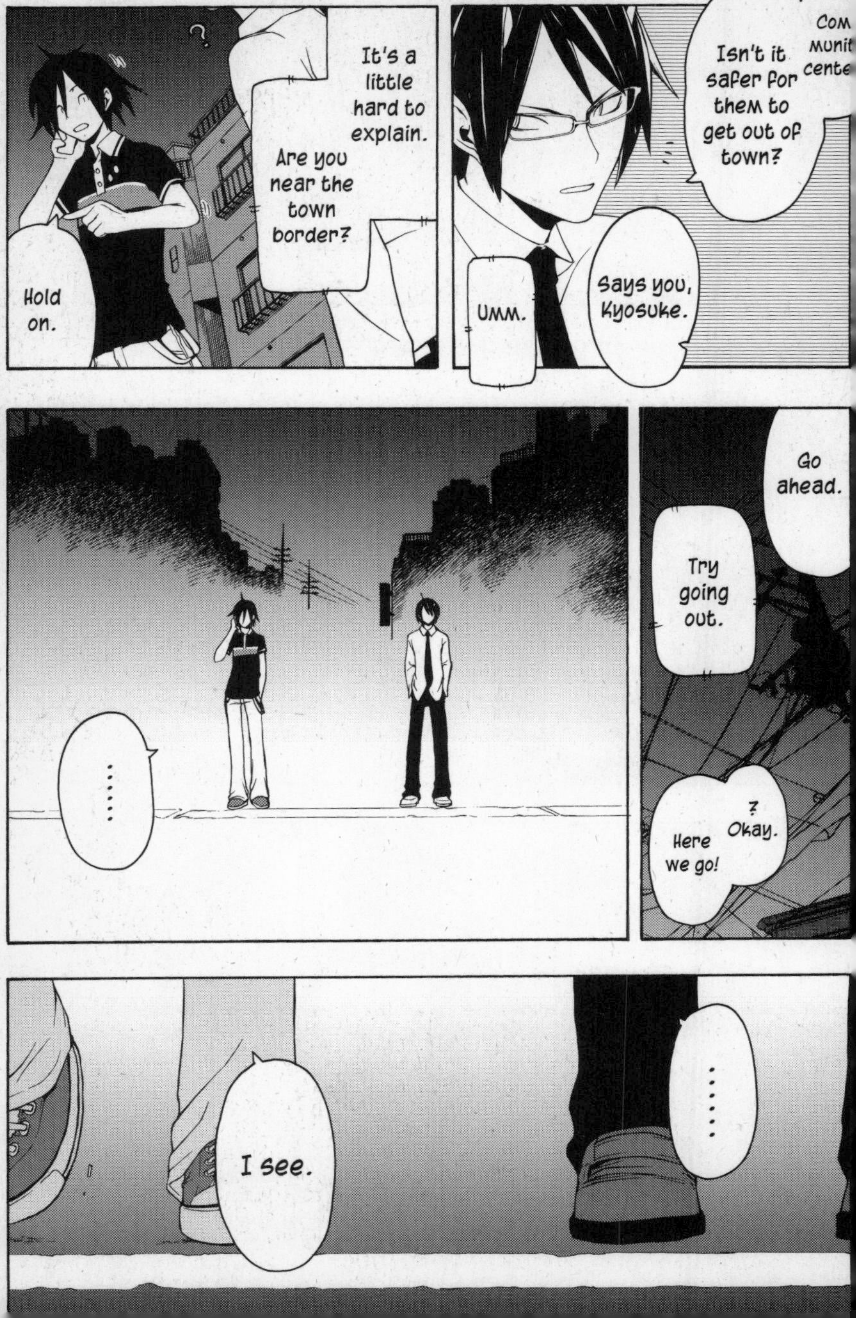
Com munit cente
Isn't it safer for them to get out of town?
Says you, Kyosuke.
Umm.
It's a little hard to explain.
Are you near the town border?
Hold on.
Go ahead.
Try going out.
? Okay.
Here we go!
......
......
I see.

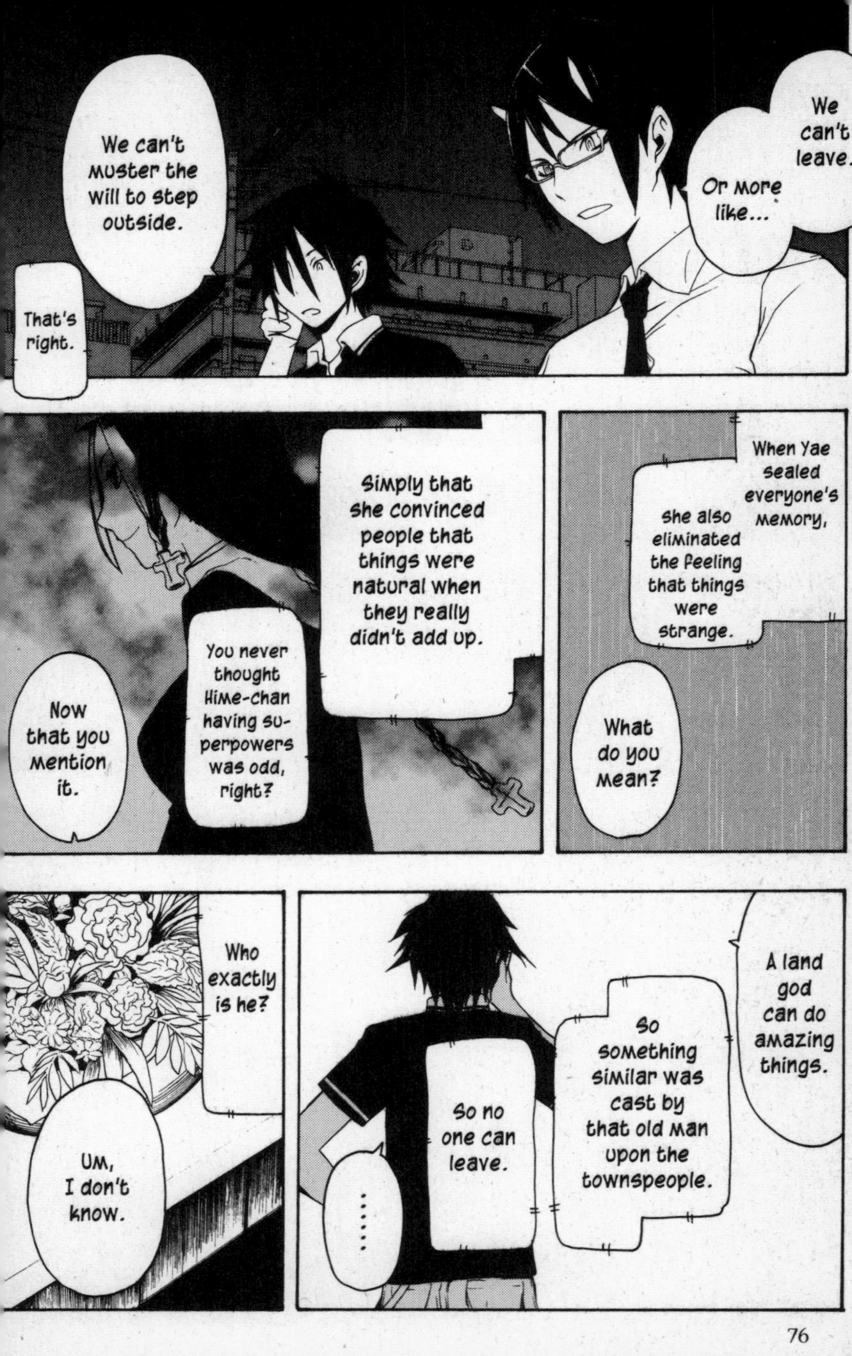
We can't leave.
Or more like...
We can't muster the will to step outside.
That's right.
When Yae sealed everyone's memory,
she also eliminated the feeling that things were strange.
What do you mean?
Simply that she convinced people that things were natural when they really didn't add up.
You never thought Hime-chan having superpowers was odd, right?
Now that you mention it.
A land god can do amazing things.
So something similar was cast by that old man upon the townspeople.
So no one can leave.
......
Who exactly is he?
Um, I don't know.

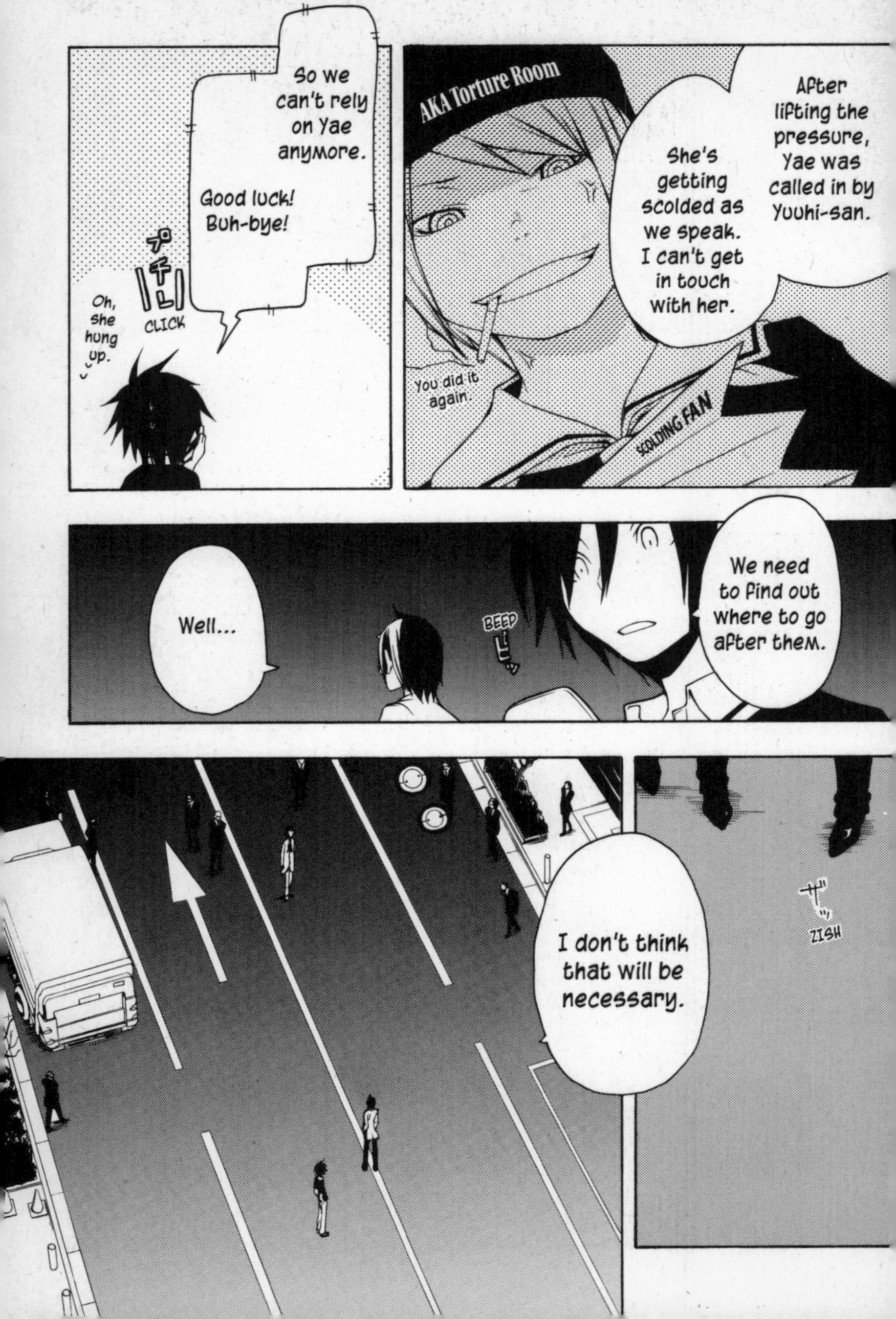
AKA Torture Room
After lifting the pressure, Yae was called in by Yuuhi-san.
She's getting scolded as we speak. I can't get in touch with her.
You did it again.
SCOLDING FAN
So we can't rely on Yae anymore.
Good luck! Buh-bye!
CLICK
Oh, she hung up.
We need to find out where to go after them.
BEEP
Well...
ZISH
I don't think that will be necessary.

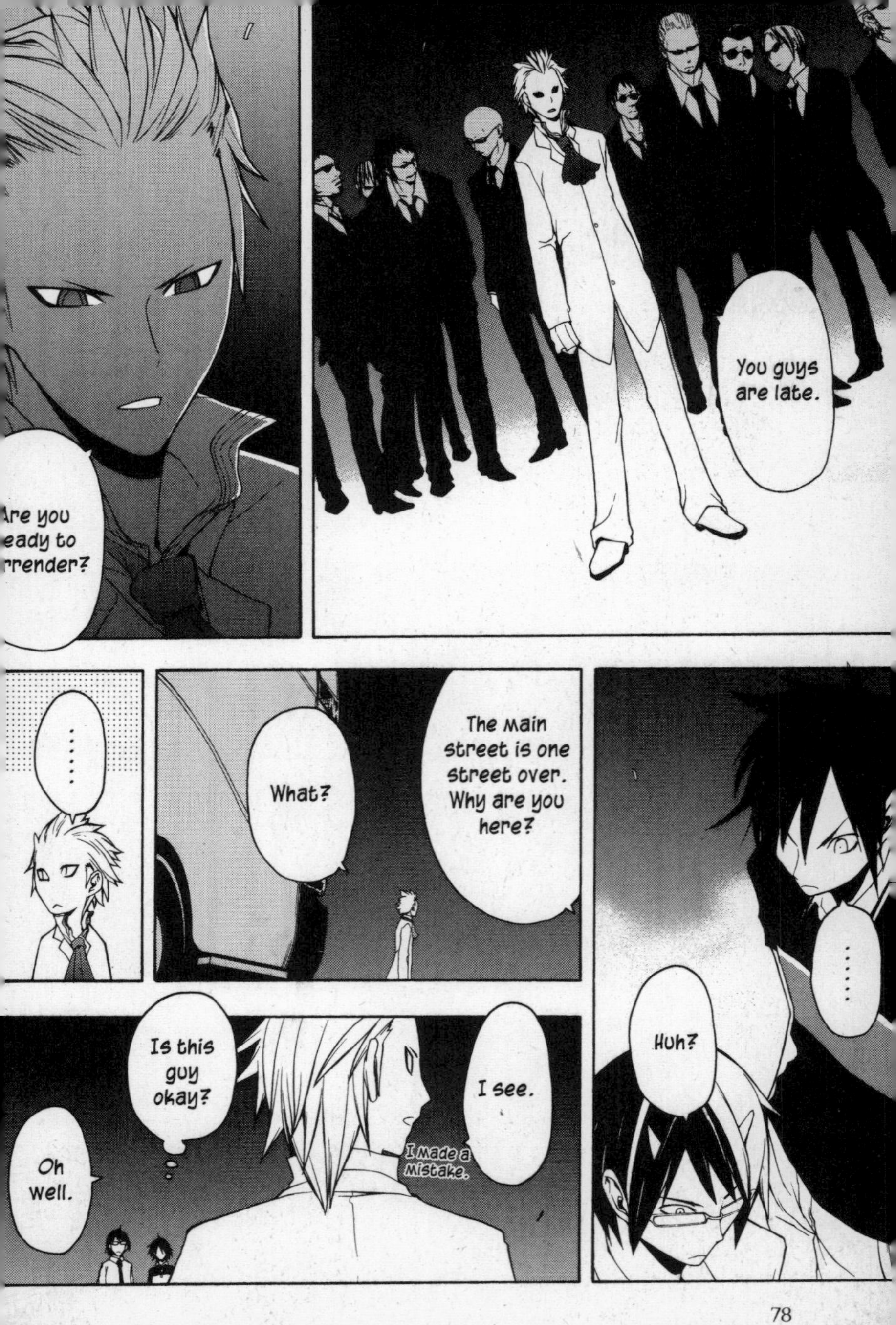
You guys are late.
Are you
eady to
rrender?
......
Huh?
The main street is one street over. Why are you here?
What?
......
I see.
I made a mistake.
Is this guy okay?
Oh well.

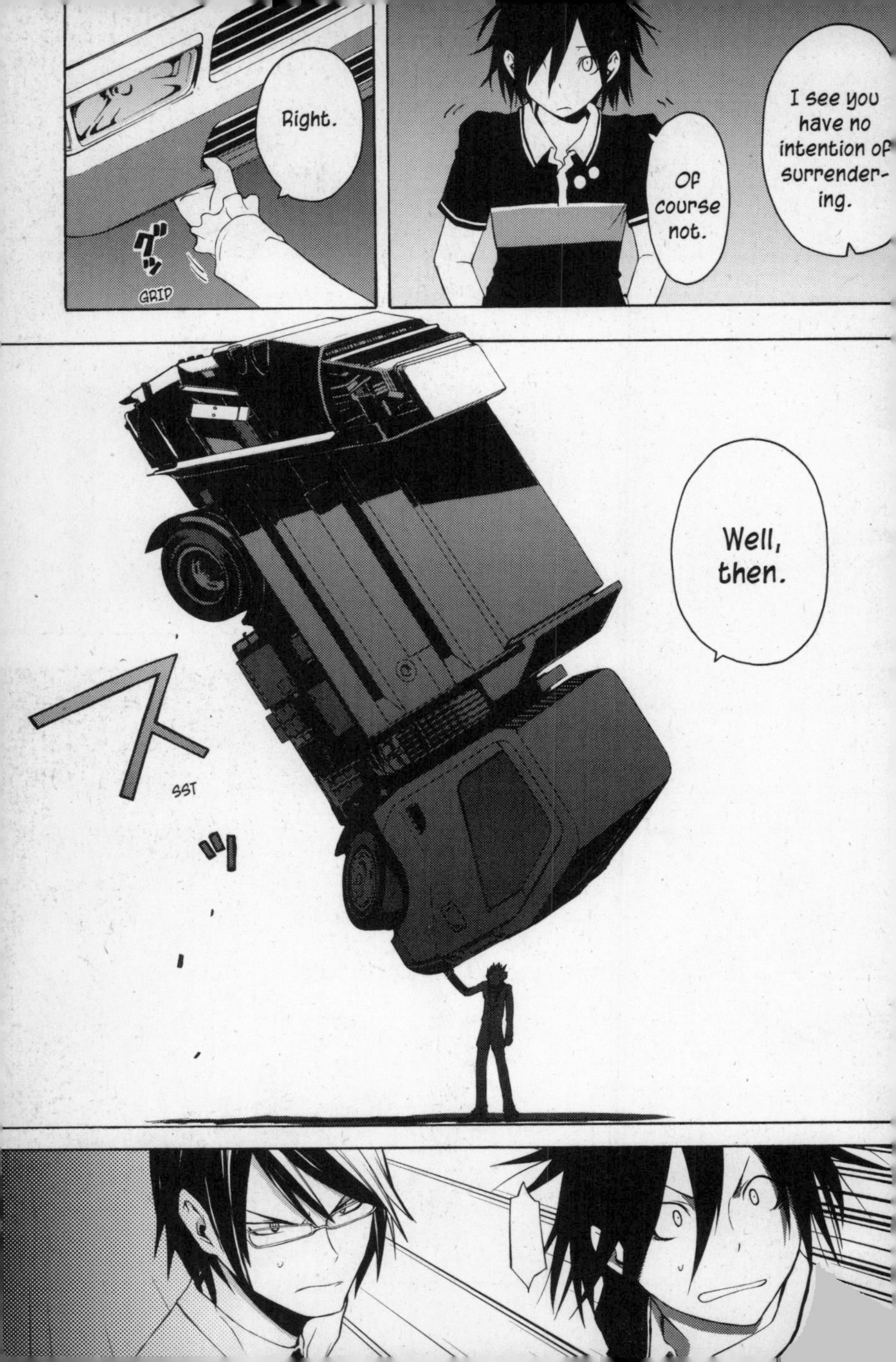
I see you have no intention of surrender-ing.
Of course not.
Right.
グッ
GRIP
Well, then.
スッ
SST

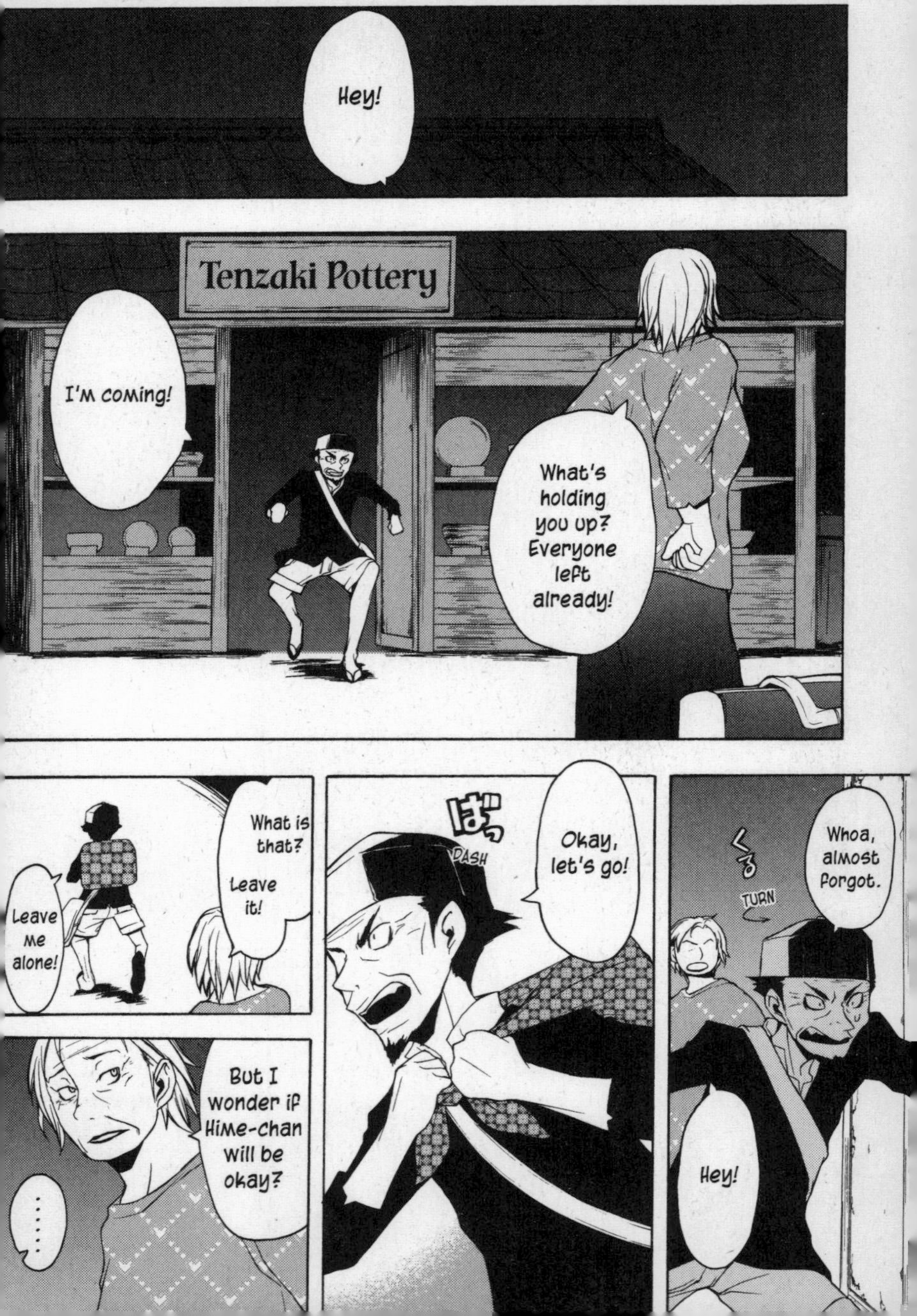
Hey!
Tenzaki Pottery
What's holding you up? Everyone left already!
I'm coming!
Whoa, almost forgot.
くる
TURN
Hey!
ばっ
DASH
Okay, let's go!
What is that?
Leave it!
Leave me alone!
But I wonder if Hime-chan will be okay?
......

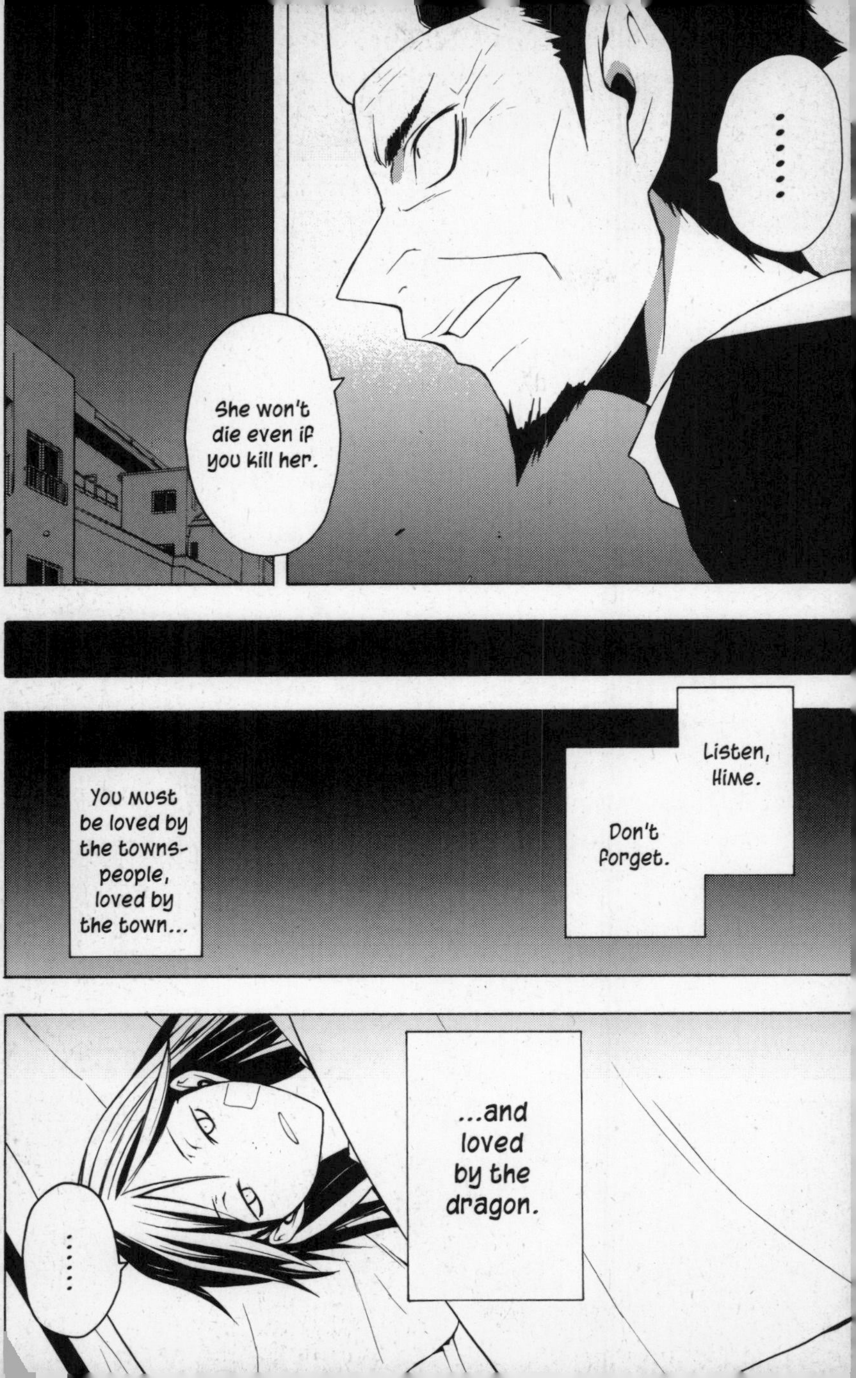
......
She won't die even if you kill her.
Listen, Hime.
Don't forget.
You must be loved by the towns-people, loved by the town...
...and loved by the dragon.
......

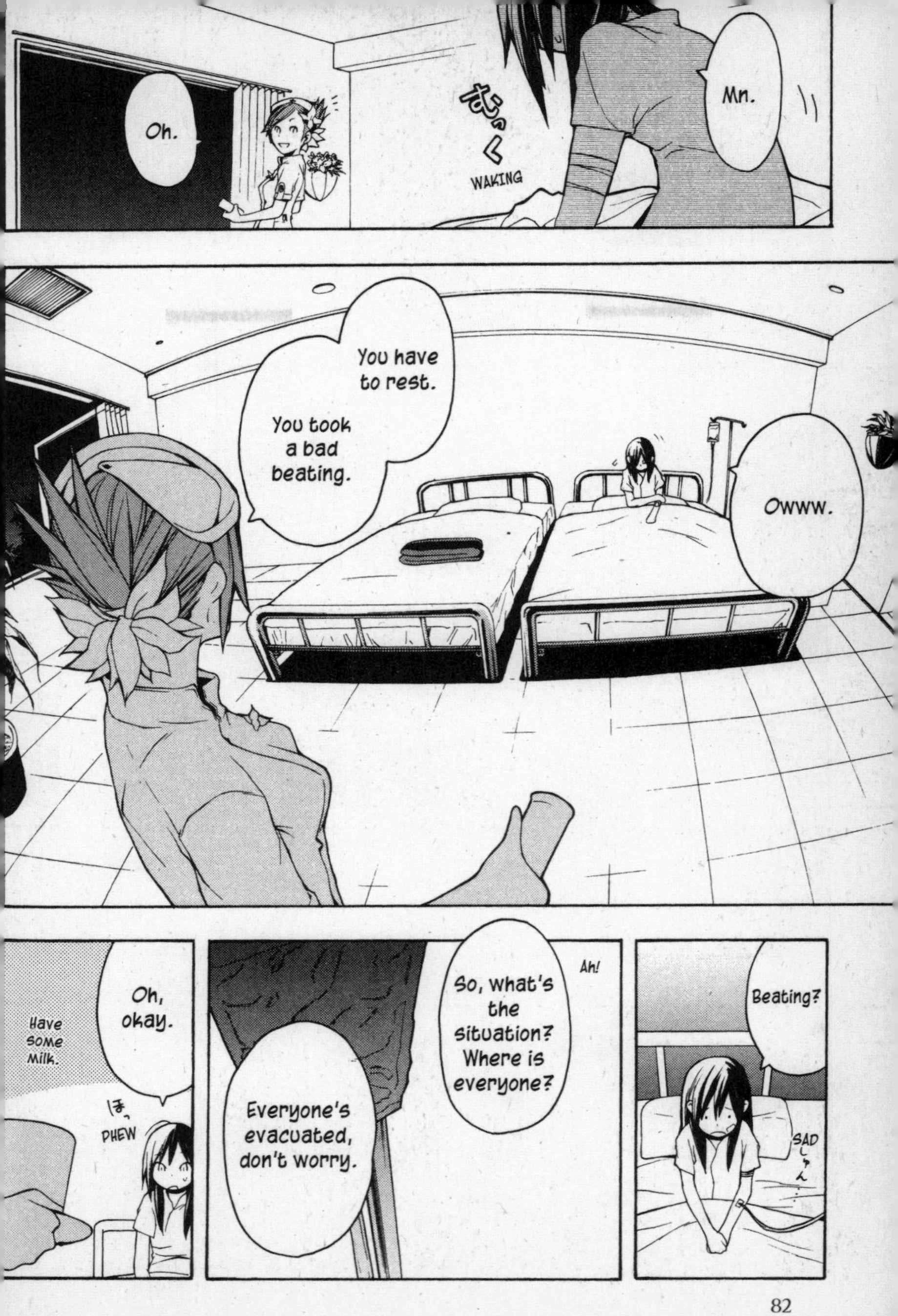
Mn.
むっく
WAKING
Oh.
Owww.
You have to rest.
You took a bad beating.
Beating?
SAD しゅん…
Ah!
So, what's the situation? Where is everyone?
Everyone's evacuated, don't worry.
Oh, okay.
Have some milk.
ほっ
PHEW

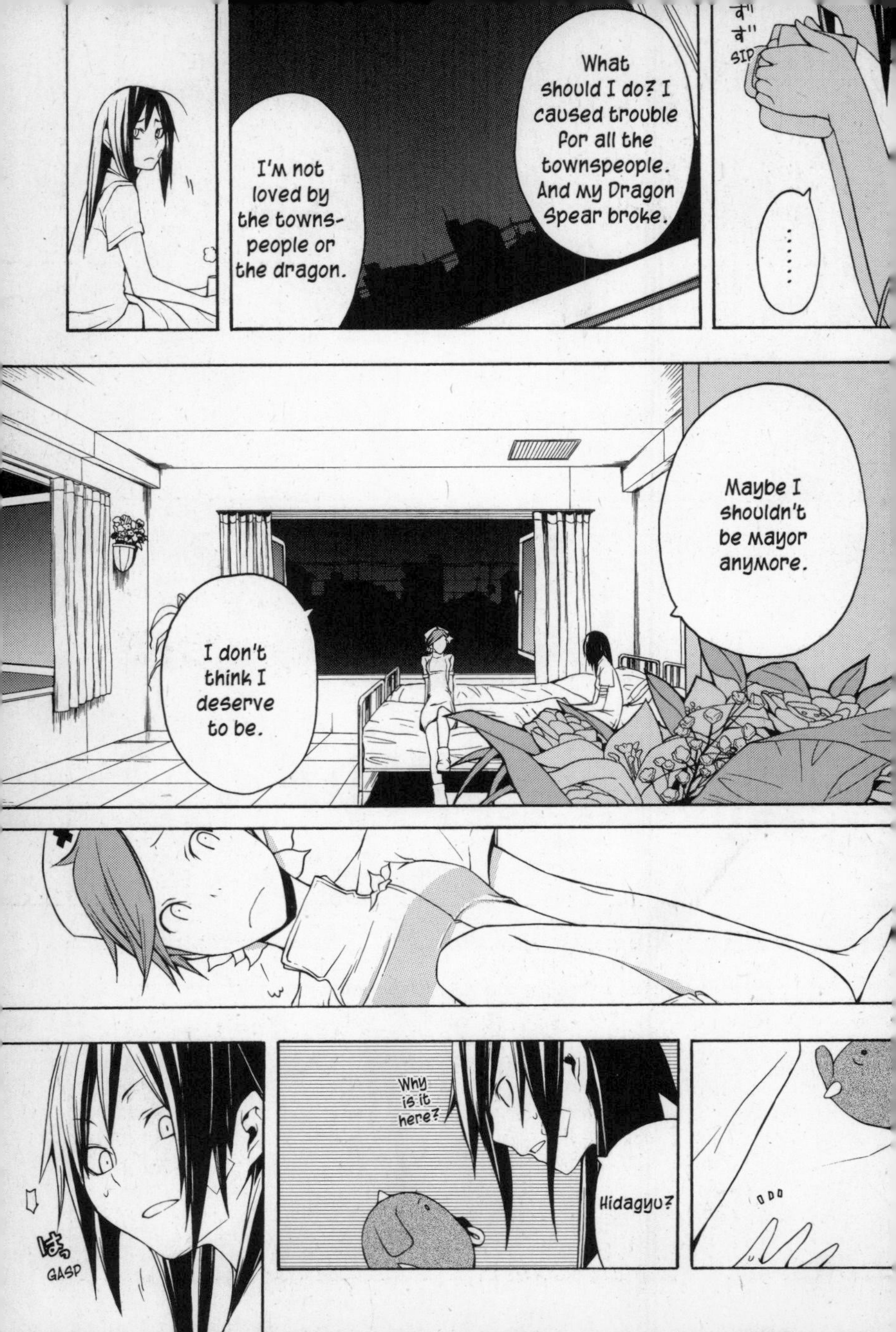
ずず
SIP
......
What should I do? I caused trouble for all the townspeople. And my Dragon Spear broke.
I'm not loved by the towns-people or the dragon.
Maybe I shouldn't be mayor anymore.
I don't think I deserve to be.
Hidagyu?
Why is it here?
はっ
GASP

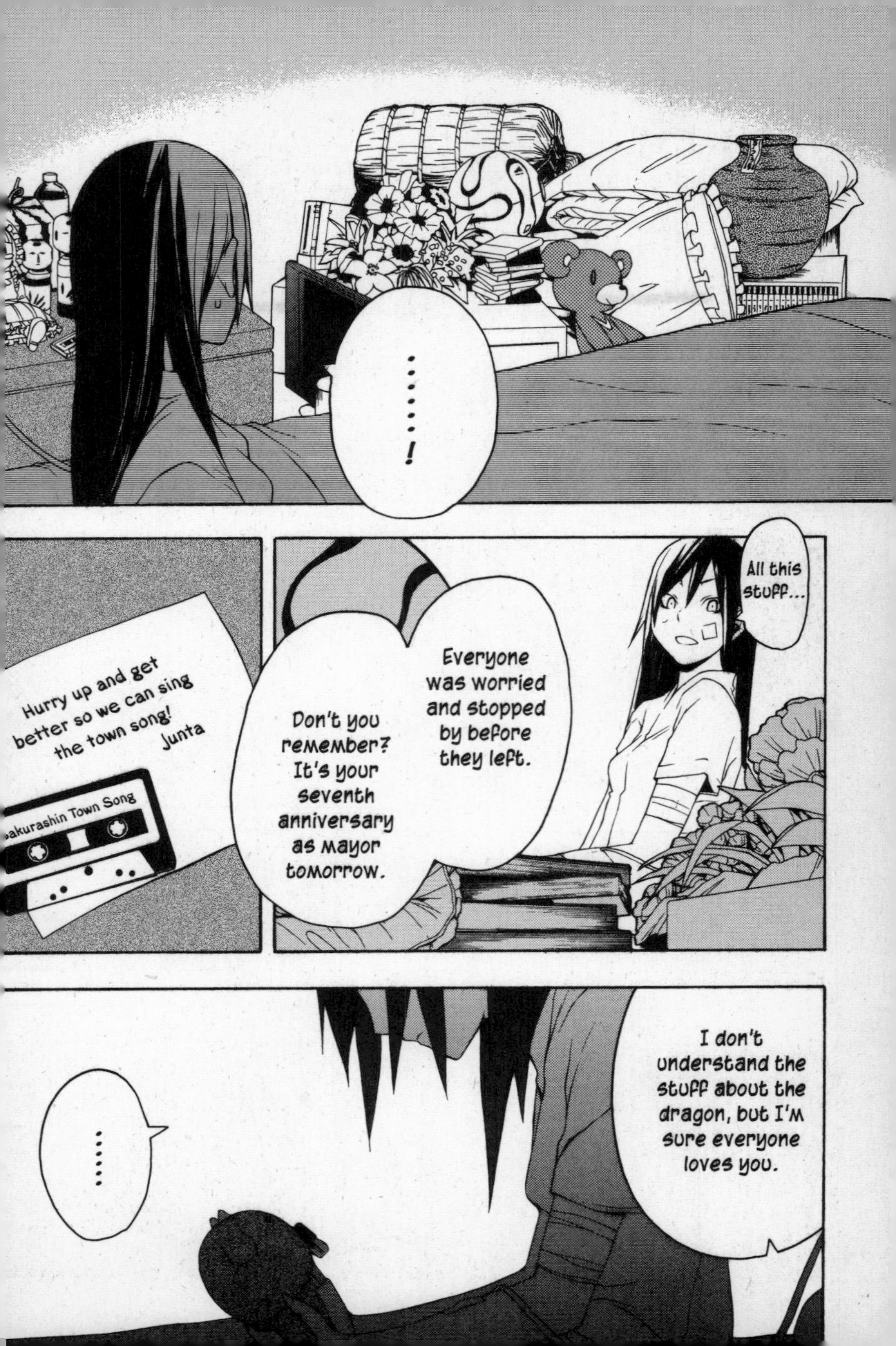
......!
All this stuff...
Everyone was worried and stopped by before they left.
Don't you remember? It's your seventh anniversary as mayor tomorrow.
Hurry up and get better so we can sing the town song! Junta
akurashin Town Song
I don't understand the stuff about the dragon, but I'm sure everyone loves you.
......

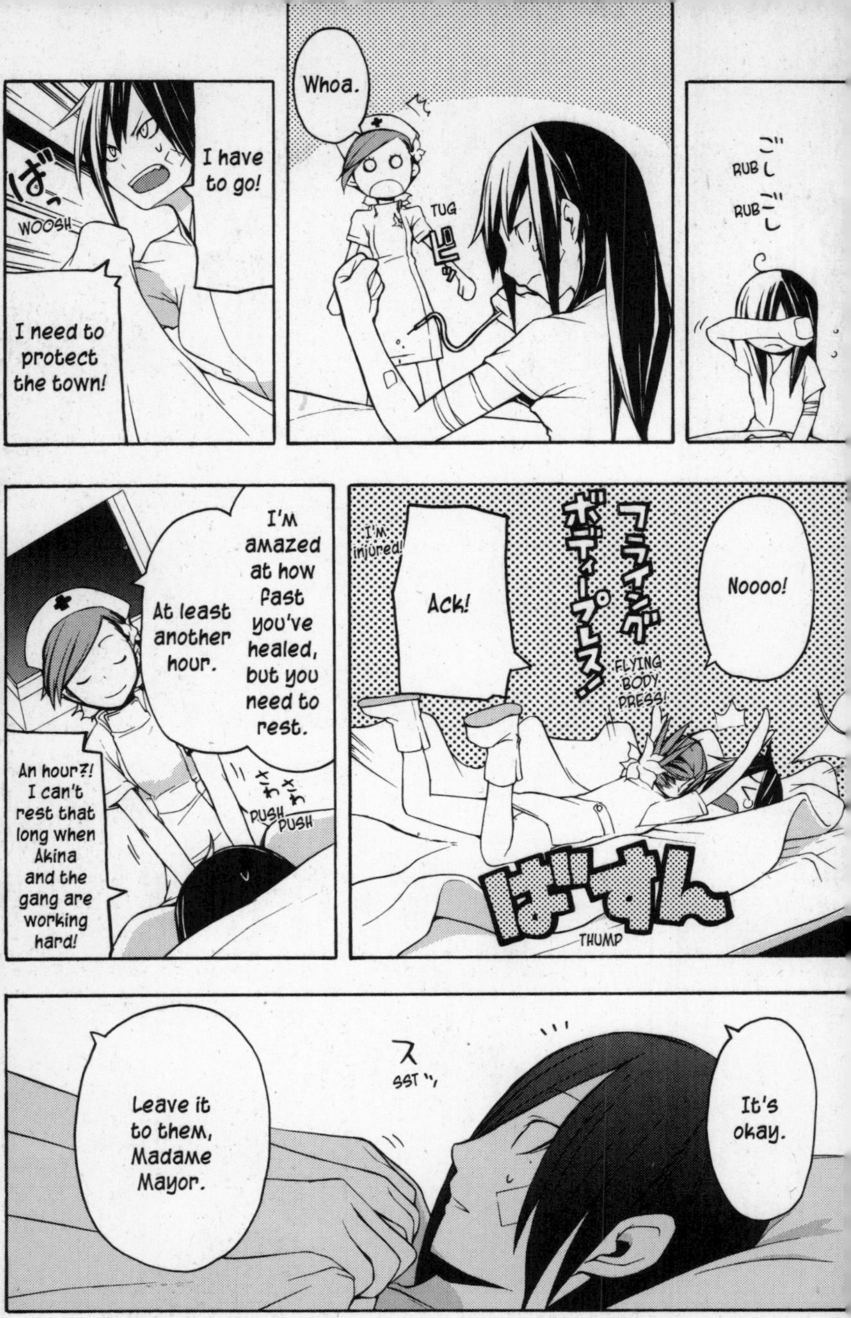

ごしごし
RUB RUB
Whoa.
TUG
ピッ
I have to go!
ばっ
WOOSH
I need to protect the town!
Noooo!
フライングボディープレス!
FLYING BODY PRESS!
I'm injured!
Ack!
ばすん
THUMP
I'm amazed at how fast you've healed, but you need to rest.
At least another hour.
さわさわ
PUSH PUSH
An hour?! I can't rest that long when Akina and the gang are working hard!
It's okay.
ス
SST
Leave it to them, Madame Mayor.

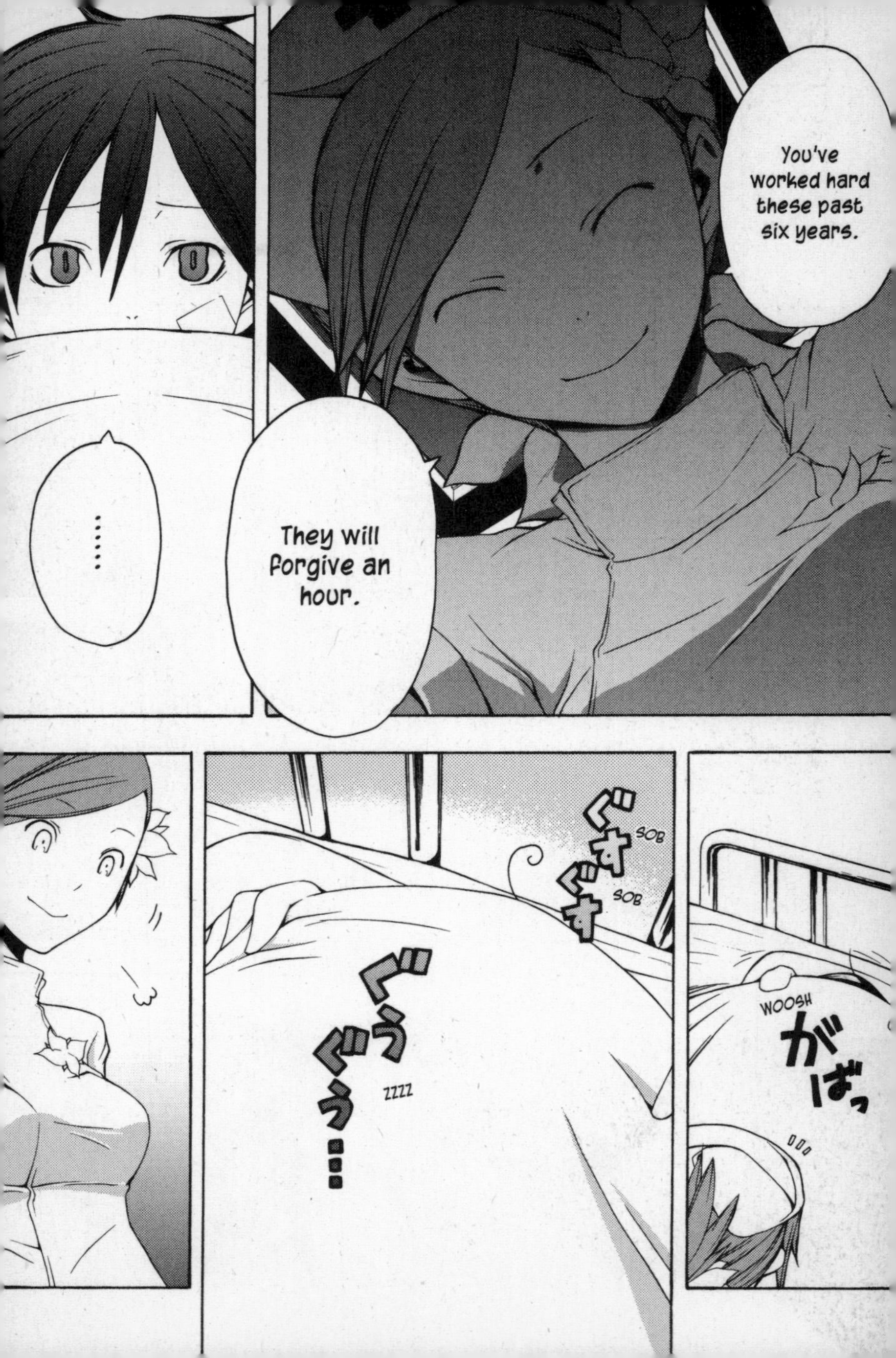

You've worked hard these past six years.
They will forgive an hour.
......
WOOSH
がばっ
ぐすぐす
SOB
SOB
ぐうぐう…
ZZZZ

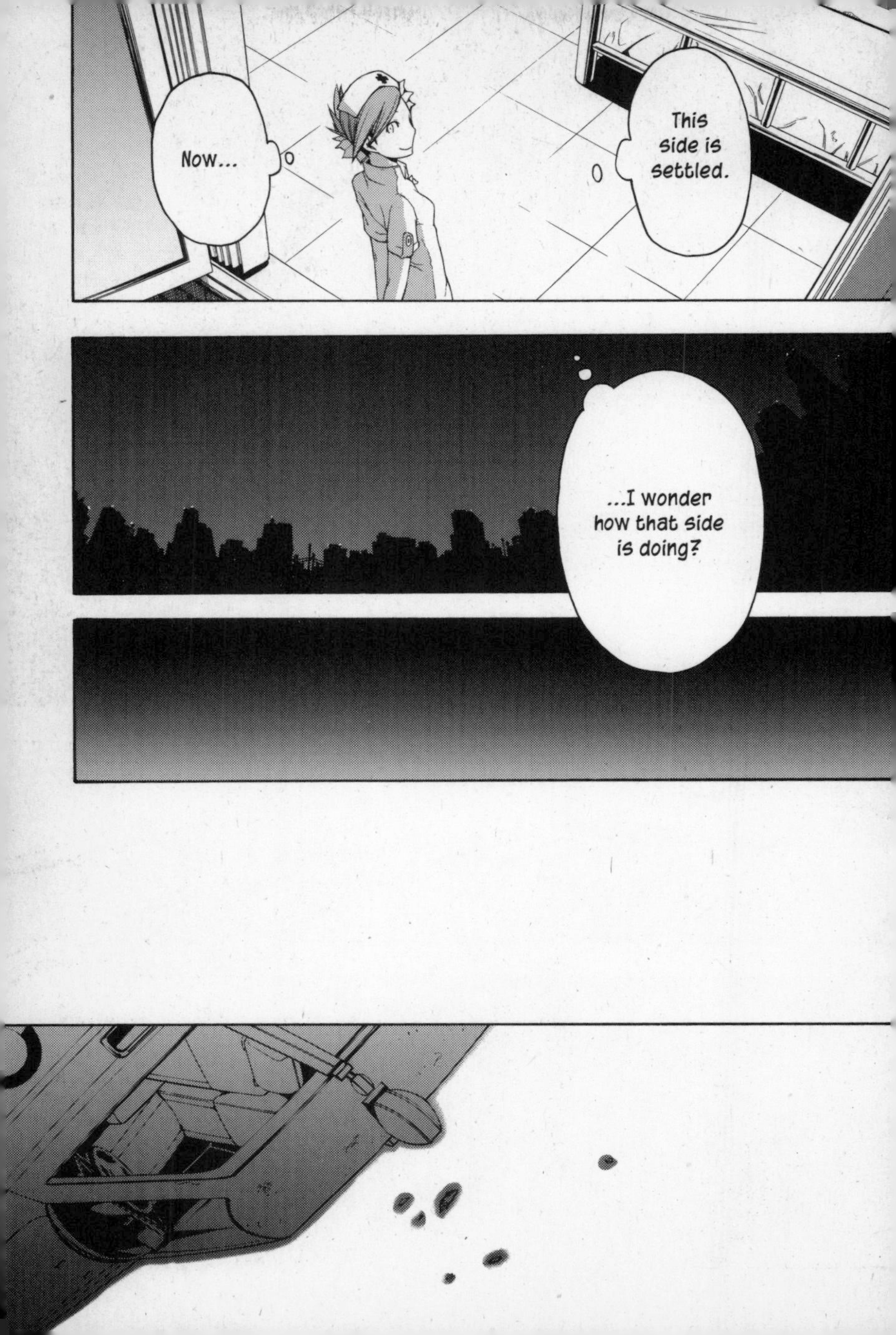
This side is settled.
Now...
...I wonder how that side is doing?

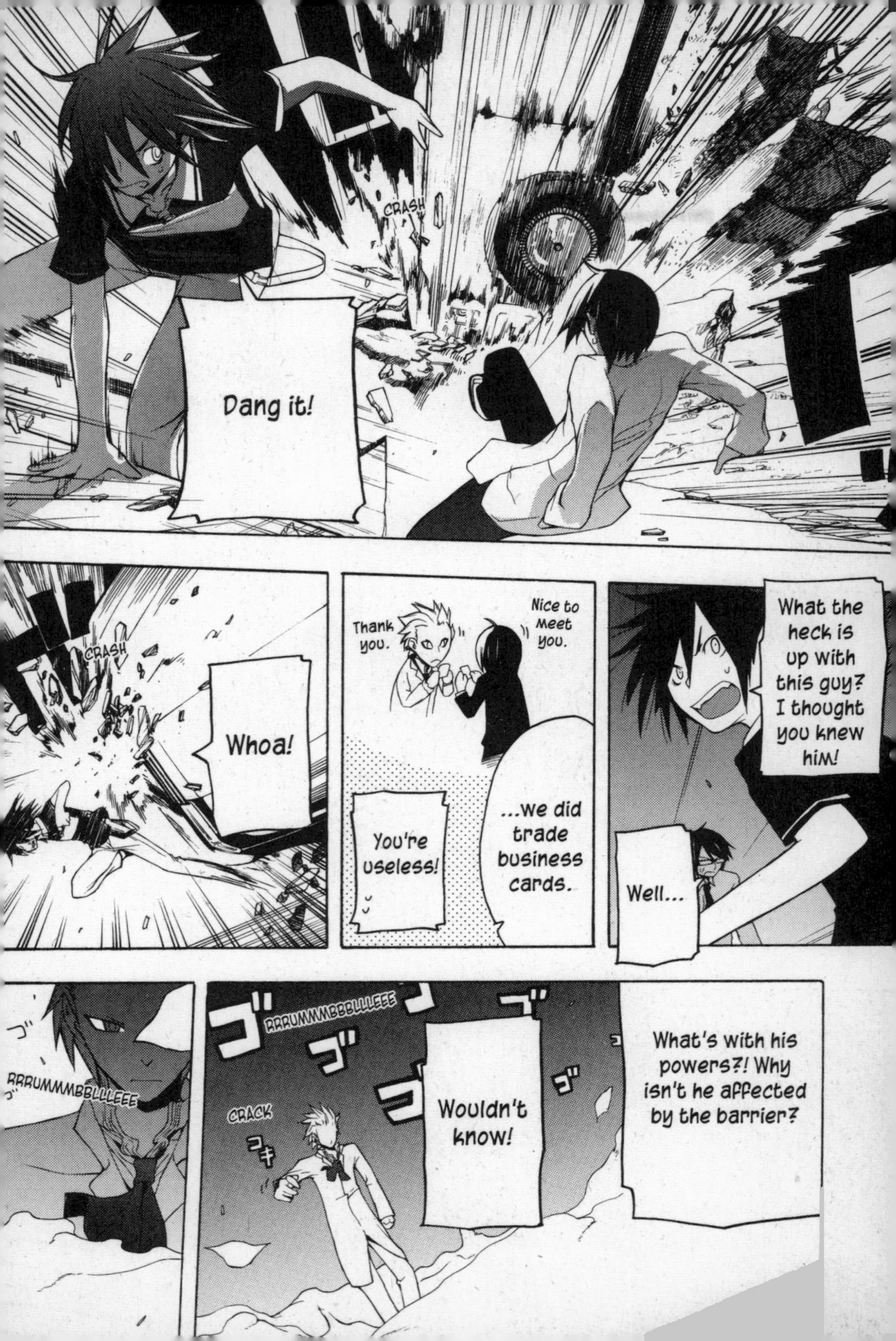
CRASH
Dang it!
What the heck is up with this guy? I thought you knew him!
Well...
Nice to meet you.
Thank you.
...we did trade business cards.
You're useless!
CRASH
Whoa!
What's with his powers?! Why isn't he affected by the barrier?
RRRUMMMBBBLLLEEE
Wouldn't know!
CRACK
コキ
RRRUMMMMBBLLLLEEE

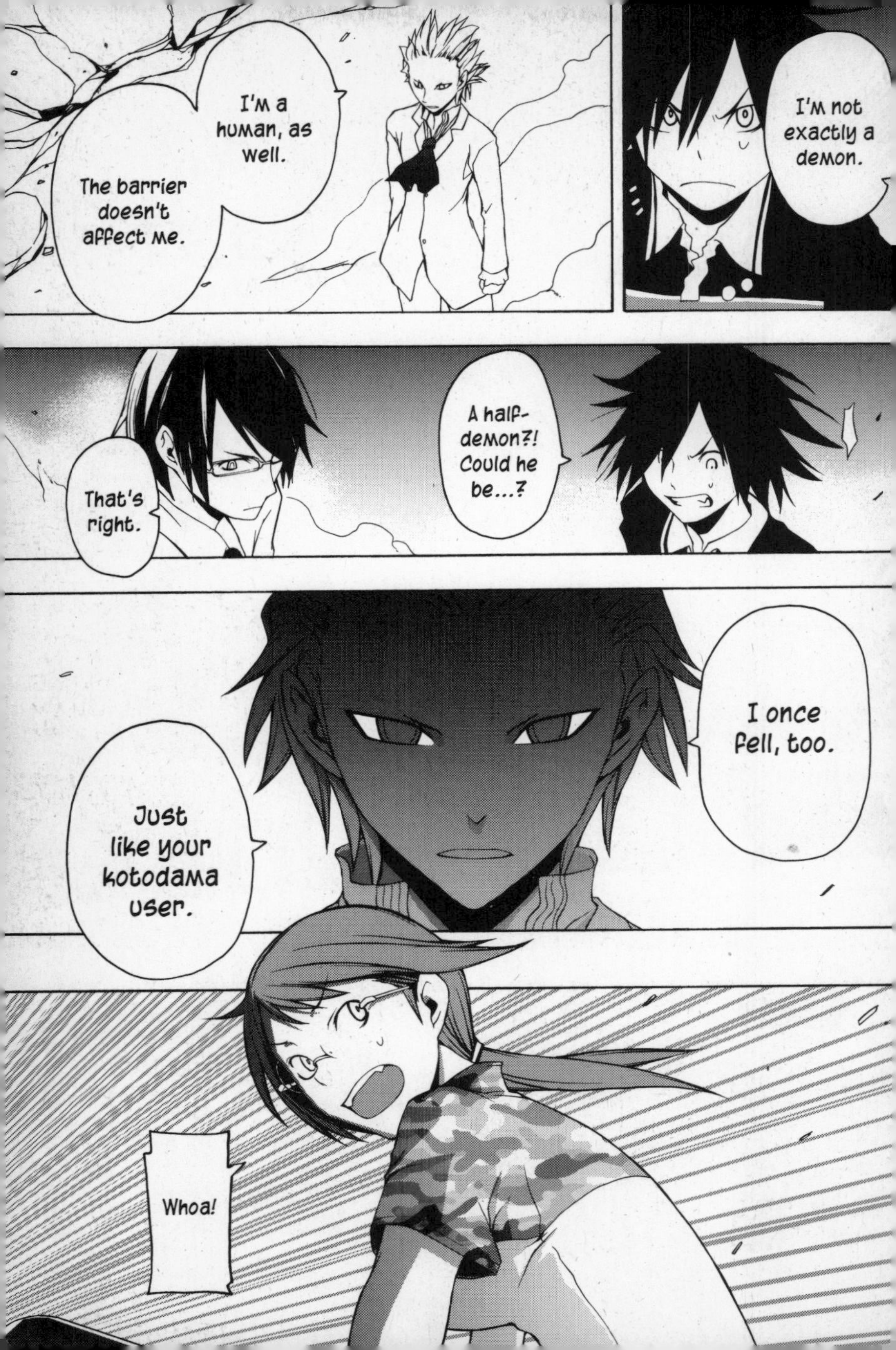
I'm not exactly a demon.
I'm a human, as well.
The barrier doesn't affect me.
A half-demon?! Could he be...?
That's right.
I once fell, too.
Just like your kotodama user.
Whoa!

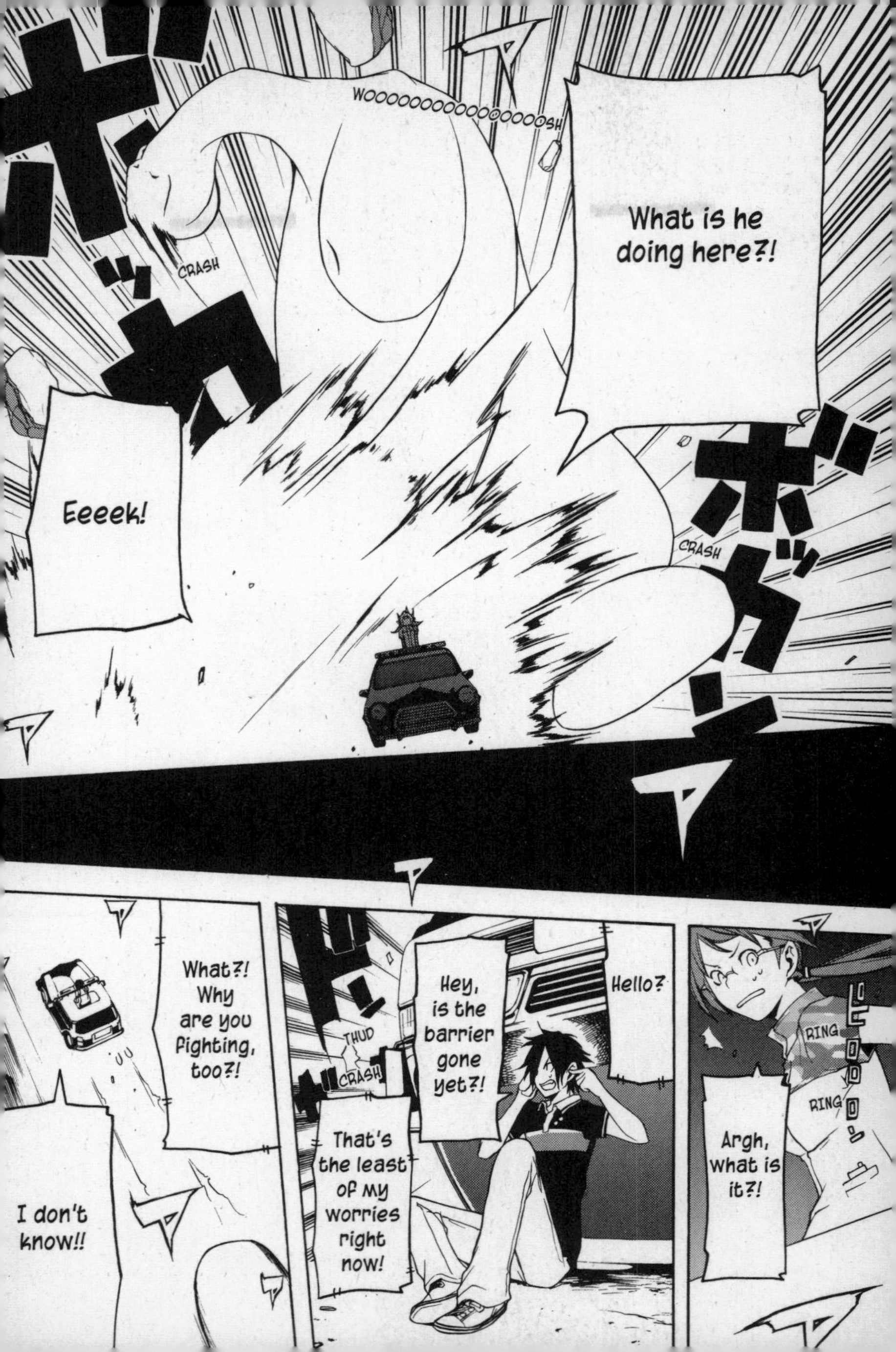
WOOOOOOOOOOOOOOOOOOSH
What is he doing here?!
CRASH
CRASH
Eeeek!
RING
RING
Argh, what is it?!
Hello?
Hey, is the barrier gone yet?!
THUD
CRASH
That's the least of my worries right now!
What?! Why are you fighting, too?!
I don't know!!

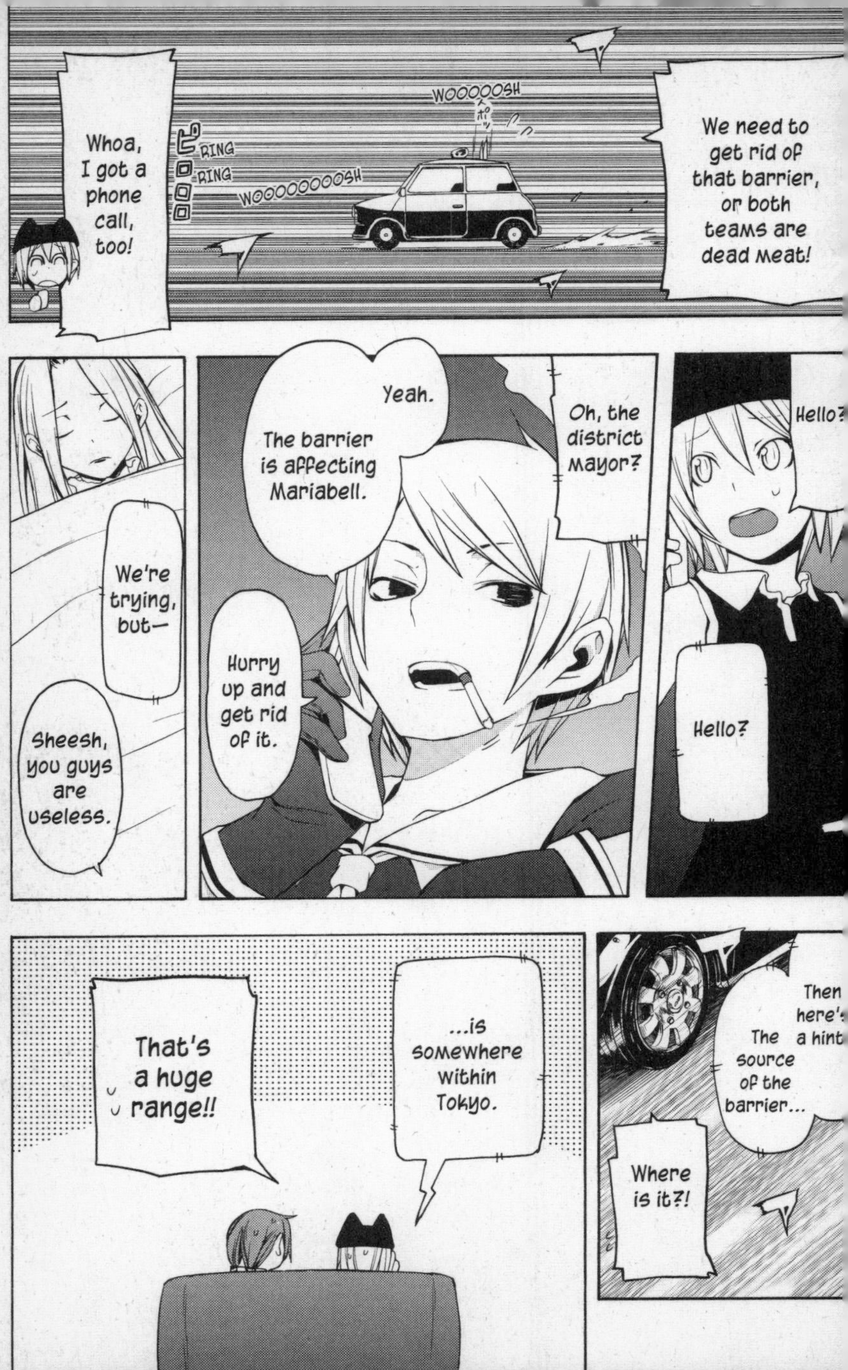
We need to get rid of that barrier, or both teams are dead meat!
WOOOOOSH
Whoa, I got a phone call, too!
RING
RING
WOOOOOOOOSH
Hello?
Hello?
Oh, the district mayor?
Yeah.
The barrier is affecting Mariabell.
Hurry up and get rid of it.
We're trying, but—
Sheesh, you guys are useless.
Then here's a hint
The source of the barrier...
Where is it?!
...is somewhere within Tokyo.
That's a huge range!!

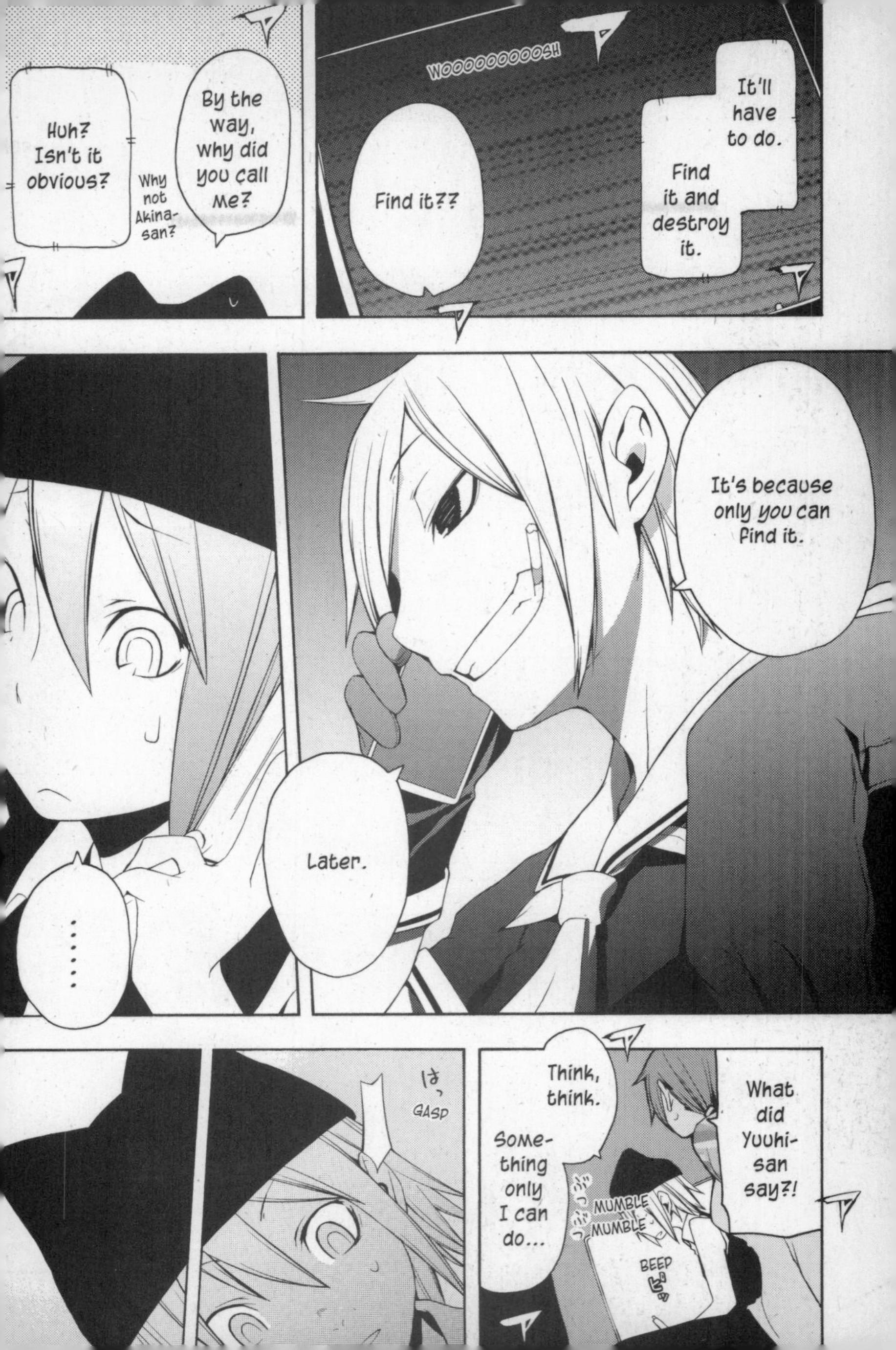
WOOOOOOOOOOSH
It'll have to do.
Find it and destroy it.
Find it??
By the way, why did you call me?
Why not Akina-san?
Huh? Isn't it obvious?
It's because only you can find it.
Later.
......
What did Yuuhi-san say?!
Think, think.
Something only I can do...
ぶつぶつ
MUMBLE MUMBLE
BEEP
ピッ
は、
GASP

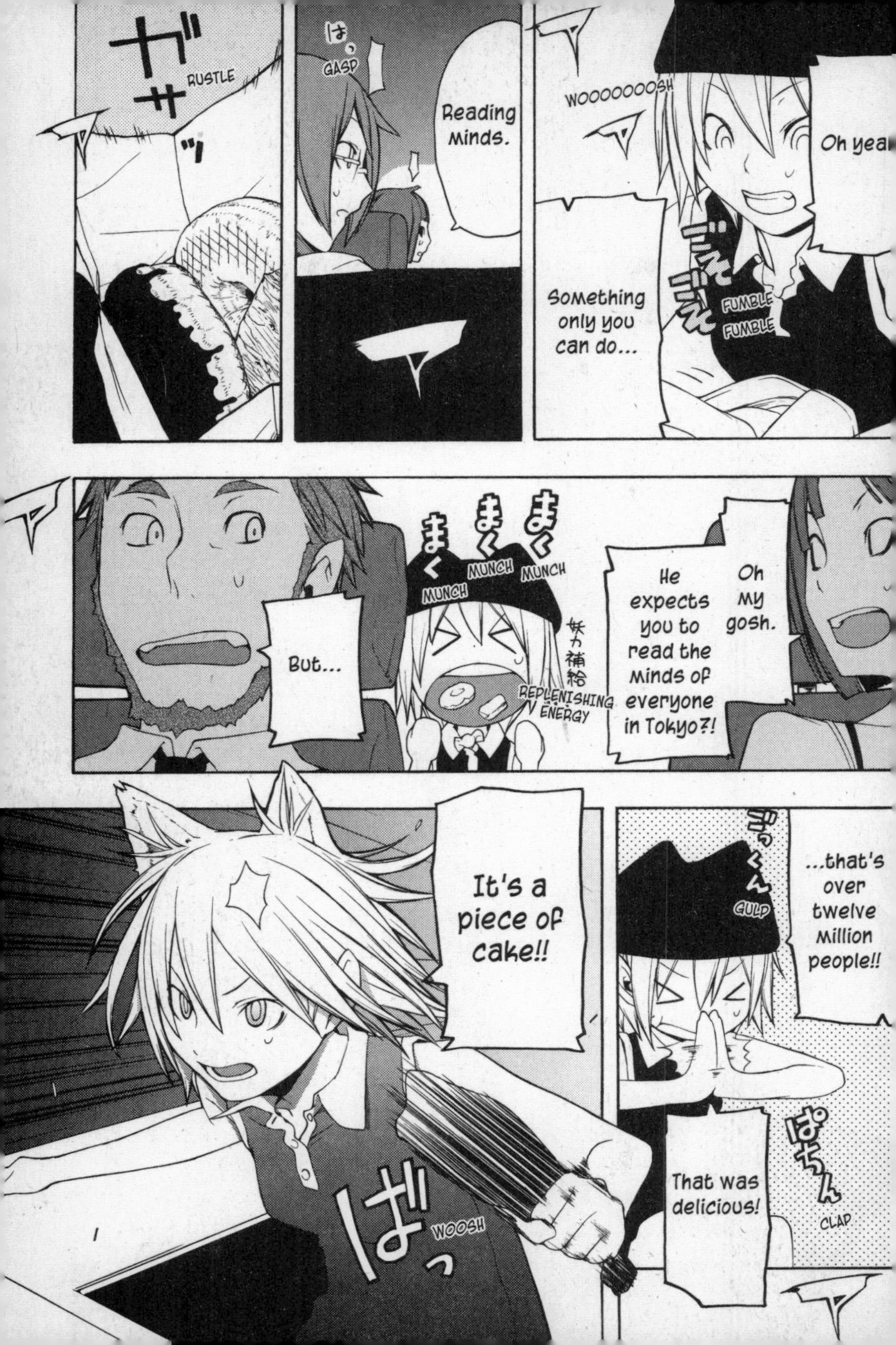
Oh yea
WOOOOOOOSH
FUMBLE FUMBLE
Something only you can do...
は、
GASP
Reading minds.
ガサッ
RUSTLE
Oh my gosh.
He expects you to read the minds of everyone in Tokyo?!
まくまくまく
MUNCH MUNCH MUNCH
妖力補給
REPLENISHING ENERGY
But...
...that's over twelve million people!!
ごっくん
GULP
ぱちん
CLAP
That was delicious!
It's a piece of cake!!
ばっ
WOOSH

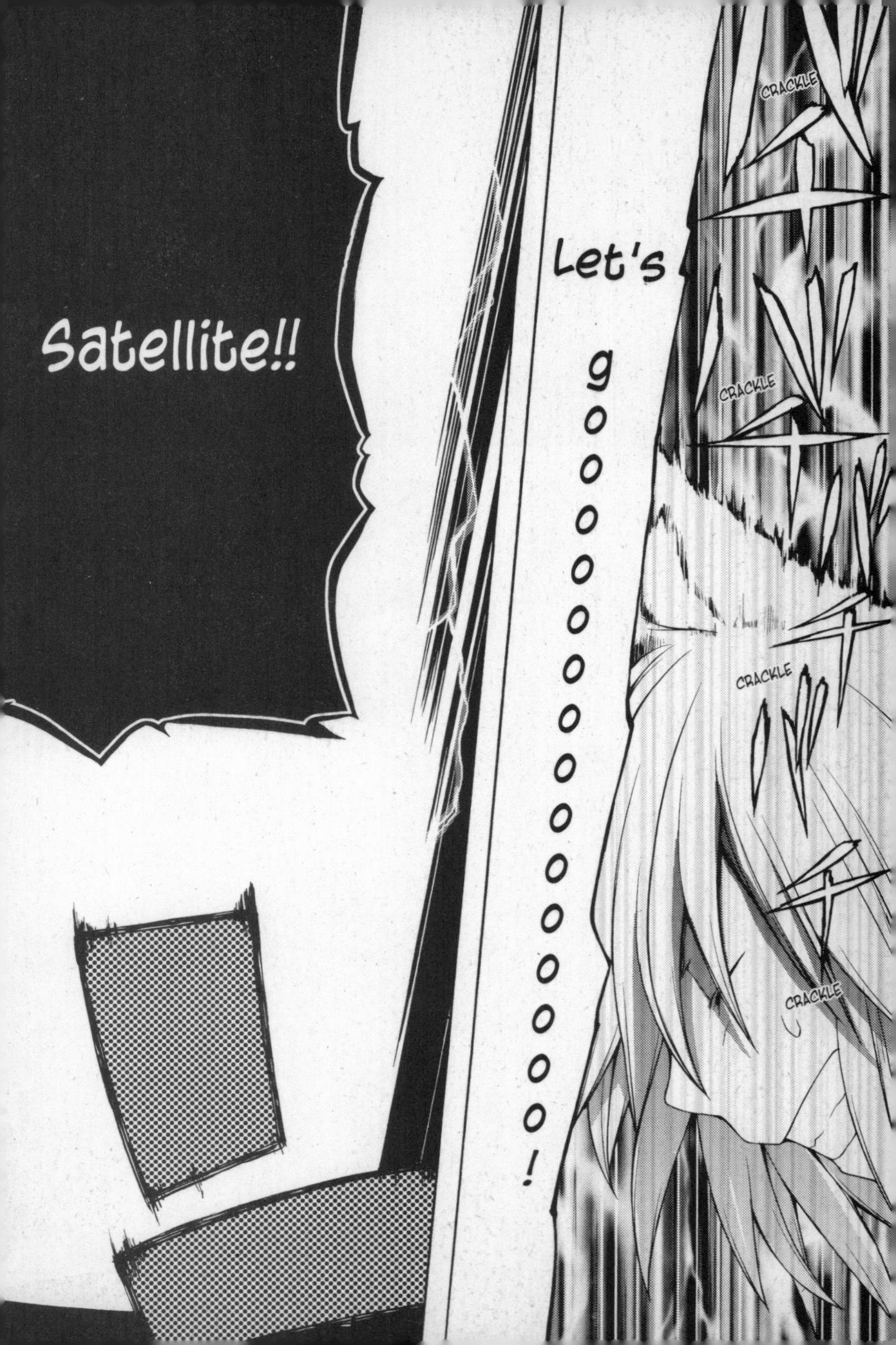
CRACKLE
Let's goooooooooooooooooooo!
CRACKLE
CRACKLE
CRACKLE
Satellite!!

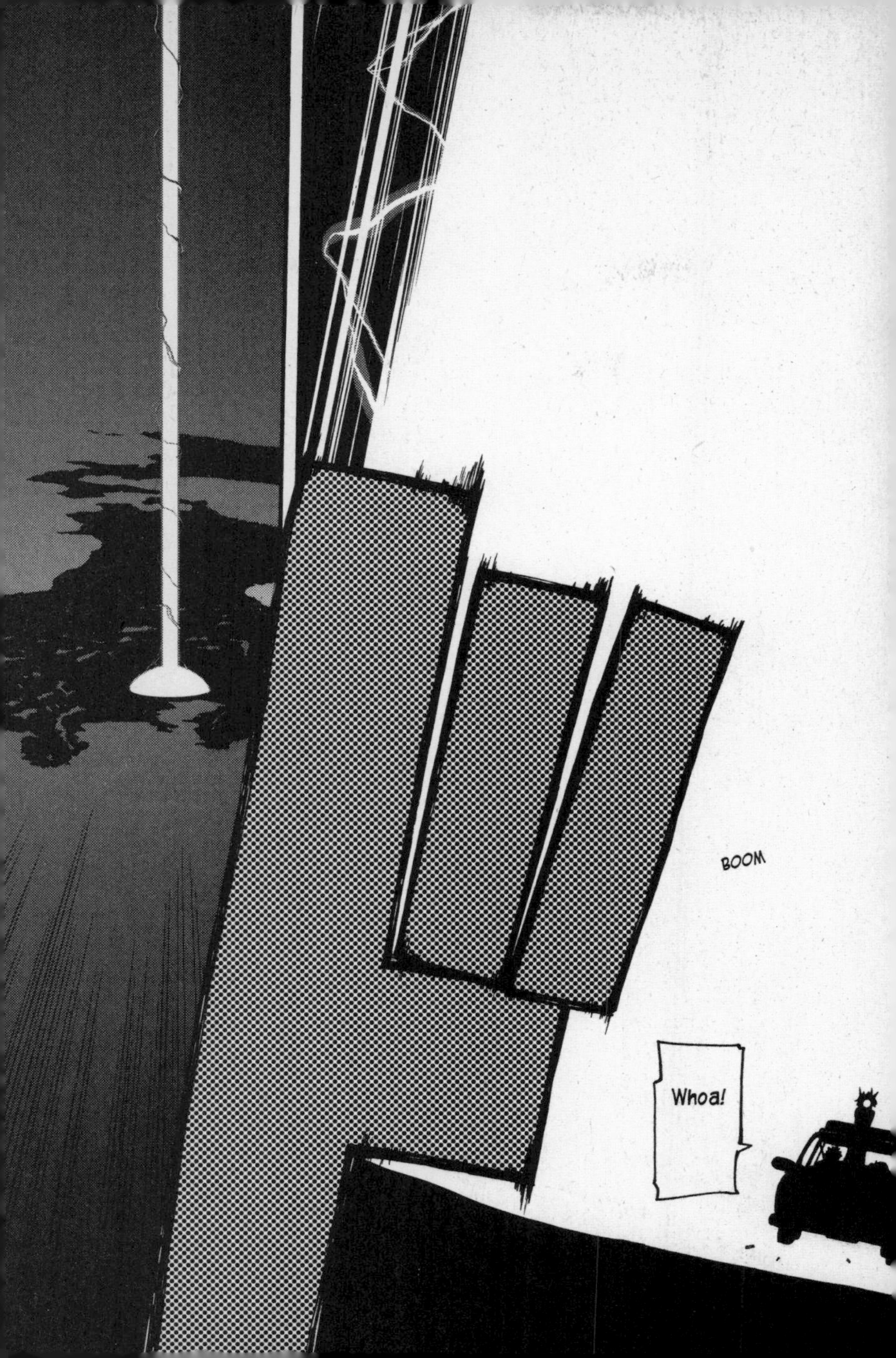
BOOM
Whoa!

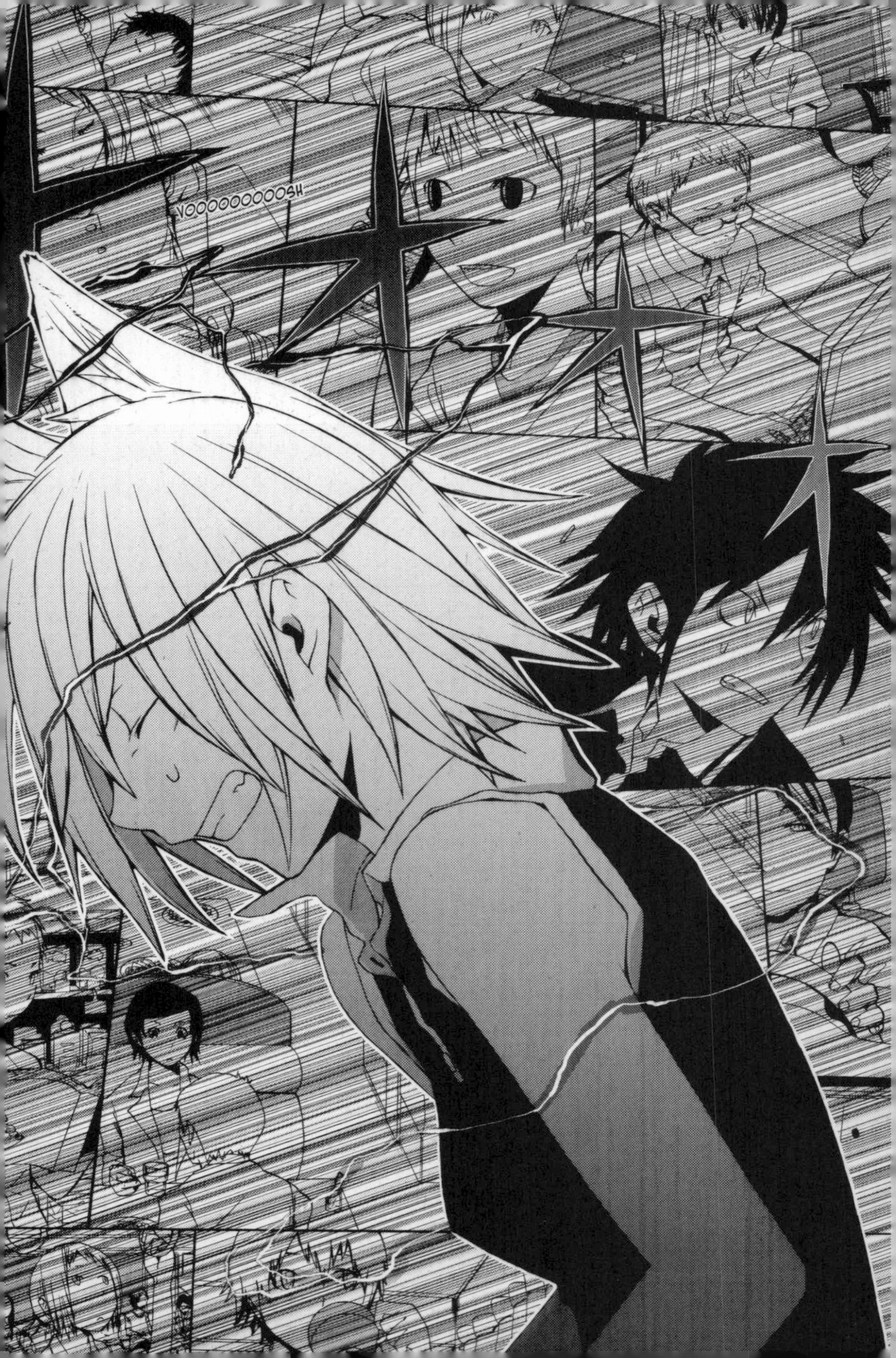
VOOOOOOOOOSH

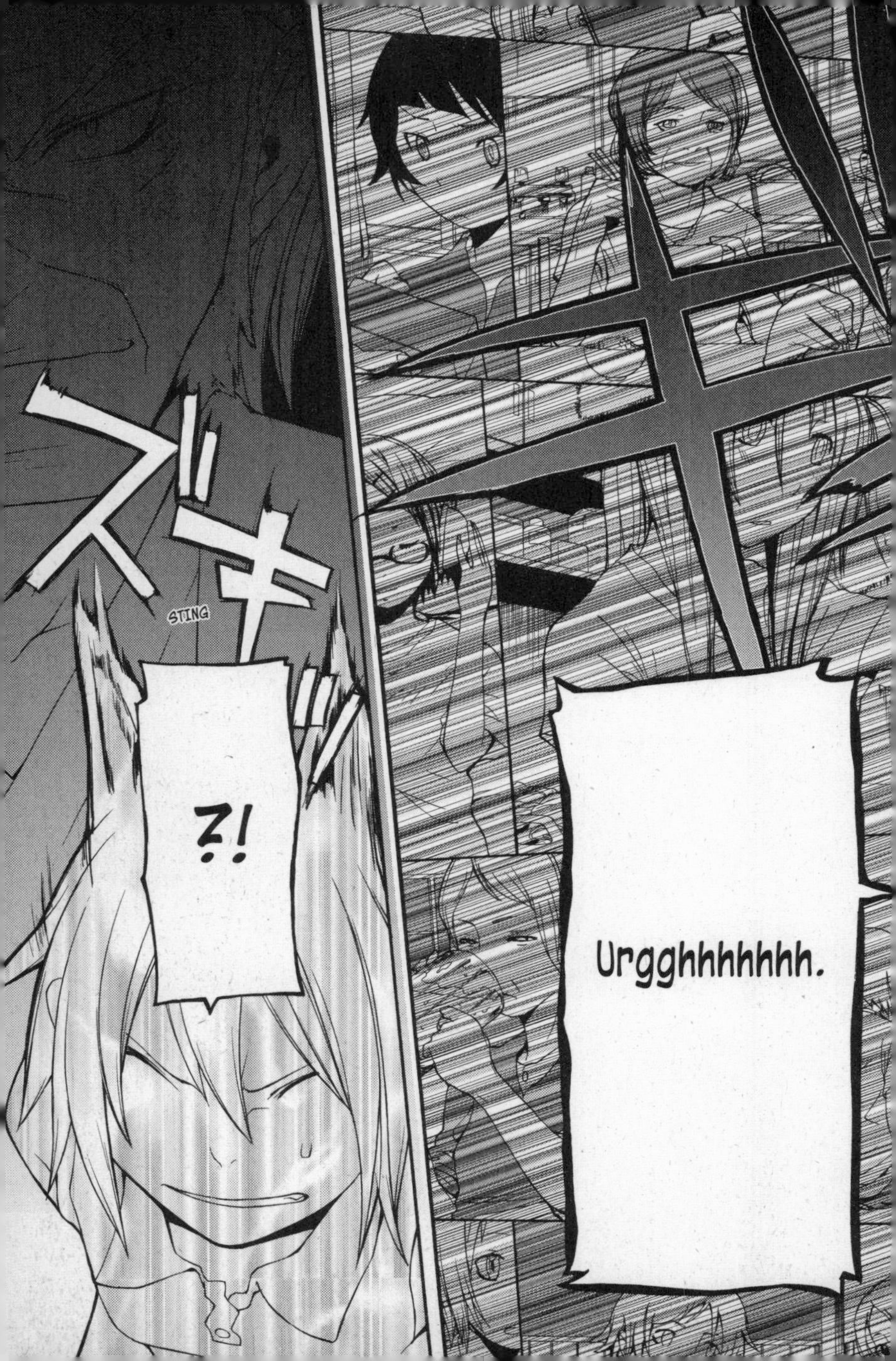
Urgghhhhhh.
ズキ
STING
?!

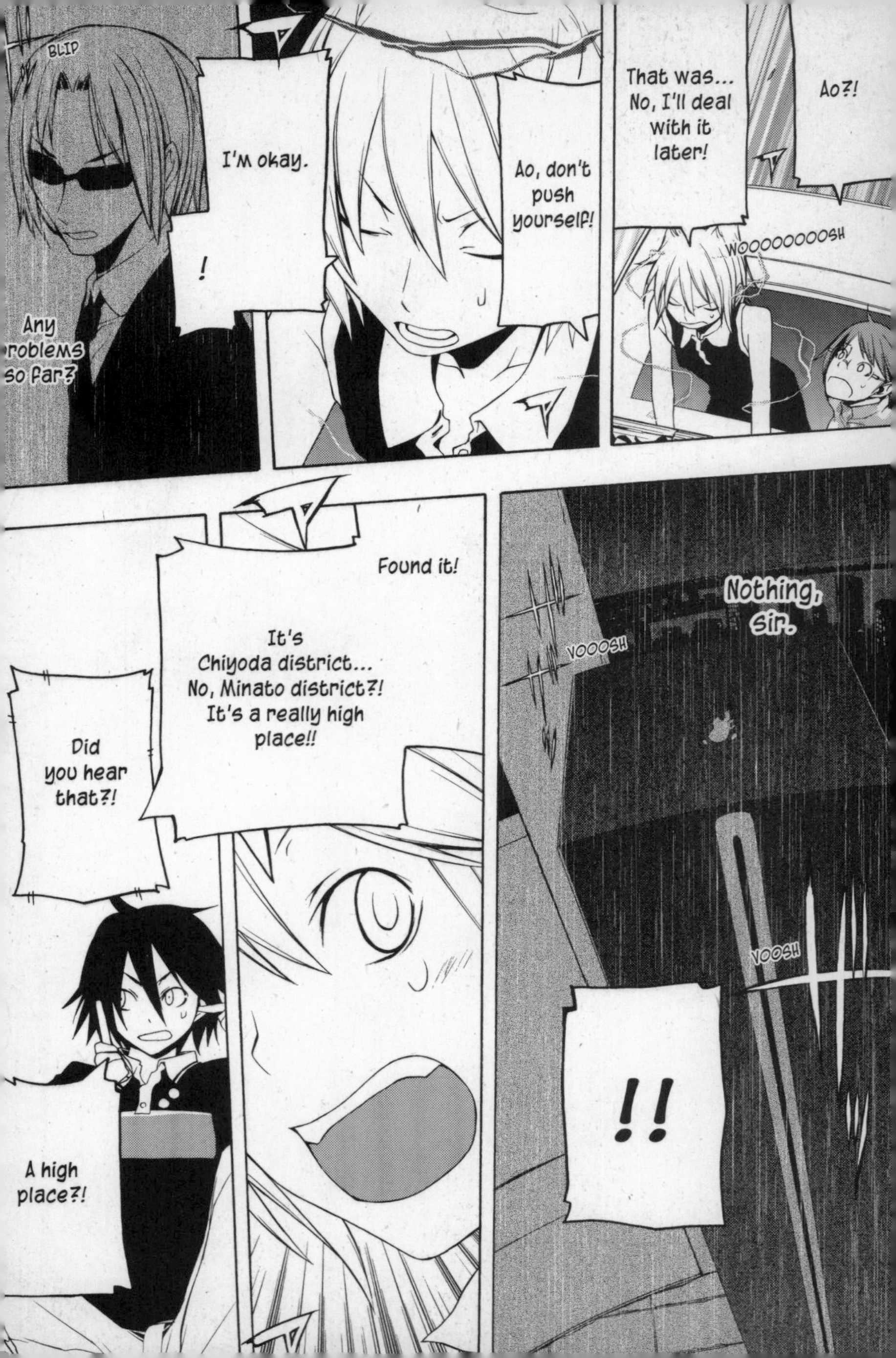

Ao?!
That was... No, I'll deal with it later!
WOOOOOOOOOSH
Ao, don't push yourself!
I'm okay.
BLIP
!
Any roblems so far?
Nothing, sir.
VOOOSH
VOOSH
!!
Found it!
It's Chiyoda district... No, Minato district?! It's a really high place!!
Did you hear that?!
A high place?!

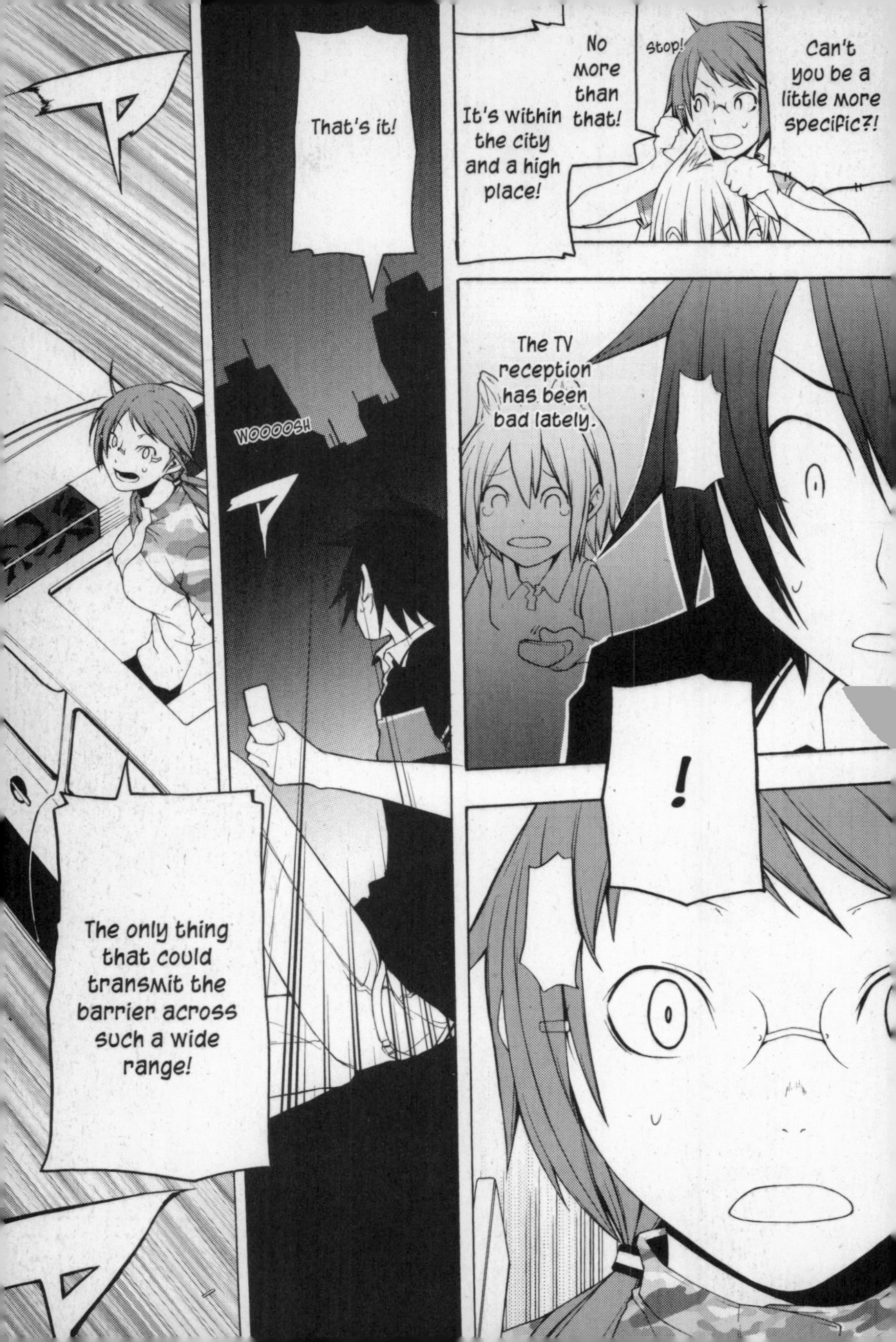
Can't you be a little more specific?!
Stop!
No more than that!
It's within the city and a high place!
The TV reception has been bad lately.
!
That's it!
WOOOOSH
The only thing that could transmit the barrier across such a wide range!

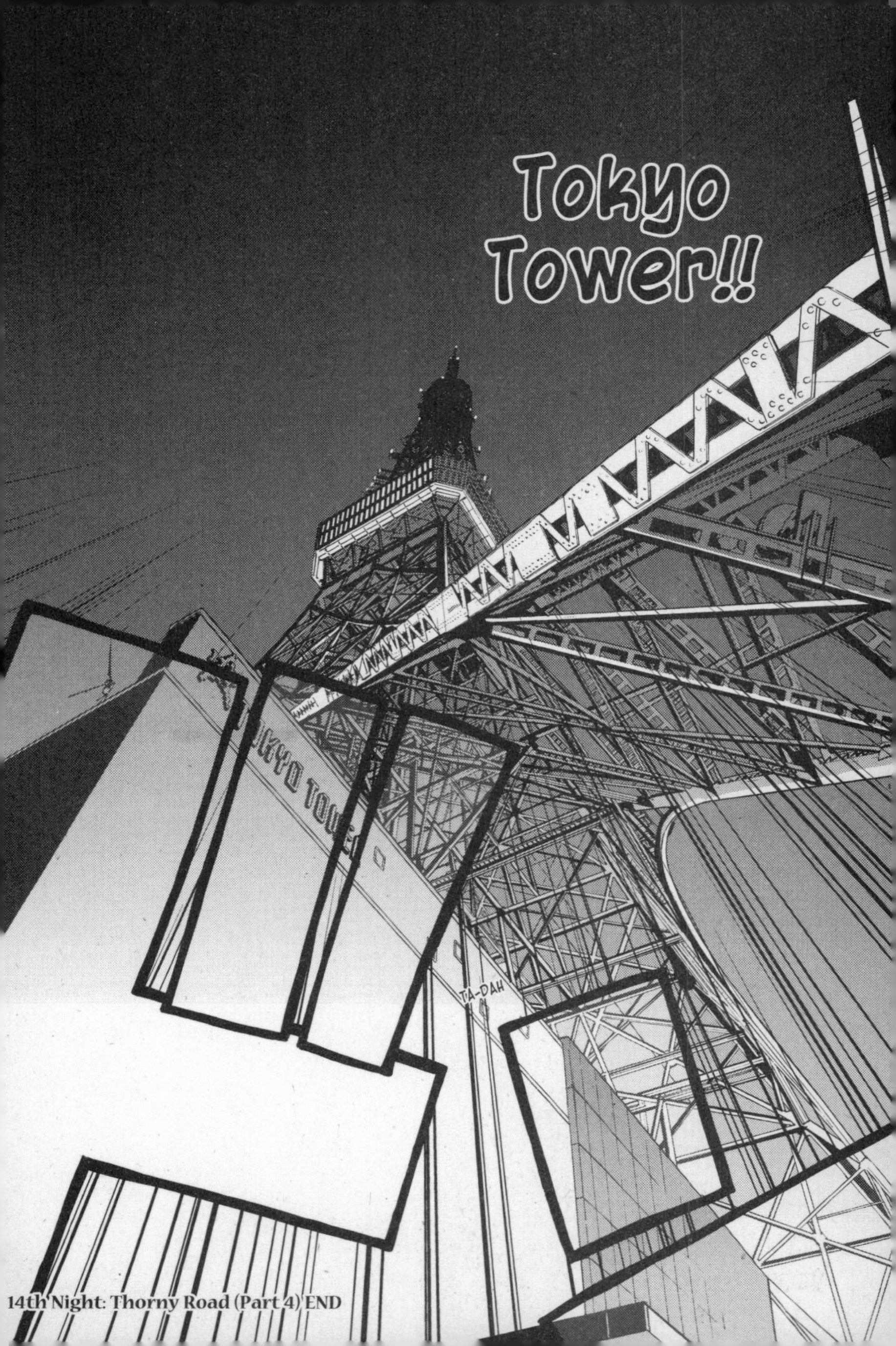
Tokyo Tower!!
TA-DAH
14th Night: Thorny Road (Part 4) END

Yozakura Quartet 3

Primary Stages of Yozakura Quartet

Mariabell

Age: *22*

Hobbies:
Cooking

Favorites

Food:
Anything

Music Group:
Kazuyoshi Nakamura

Comedian:
Dayan

Uchi-P Member:
Parachute Troop

Little-Known Fact:
She likes Japanese food for
breakfast (and gets mad if she
doesn't get it).

I didn't have any early
sketches of her.

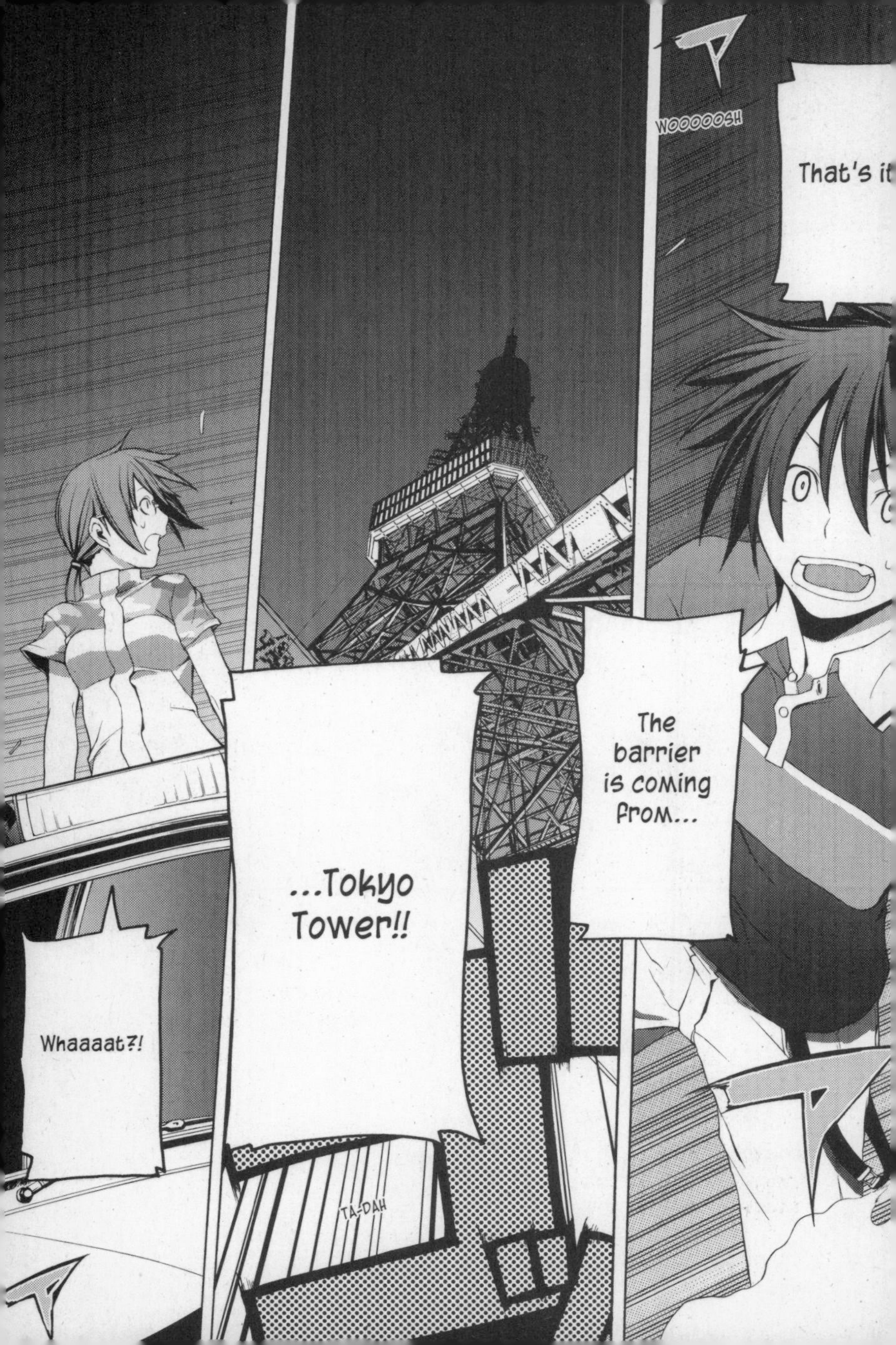
WOOOOOSH
That's it
The barrier is coming from...
...Tokyo Tower!!
TA-DAH
Whaaaat?!

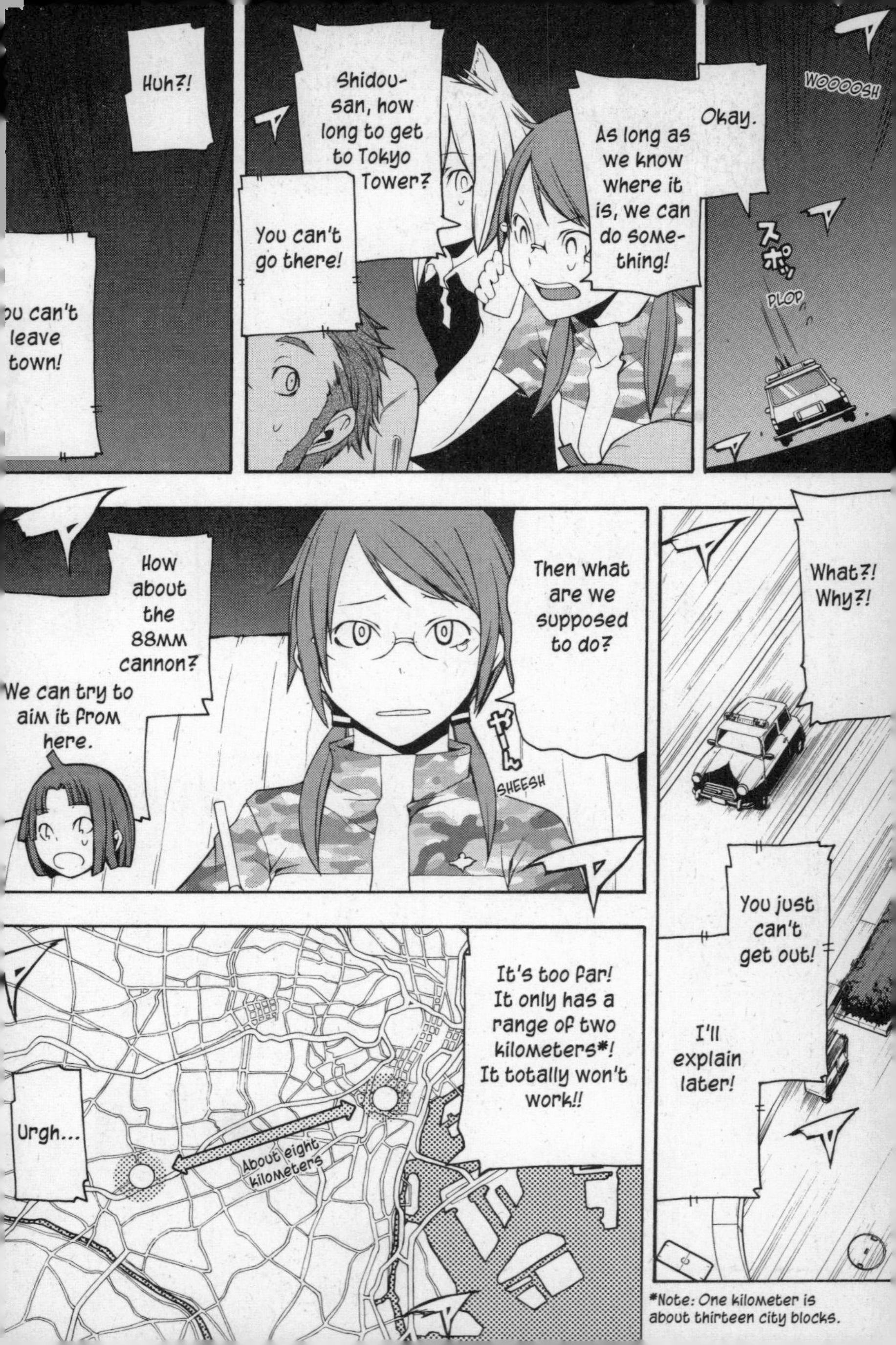
WOOOOSH
スポッ
PLOP
Okay. As long as we know where it is, we can do something!
Shidou-san, how long to get to Tokyo Tower?
You can't go there!
Huh?!
ou can't leave town!
What?! Why?!
You just can't get out!
I'll explain later!
Then what are we supposed to do?
SHEESH
How about the 88MM cannon?
We can try to aim it from here.
It's too far! It only has a range of two kilometers*! It totally won't work!!
About eight kilometers
Urgh...

*Note: One kilometer is about thirteen city blocks.

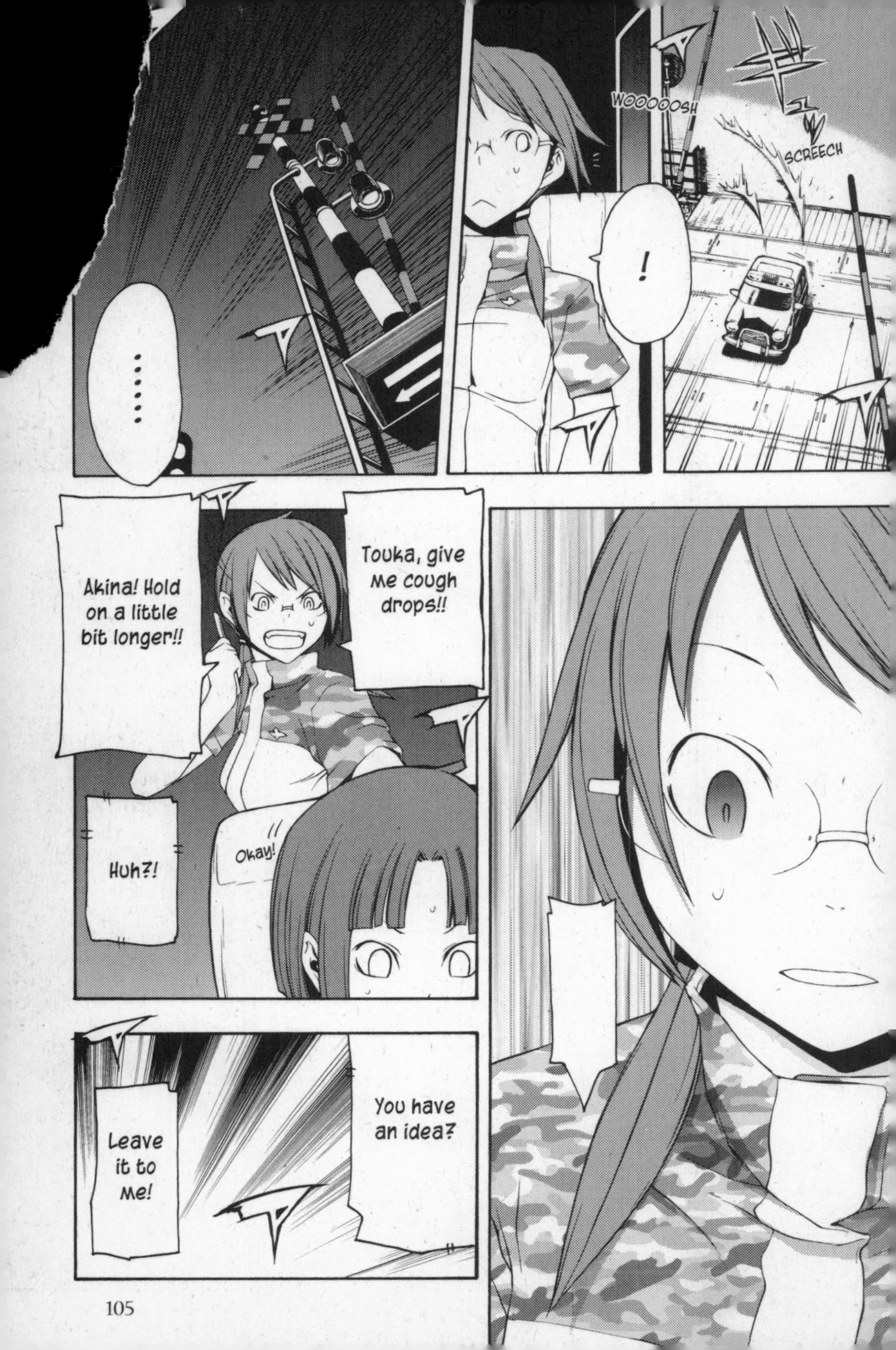
SCREECH
WOOOOOSH
!
......
Touka, give me cough drops!!
Akina! Hold on a little bit longer!!
Okay!
Huh?!
You have an idea?
Leave it to me!

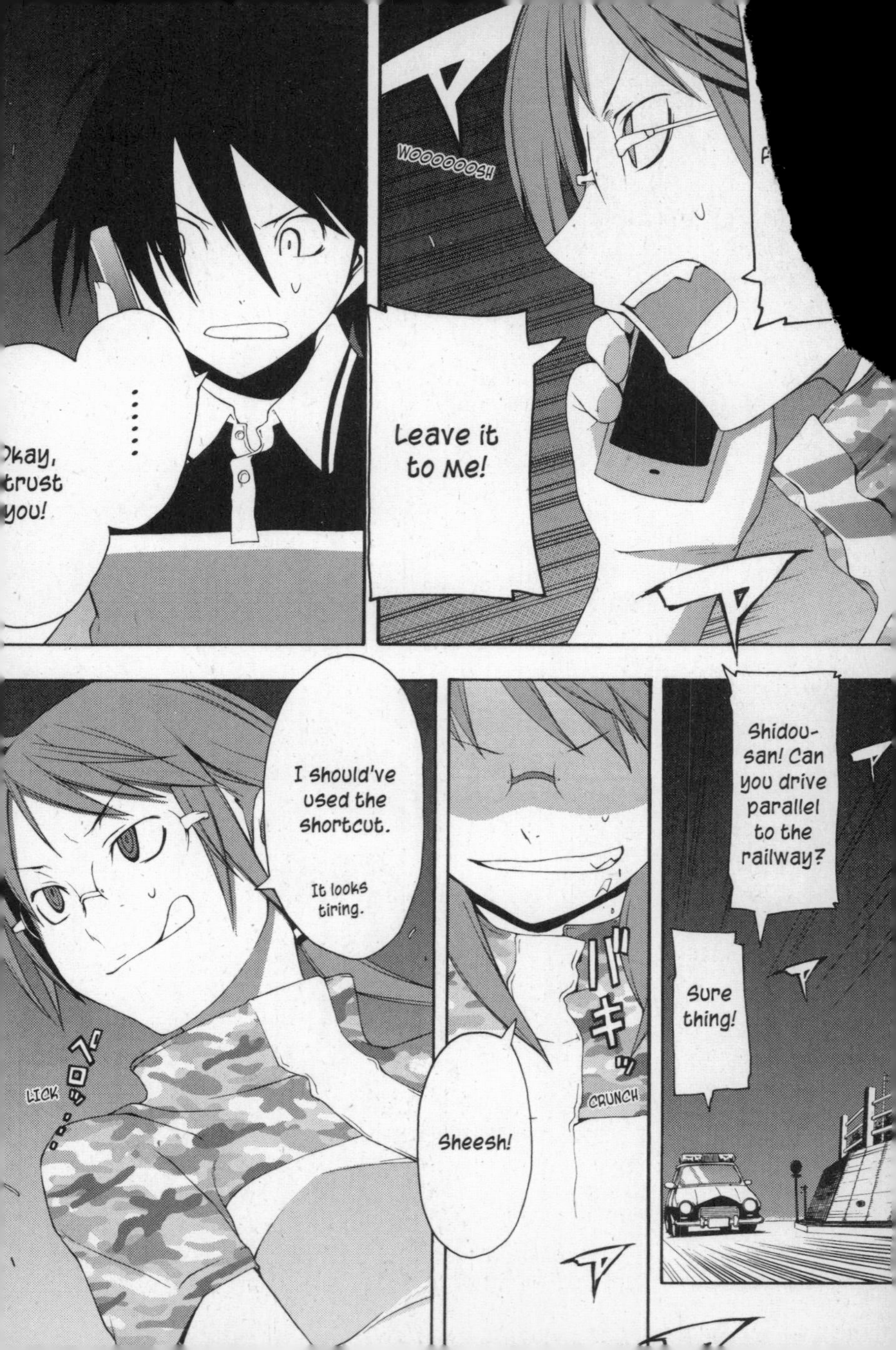

WOOOOOOSH
Leave it to Me!
......
Okay, trust you!
Shidou-san! Can you drive parallel to the railway?
Sure thing!
CRUNCH
Sheesh!
I should've used the shortcut.
It looks tiring.
LICK

15th Night:
Thorny Road
(Part 5)

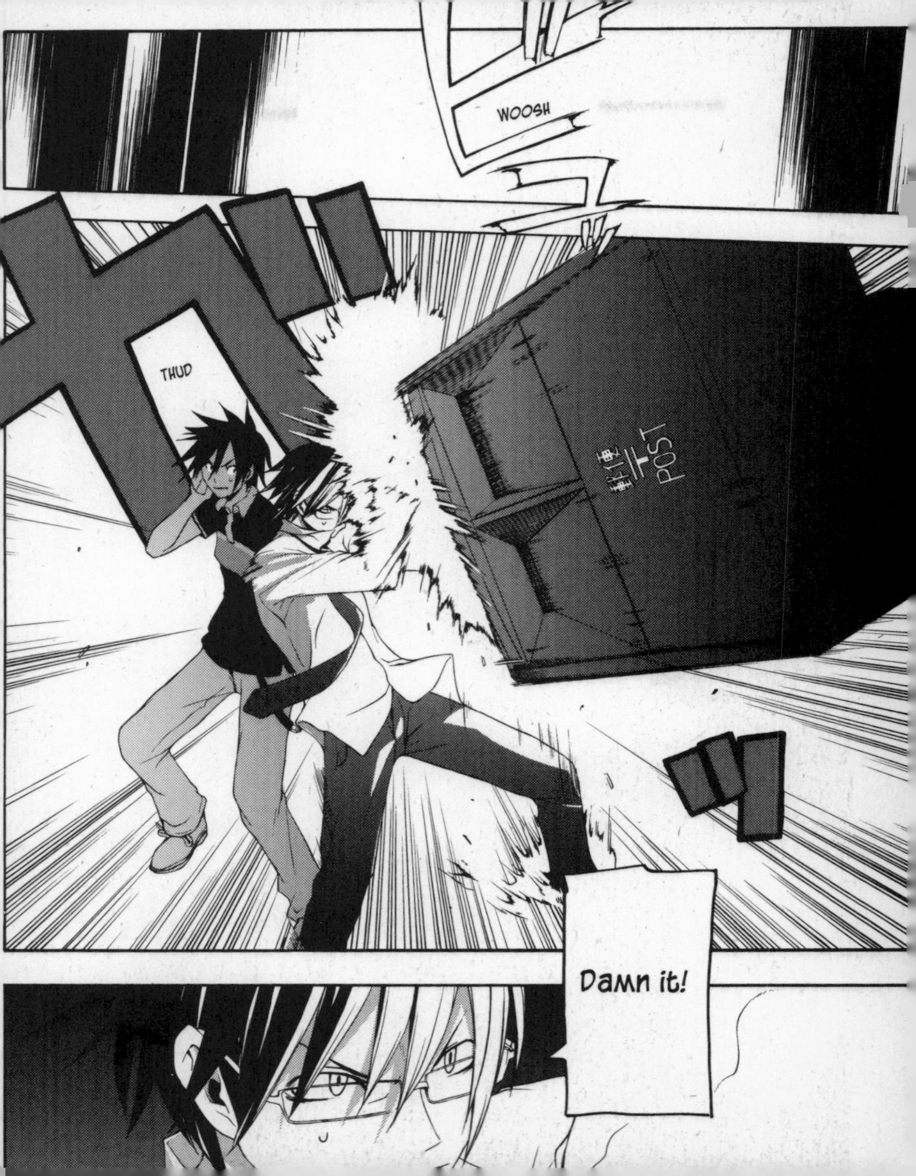
WOOSH
THUD
POST
Damn it!

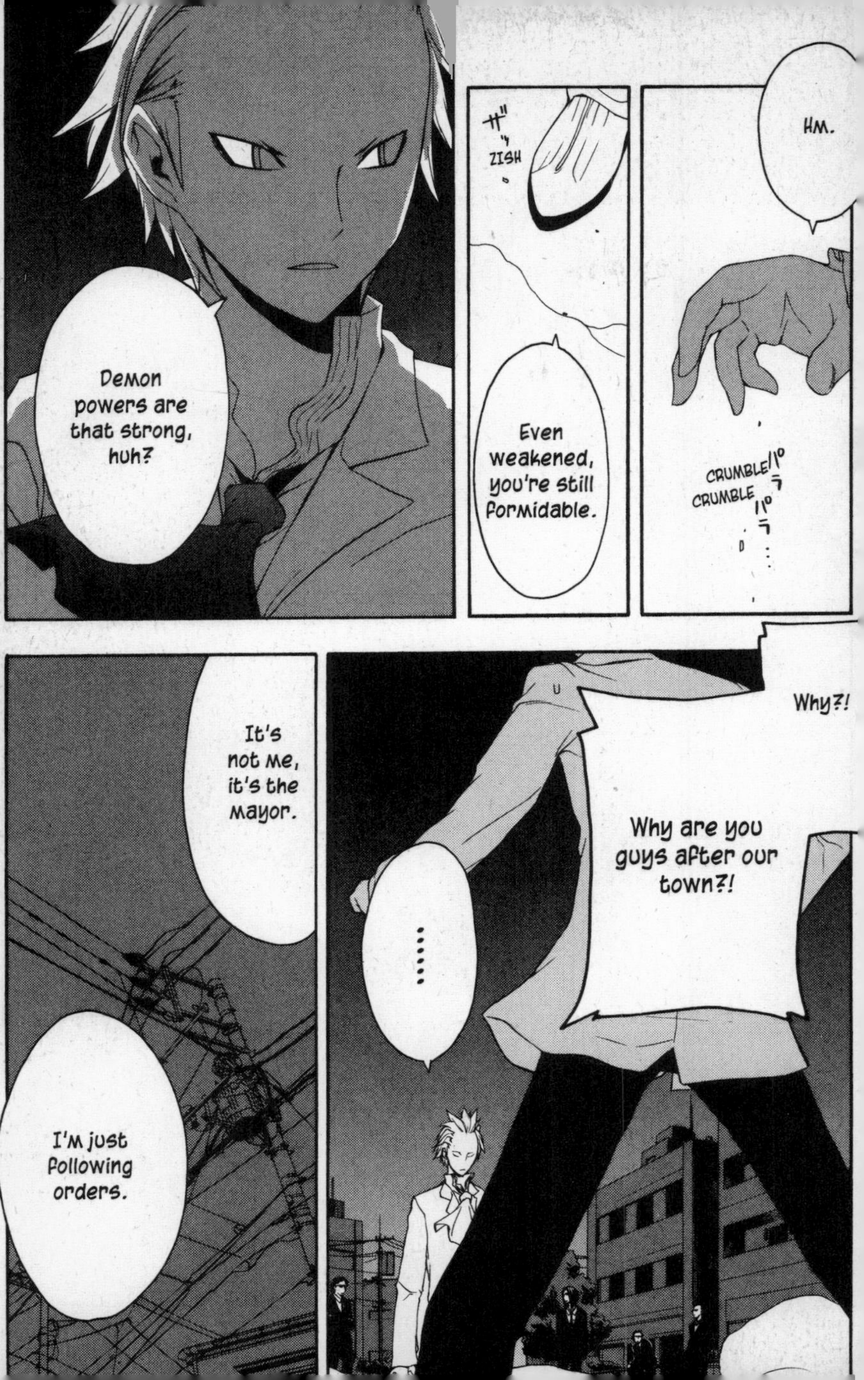
HM.
CRUMBLE CRUMBLE
パラ パラ
ザッ
ZISH
Even weakened, you're still formidable.
Demon powers are that strong, huh?
Why?!
Why are you guys after our town?!
......
It's not me, it's the mayor.
I'm just following orders.

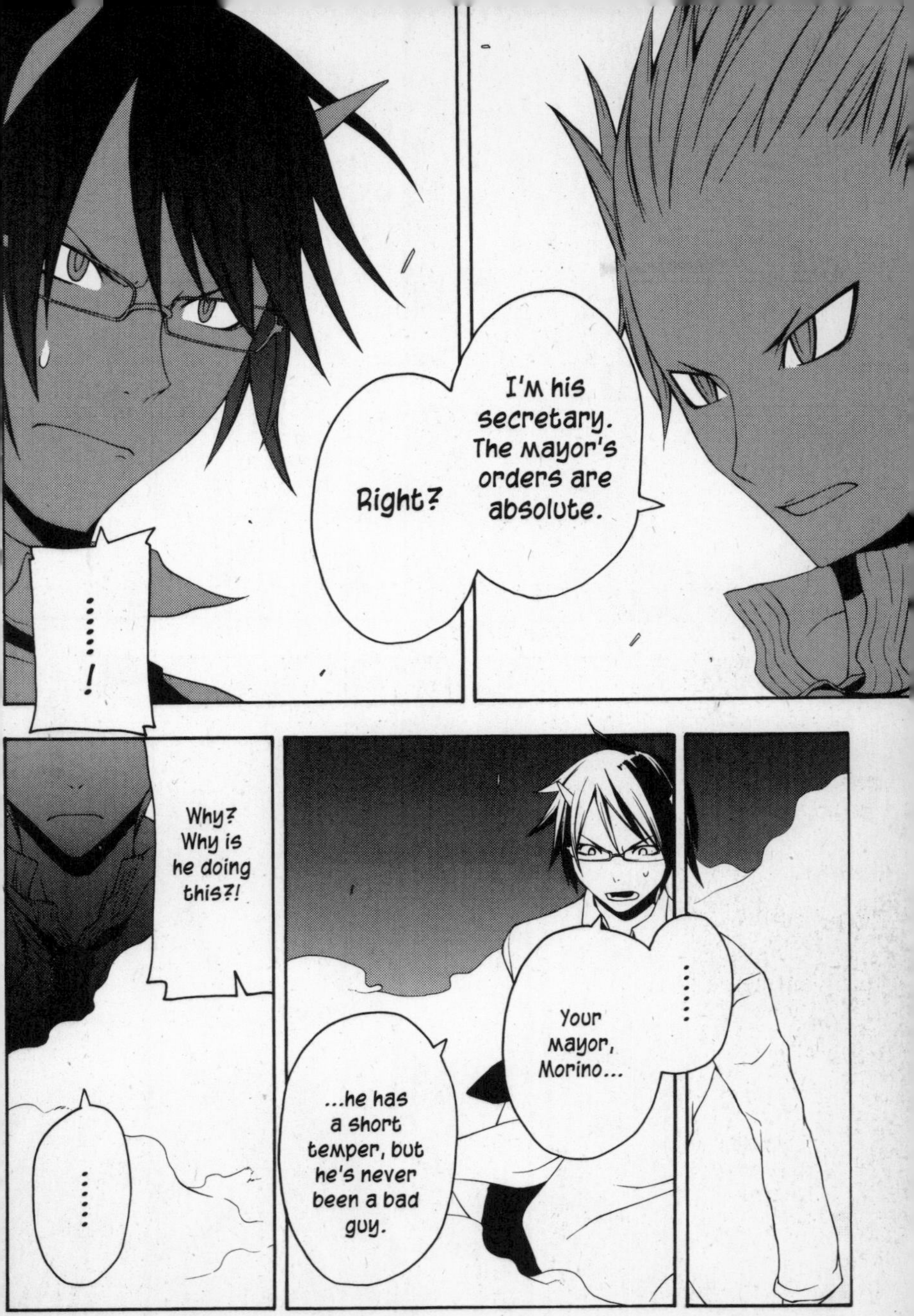
I'm his secretary. The mayor's orders are absolute.
Right?
......!
...... Your mayor, Morino...
...he has a short temper, but he's never been a bad guy.
Why? Why is he doing this?!
......

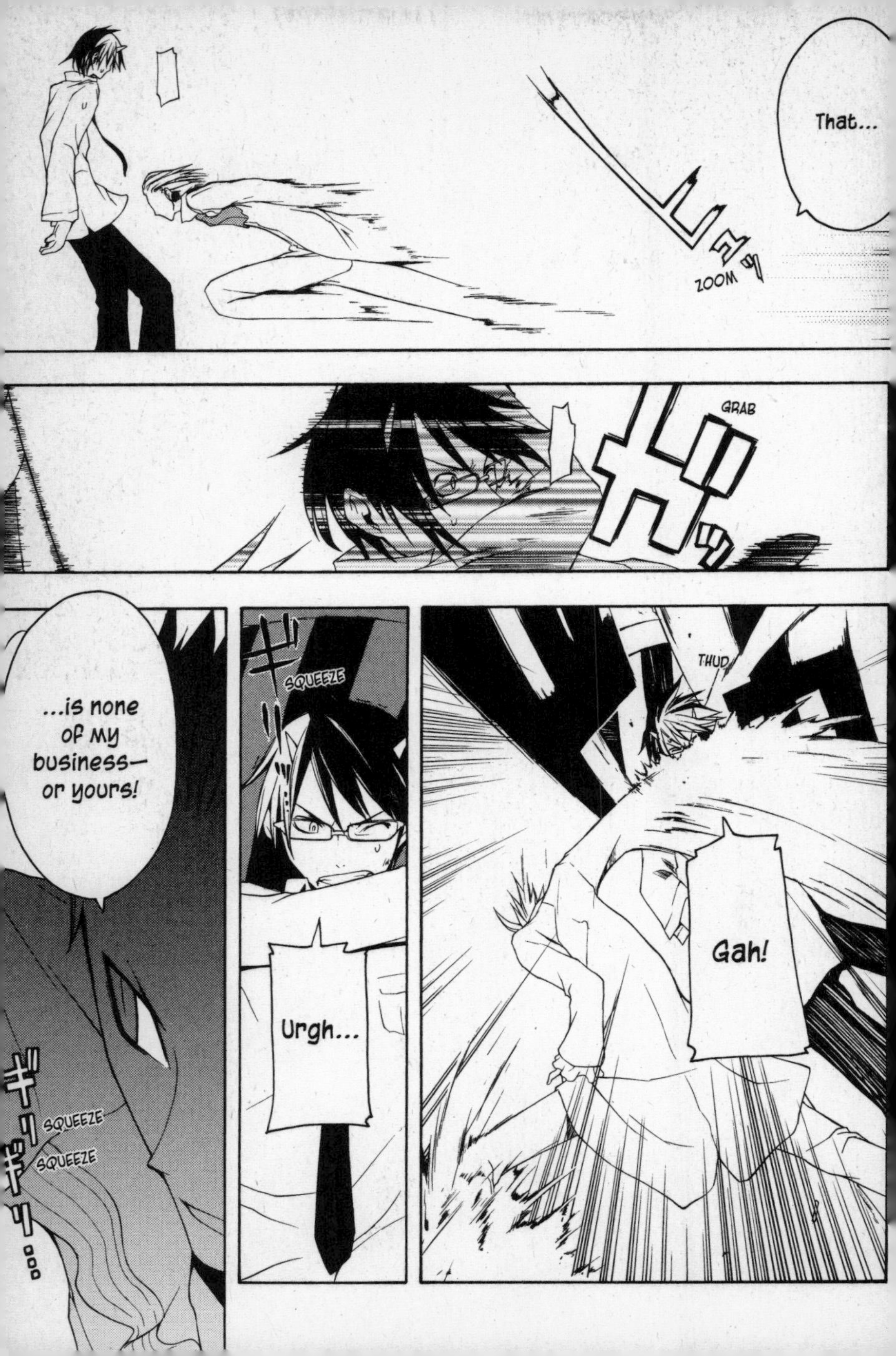
That...
ZOOM
GRAB
THUD
Gah!
SQUEEZE
Urgh...
...is none of my business—or yours!
SQUEEZE
SQUEEZE

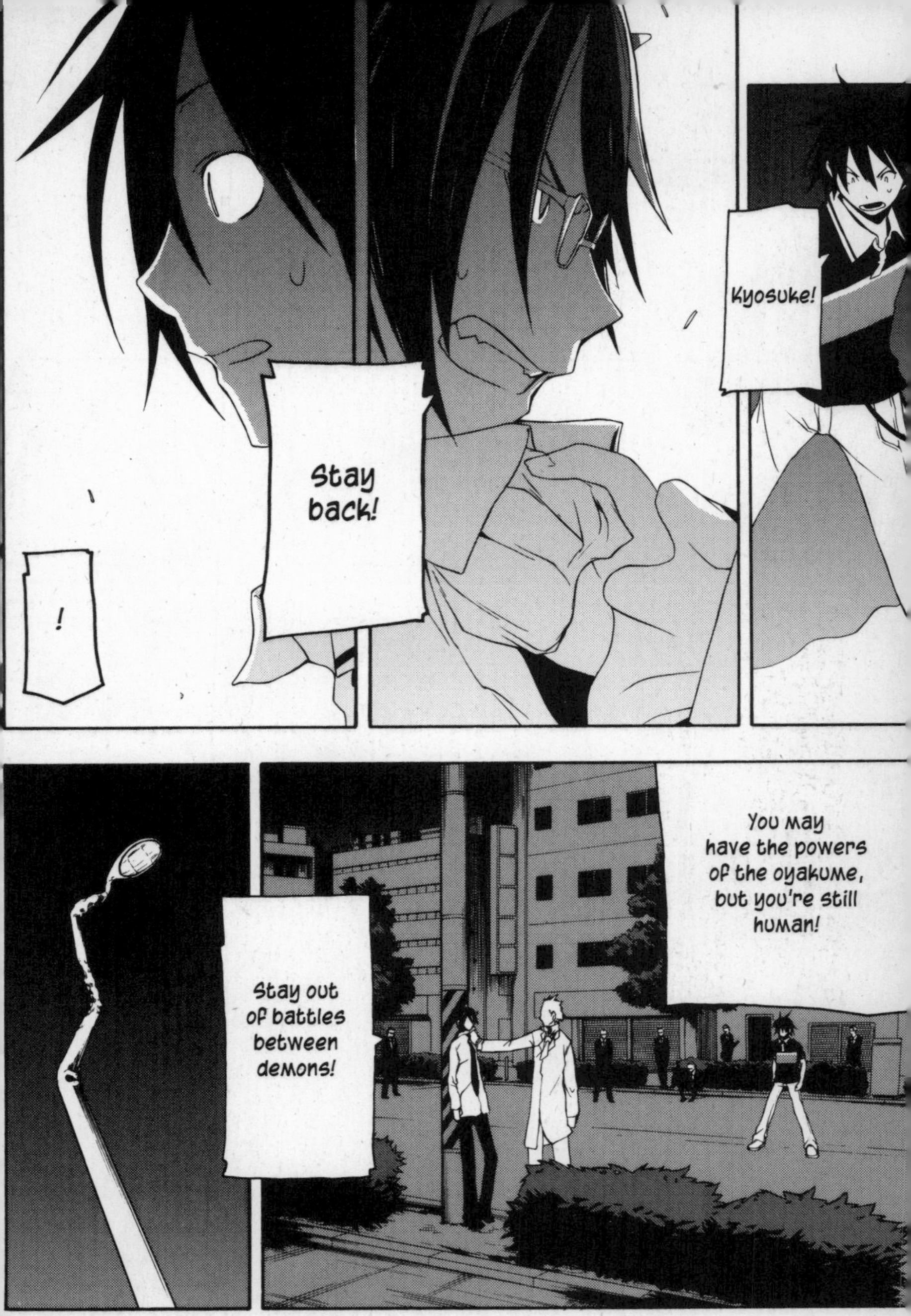
Kyosuke!
Stay back!
!
You may have the powers of the oyakume, but you're still human!
Stay out of battles between demons!

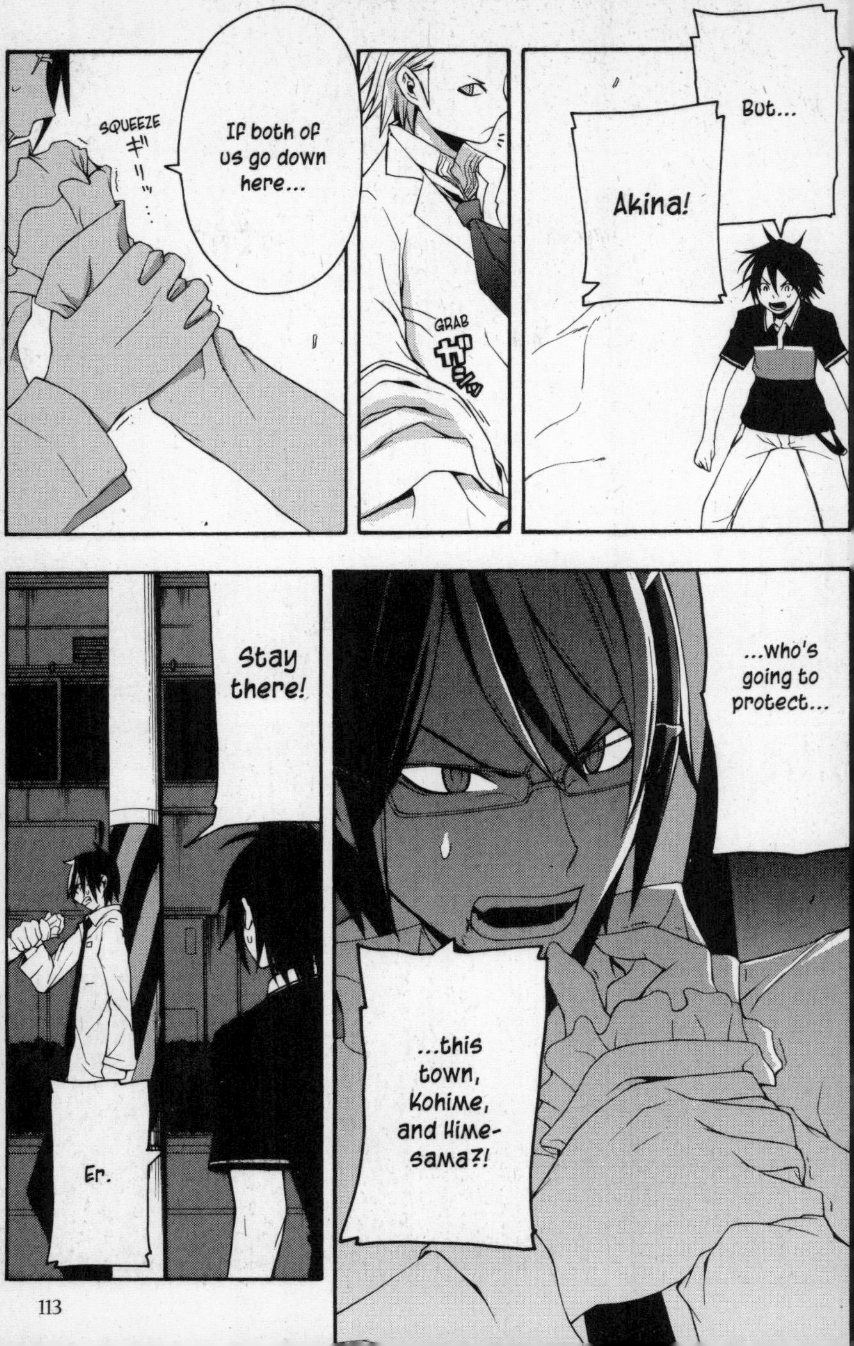
But...
Akina!
GRAB
ガシッ
If both of us go down here...
SQUEEZE
ギリッ
...who's going to protect...
...this town, Kohime, and Hime-sama?!
Stay there!
Er.

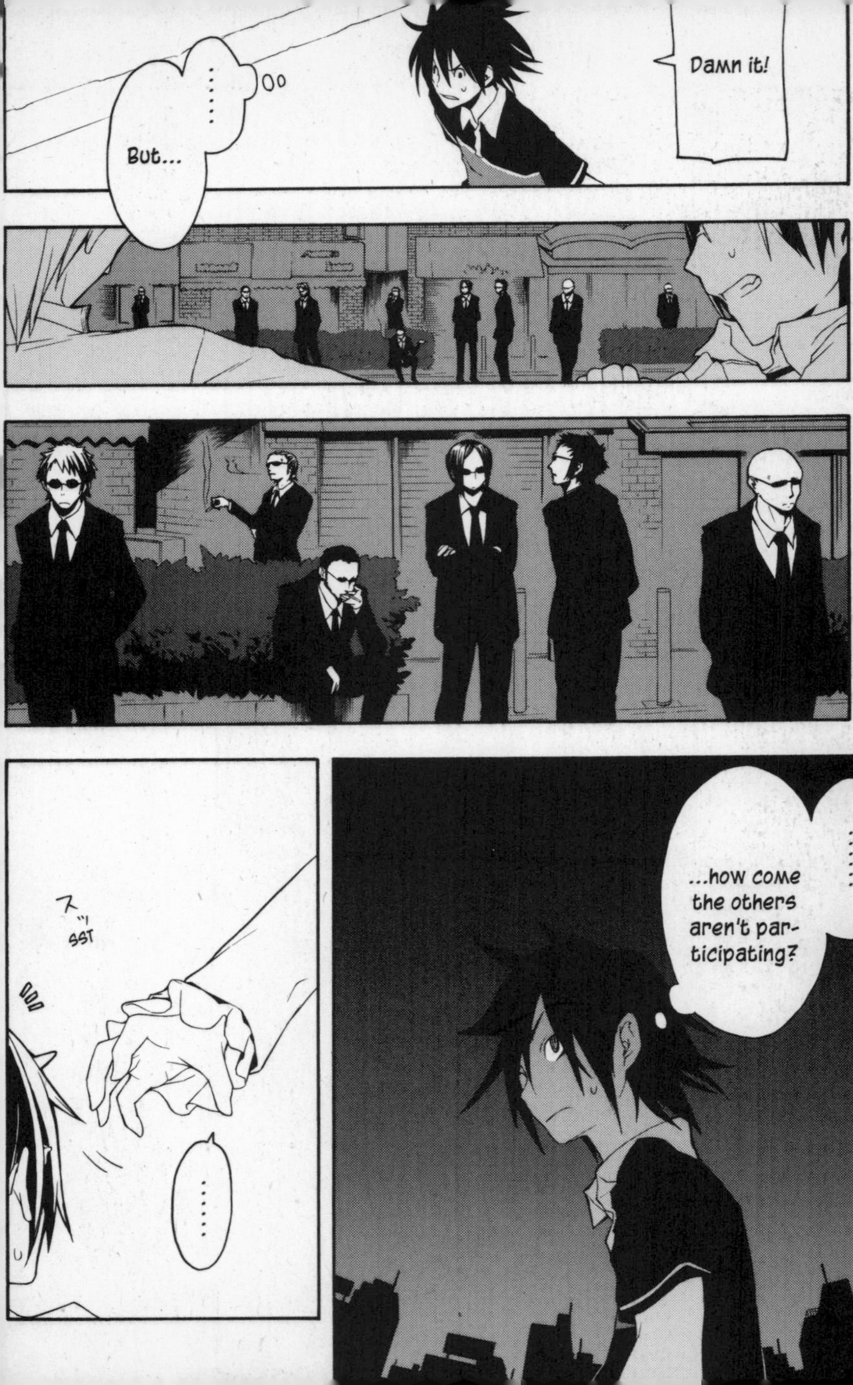
Damn it!
......
But...
......
...how come the others aren't participating?
スッ
SST
......

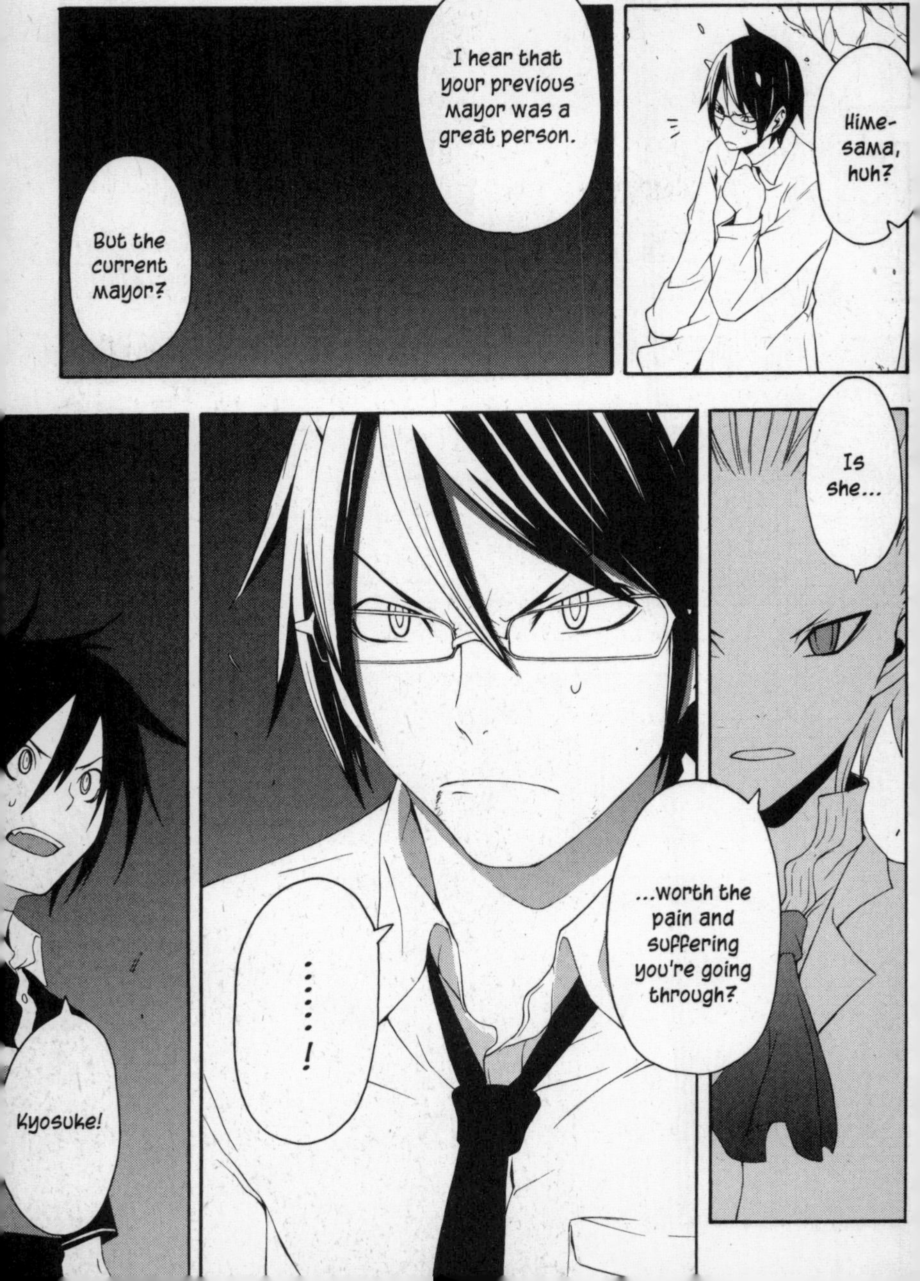
Hime-sama, huh?
I hear that your previous mayor was a great person.
But the current mayor?
Is she...
...worth the pain and suffering you're going through?
......!
Kyosuke!

Noodles!

Give me noodles!

I'm hungry!
I'm hungry!

Kyosuke! You have to try to remember the good things!!

Think positive!

UMMM.

BOB
BOB

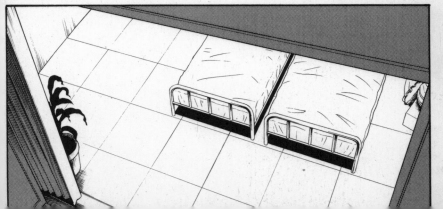

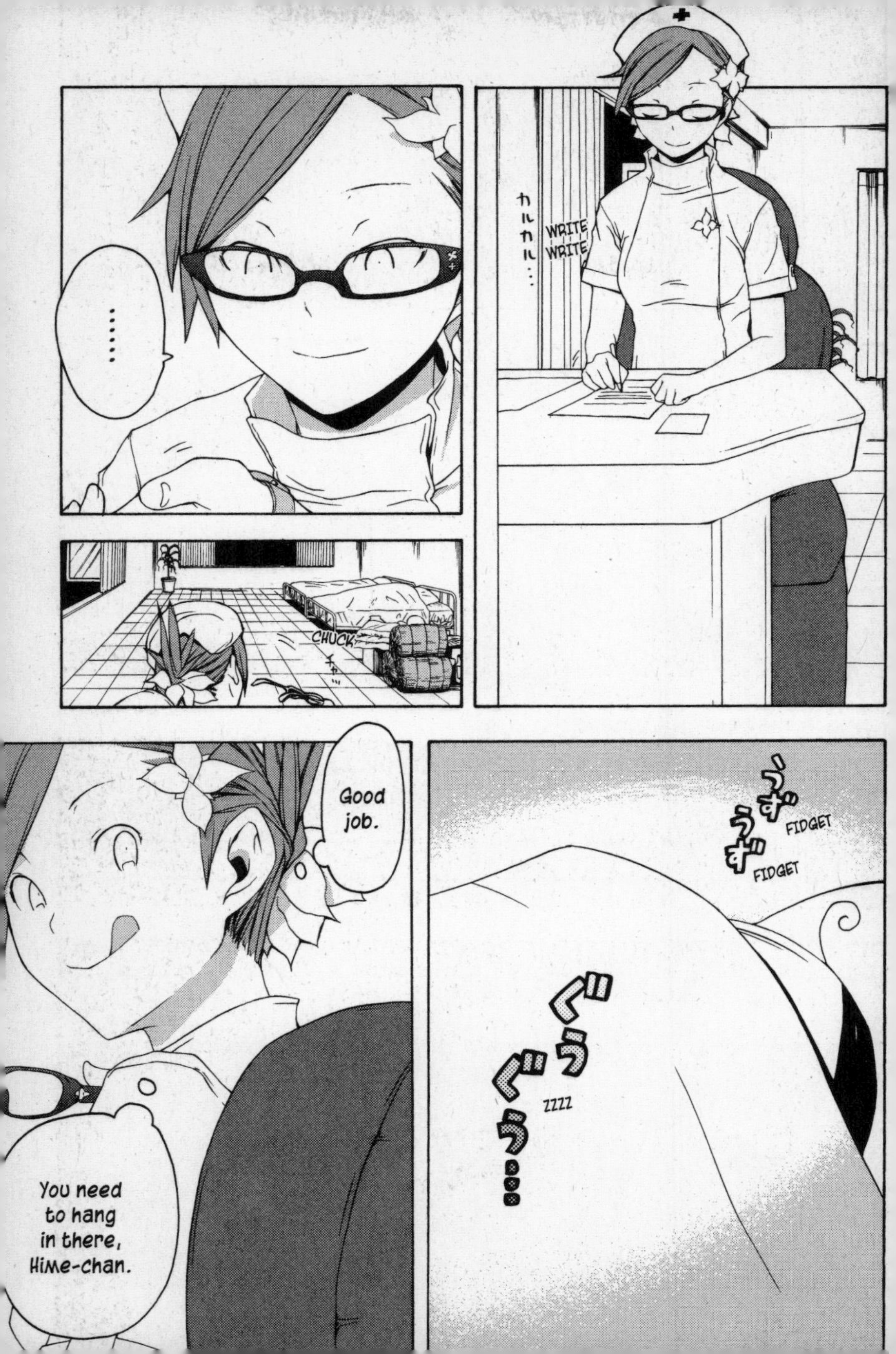
カルカル…
WRITE WRITE
……
CHUCK
うずうず
FIDGET FIDGET
ぐうぐう…
ZZZZ
Good job.
You need to hang in there, Hime-chan.

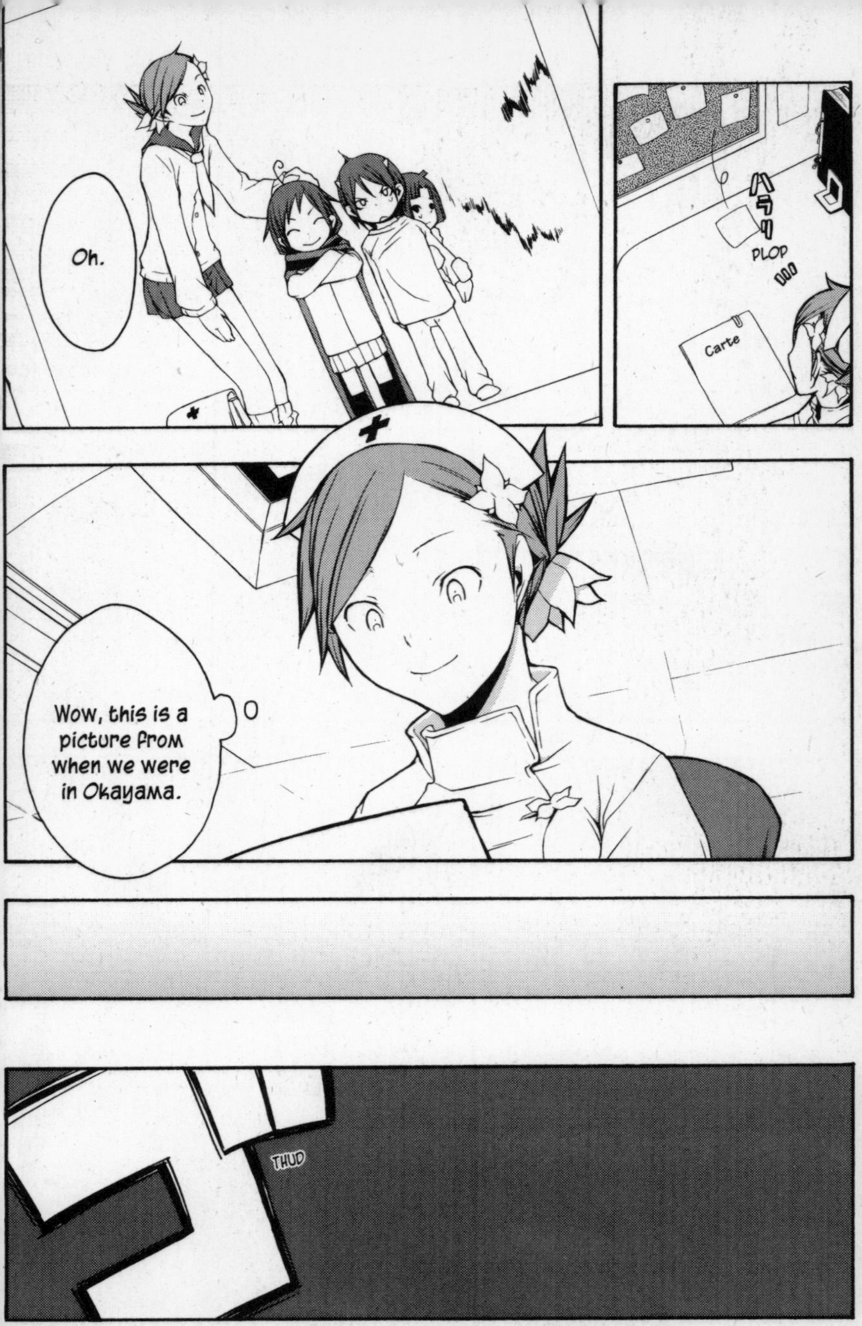
ハラリ
PLOP
Carte
Oh.
Wow, this is a picture from when we were in Okayama.
THUD

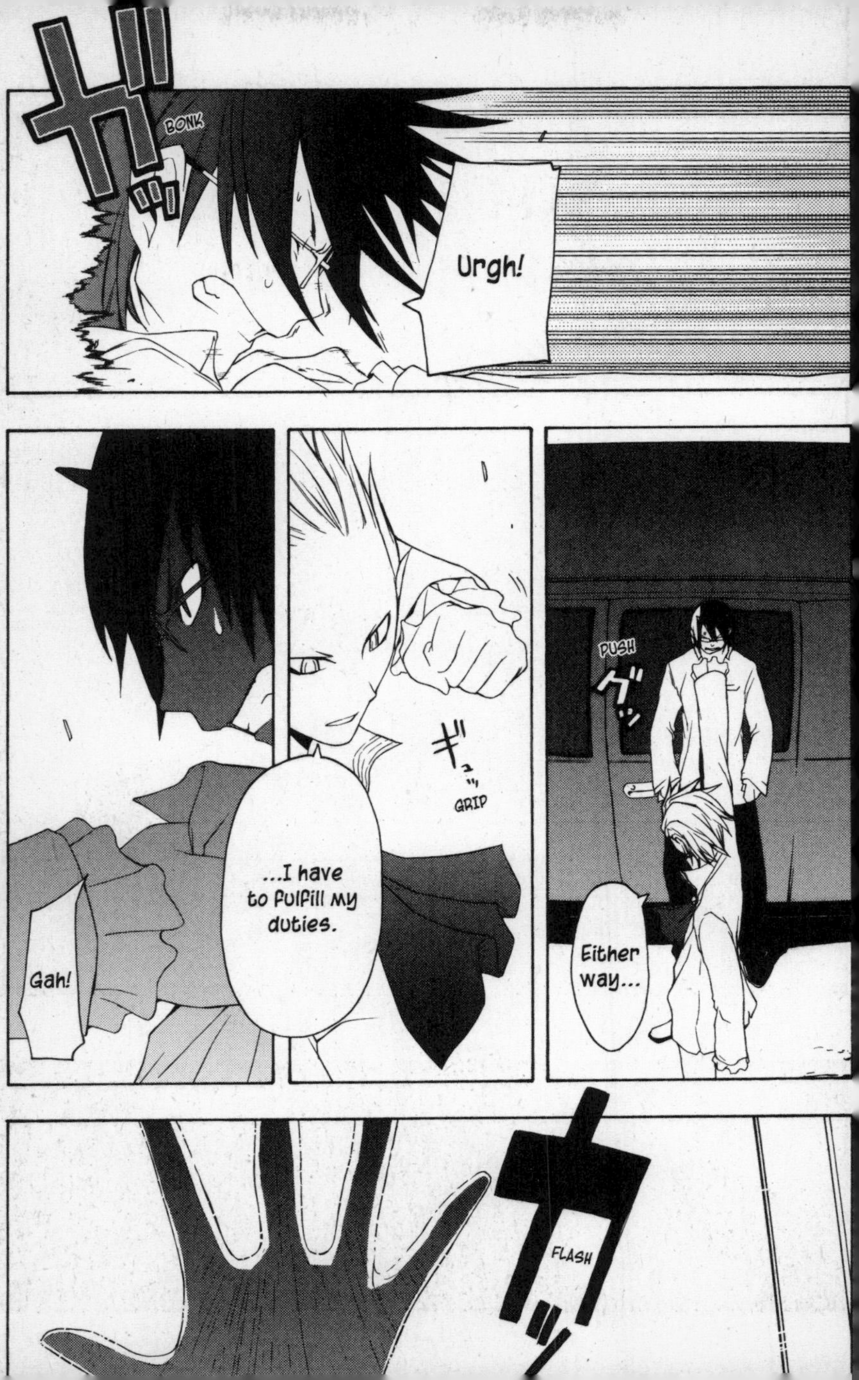
BONK
Urgh!
PUSH
Either way...
GRIP
...I have to fulfill my duties.
Gah!
FLASH

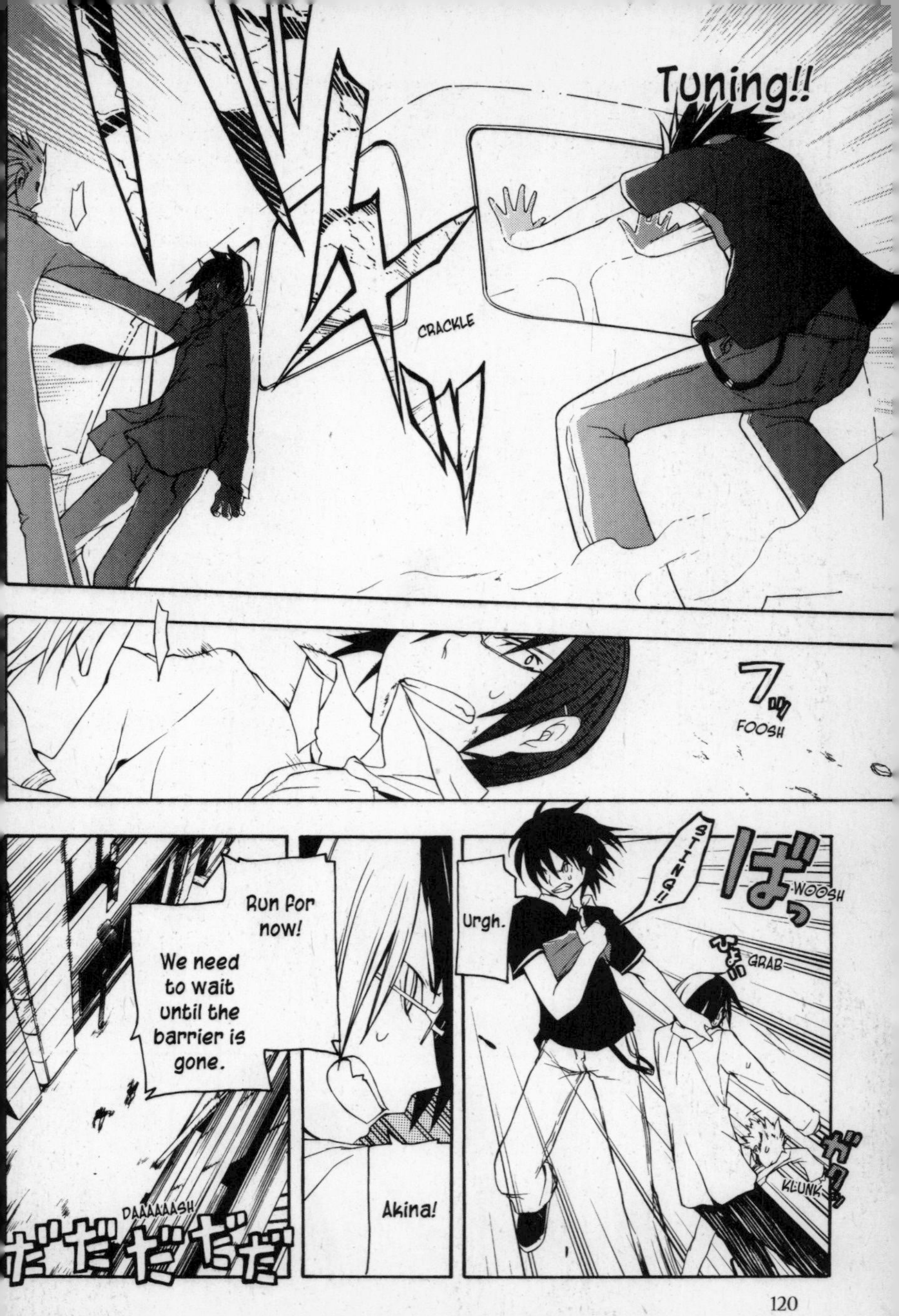
Tuning!!
CRACKLE
FOOSH
ばっ
WOOSH
STING!!
Urgh.
GRAB
KLUNK
Akina!
Run for now!
We need to wait until the barrier is gone.
DAAAAAASH
だだだだだ

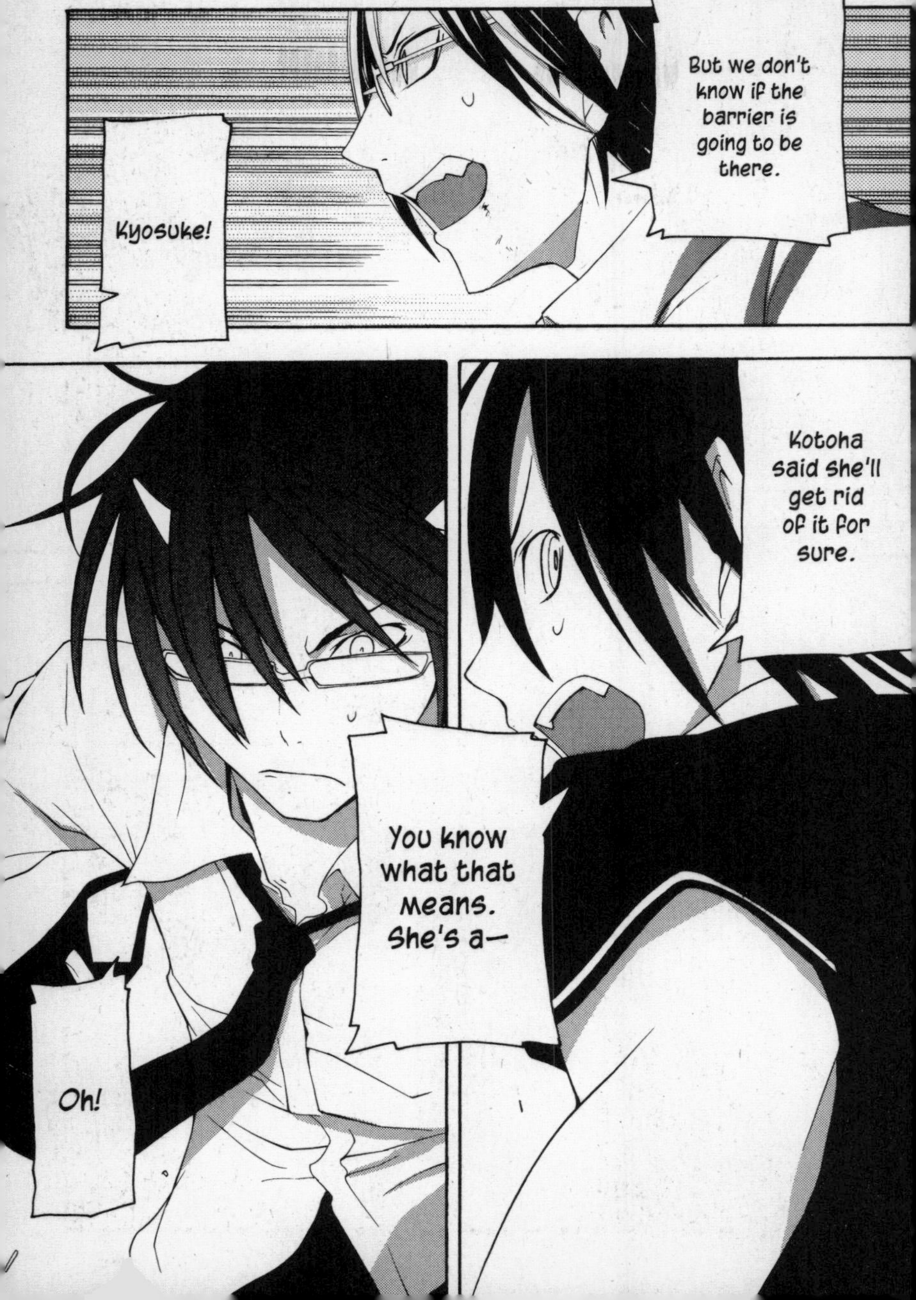
But we don't know if the barrier is going to be there.
Kyosuke!
Kotoha said she'll get rid of it for sure.
You know what that means. She's a—
Oh!

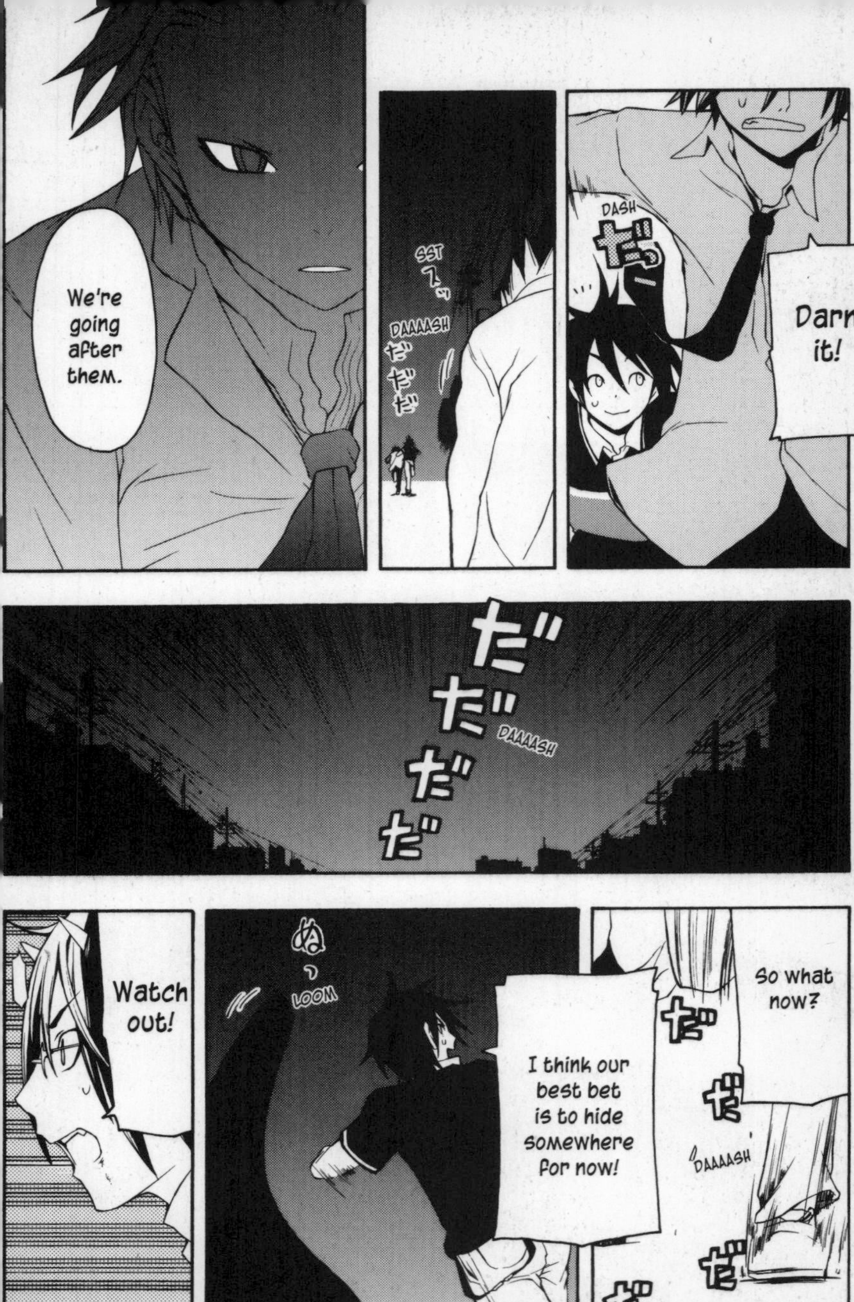
DASH
だっ
Darn it!
SST
スッ
DAAAASH
だだだ
We're going after them.
だだだだ
DAAAASH
So what now?
だだだだ
DAAAASH
ぬっ
LOOM
I think our best bet is to hide somewhere for now!
Watch out!

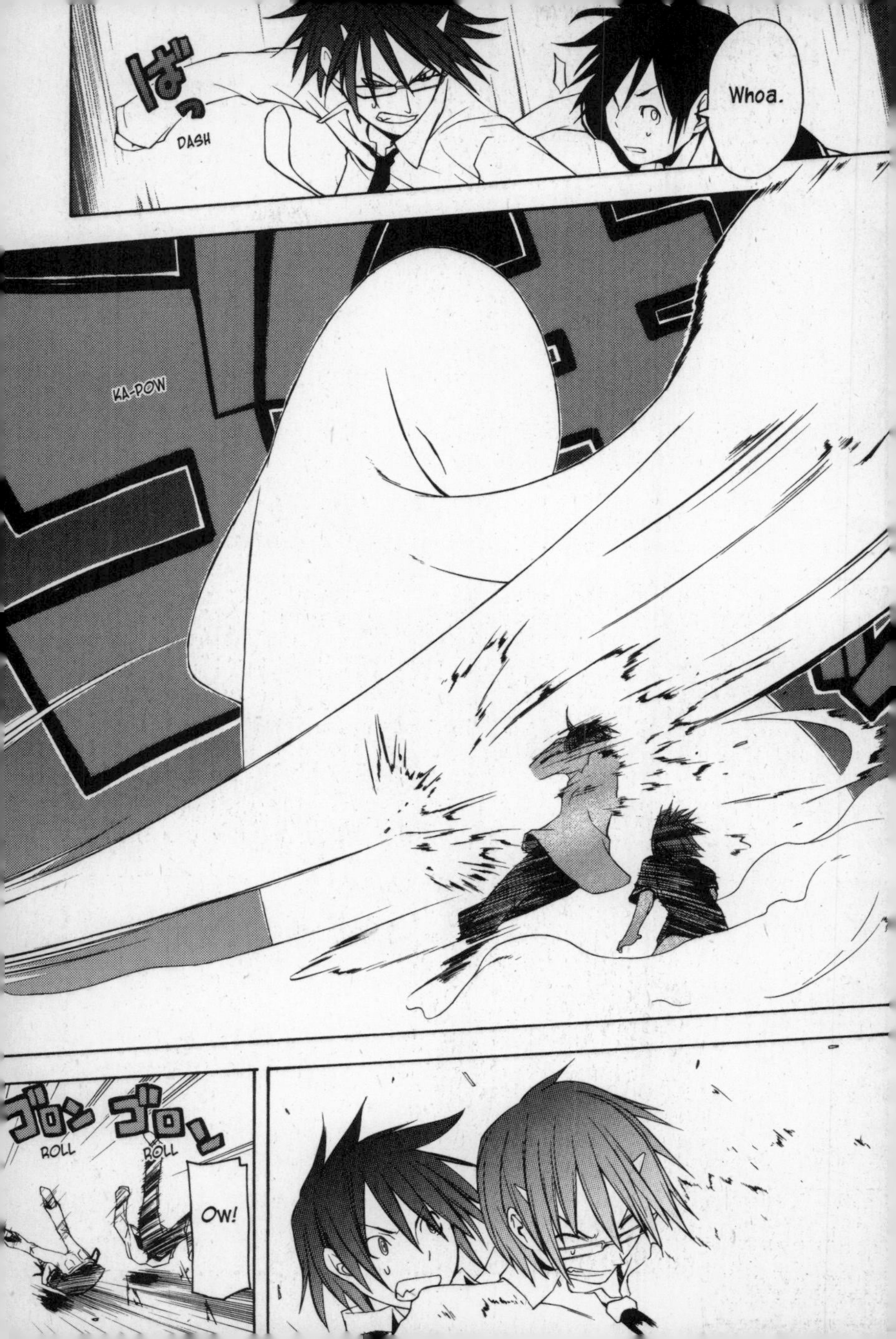
Whoa.
ばっ
DASH
KA-POW
ゴロン
ROLL
ゴロン
ROLL
Ow!

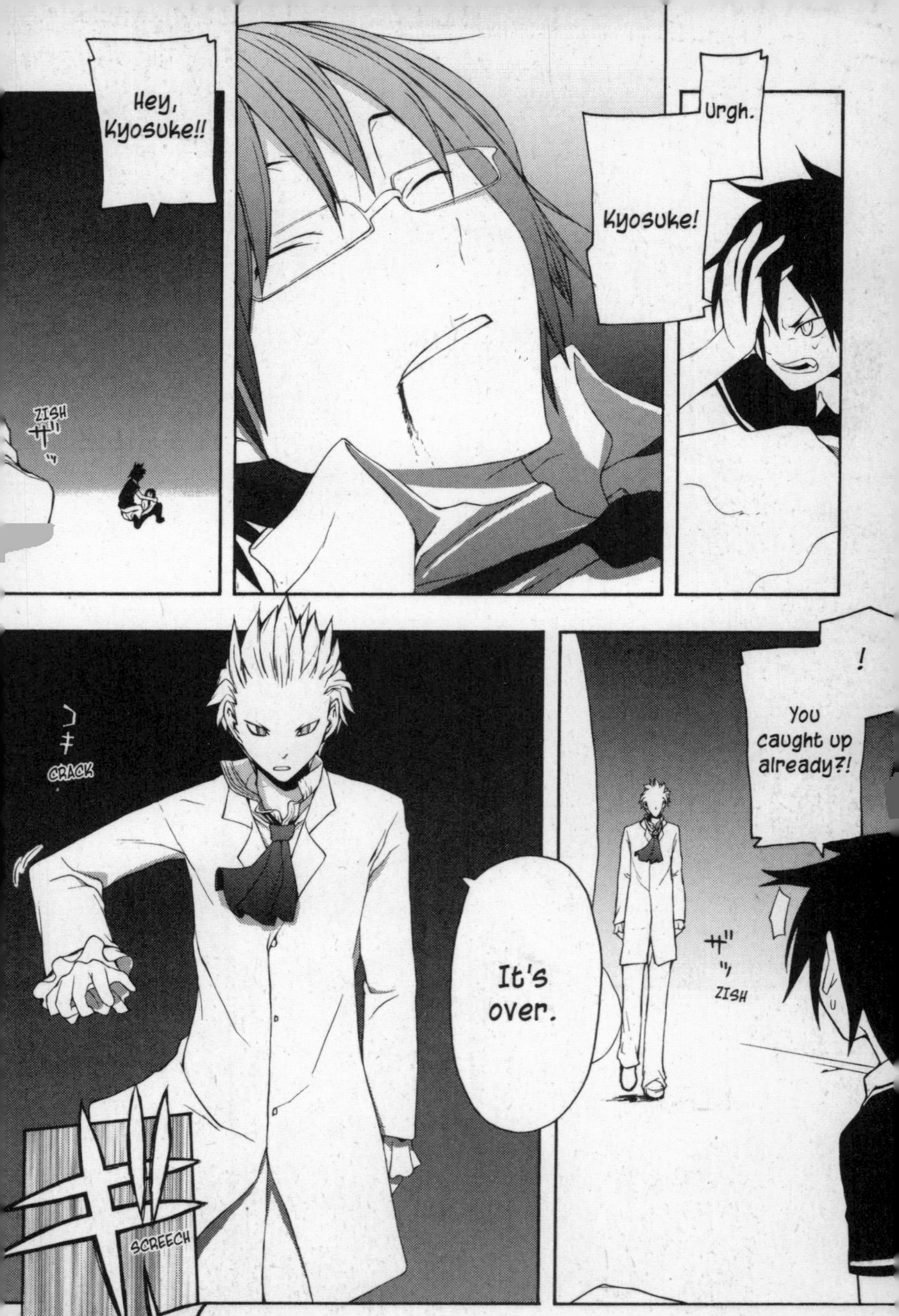
Urgh.
Kyosuke!
Hey, Kyosuke!!
ZISH
!
You caught up already?!
It's over.
ZISH
CRACK
SCREECH

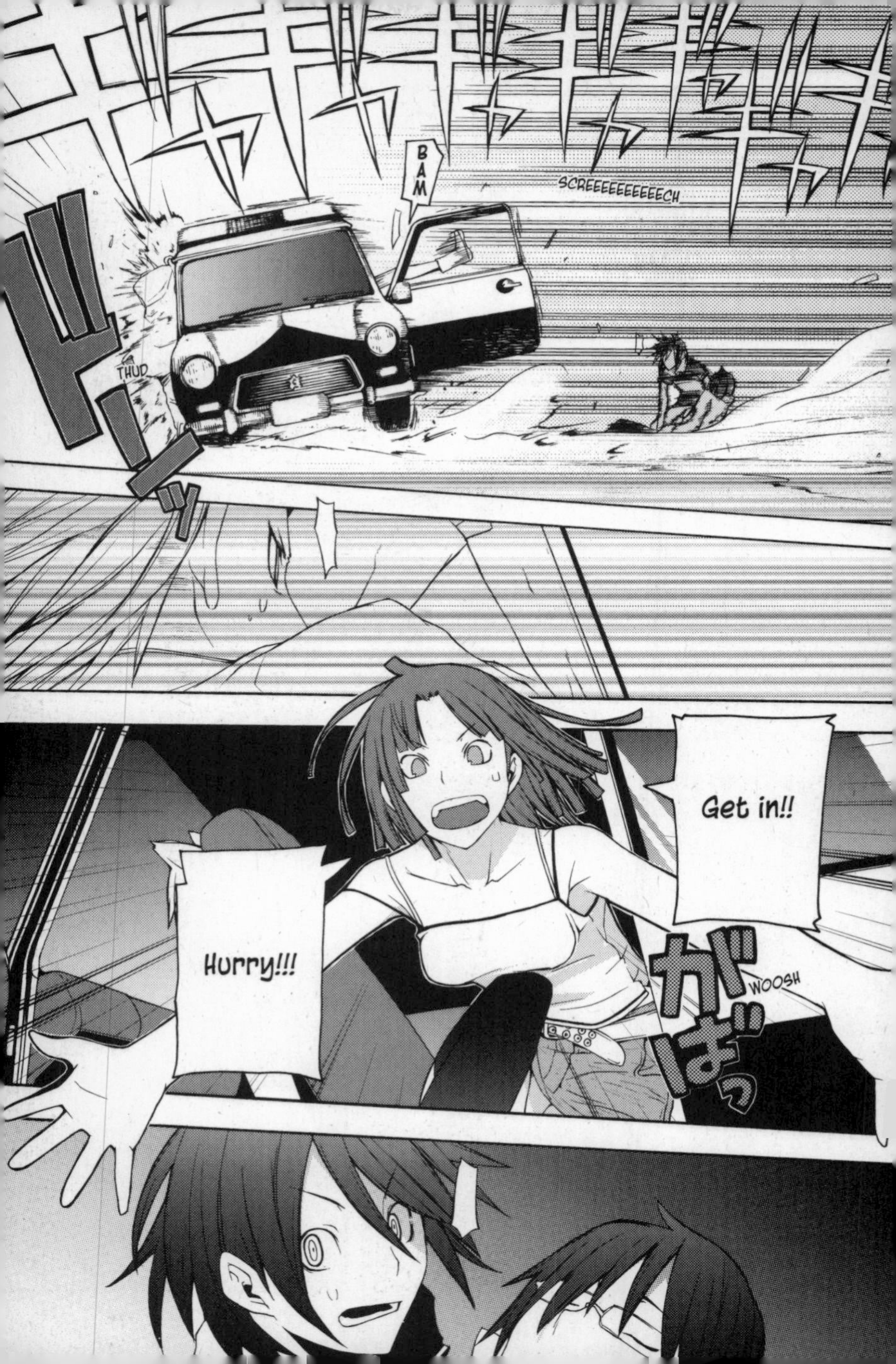
SCREEEEEEEEEEEECH
BAM
ドッ
THUD
Get in!!
がばっ
WOOSH
Hurry!!!

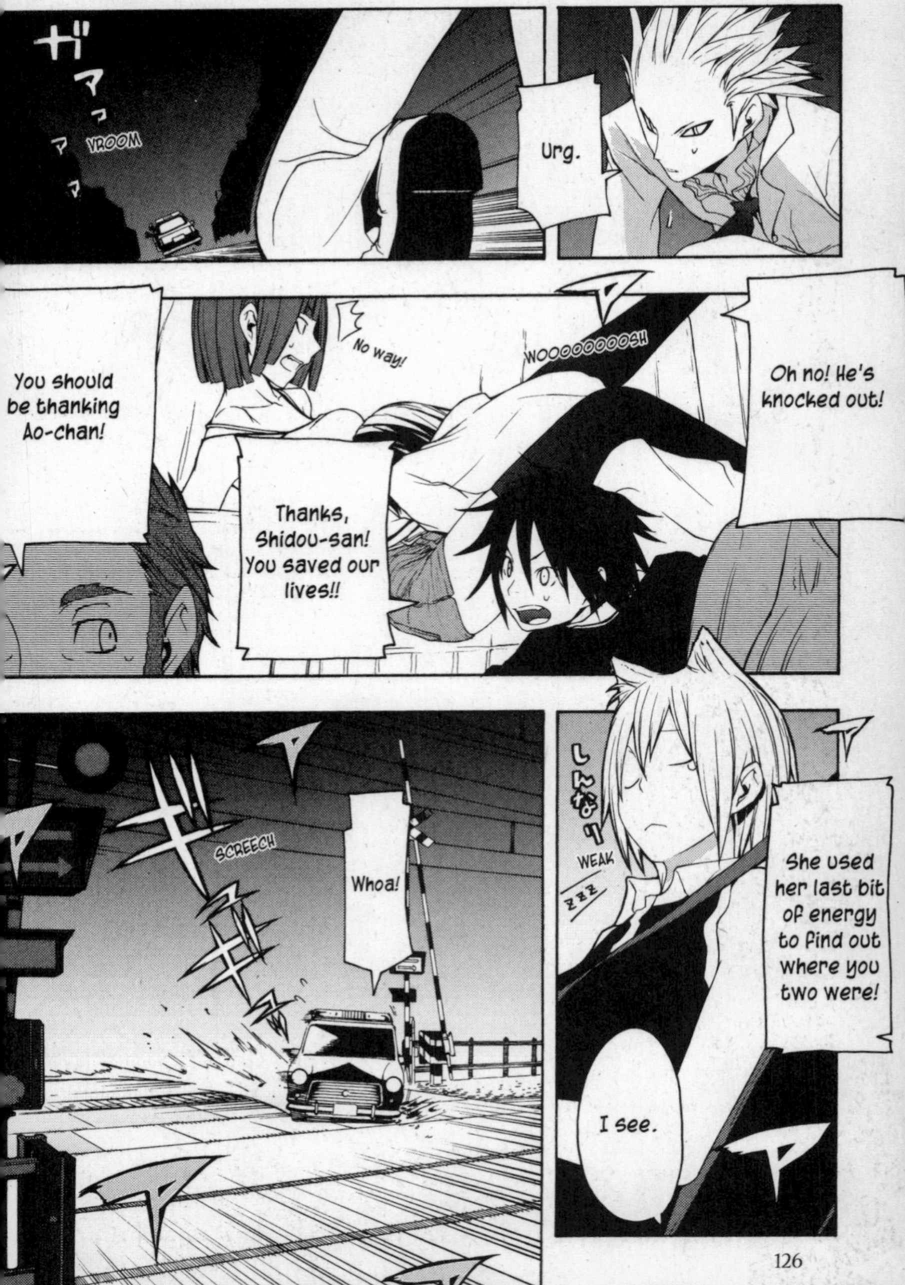
Urg.
ガァァァ
VROOM
Oh no! He's knocked out!
WOOOOOOOOOSH
No way!
Thanks, Shidou-san! You saved our lives!!
You should be thanking Ao-chan!
She used her last bit of energy to find out where you two were!
しんなり
WEAK
zzz
I see.
Whoa!
SCREECH

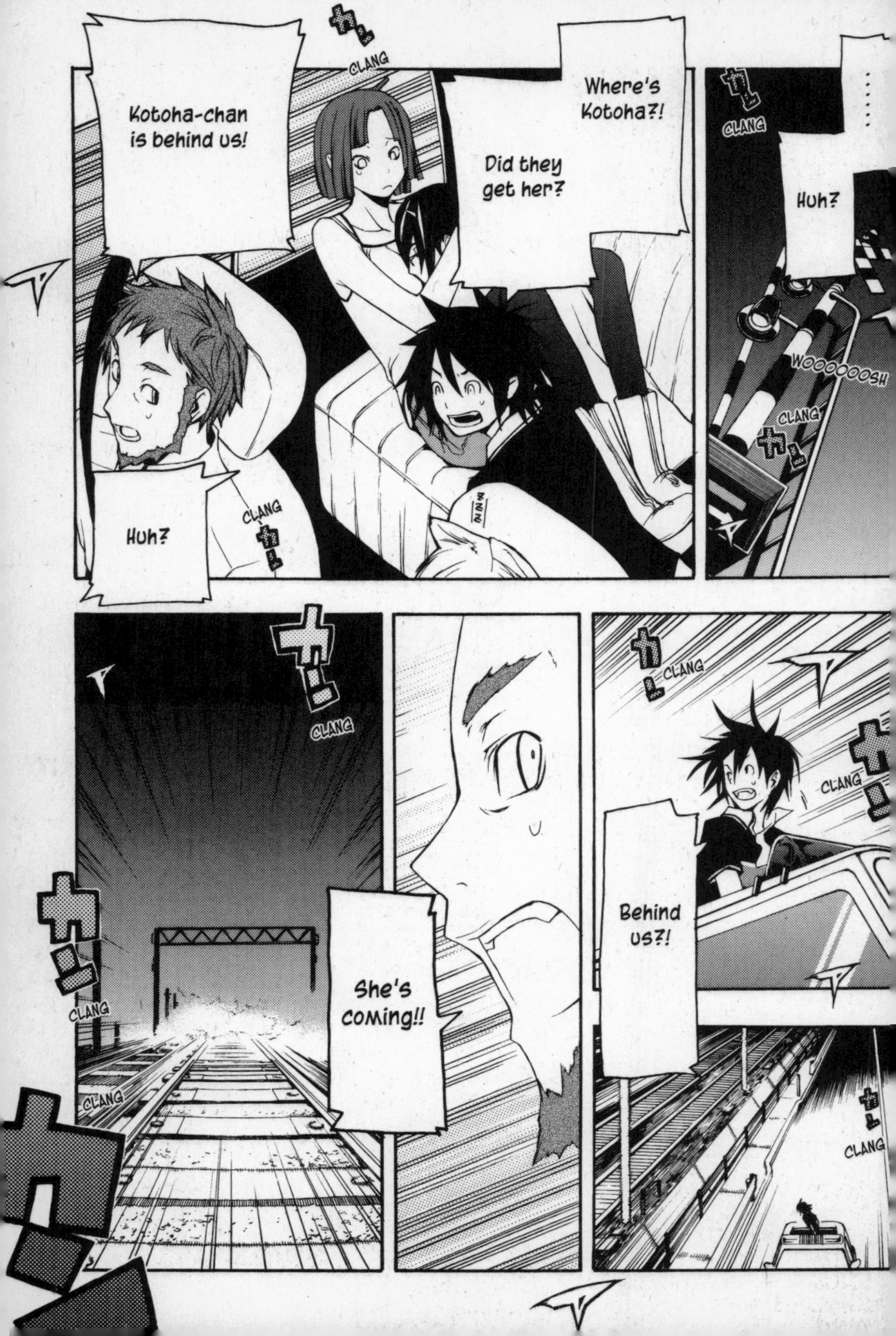
......
Huh?
CLANG
WOOOOOOSH
CLANG
CLANG
Where's Kotoha?!
Did they get her?
Kotoha-chan is behind us!
Huh?
CLANG
CLANG
CLANG
Behind us?!
CLANG
She's coming!!
CLANG
CLANG
CLANG

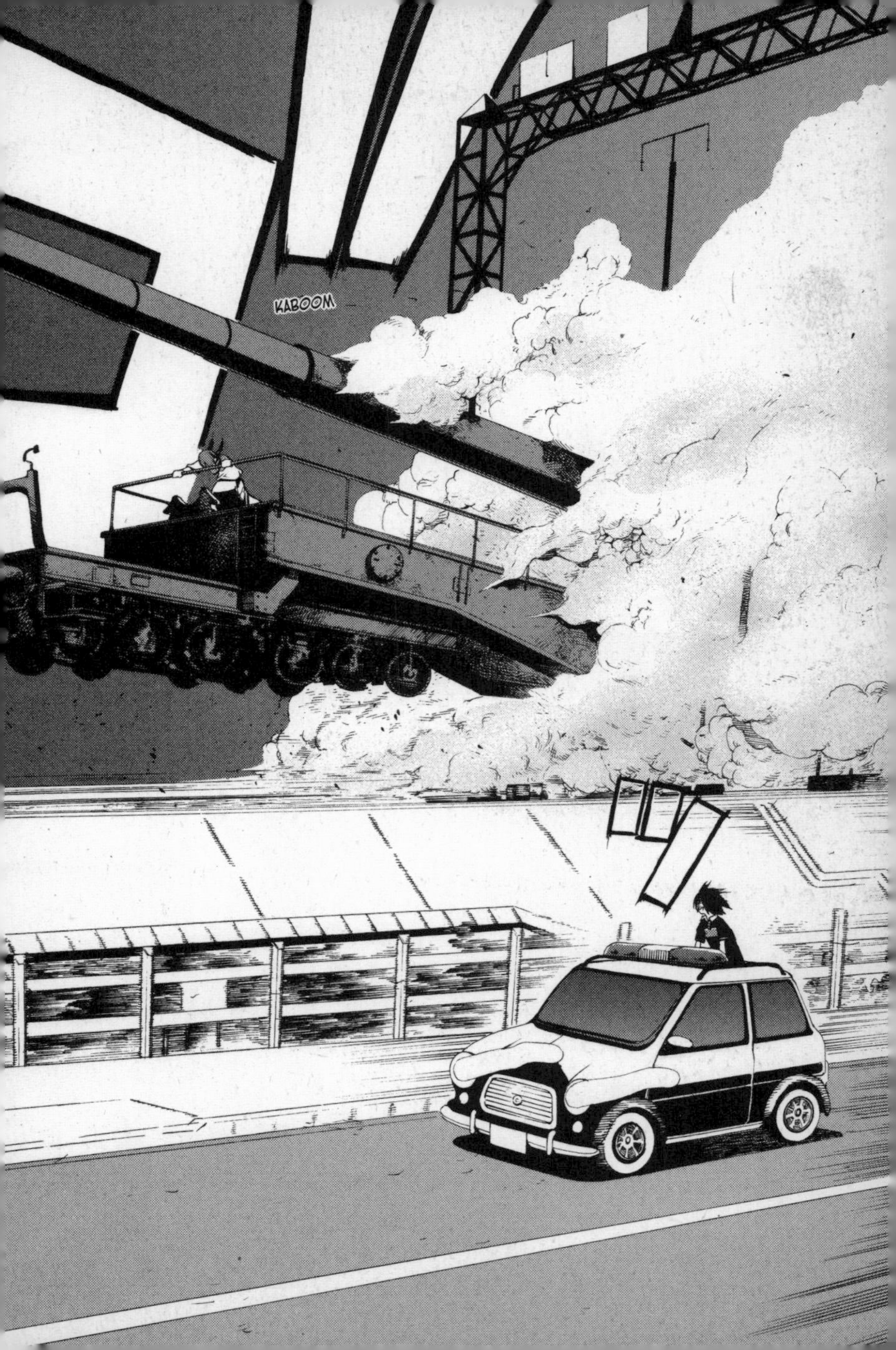
KABOOM

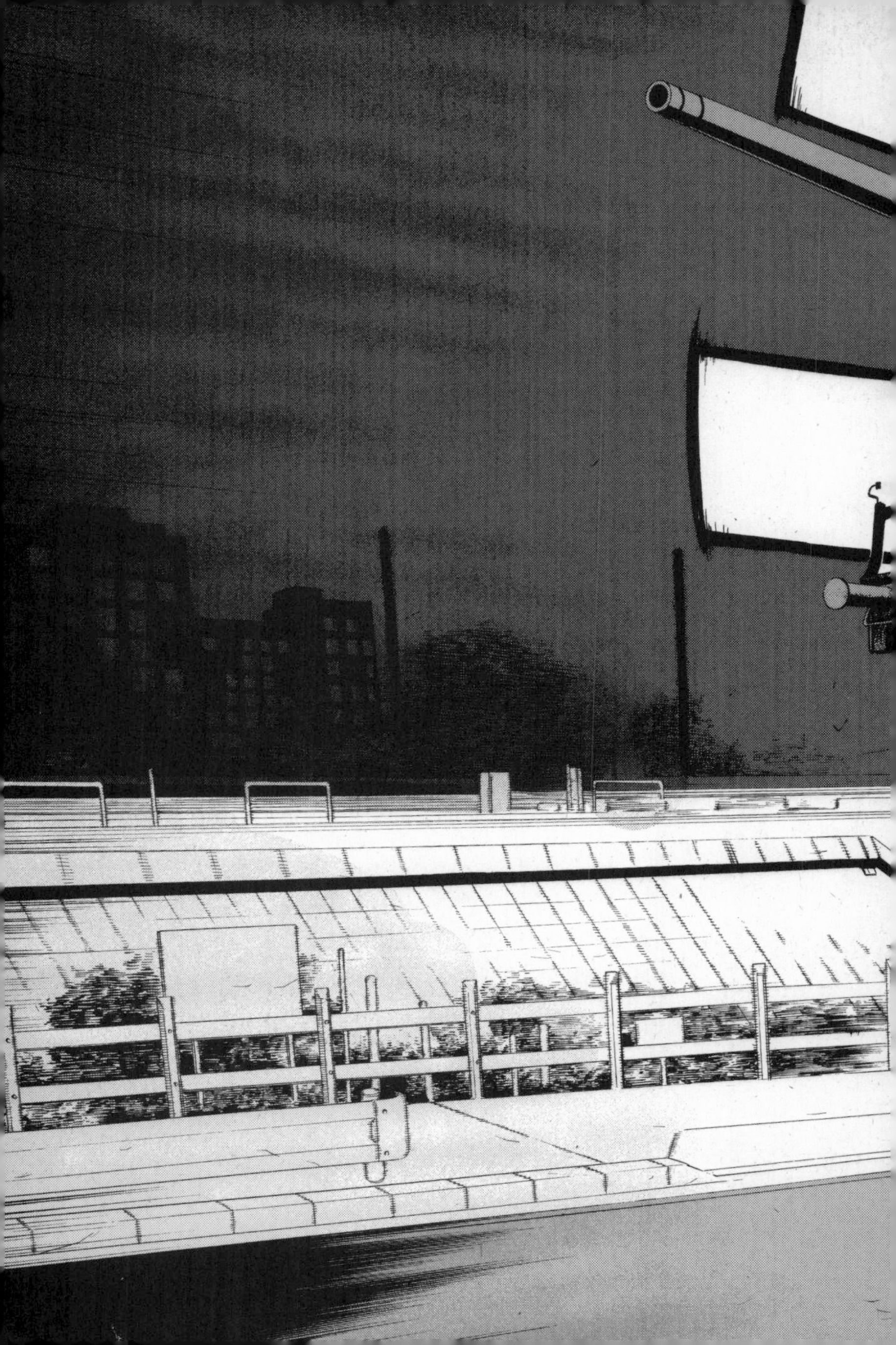

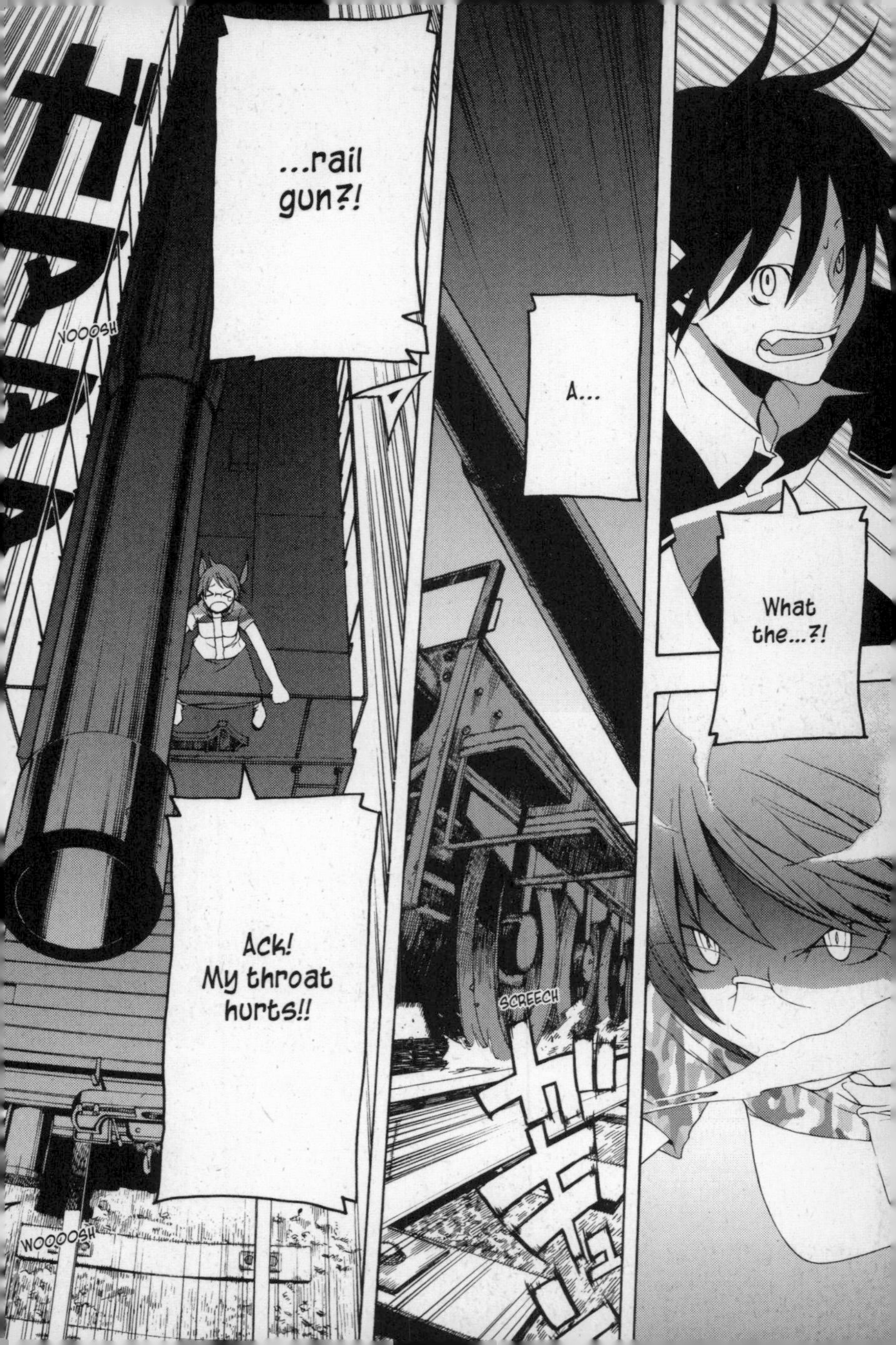
What the...?!
A...
SCREECH
...rail gun?!
VOOOSH
Ack! My throat hurts!!
WOOOOSH

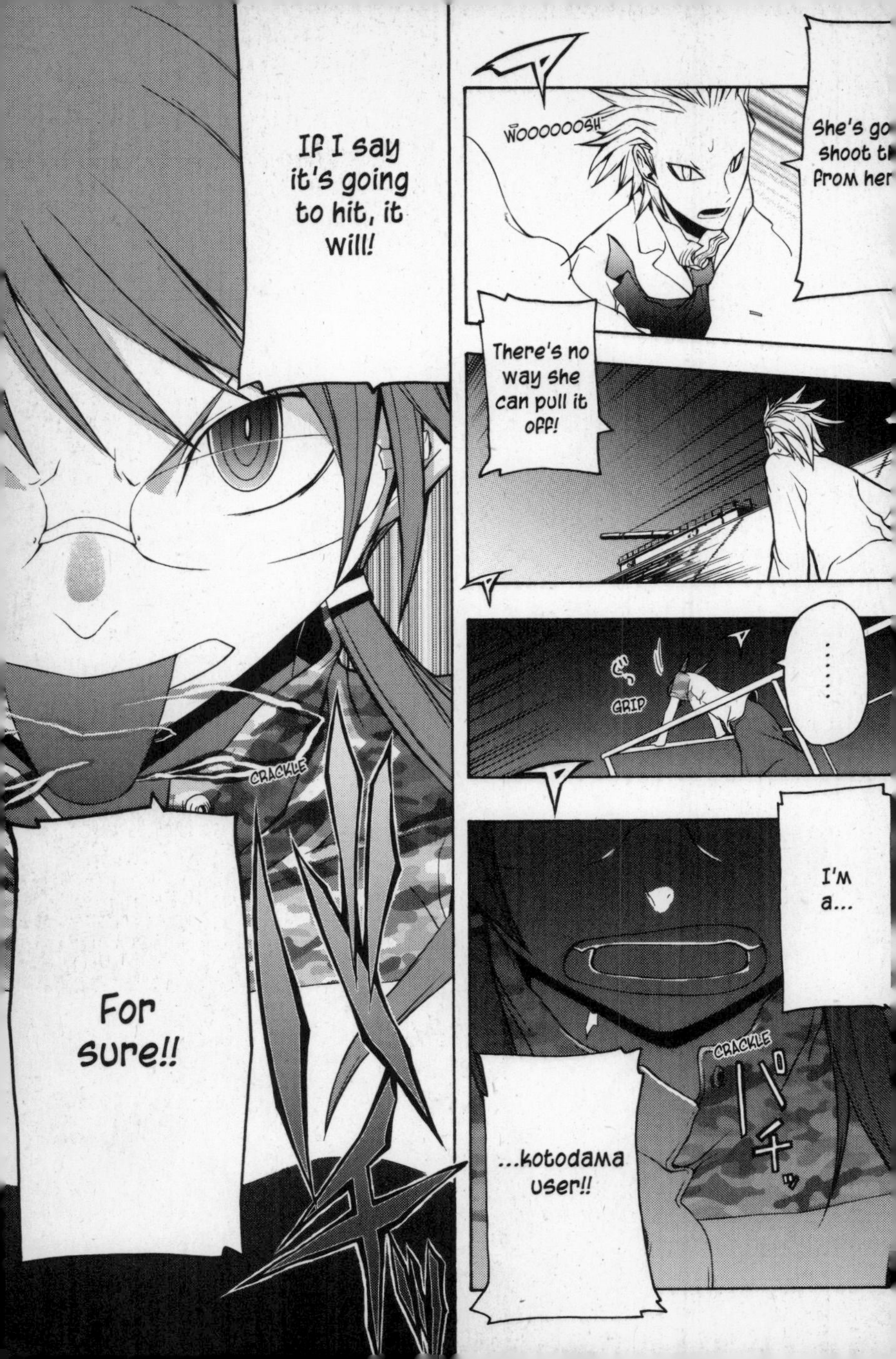
She's go shoot t from her
WOOOOOOOSH
There's no way she can pull it off!
......
GRIP
I'm a...
...kotodama user!!
CRACKLE
If I say it's going to hit, it will!
CRACKLE
For sure!!

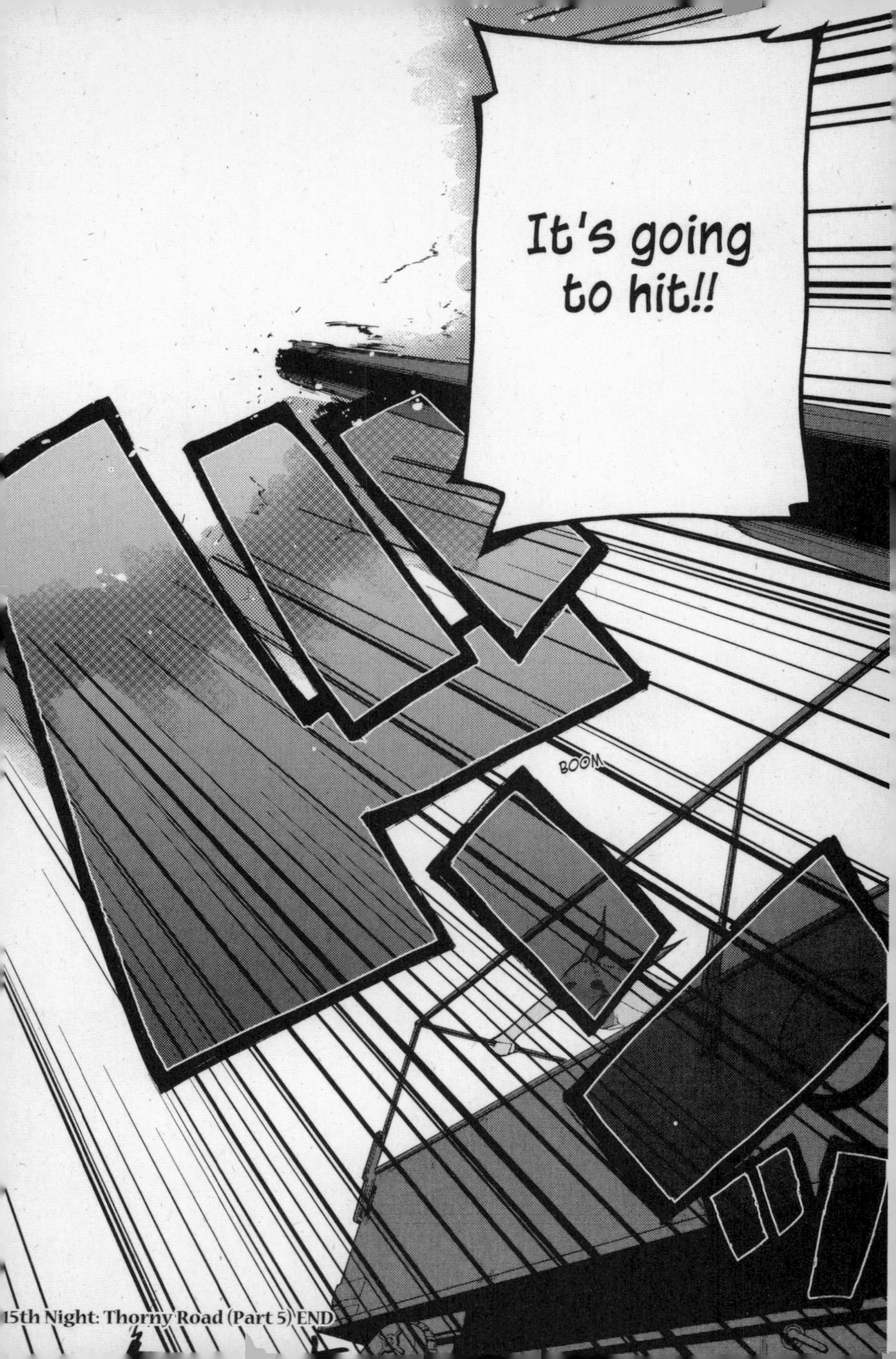
It's going to hit!!
BOOM

15th Night: Thorny Road (Part 5) END

Yozakura Quartet

Primary Stages of Yozakura Quartet

Shidou Mizuki
-san

Age: *28*

Hobbies:
Gardening

Favorites

Food:
Meaty things

Music Group:
Baker Brothers

Comedian:
Kamaitachi

Uchi-P Member:
Sekiya

Little-Known Fact:
He is a heavy drinker.

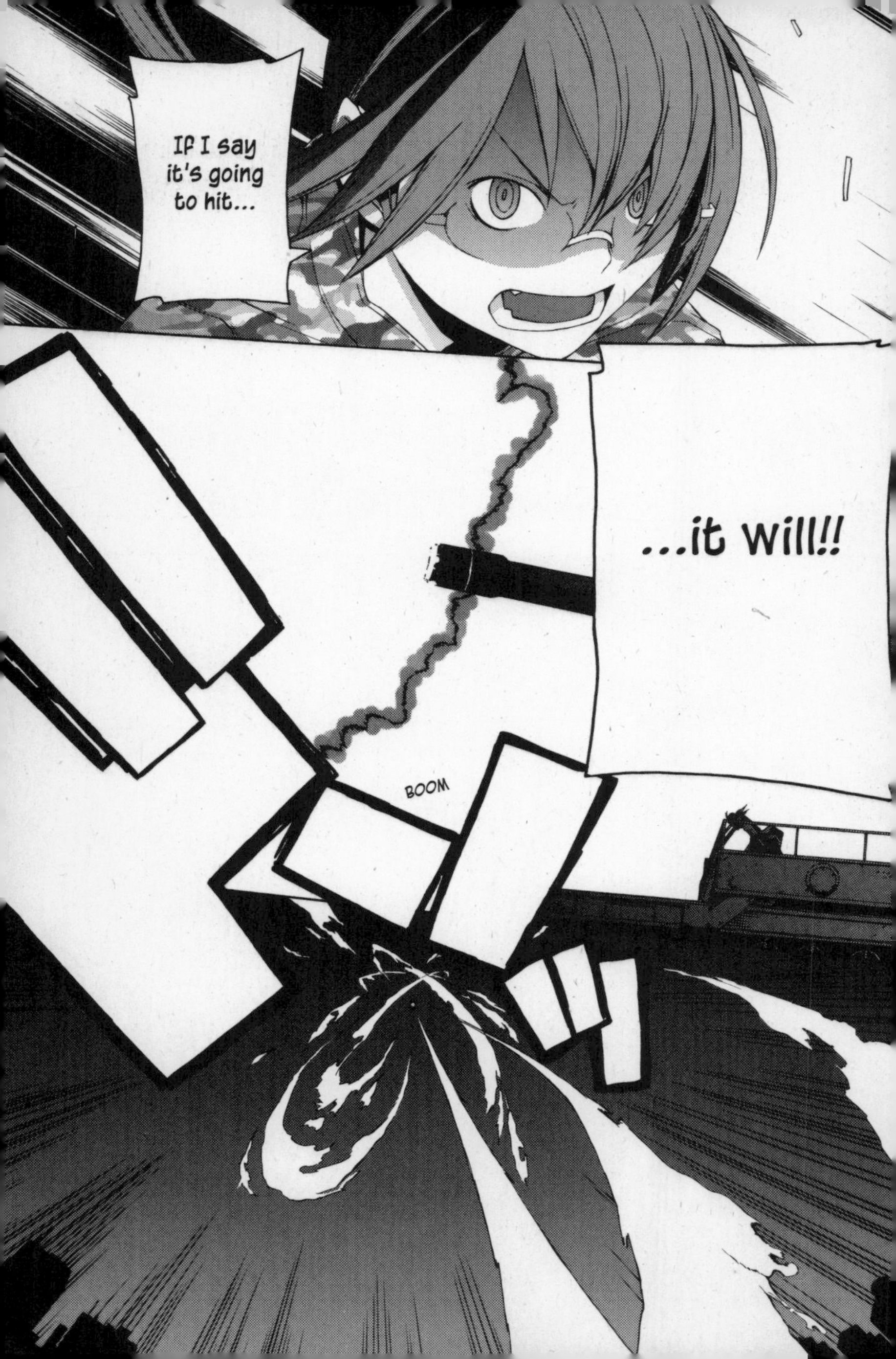
If I say it's going to hit...
...it will!!
BOOM

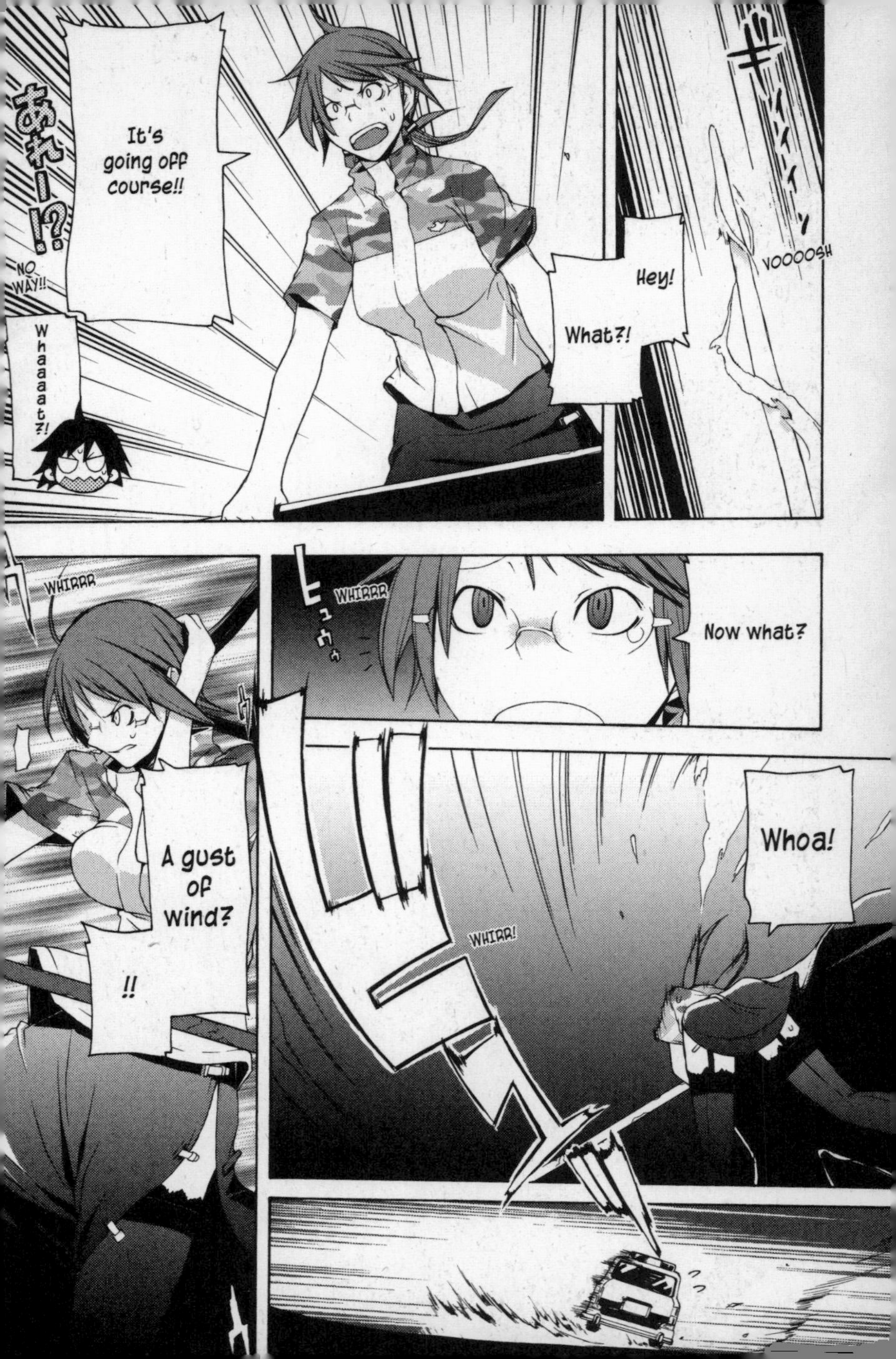
VOOOOSH
Hey!
What?!
It's going off course!!
あれー!?
NO WAY!!
Whaaaaat?!
WHIRRR
Now what?
Whoa!
WHIRR!
WHIRRR
A gust of wind?
!!

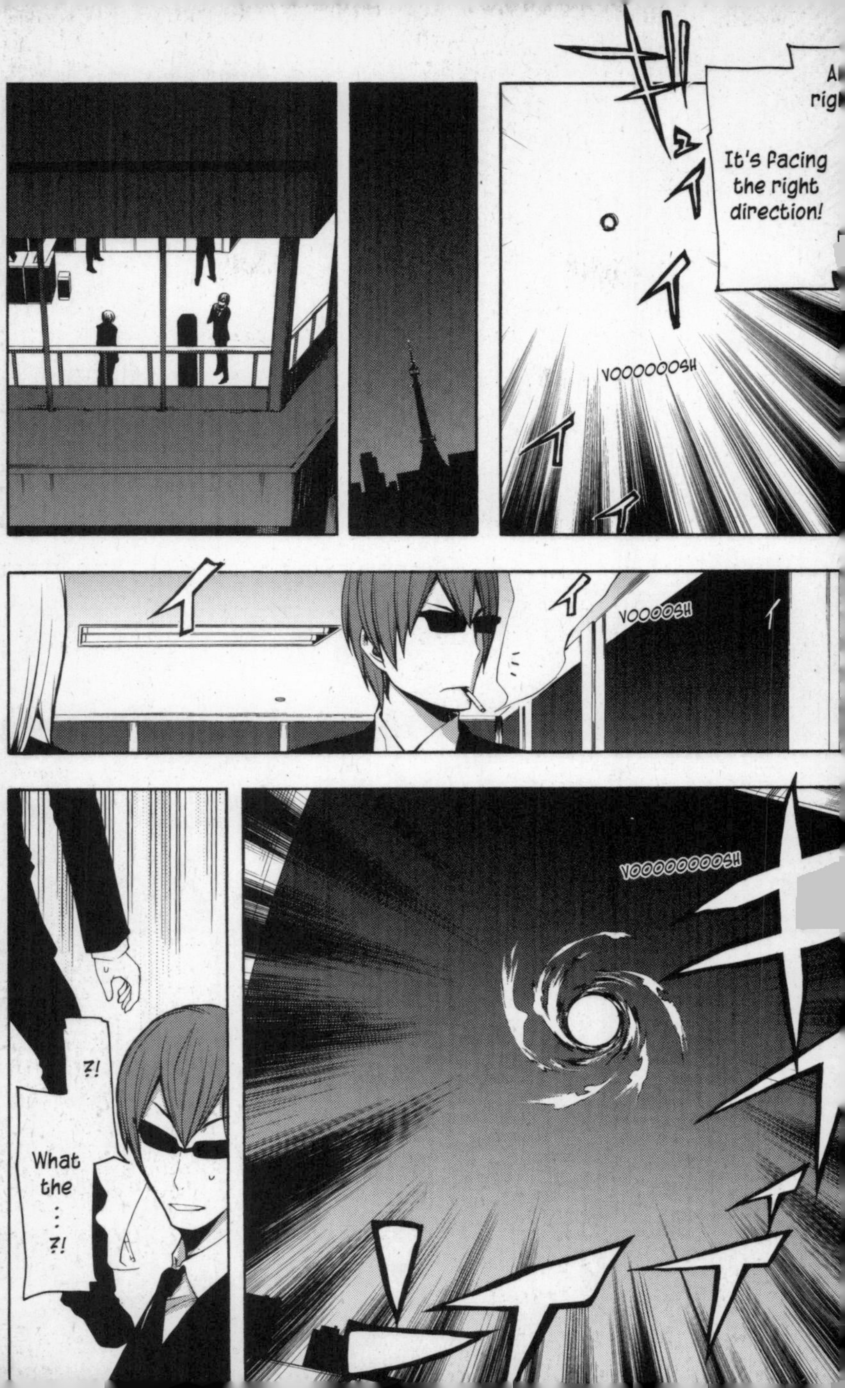
It's facing the right direction!
VOOOOOOSH
VOOOOSH
VOOOOOOOOOSH
?!
What the ...?!

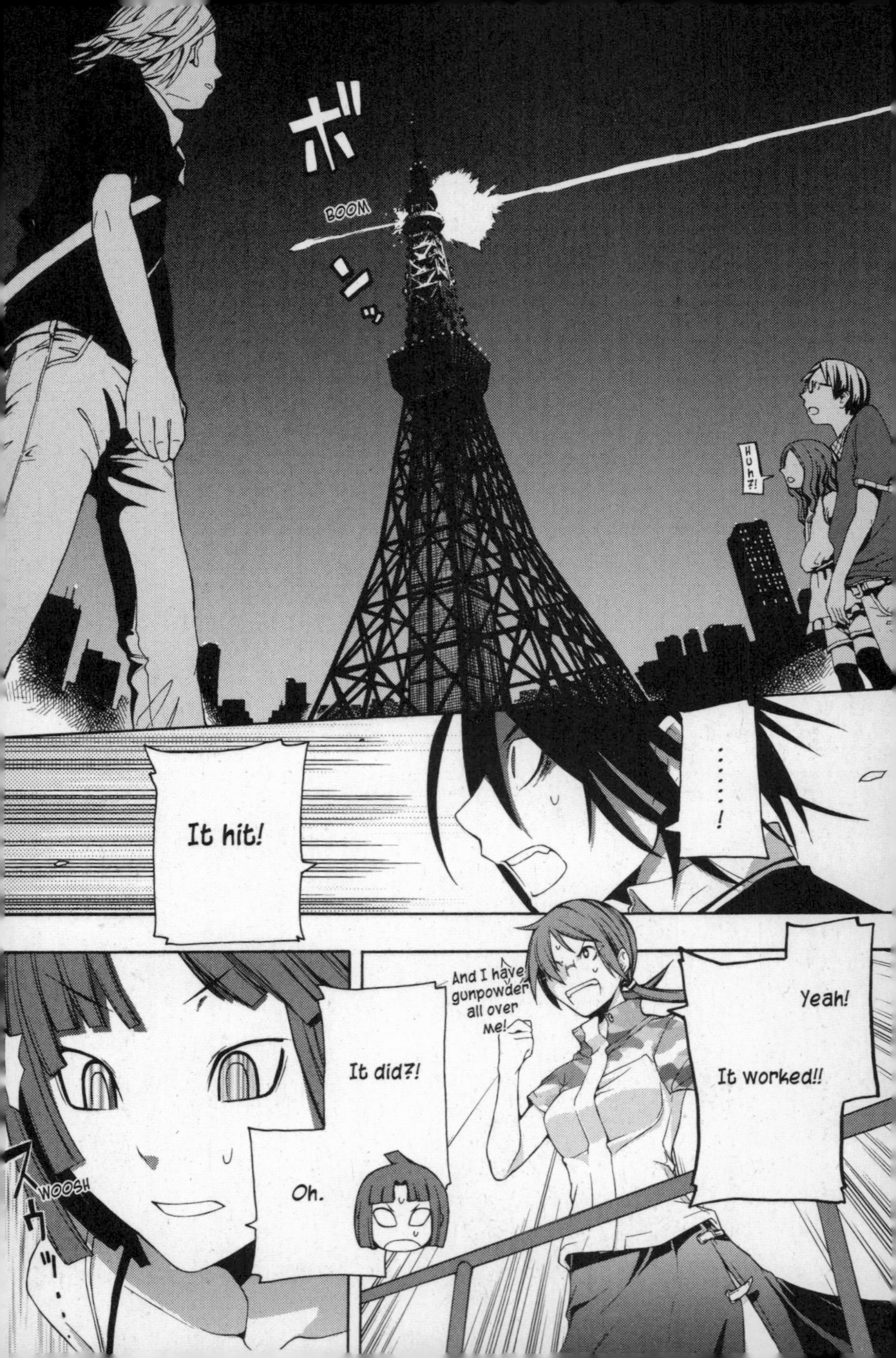
ボ
BOOM
ンッ
Huh?!
......!
It hit!
Yeah!
It worked!!
And I have gunpowder all over me!
It did?!
Oh.
WOOSH

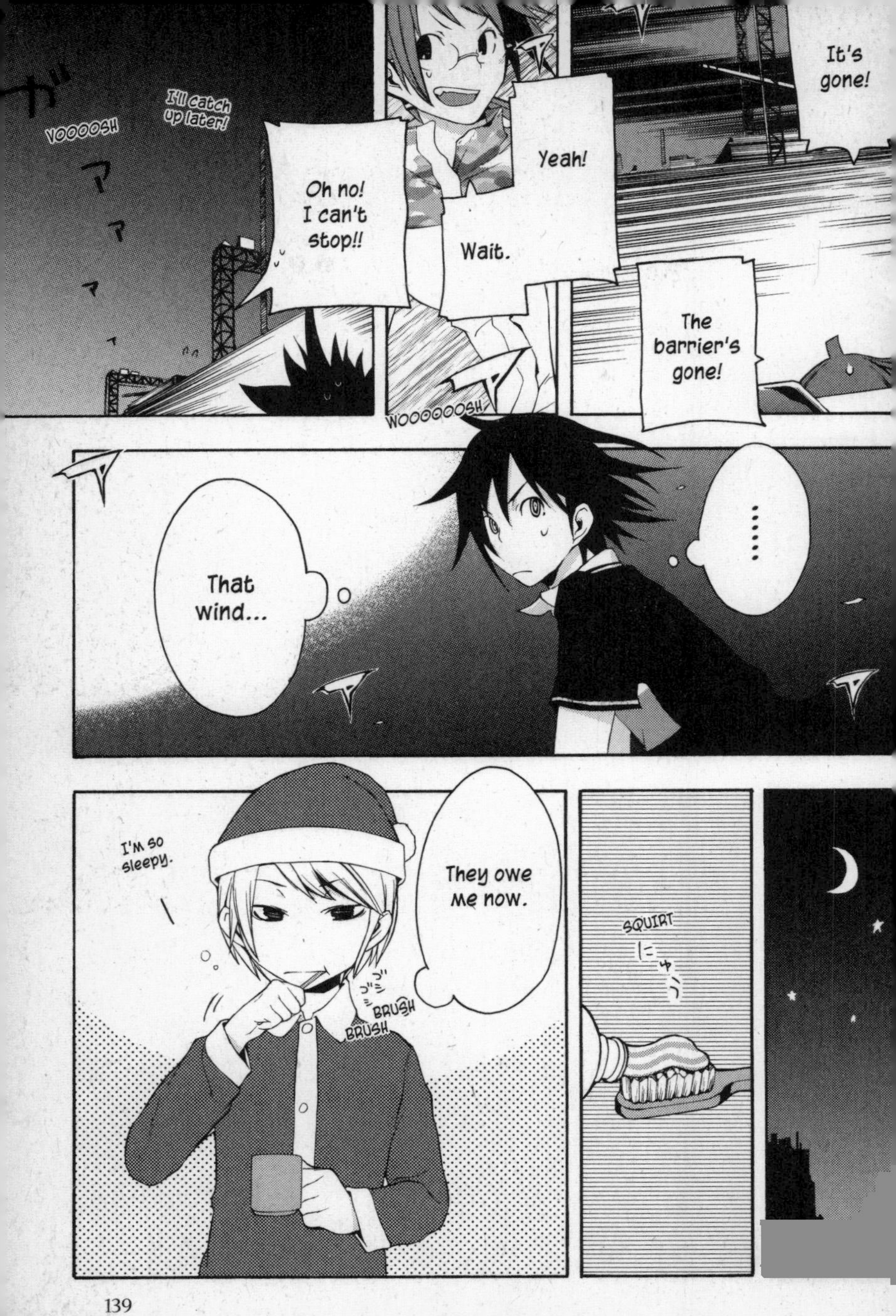
It's gone!
The barrier's gone!
Yeah!
Wait.
WOOOOOOSH
Oh no! I can't stop!!
I'll catch up later!
VOOOOSH
......
That wind...
SQUIRT
They owe me now.
BRUSH
BRUSH
I'm so sleepy.

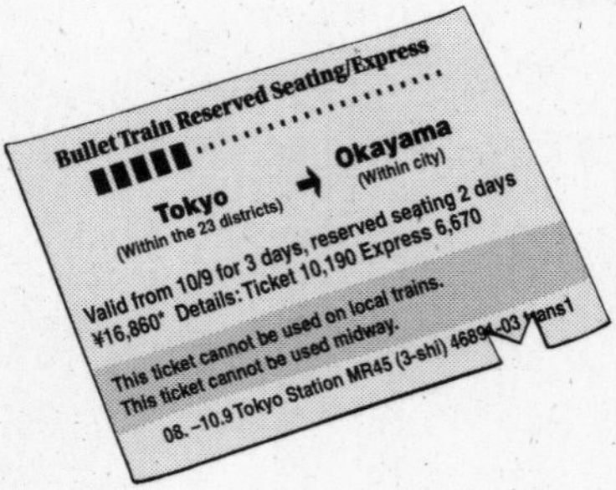
Bullet Train Reserved Seating/Express
Tokyo
(Within the 23 districts)
Okayama
(Within city)
Valid from 10/9 for 3 days, reserved seating 2 days
¥16,860* Details: Ticket 10,190 Express 6,670
This ticket cannot be used on local trains.
This ticket cannot be used midway.
08. –10.9 Tokyo Station MR45 (3-shi)

16th Night: Thorny Road (Part 6)

*equals approx. $169

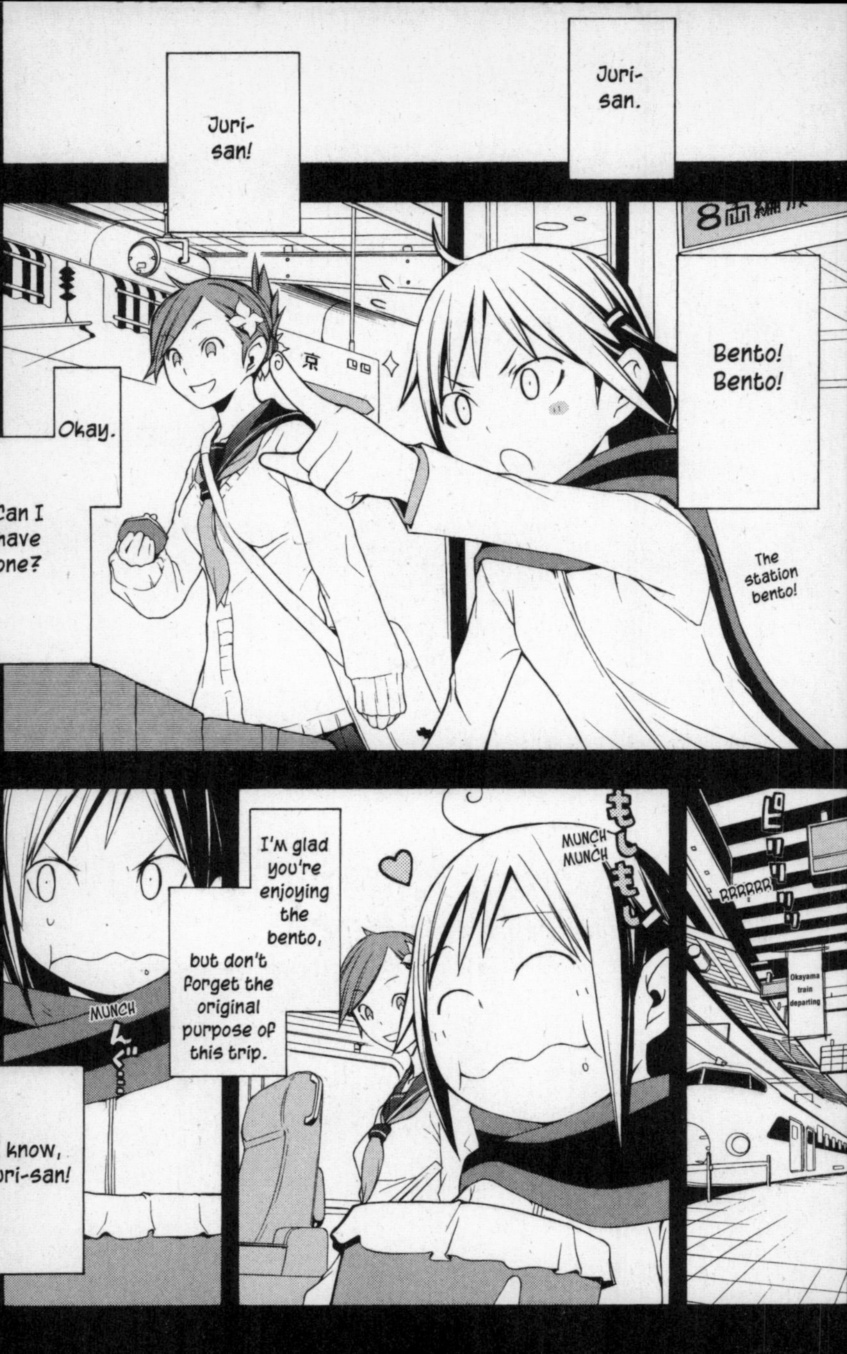
Juri-san.
Juri-san!
Bento! Bento!
The station bento!
Can I have one?
Okay.
ピリリリリ
BRRRRRR
Okayama train departing
もしもし
MUNCH MUNCH
I'm glad you're enjoying the bento, but don't forget the original purpose of this trip.
MUNCH
んぐ…
I know, Juri-san!

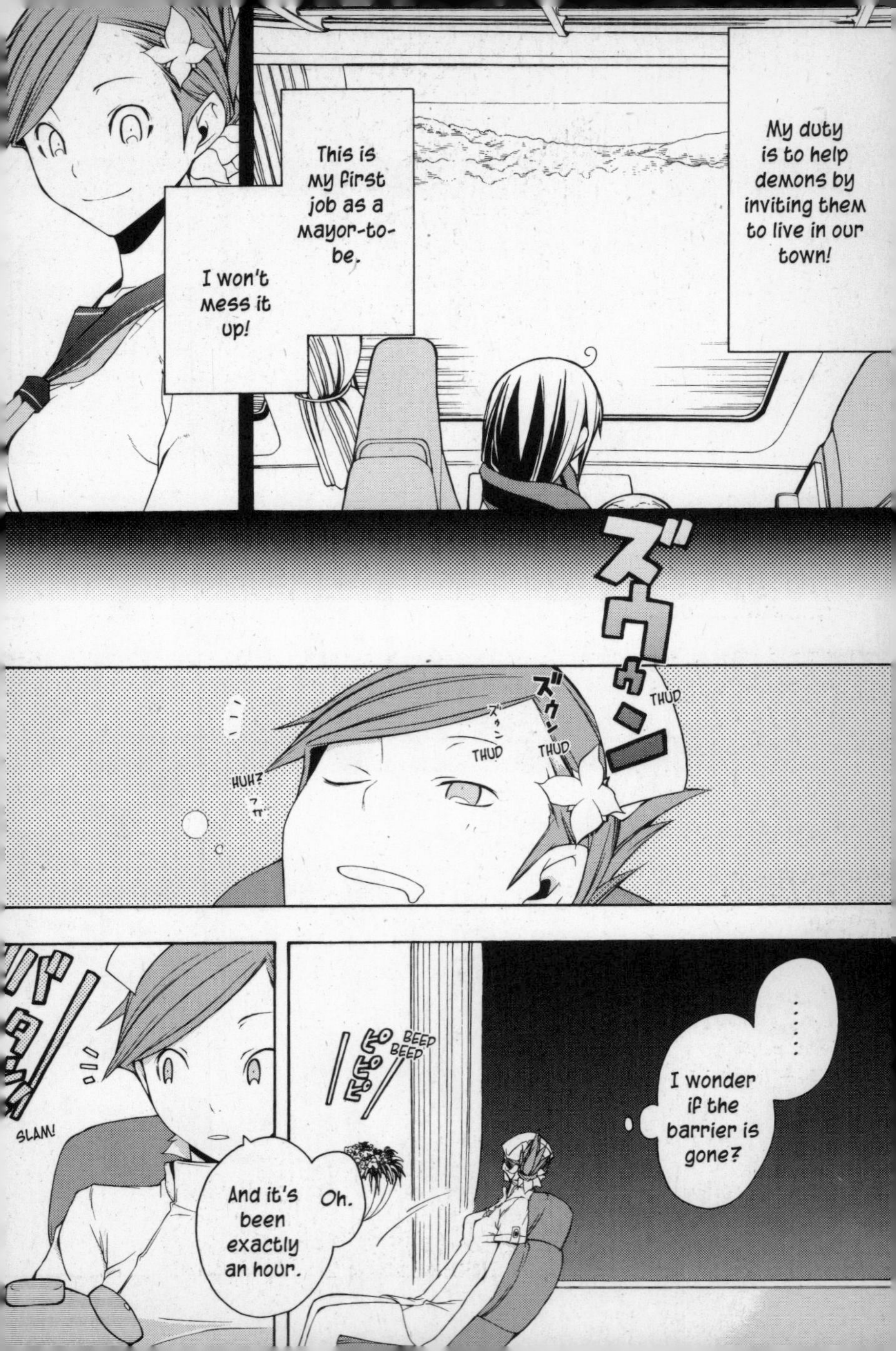
My duty is to help demons by inviting them to live in our town!
This is my first job as a mayor-to-be.
I won't mess it up!
THUD
THUD
THUD
HUH?
I wonder if the barrier is gone?
Oh.
And it's been exactly an hour.
BEEP BEEP
SLAM!

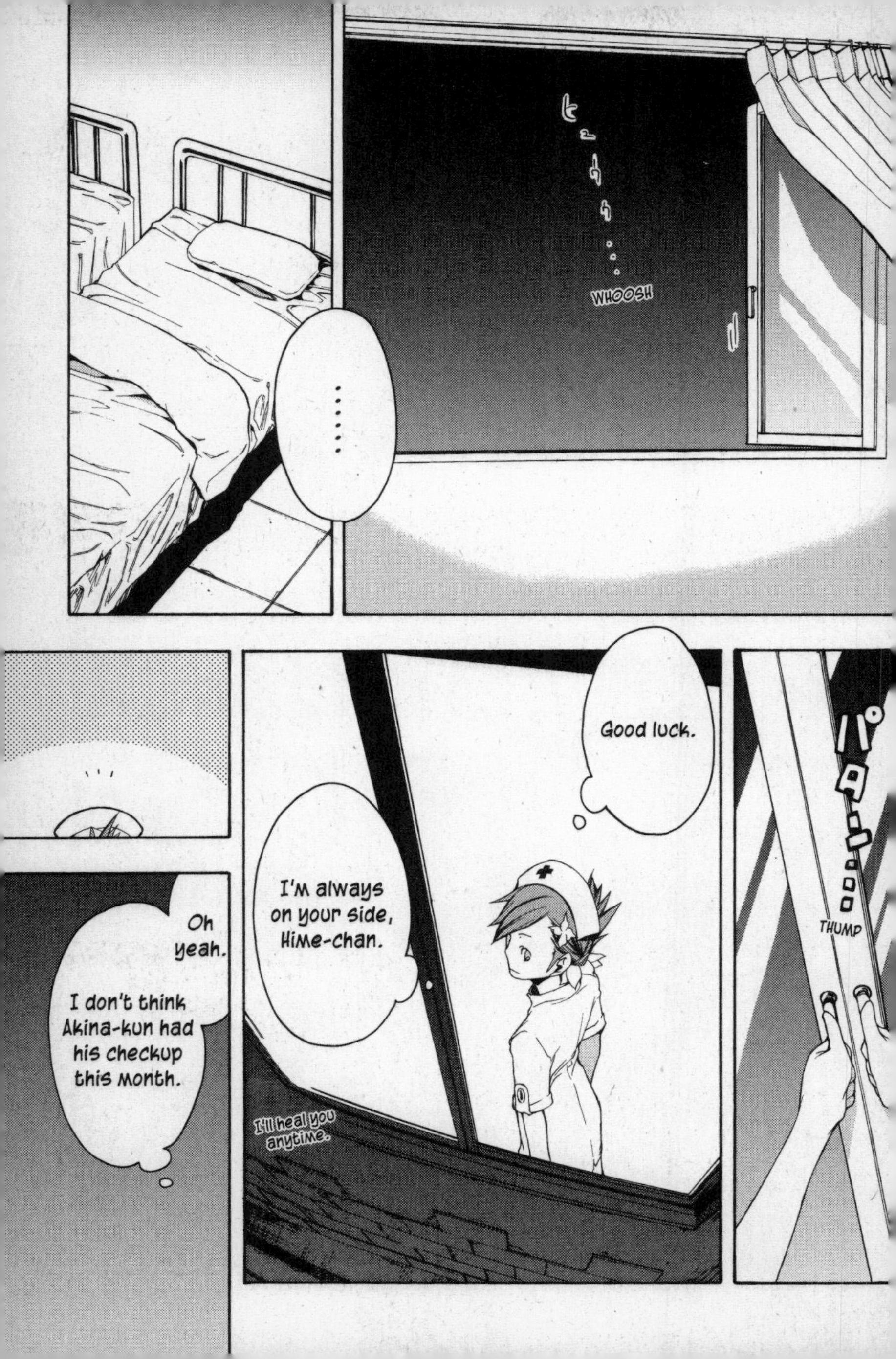
WHOOSH
......
THUMP
Good luck.
I'm always on your side, Hime-chan.
I'll heal you anytime.
Oh yeah.
I don't think Akina-kun had his checkup this month.

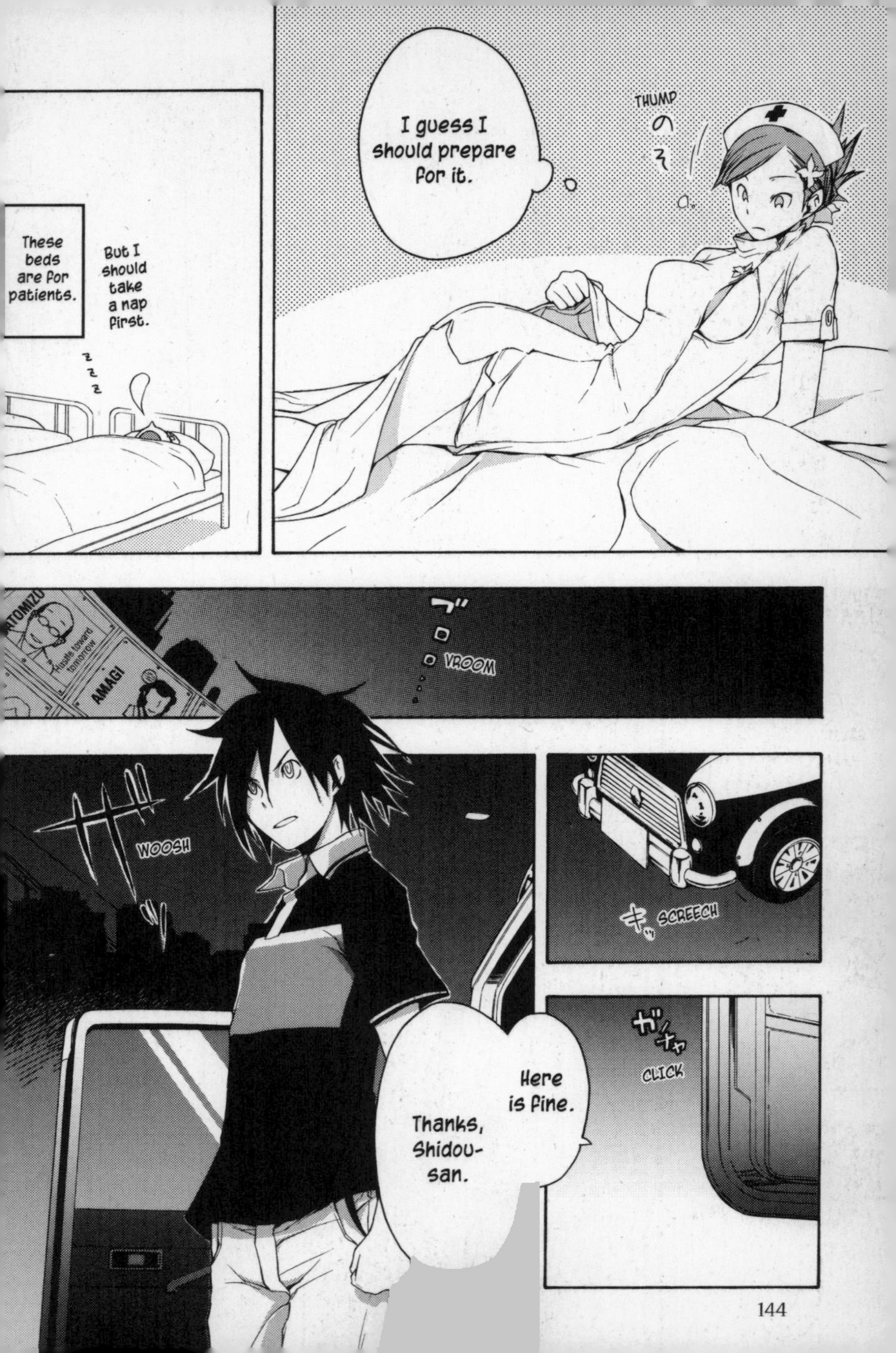

I guess I should prepare for it.
THUMP
These beds are for patients.
But I should take a nap first.
z z z
ATOMIZU
AMAGI
VROOM
SCREECH
CLICK
WOOSH
Here is fine.
Thanks, Shidou-san.

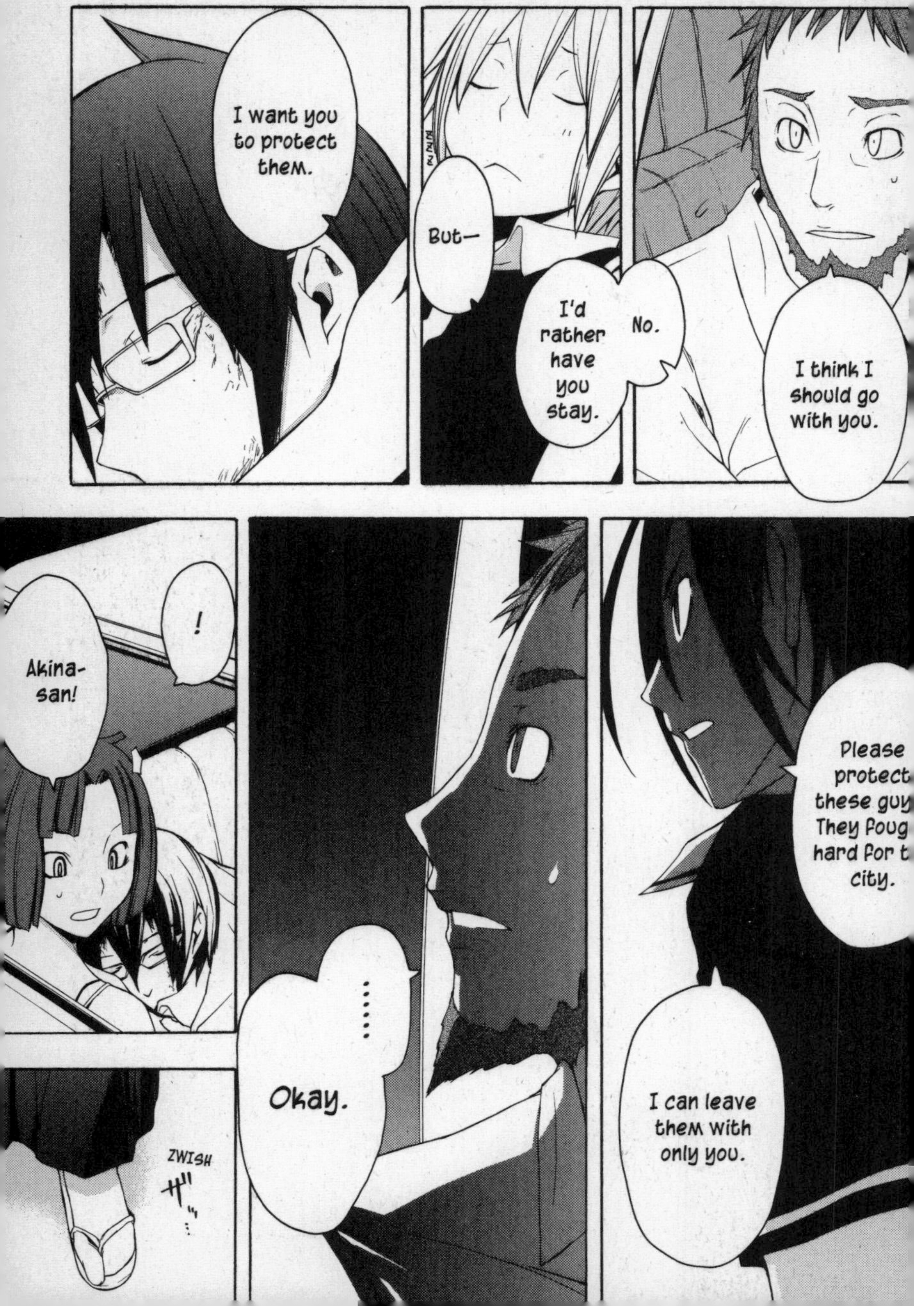
I think I should go with you.
No.
I'd rather have you stay.
But—
I want you to protect them.
Please protect these guy They foug hard for t city.
I can leave them with only you.
......
Okay.
!
Akina-san!
ZWISH
ザッ

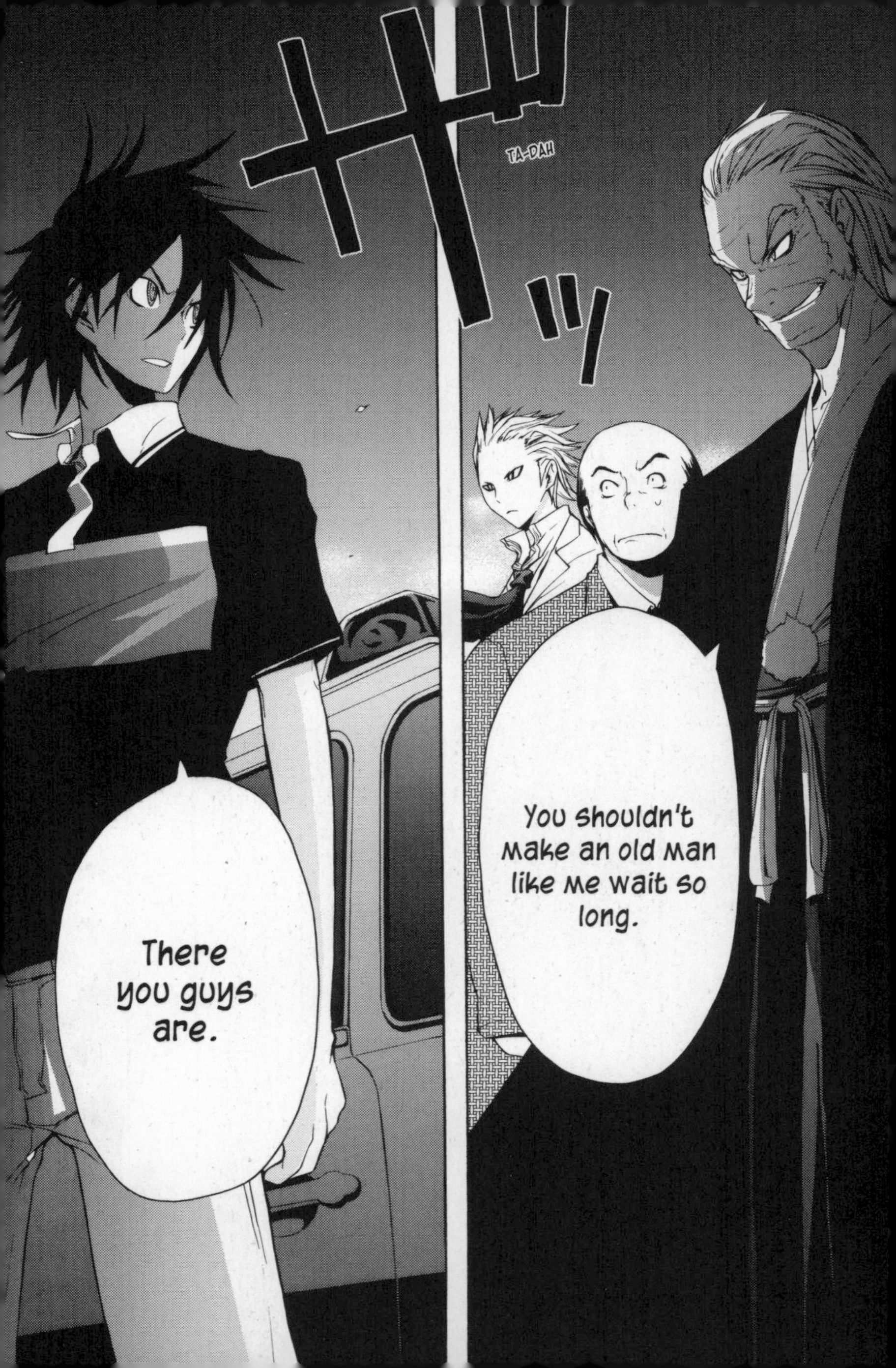
TA-DAH
You shouldn't make an old man like me wait so long.
There you guys are.

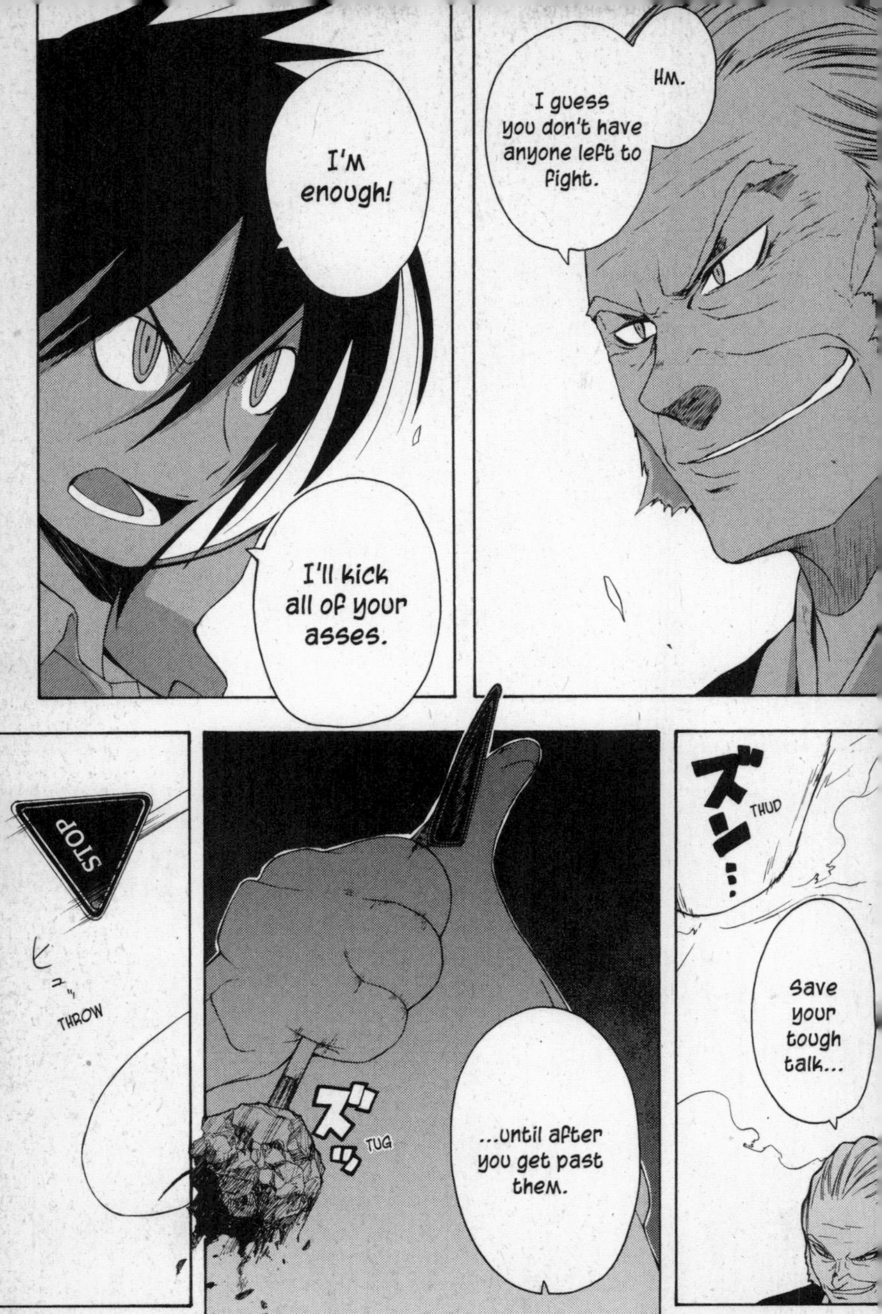
HM.
I guess you don't have anyone left to fight.
I'M enough!
I'll kick all of your asses.
ズン…
THUD
Save your tough talk...
ズッ
TUG
...until after you get past them.
STOP
ヒュッ
THROW

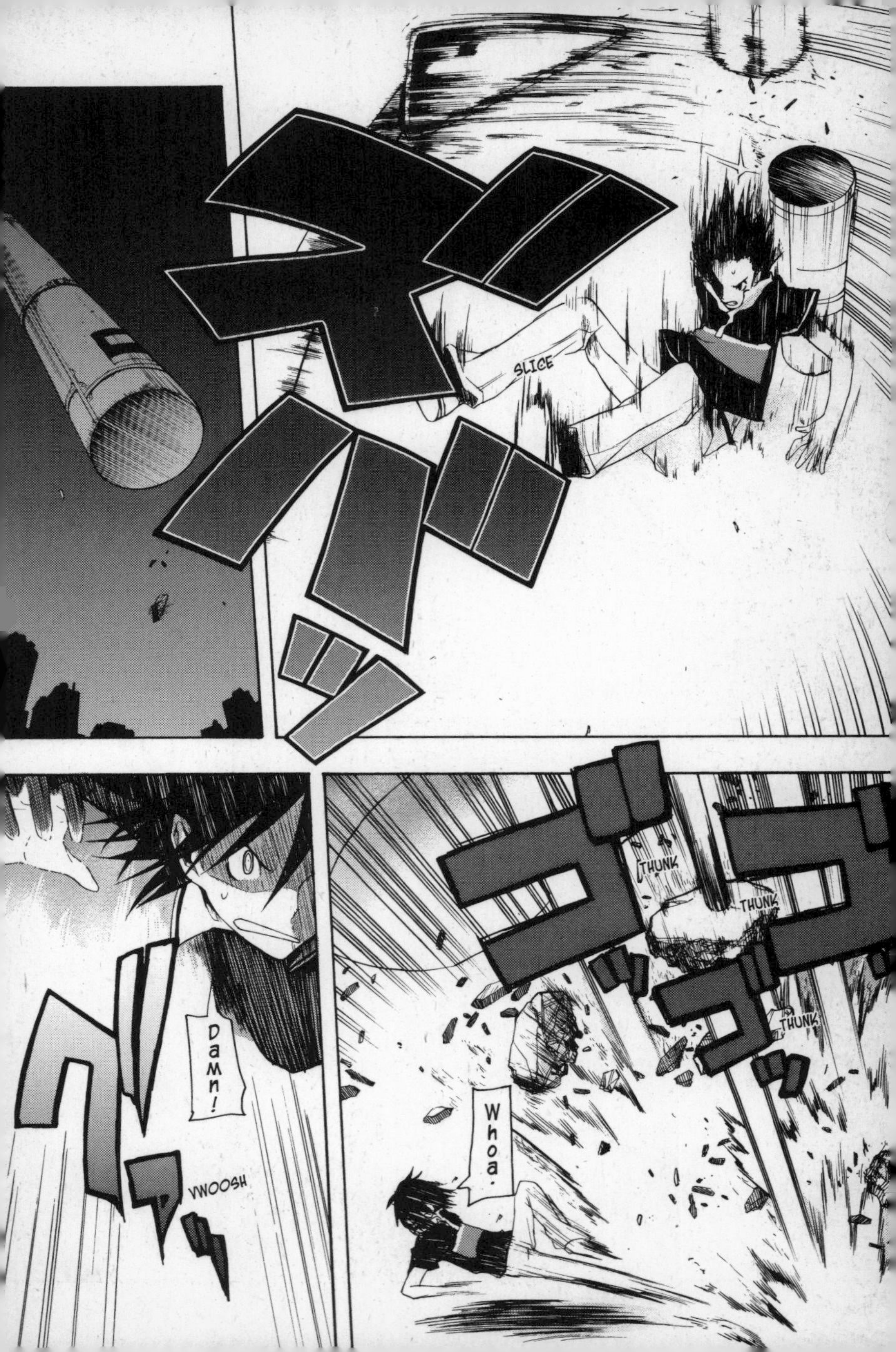
SLICE
THUNK
THUNK
THUNK
Whoa.
Damn!
VWOOSH

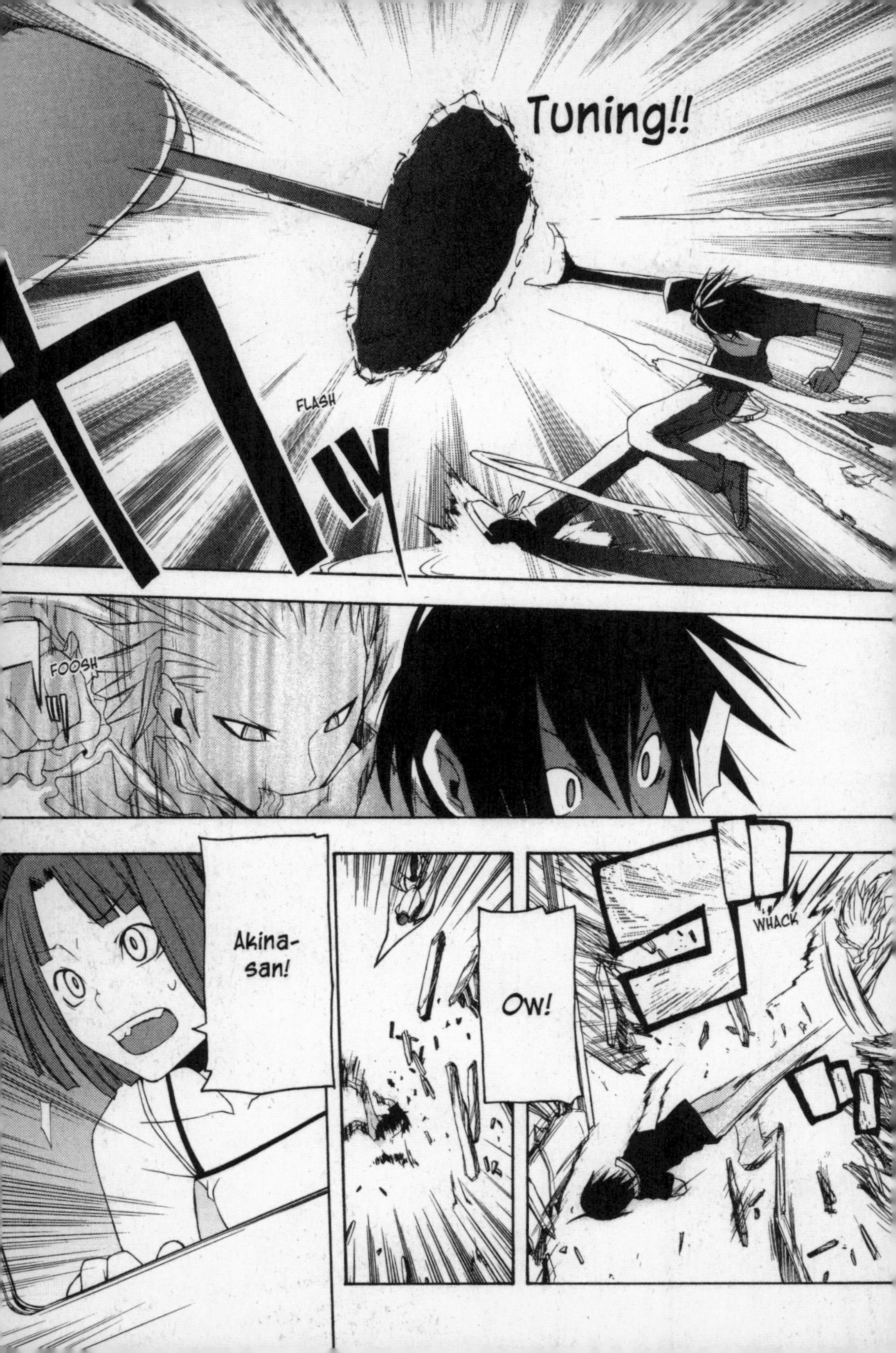
Tuning!!
FLASH
FOOSH
WHACK
OW!
Akina-san!

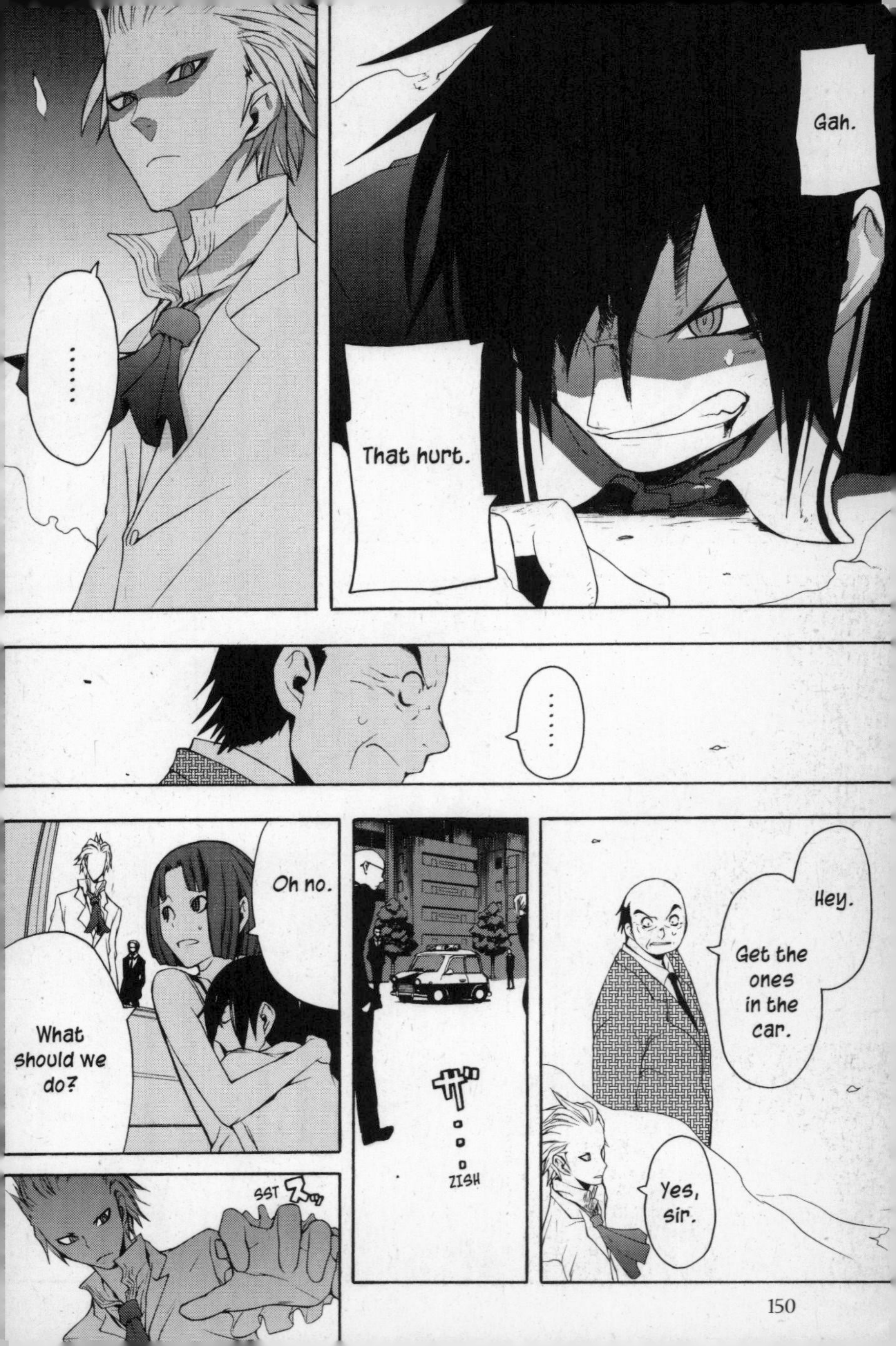
Gah.
That hurt.
......
......
Hey.
Get the ones in the car.
Yes, sir.
ZISH
Oh no.
What should we do?
SST

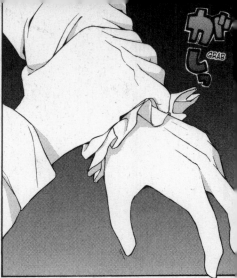

SQUEEZE

!

SQUEEEEZE

...!

...I don't know if I'll be able to restrain myself.

Please don't.

If something happens to them...

Heh.

You shouldn't do that.

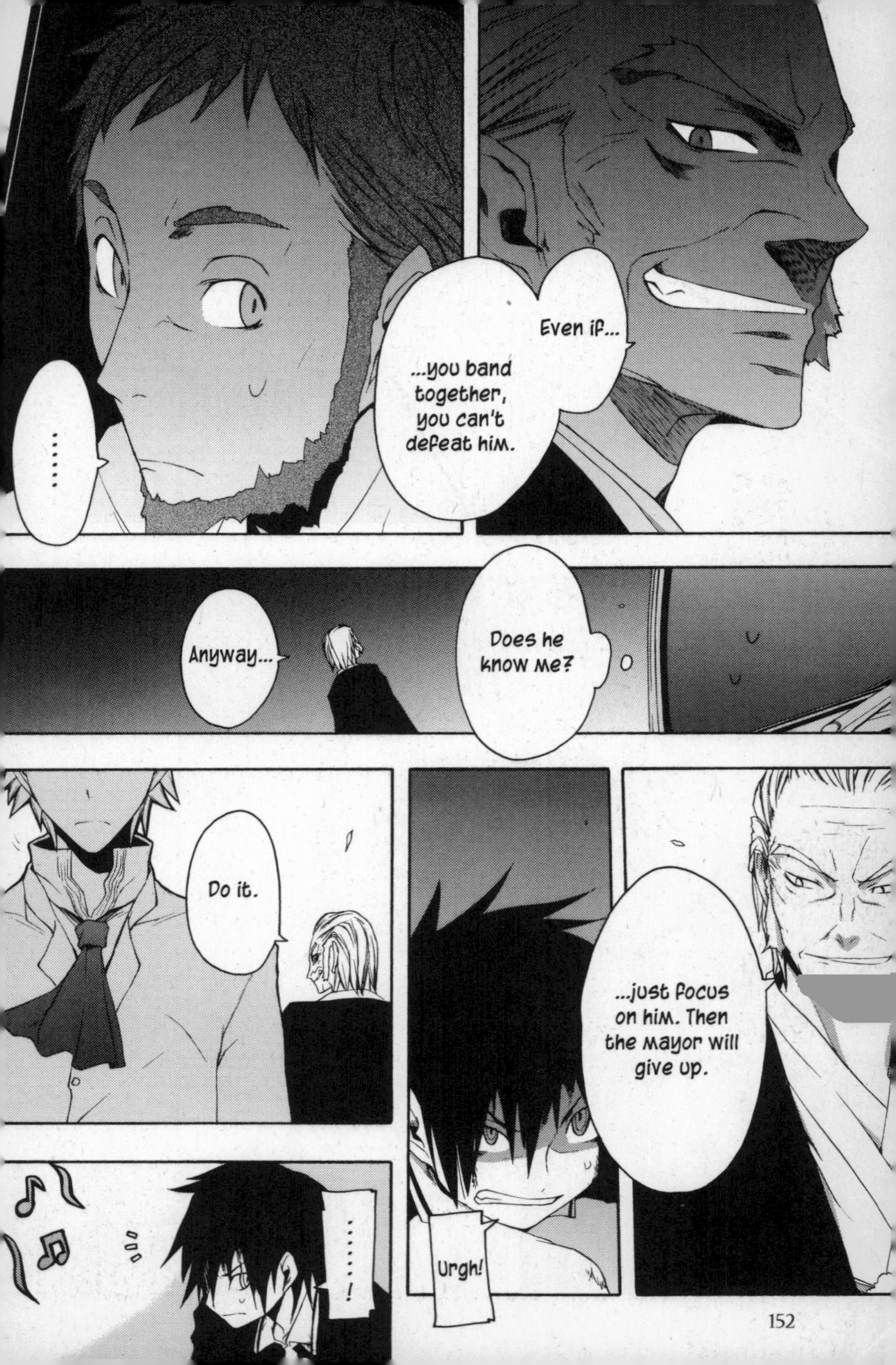
Even if...
...you band together, you can't defeat him.
......
Does he know me?
Anyway...
...just focus on him. Then the mayor will give up.
Urgh!
Do it.
......!

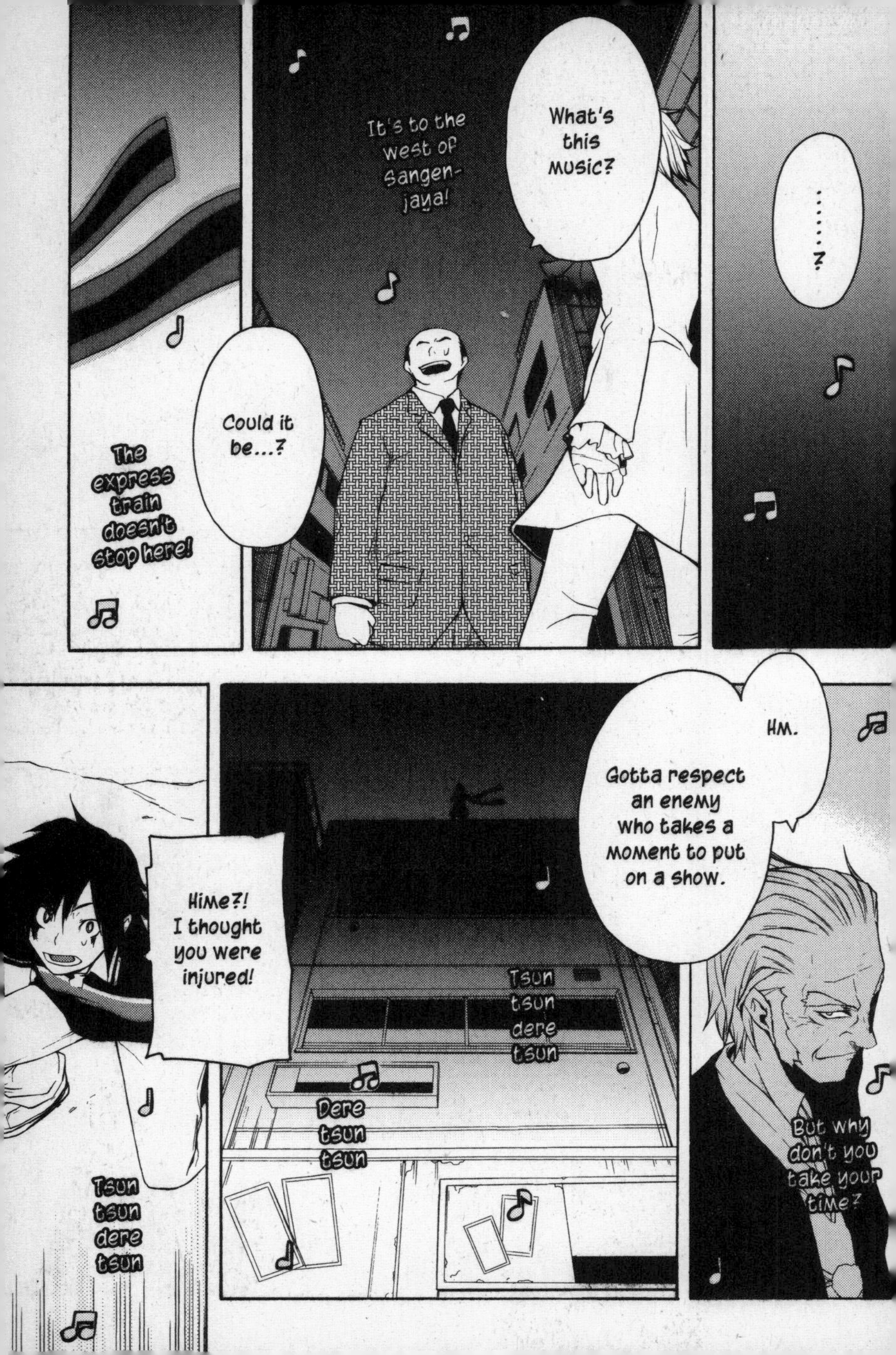
......?
What's this music?
It's to the west of Sangen-jaya!
Could it be...?
The express train doesn't stop here!
Hm.
Gotta respect an enemy who takes a moment to put on a show.
But why don't you take your time?
Tsun tsun dere tsun
Dere tsun tsun
Hime?! I thought you were injured!
Tsun tsun dere tsun

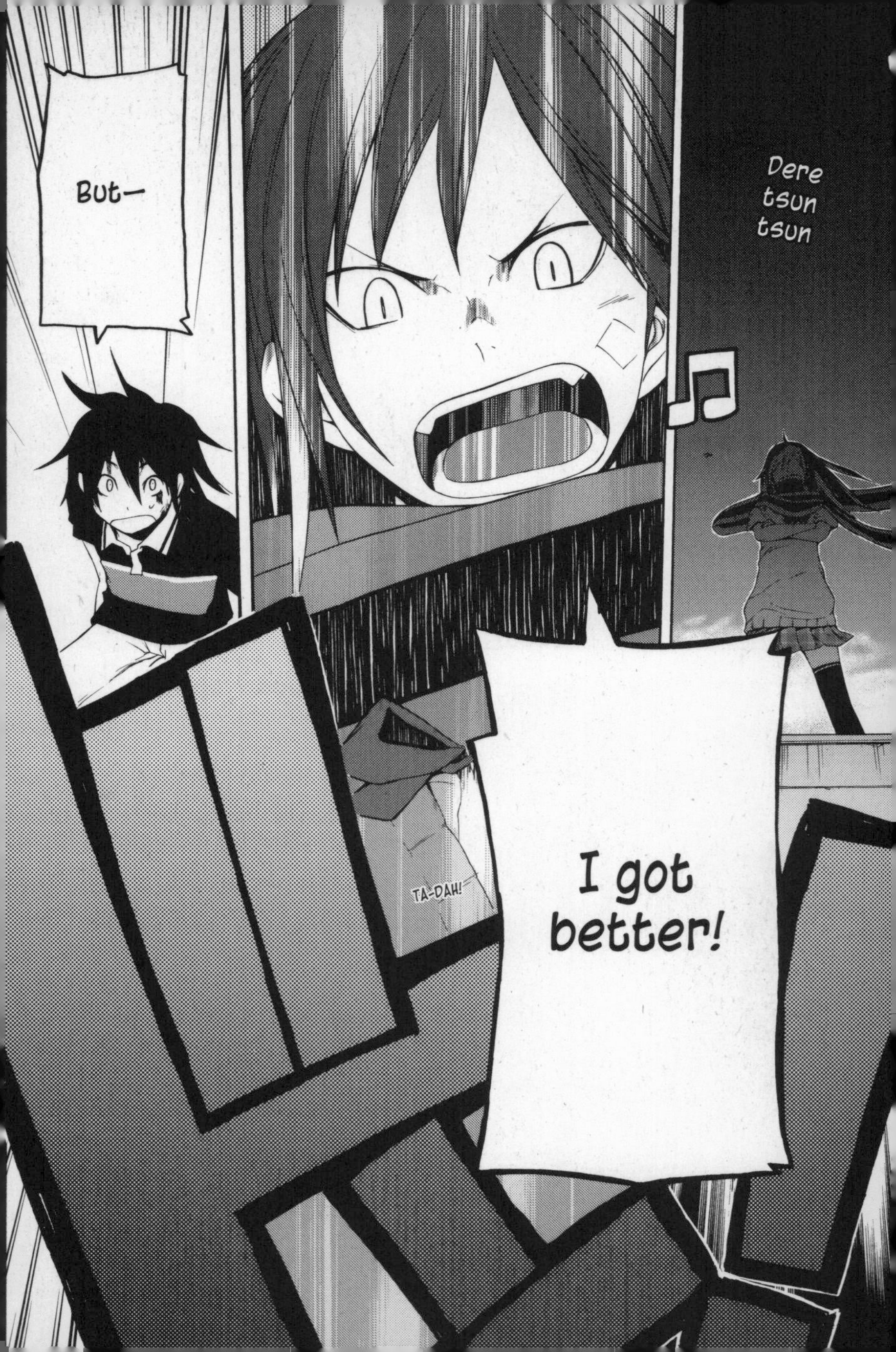
Dere tsun tsun
I got better!
TA-DAH!
But—

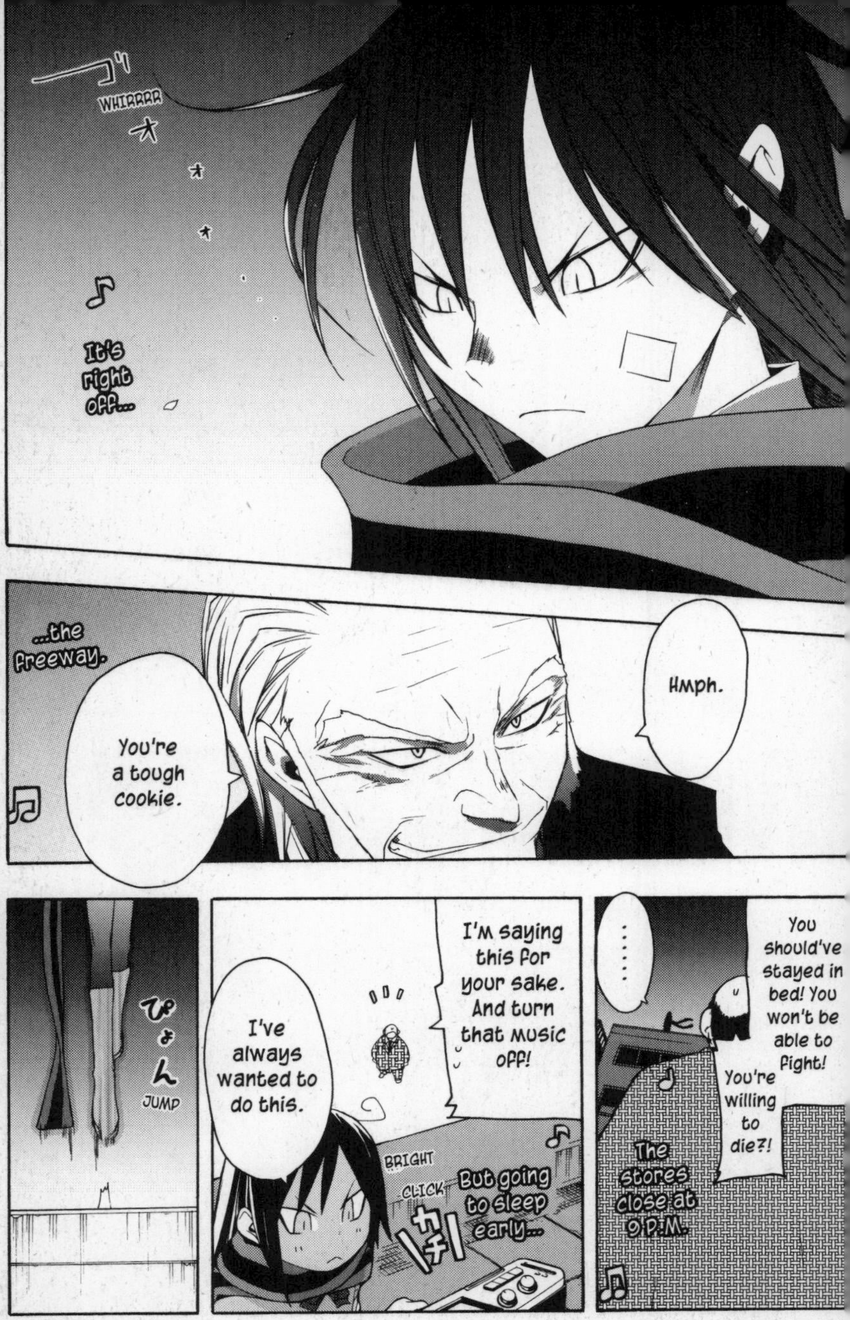
WHIRRRR
It's right off...
Hmph.
...the freeway.
You're a tough cookie.
You should've stayed in bed! You won't be able to fight!
......
You're willing to die?!
The stores close at 9 P.M.
I'm saying this for your sake. And turn that music off!
I've always wanted to do this.
BRIGHT
CLICK
But going to sleep early...
JUMP

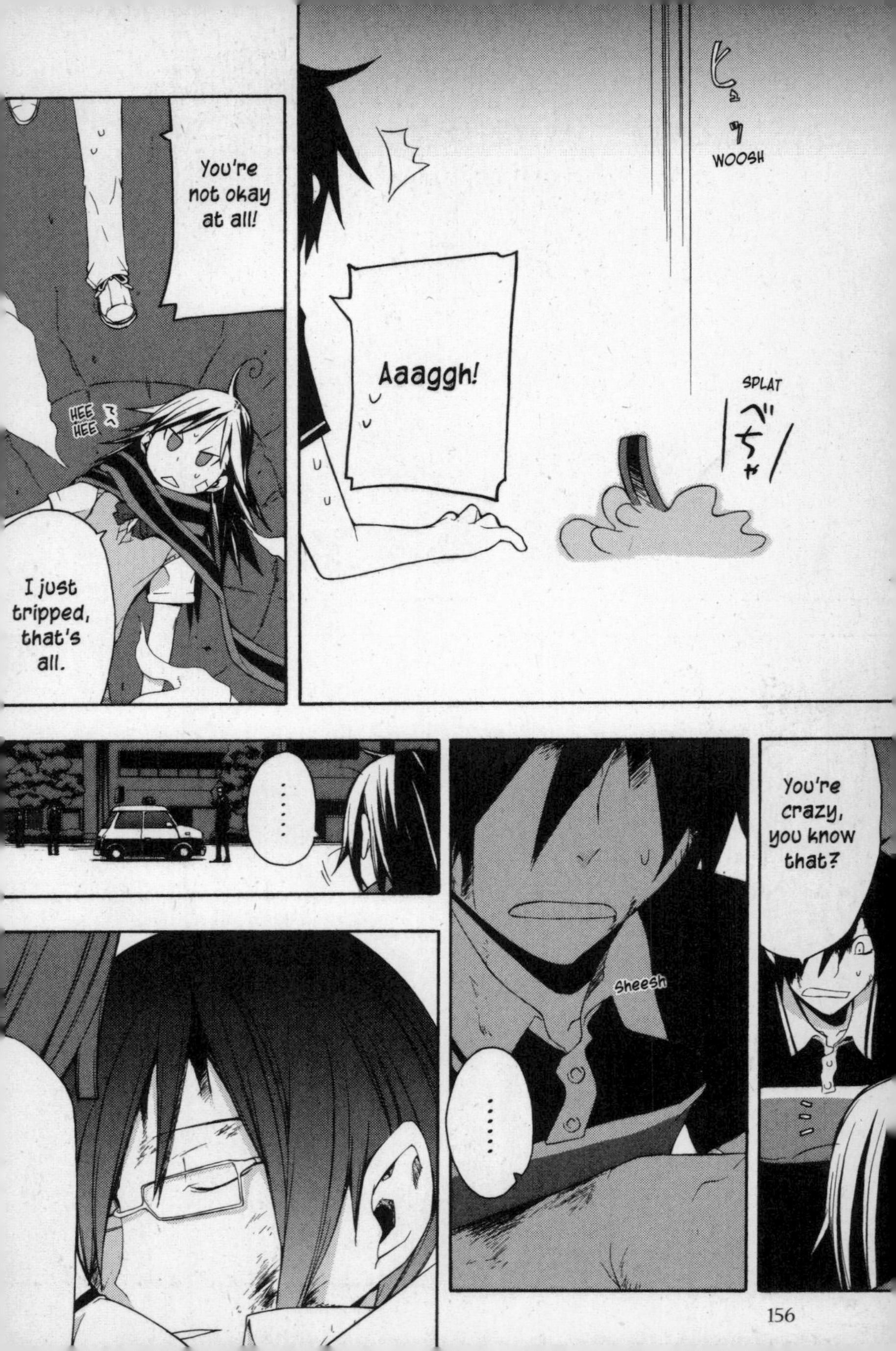

ひゅっ
WOOSH
SPLAT
べちゃ
Aaaggh!
You're not okay at all!
HEE HEE
へへ
I just tripped, that's all.
You're crazy, you know that?
Sheesh
......
......

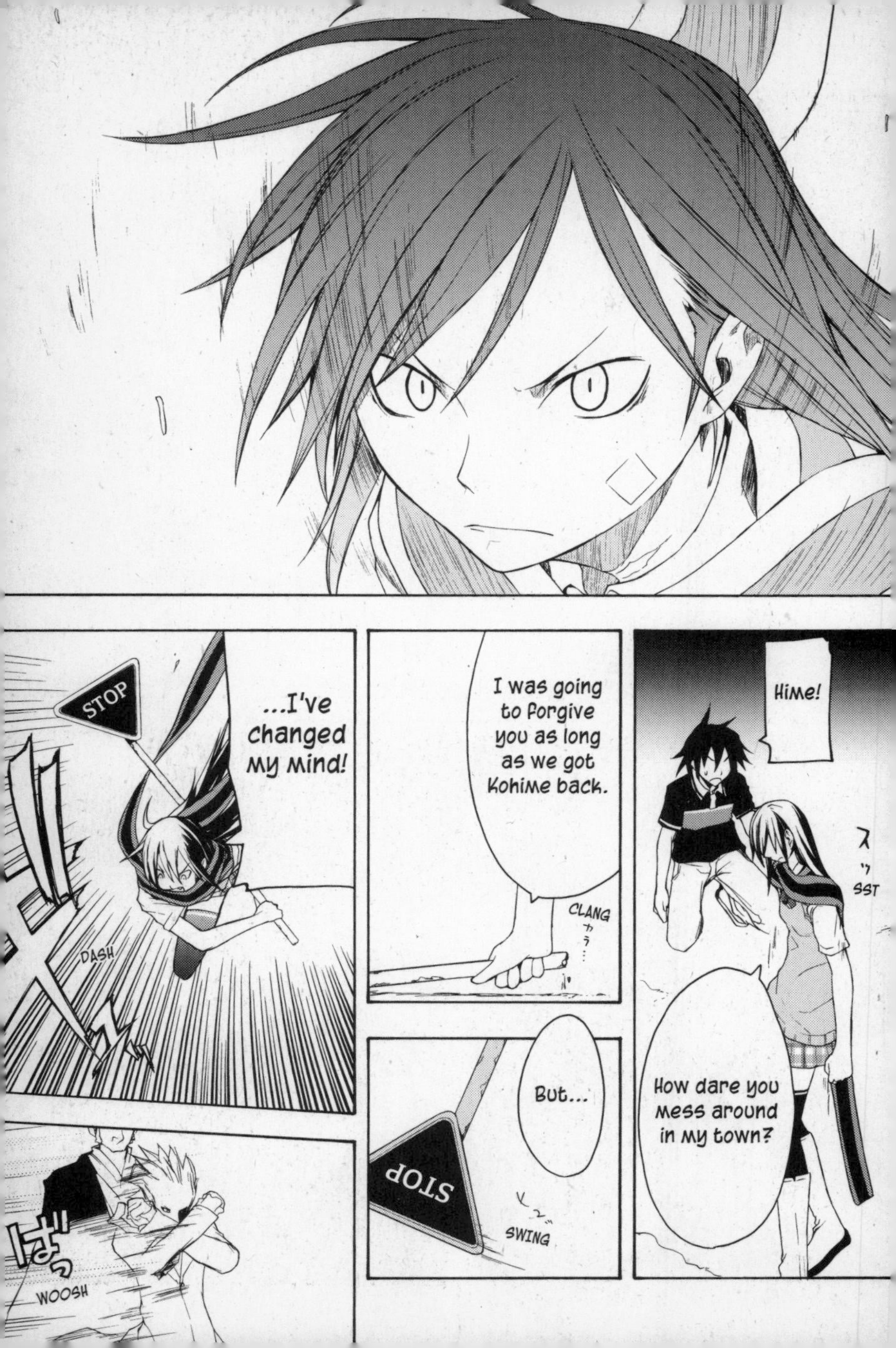
Hime!
SST
How dare you mess around in my town?
I was going to forgive you as long as we got Kohime back.
CLANG
But...
STOP
SWING
...I've changed my mind!
STOP
DASH
ばっ
WOOSH

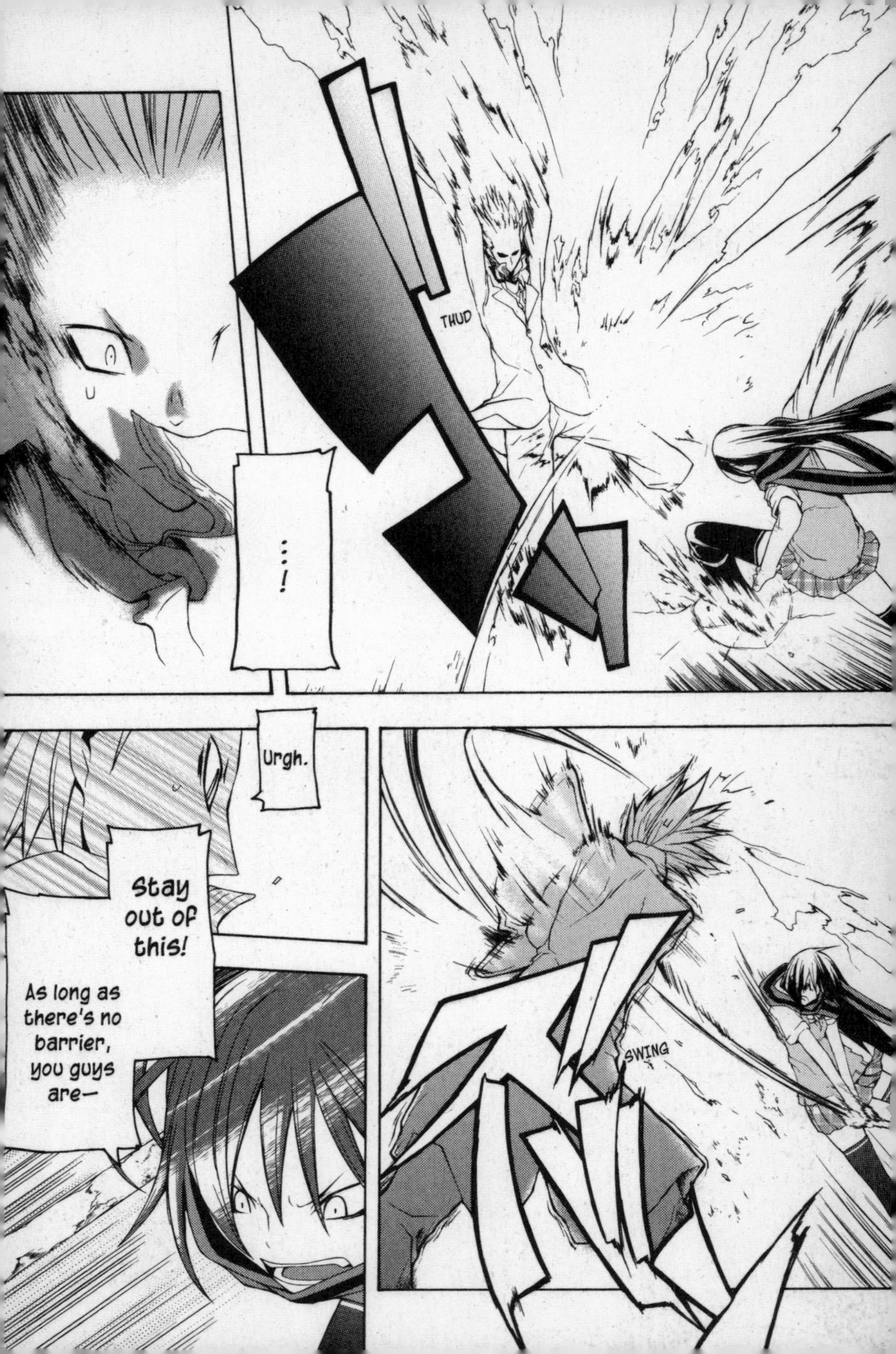
THUD
...!
SWING
Urgh.
Stay out of this!
As long as there's no barrier, you guys are—

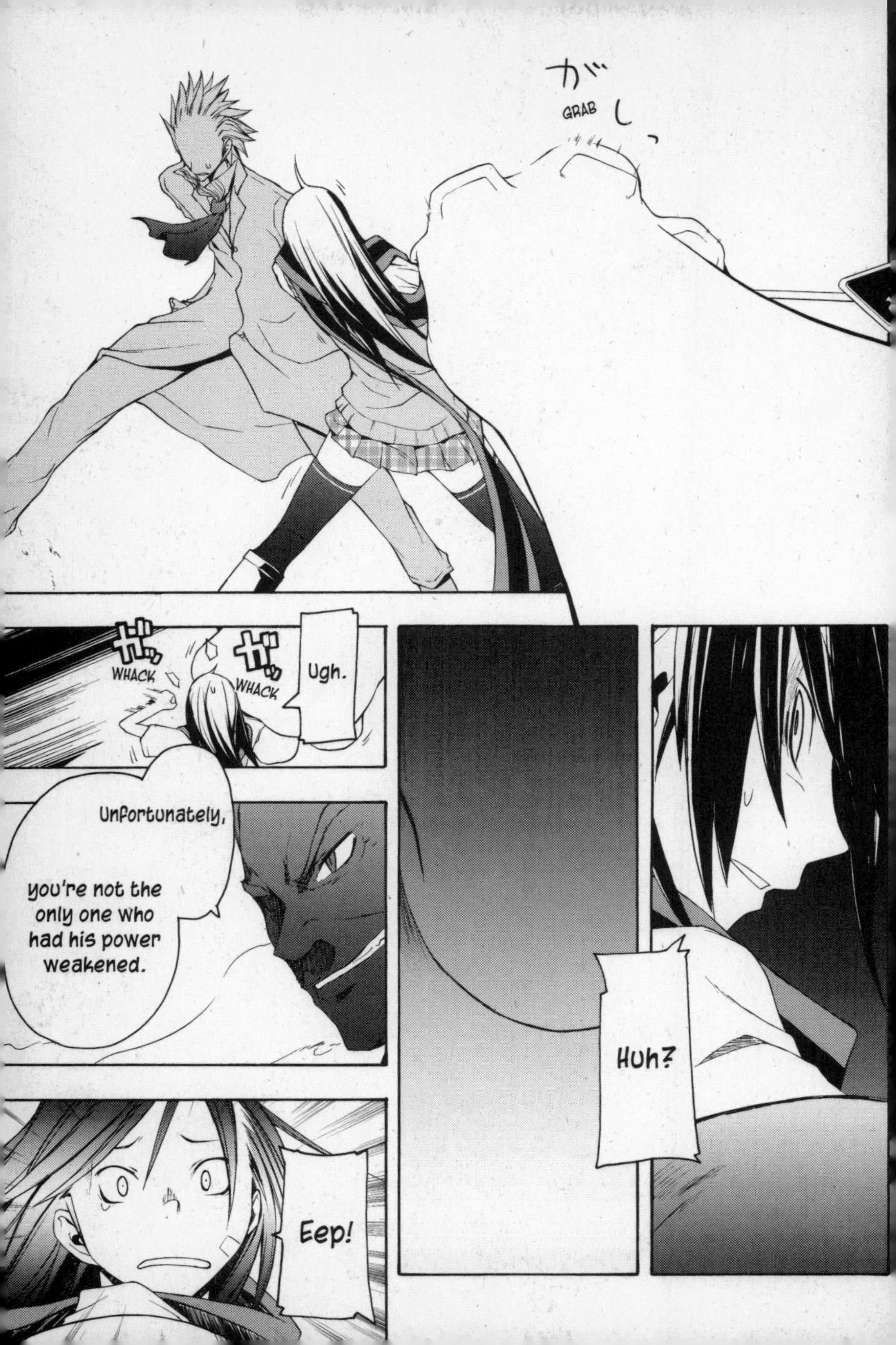

ガし
GRAB
Huh?
ガッ
WHACK
ガッ
WHACK
Ugh.
Unfortunately,
you're not the only one who had his power weakened.
Eep!

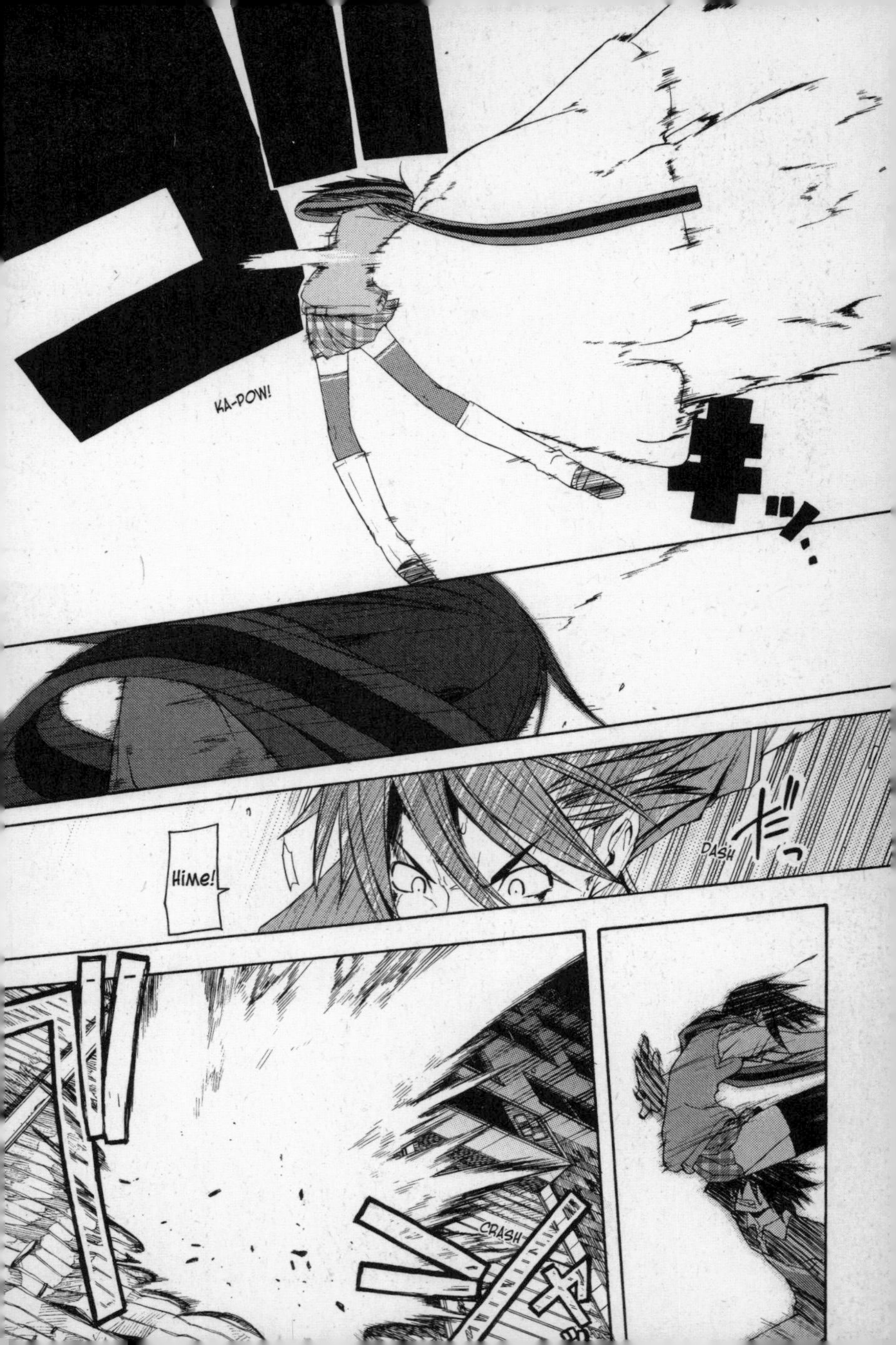
KA-POW!
DASH
Hime!
CRASH

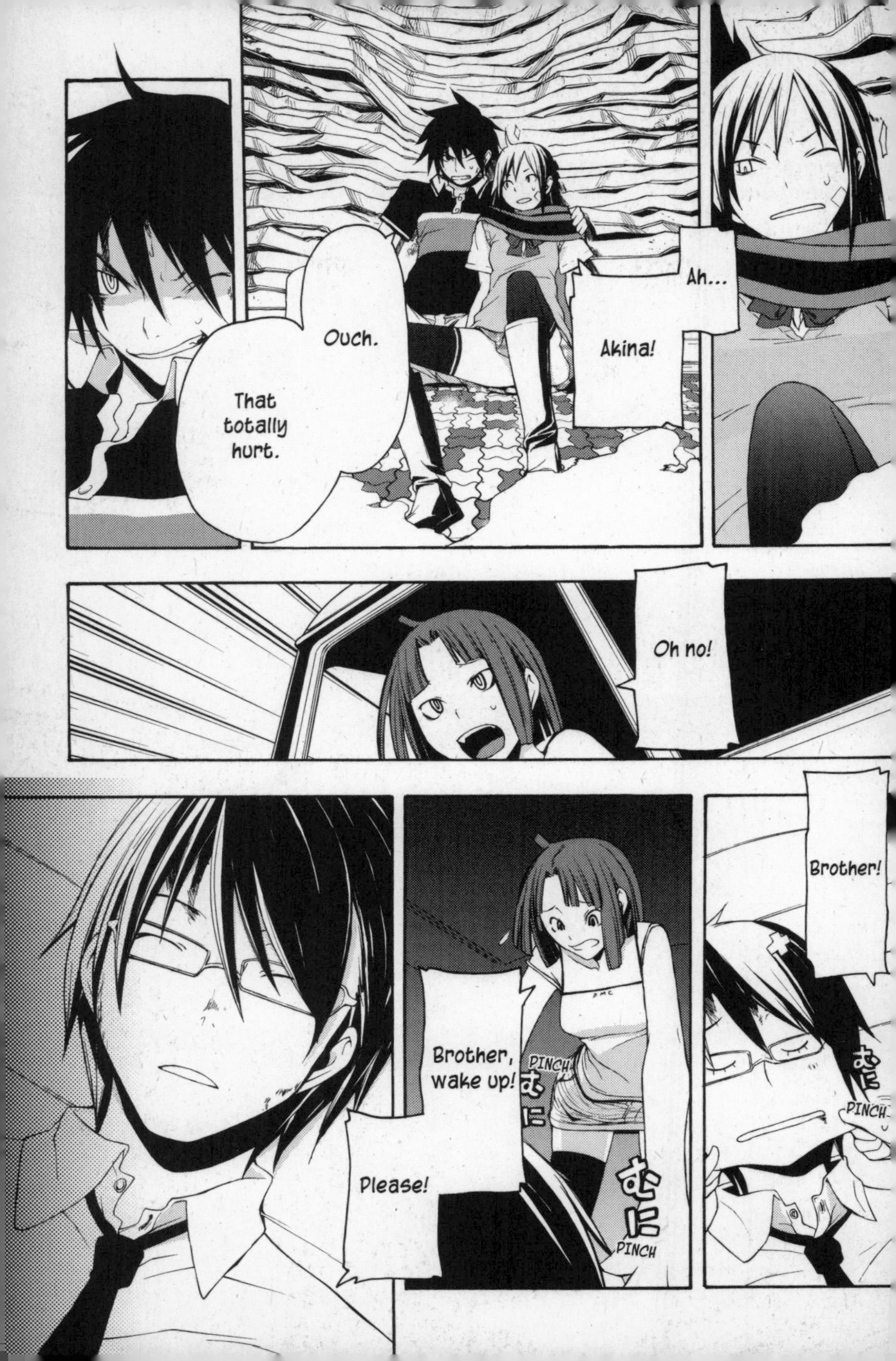
Ah...
Akina!
Ouch.
That totally hurt.
Oh no!
Brother!
PINCH
Brother, wake up!
PINCH
むに
むに
PINCH
Please!

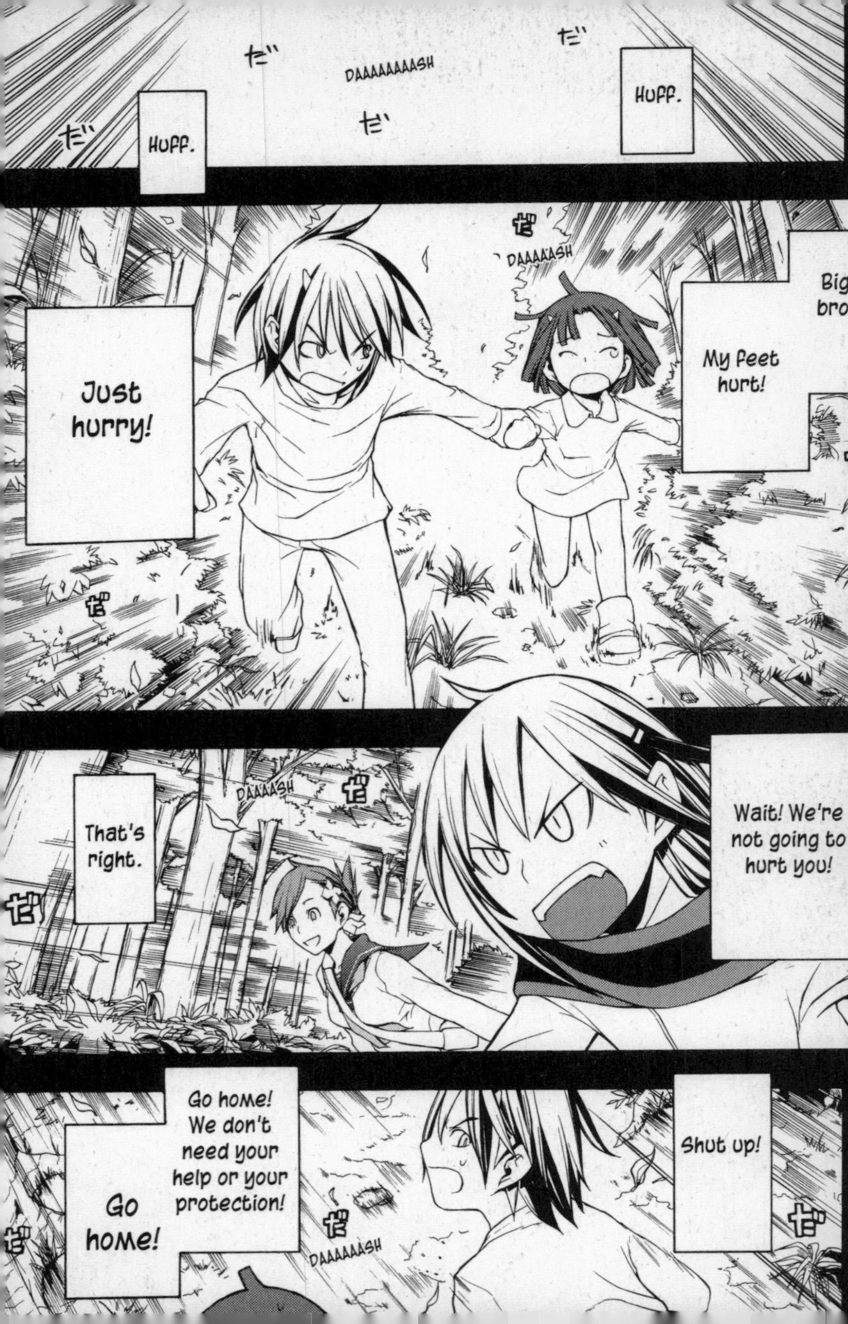
だ
Huff.
だ
DAAAAAAAASH
だ
だ
Huff.
だ
DAAAAASH
Big bro!
My feet hurt!
だ
Just hurry!
だ
Wait! We're not going to hurt you!
だ
DAAAASH
That's right.
だ
Shut up!
だ
だ
DAAAAAASH
Go home! We don't need your help or your protection!
Go home!
だ

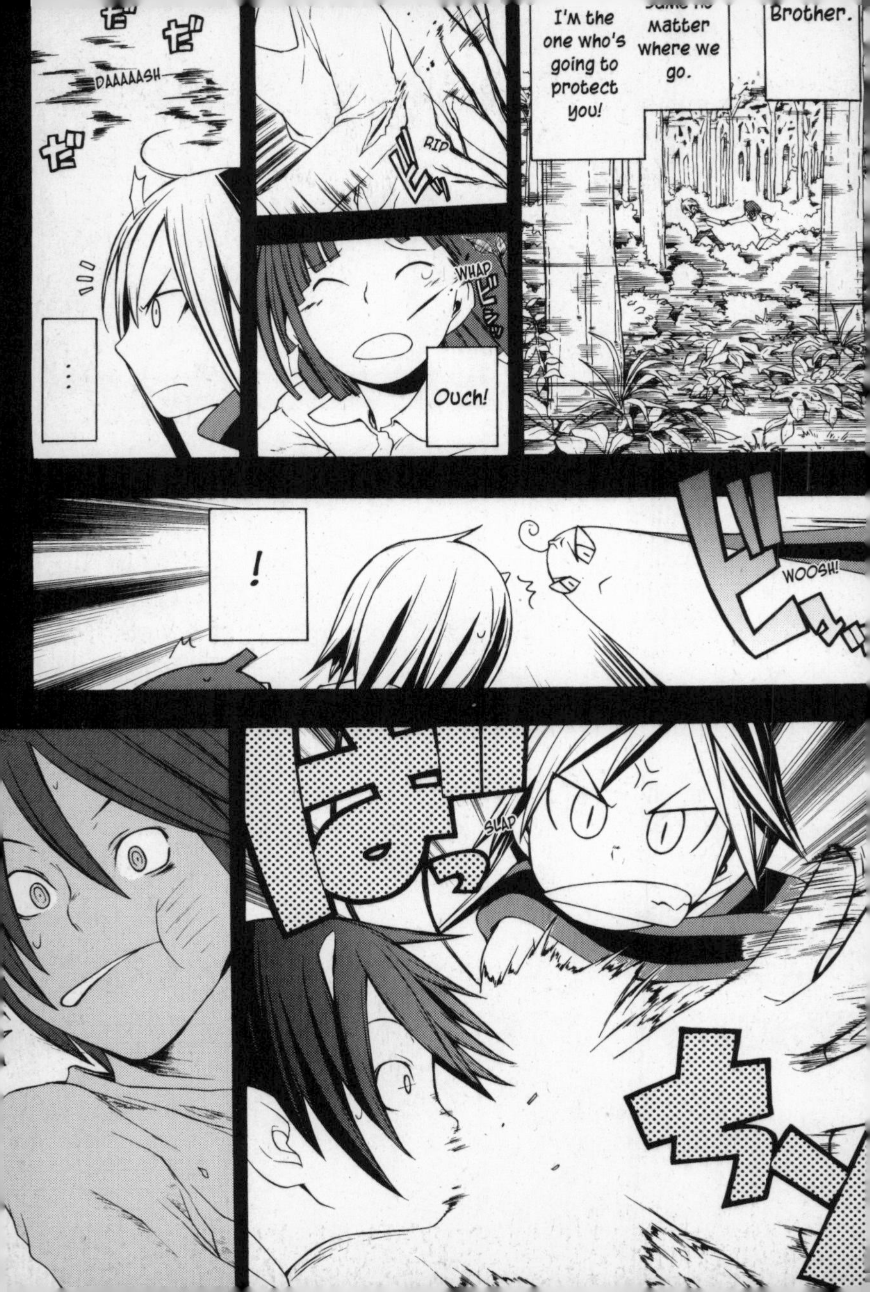
Brother.
matter where we go.
I'm the one who's going to protect you!
RIP
WHAP
Ouch!
DAAAAASH
...
WOOSH!
!
SLAP

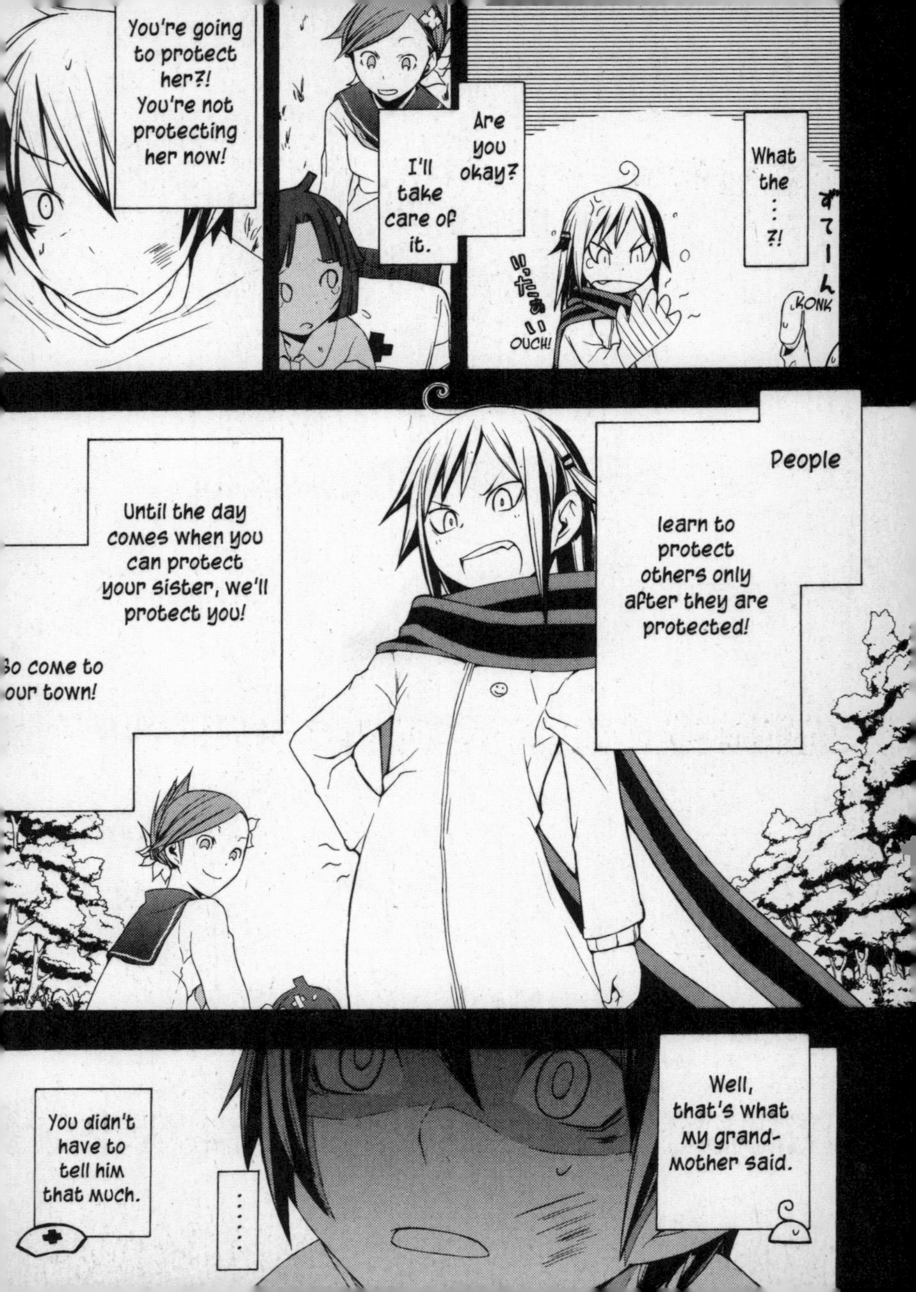
What the . . . ?!
ずてーん
KONK
いだぁい
OUCH!
Are you okay?
I'll take care of it.
You're going to protect her?! You're not protecting her now!
People learn to protect others only after they are protected!
Until the day comes when you can protect your sister, we'll protect you!
So come to our town!
Well, that's what my grand-mother said.
......
You didn't have to tell him that much.

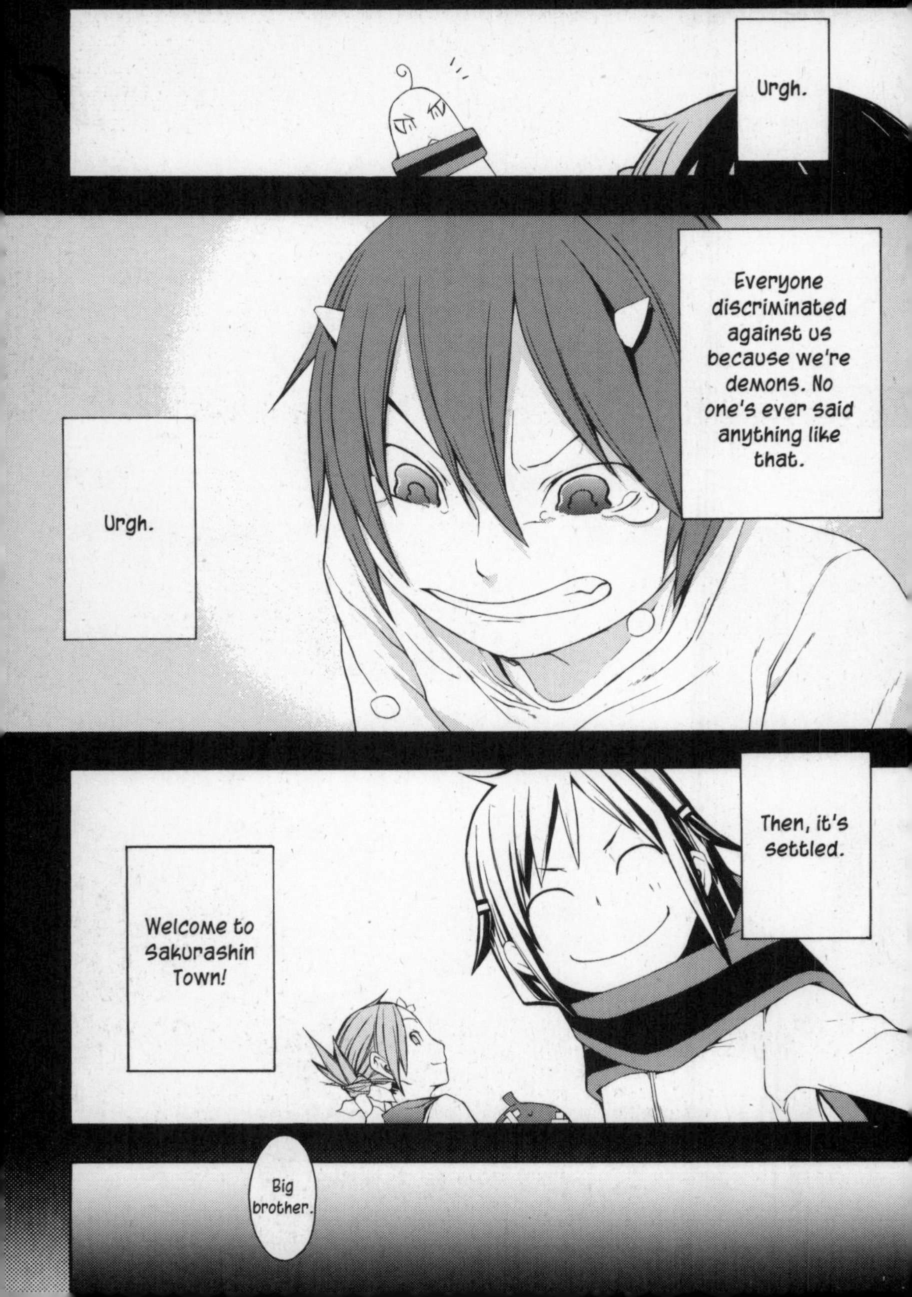
Urgh.
Everyone discriminated against us because we're demons. No one's ever said anything like that.
Urgh.
Then, it's settled.
Welcome to Sakurashin Town!
Big brother.

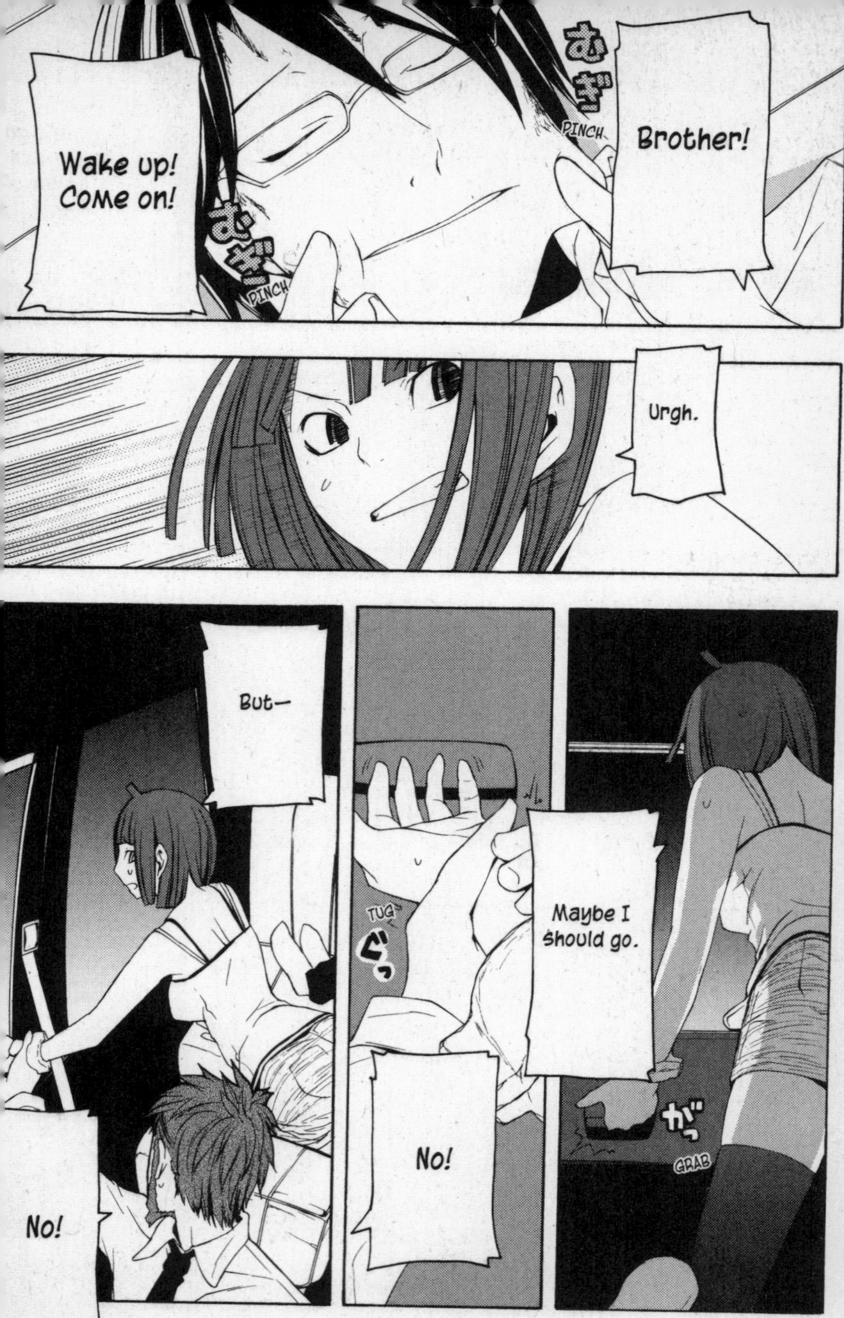

Brother!
むぎ
PINCH
Wake up! Come on!
むぎ
PINCH
Urgh.
Maybe I should go.
がっ
GRAB
ぐっ
TUG
No!
But—
No!

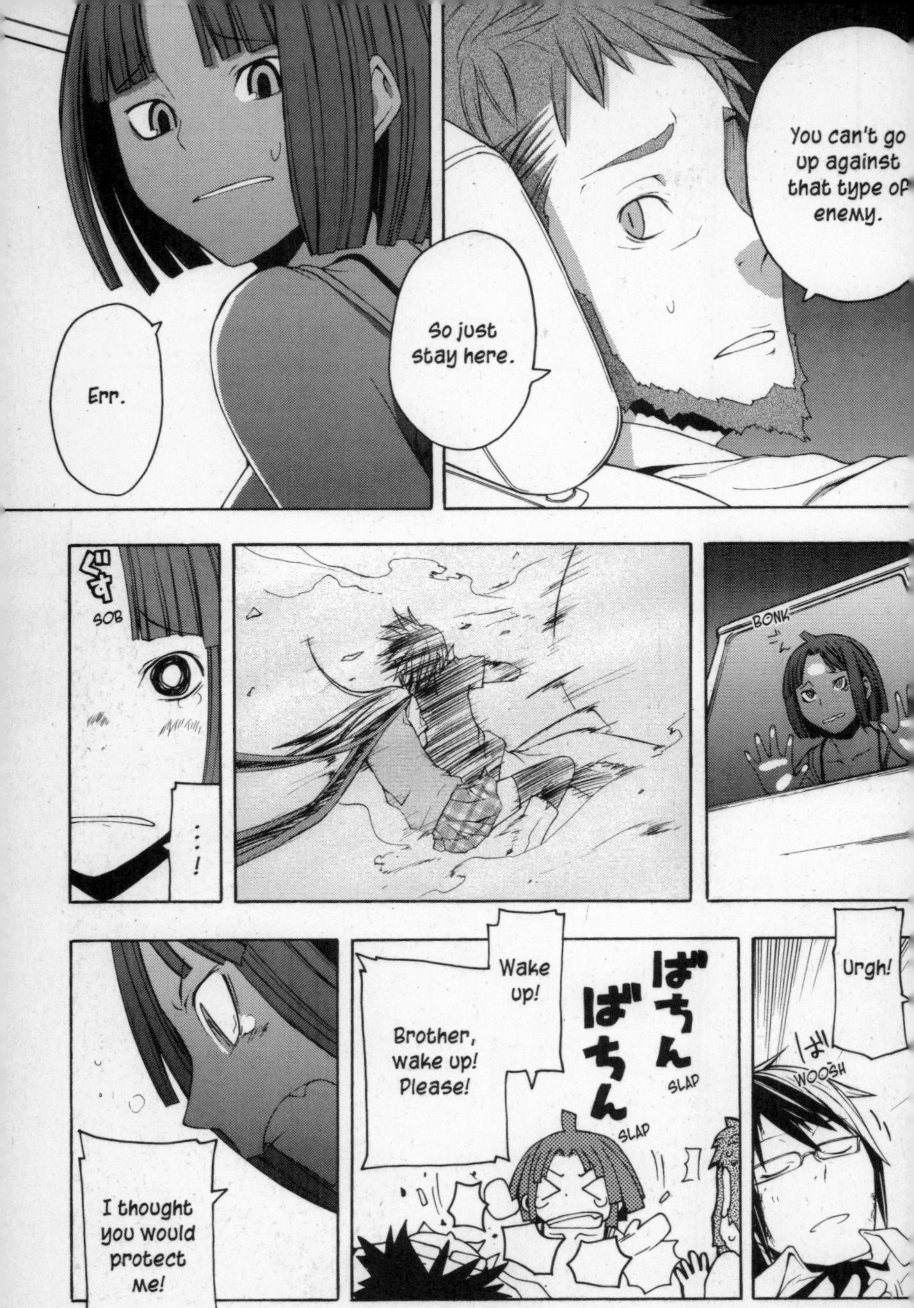
You can't go up against that type of enemy.
So just stay here.
Err.
BONK
ぐす
SOB
...!
Urgh!
ば
WOOSH
Wake up!
Brother, wake up! Please!
ばちん
SLAP
ばちん
SLAP
I thought you would protect me!

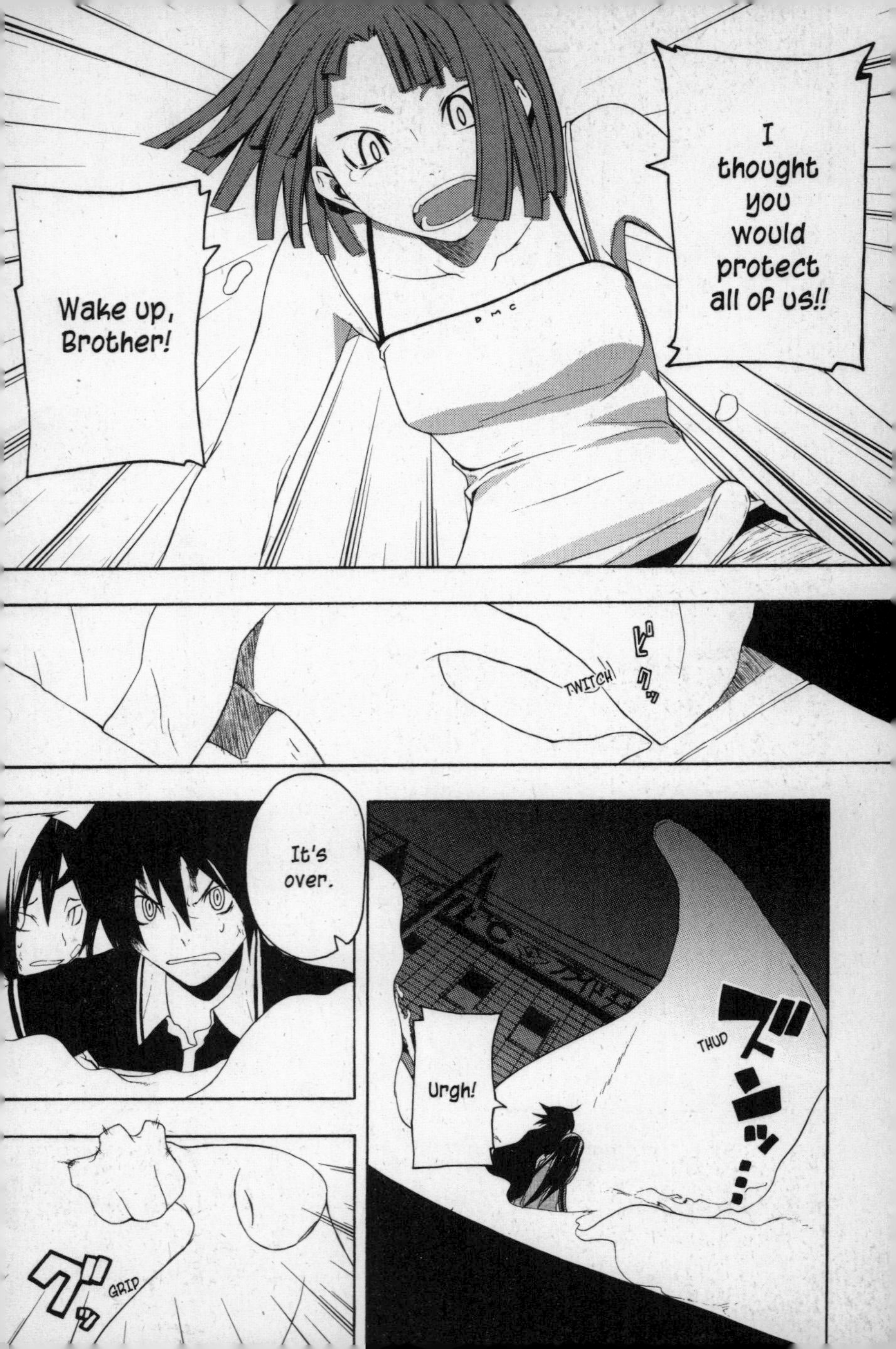
I thought you would protect all of us!!
Wake up, Brother!
ピクッ
TWITCH
ズンッ…
THUD
Urgh!
It's over.
グッ
GRIP

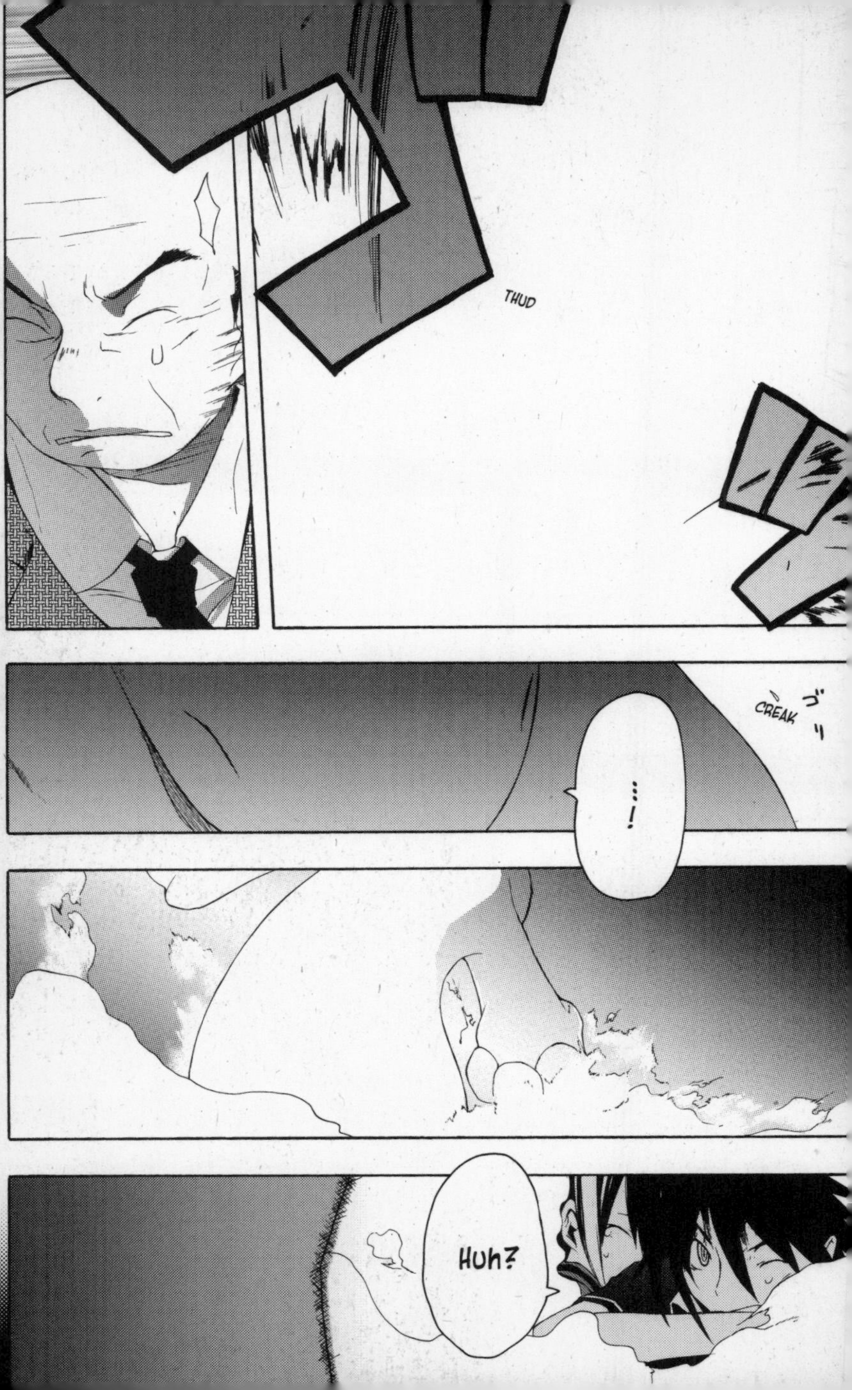
THUD
CREAK
ゴリ
...!
Huh?

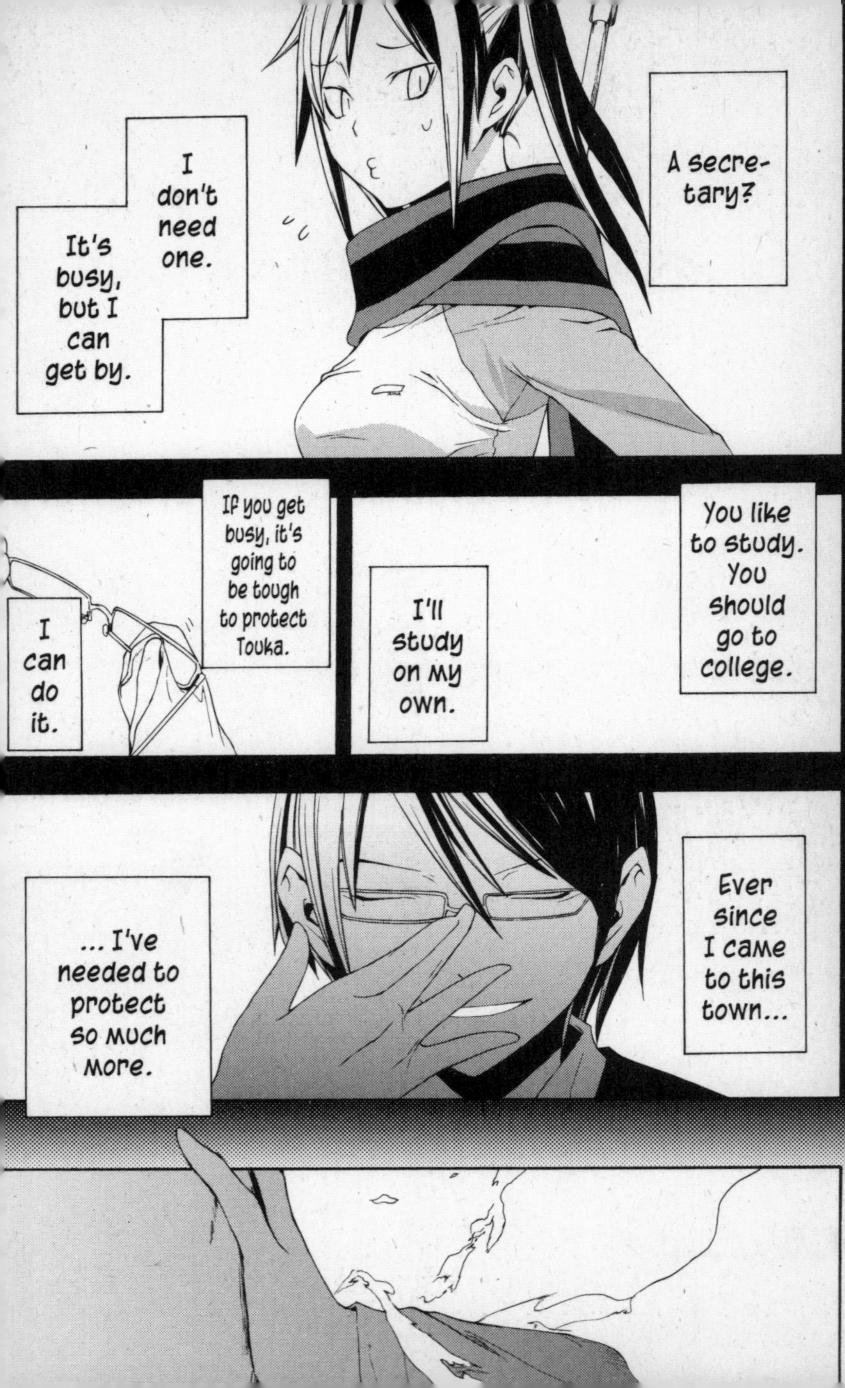
A secretary?
I don't need one.
It's busy, but I can get by.
You like to study. You should go to college.
I'll study on my own.
If you get busy, it's going to be tough to protect Touka.
I can do it.
Ever since I came to this town...
... I've needed to protect so much more.

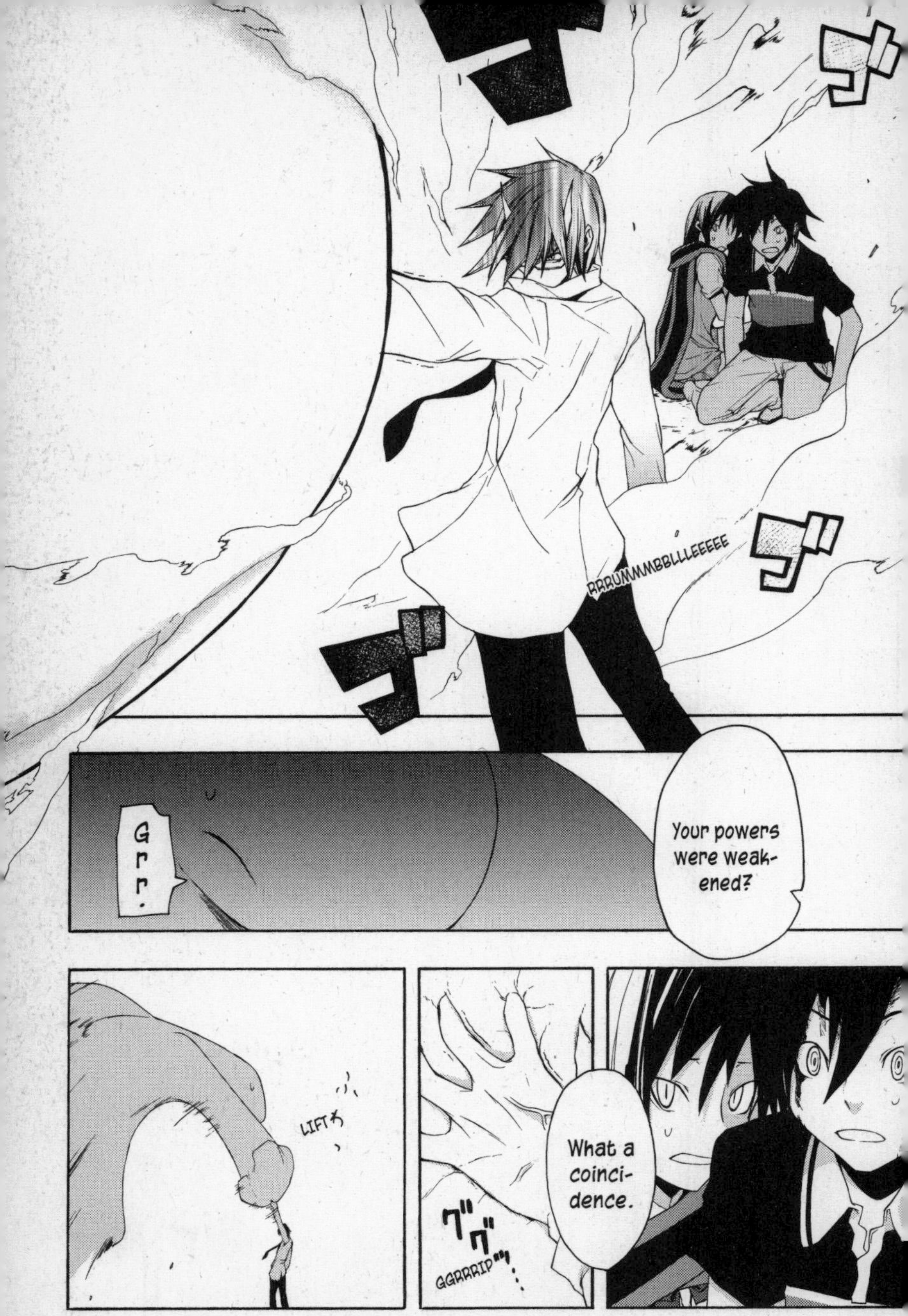
RRRUMMMMBBLLLEEEEE
Your powers were weak-ened?
Grr.
What a coinci-dence.
GGRRRIP
LIFT

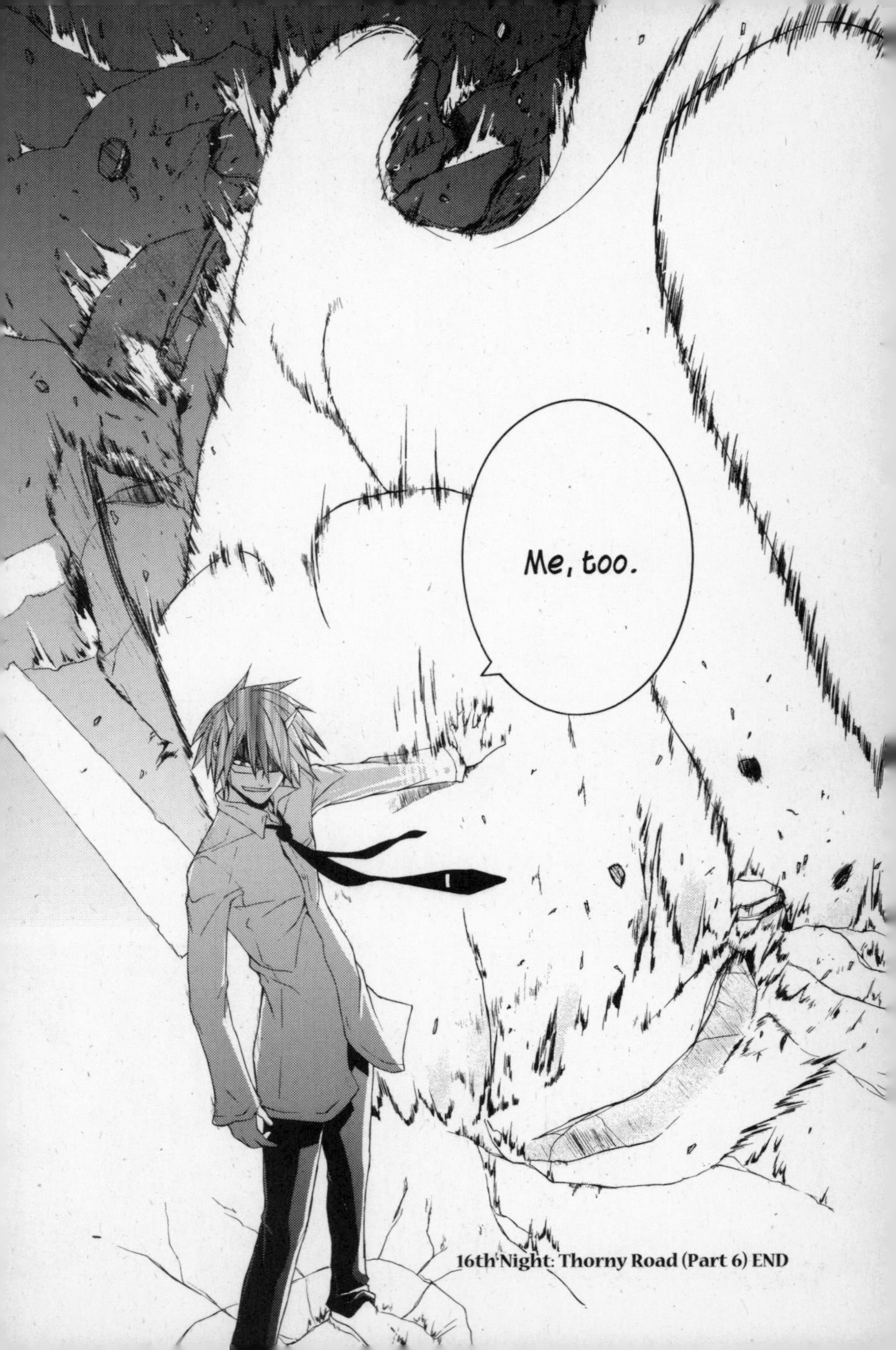
Me, too.

16th Night: Thorny Road (Part 6) END

Yozakura Quartet *3*

Yozakura Quartet 3

Sakurashin Town Song

Music and lyrics by Hime Yarizakura

1

It's to the west of
Sangen-jaya
The express train doesn't
stop here
But why don't you take
your time?
Tsun tsun dere tsun dere
tsun tsun
Tsun tsun dere tsun dere
tsun tsun

2

It's right off the freeway
The stores close at 9 P.M.
But sleeping early and
waking up early is good for
your health
Tsun tsun dere tsun dere
tsun tsun
Tsun tsun dere tsun dere
tsun tsun

3

Old streets, main streets, we
have lots of streets
The buildings here may
be low
But you can see the sky more
clearly
Tsun tsun dere tsun dere
tsun tsun
Tsun tsun dere tsun dere
tsun tsun
Tsun tsun dere tsun dere
tsun tsun
Tsun tsun dere tsun dere
tsun tsun

You can all sing along!
Make up your own Melody!

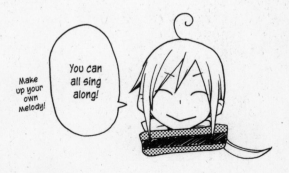

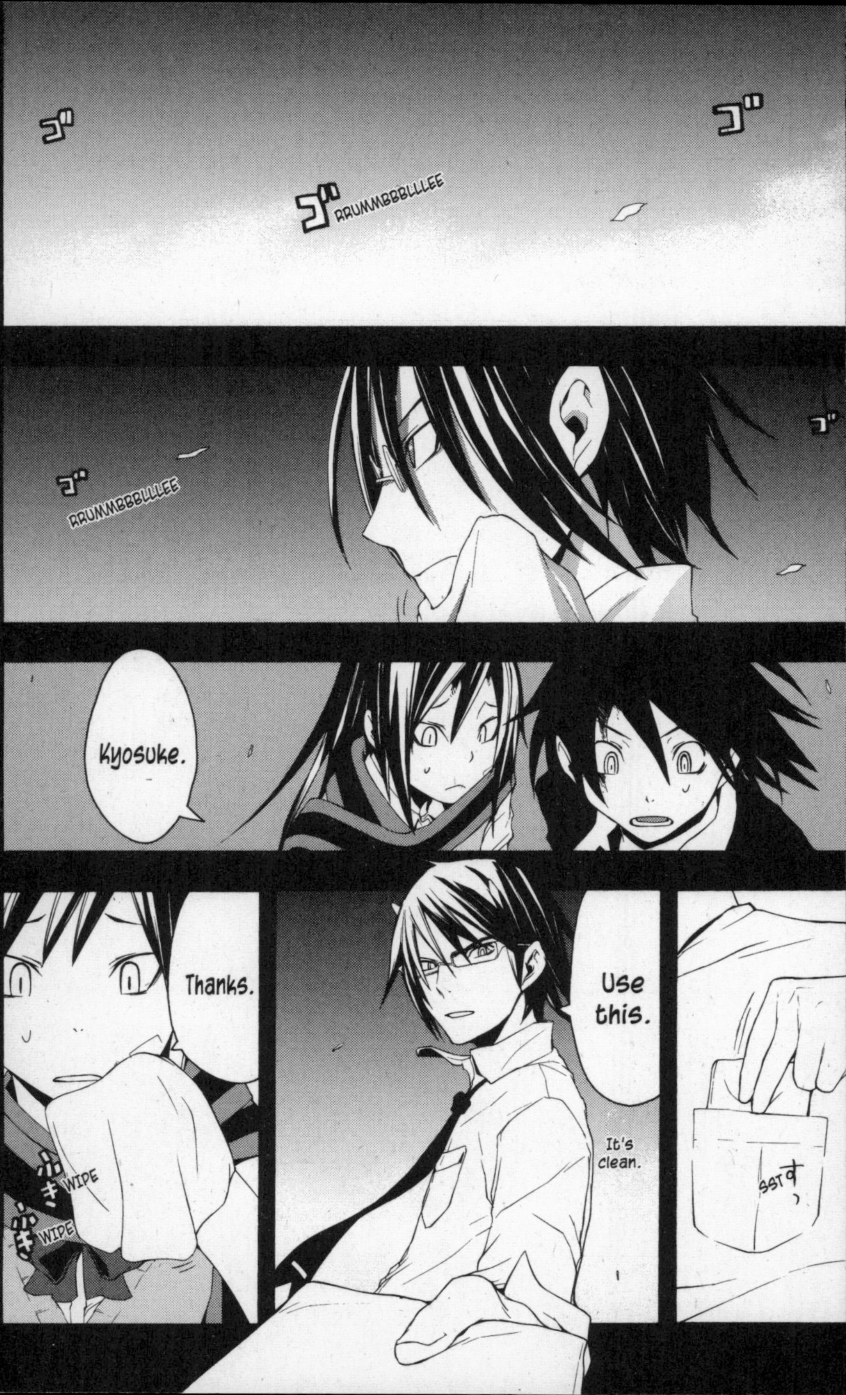

ゴ
ゴ
ゴ RRUMMBBBLLLEE
ゴ
ゴ RRUMMBBBLLLEE
Kyosuke.
SST すっ
Use this.
It's clean.
Thanks.
ふき WIPE
ふき WIPE

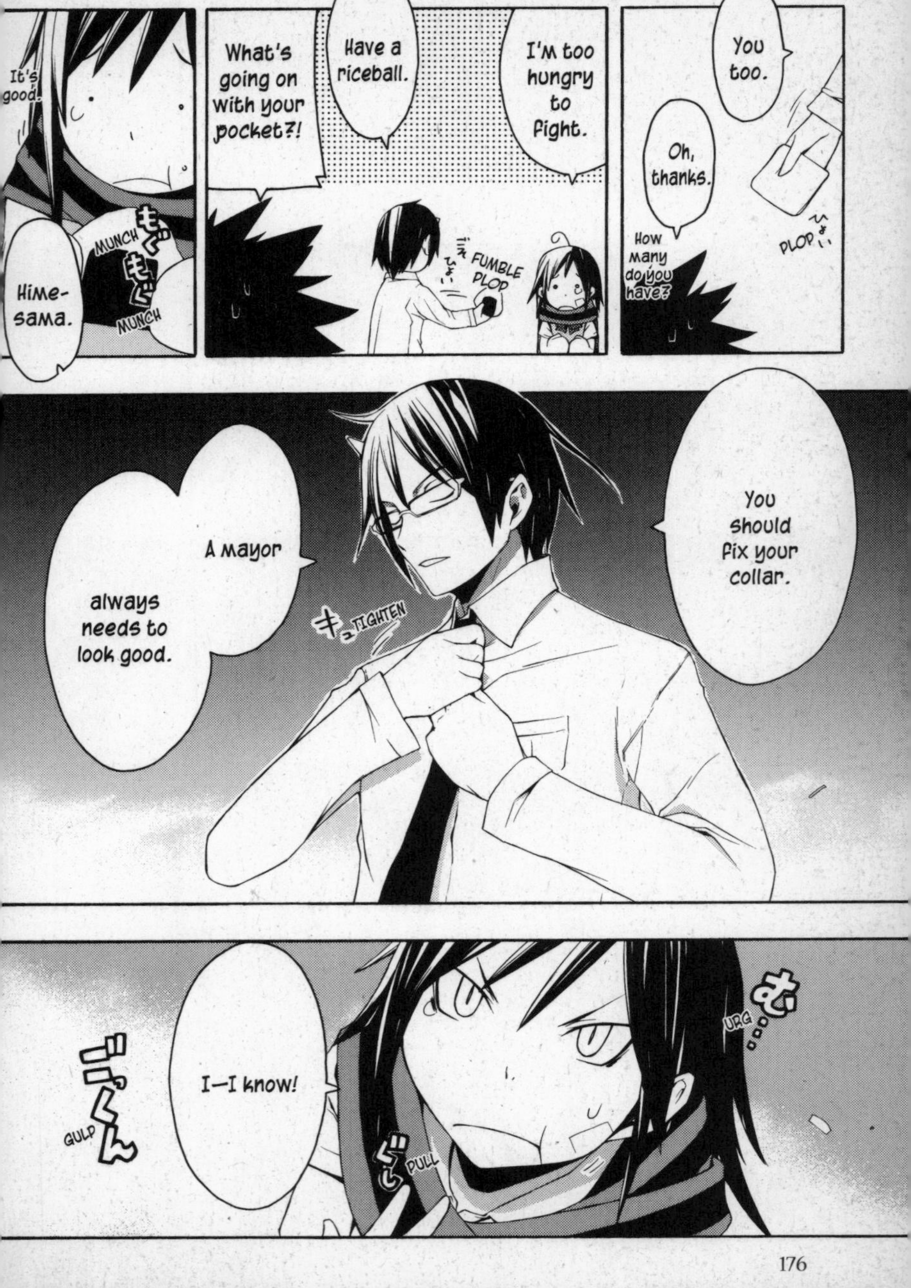
You too.
Oh, thanks.
How many do you have?
PLOP
I'm too hungry to fight.
Have a riceball.
What's going on with your pocket?!
FUMBLE PLOP
It's good.
MUNCH
MUNCH
Hime-sama.
You should fix your collar.
A mayor always needs to look good.
TIGHTEN
URG...
I—I know!
PULL
GULP

17th Night:
Thorny Road
(Part 7)

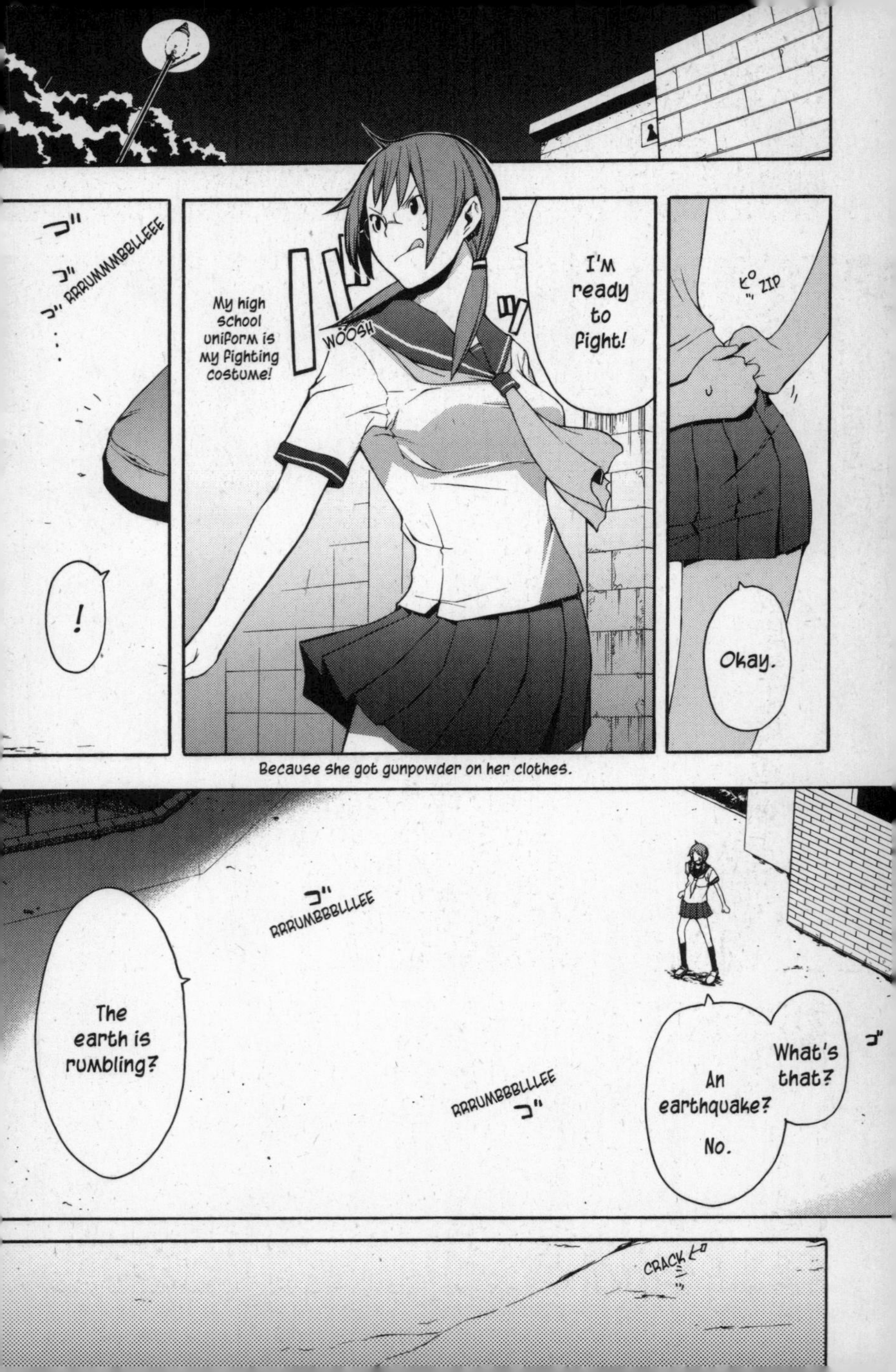
ピ" ZIP
Okay.
I'm ready to fight!
WOOSH
My high school uniform is my fighting costume!
ゴ" ゴ" ゴ" RRRUMMMBBLLEEE
...
!
Because she got gunpowder on her clothes.
ゴ"
What's that?
An earthquake?
No.
ゴ" RRRUMBBBLLLEE
ゴ" RRRUMBBBLLLEE
The earth is rumbling?
CRACK ピ"

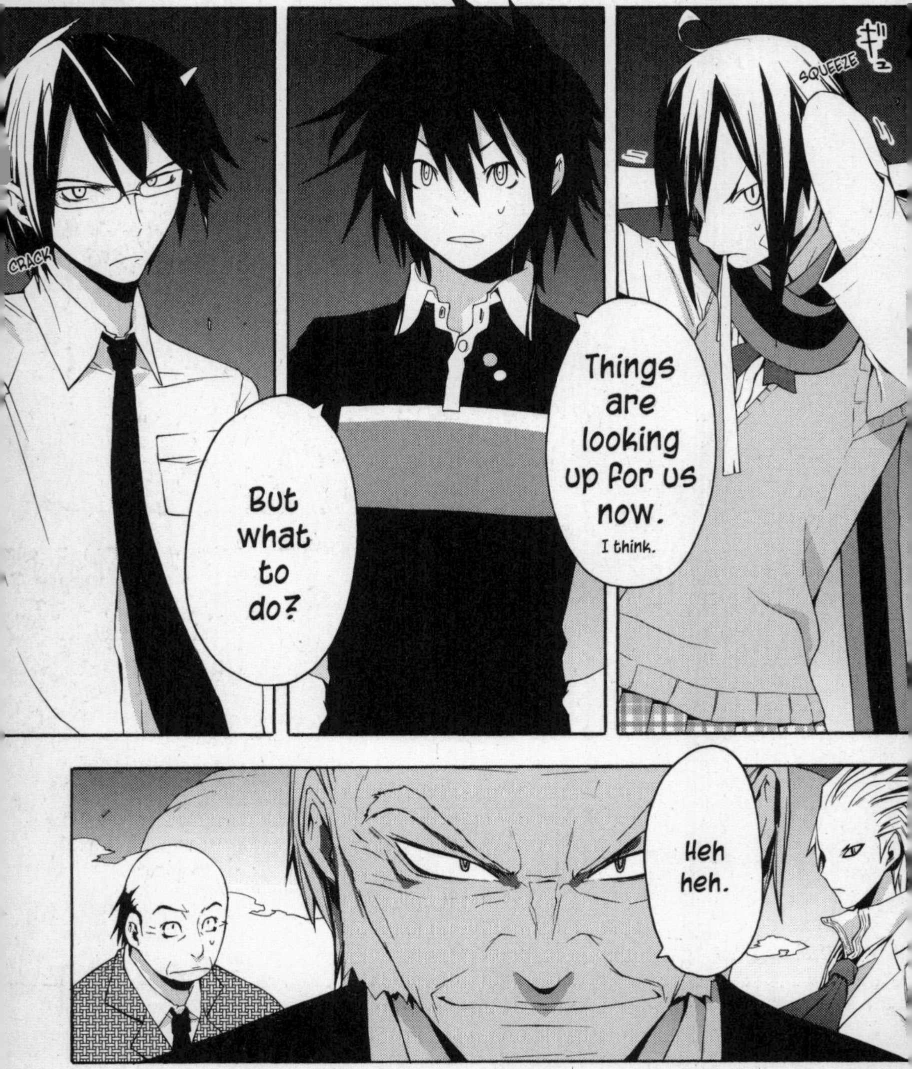
ギュ
SQUEEZE
Things are looking up for us now.
I think.
But what to do?
CRACK
Heh heh.

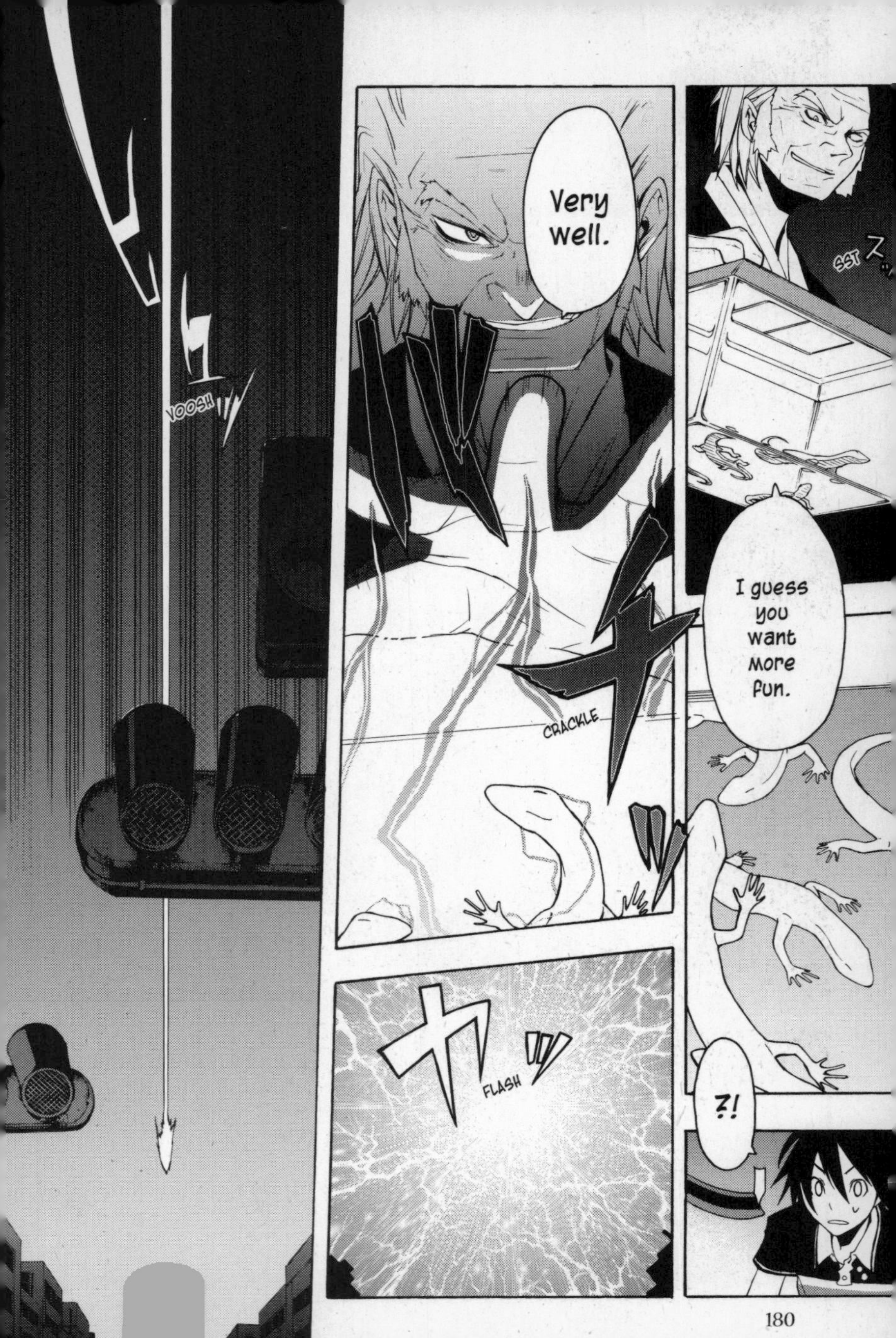
SST
I guess you want more fun.
?!
Very well.
CRACKLE
FLASH
VOOSH

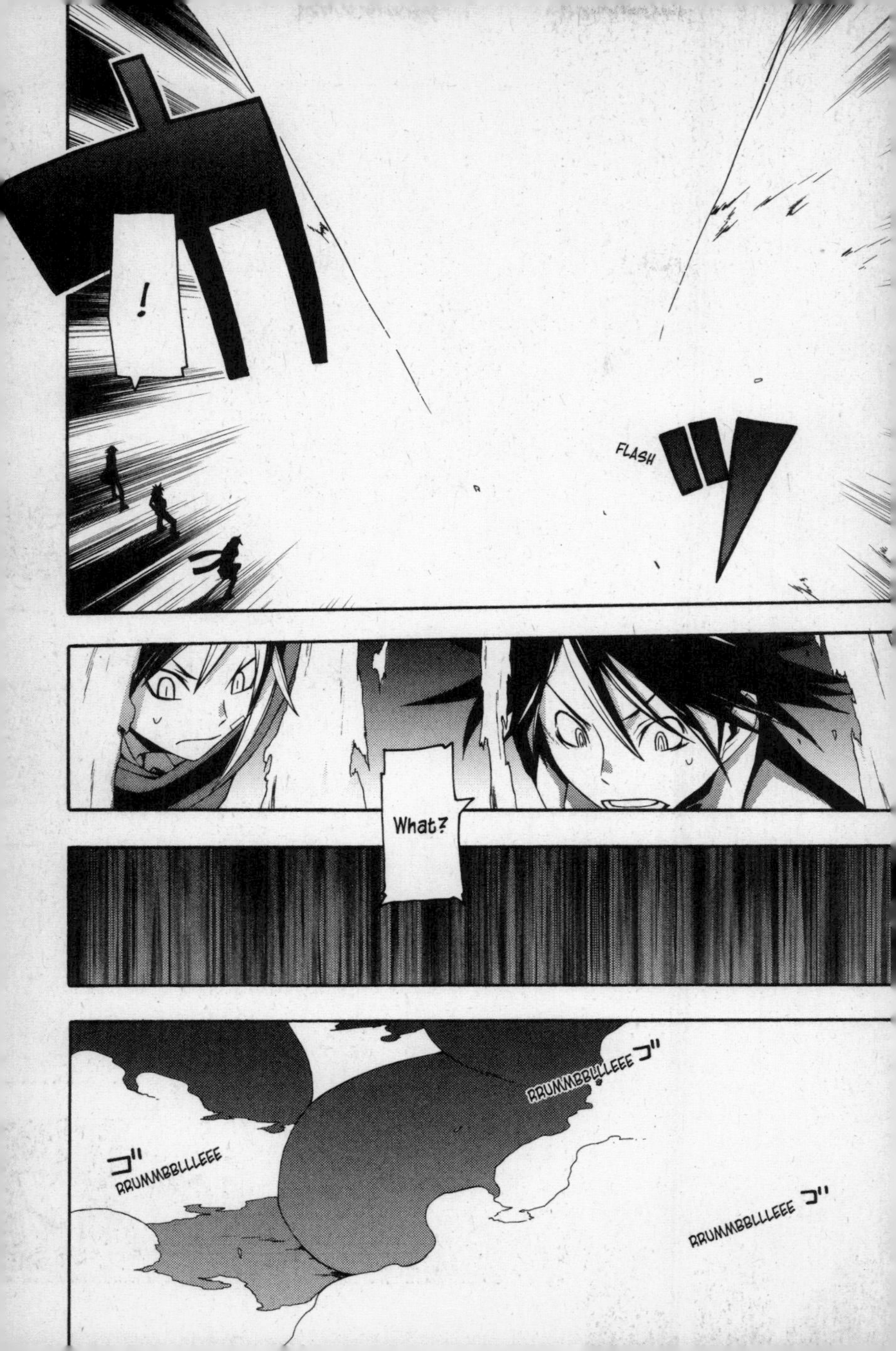
FLASH
!
What?
RRUMMBBLLLEEE ゴ
RRUMMBBLLLEEE ゴ
ゴ RRUMMBBLLLEEE

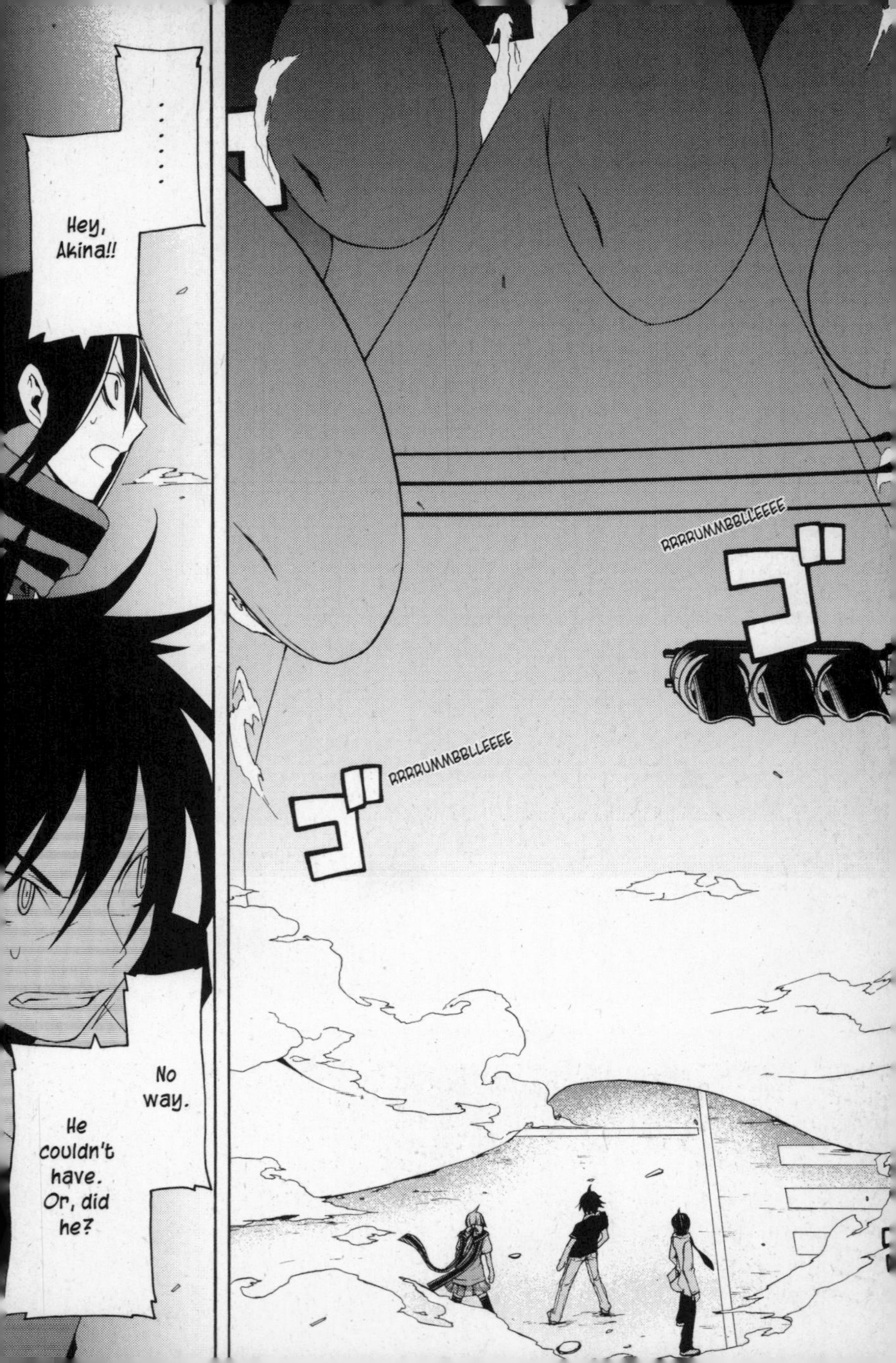
RRRRUMMBBLLEEEE
ゴゴ
RRRRUMMBBLLEEEE
ゴゴ
......
Hey, Akina!!
No way.
He couldn't have. Or, did he?

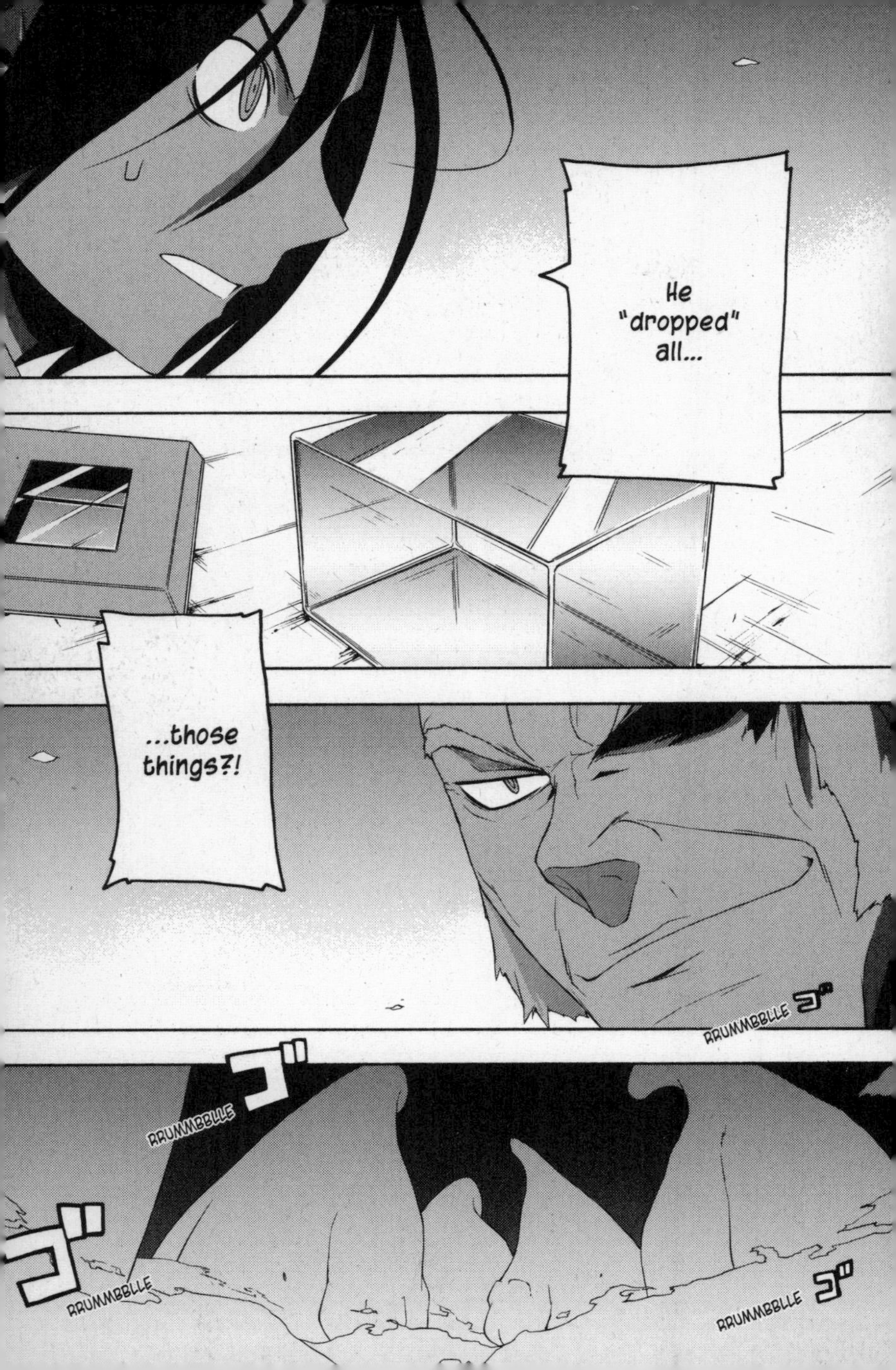
He "dropped" all...
...those things?!
RRUMMBBLLE ゴ
ゴ RRUMMBBLLE
ゴ RRUMMBBLLE
RRUMMBBLLE ゴ

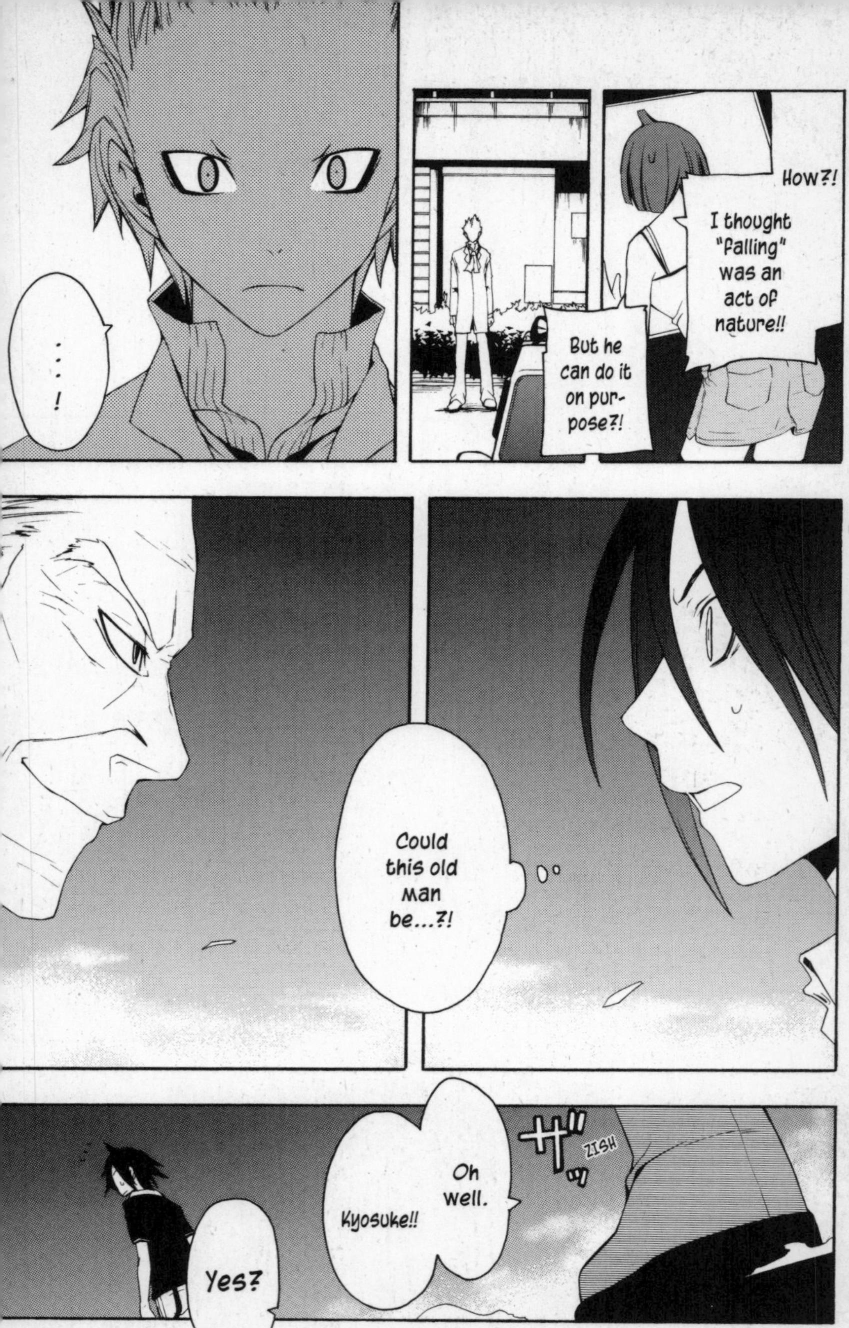
How?!
I thought "falling" was an act of nature!!
But he can do it on pur-pose?!
...!
Could this old man be...?!
Oh well.
ZISH
Kyosuke!!
Yes?

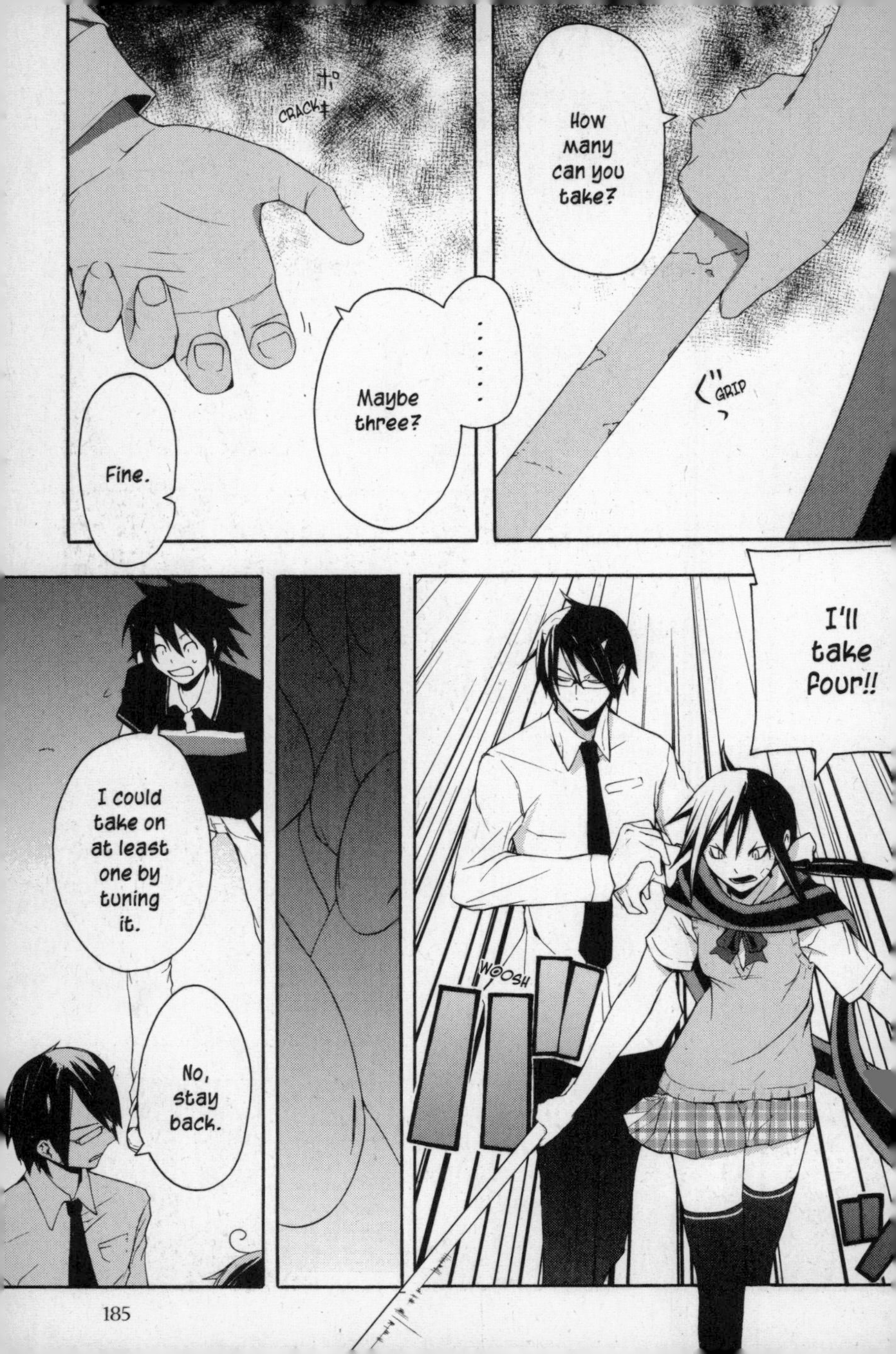
How many can you take?
GRIP
......
Maybe three?
CRACK
Fine.
I'll take four!!
WOOSH
I could take on at least one by tuning it.
No, stay back.

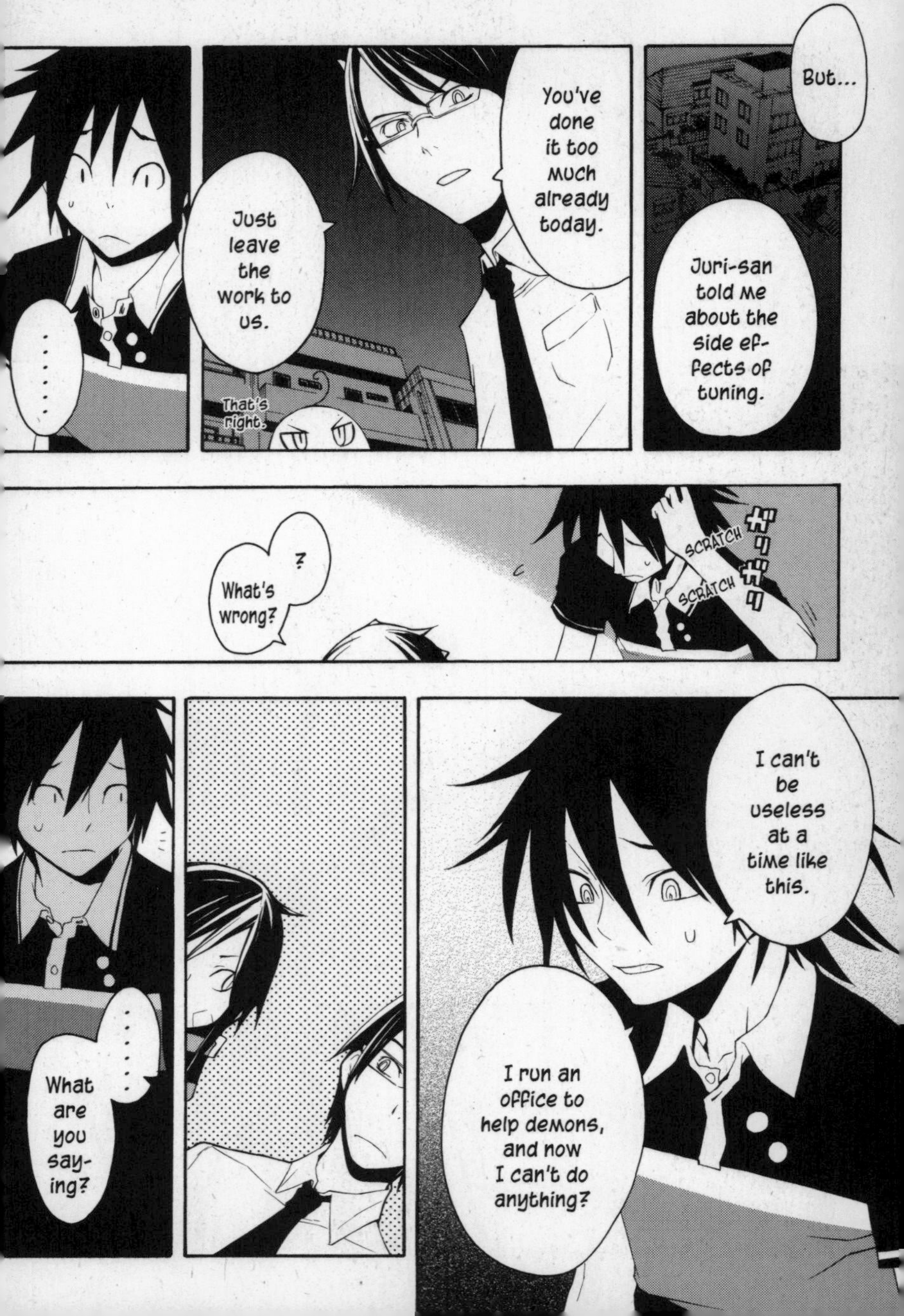
But...
Juri-san told me about the side ef-fects of tuning.
You've done it too much already today.
Just leave the work to us.
That's right.
......
ガリ SCRATCH
ガリ SCRATCH
? What's wrong?
I can't be useless at a time like this.
I run an office to help demons, and now I can't do anything?
......
What are you say-ing?

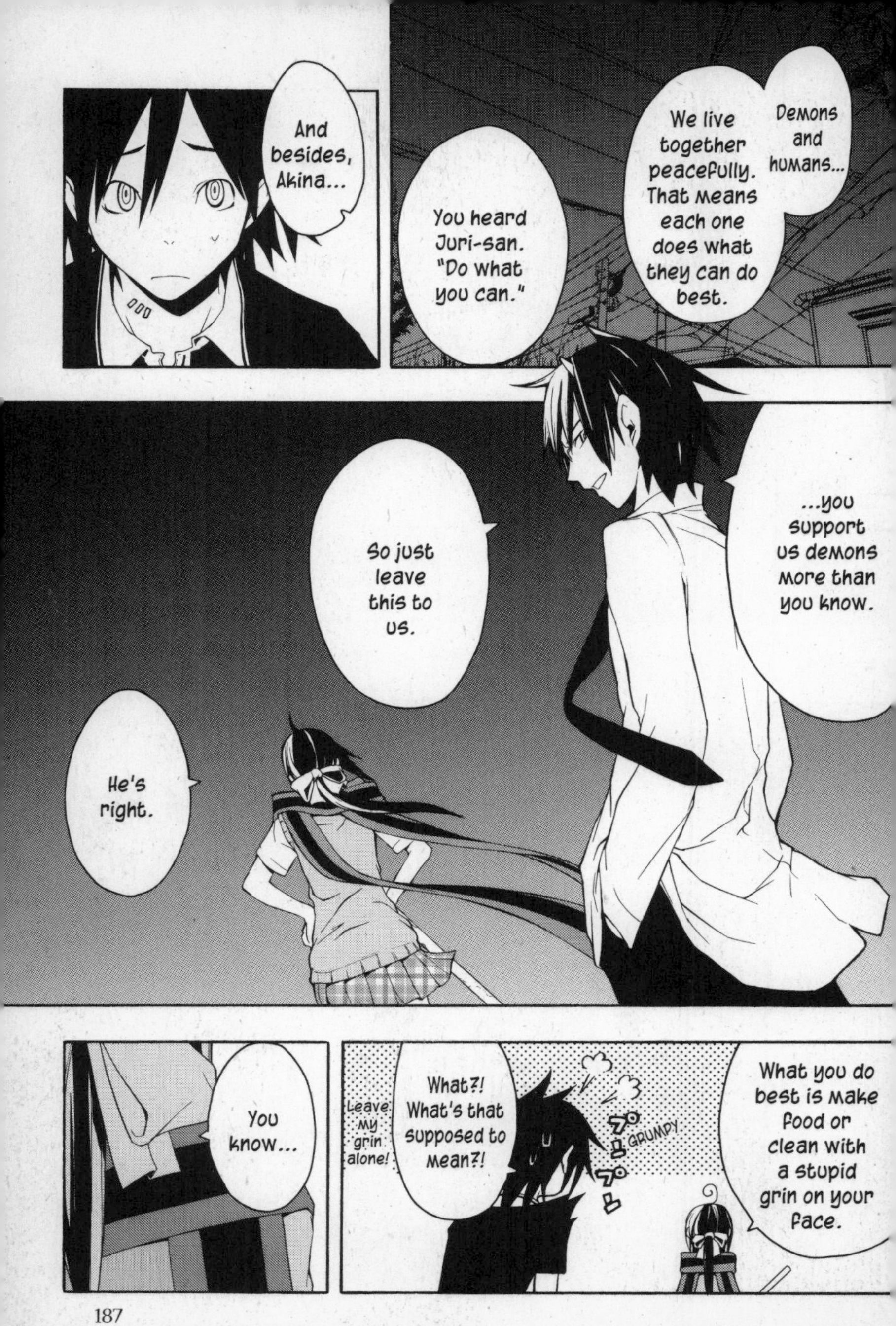
Demons and humans...
We live together peacefully. That means each one does what they can do best.
You heard Juri-san. "Do what you can."
And besides, Akina...
...you support us demons more than you know.
So just leave this to us.
He's right.
What you do best is make food or clean with a stupid grin on your face.
What?! What's that supposed to mean?!
Leave my grin alone!
GRUMPY
You know...

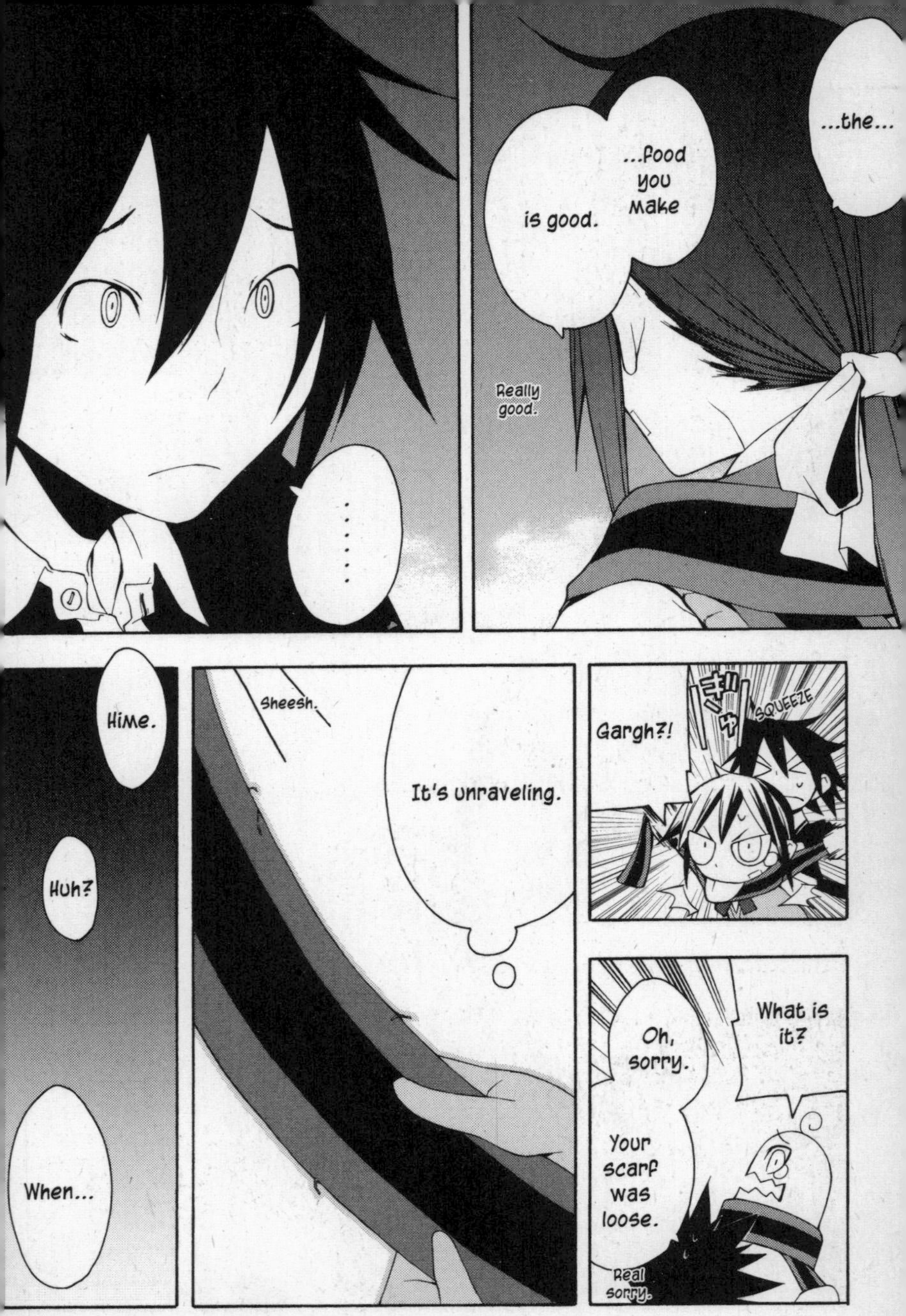
...the...
...food you make is good.
Really good.
......
SQUEEZE
Gargh?!
What is it?
Oh, sorry.
Your scarf was loose.
Real sorry.
It's unraveling.
Sheesh.
Hime.
Huh?
When...

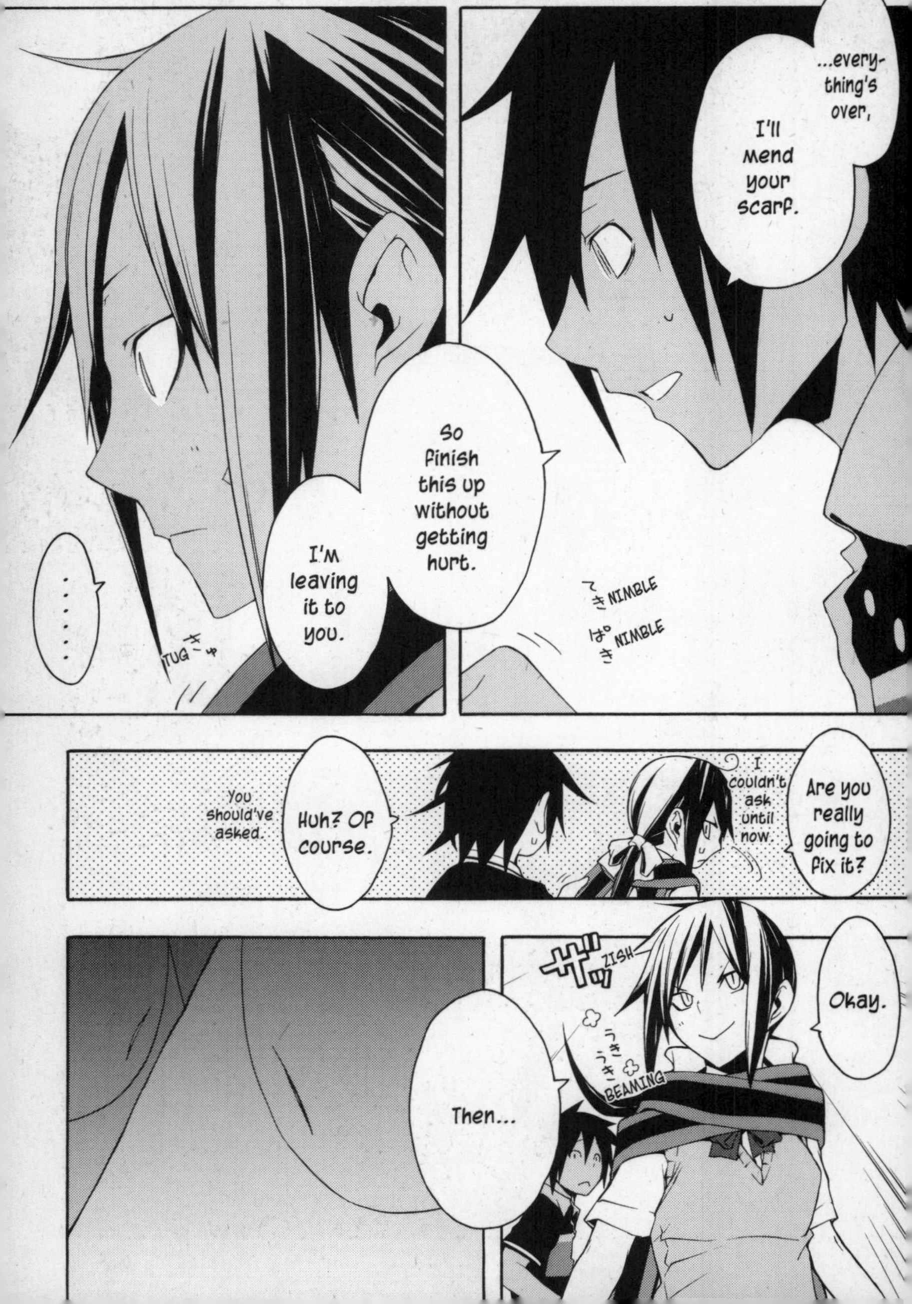
...every-thing's over,
I'll mend your scarf.
てき NIMBLE
ぱき NIMBLE
So finish this up without getting hurt.
I'm leaving it to you.
きゅ TUG
......
Are you really going to fix it?
I couldn't ask until now.
Huh? Of course.
You should've asked.
Okay.
ザッ ZISH
うき うき BEAMING
Then...

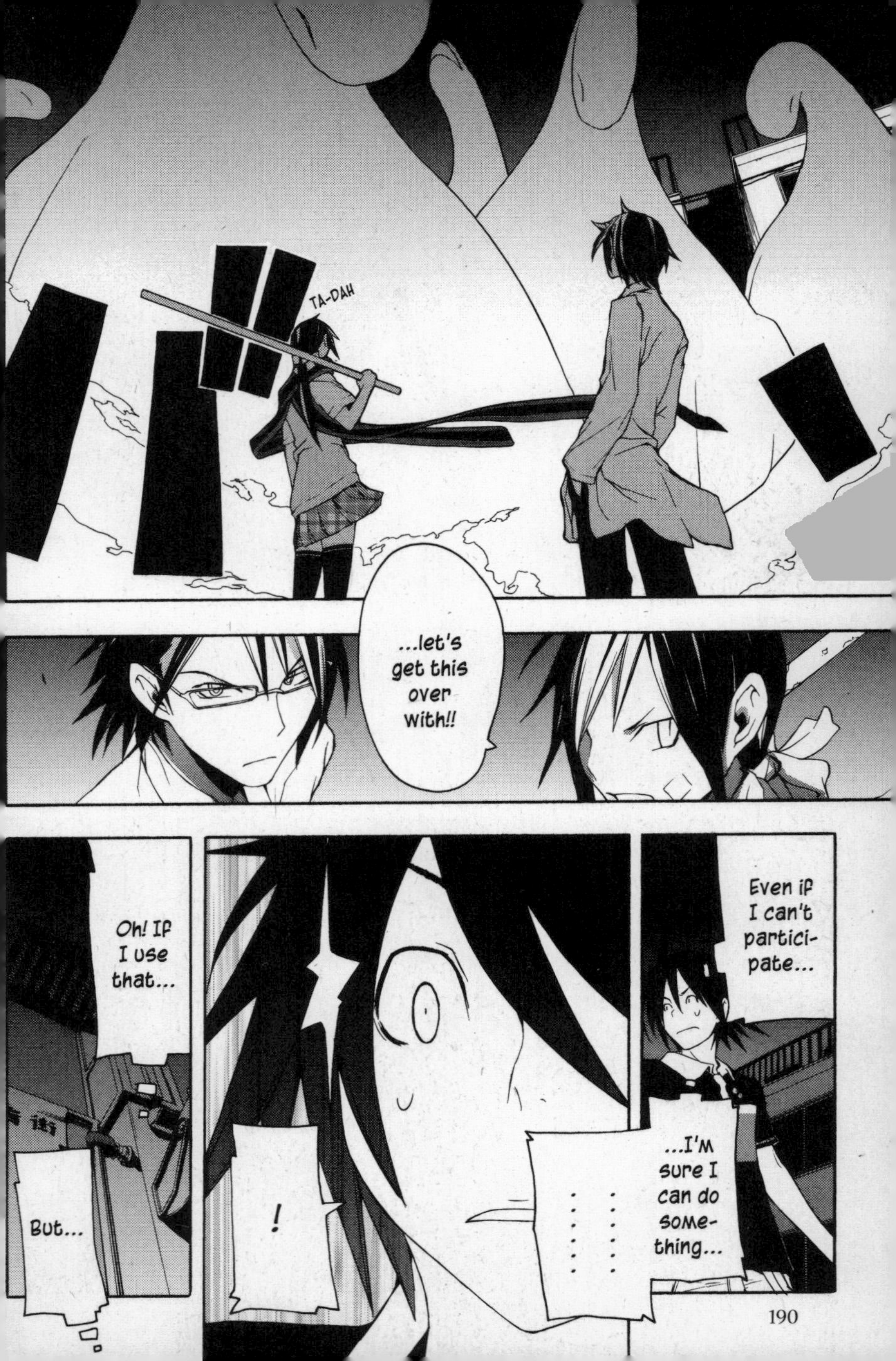
TA-DAH
...let's get this over with!!
Even if I can't partici- pate...
...I'M sure I can do some- thing...
!
......
Oh! If I use that...
But...

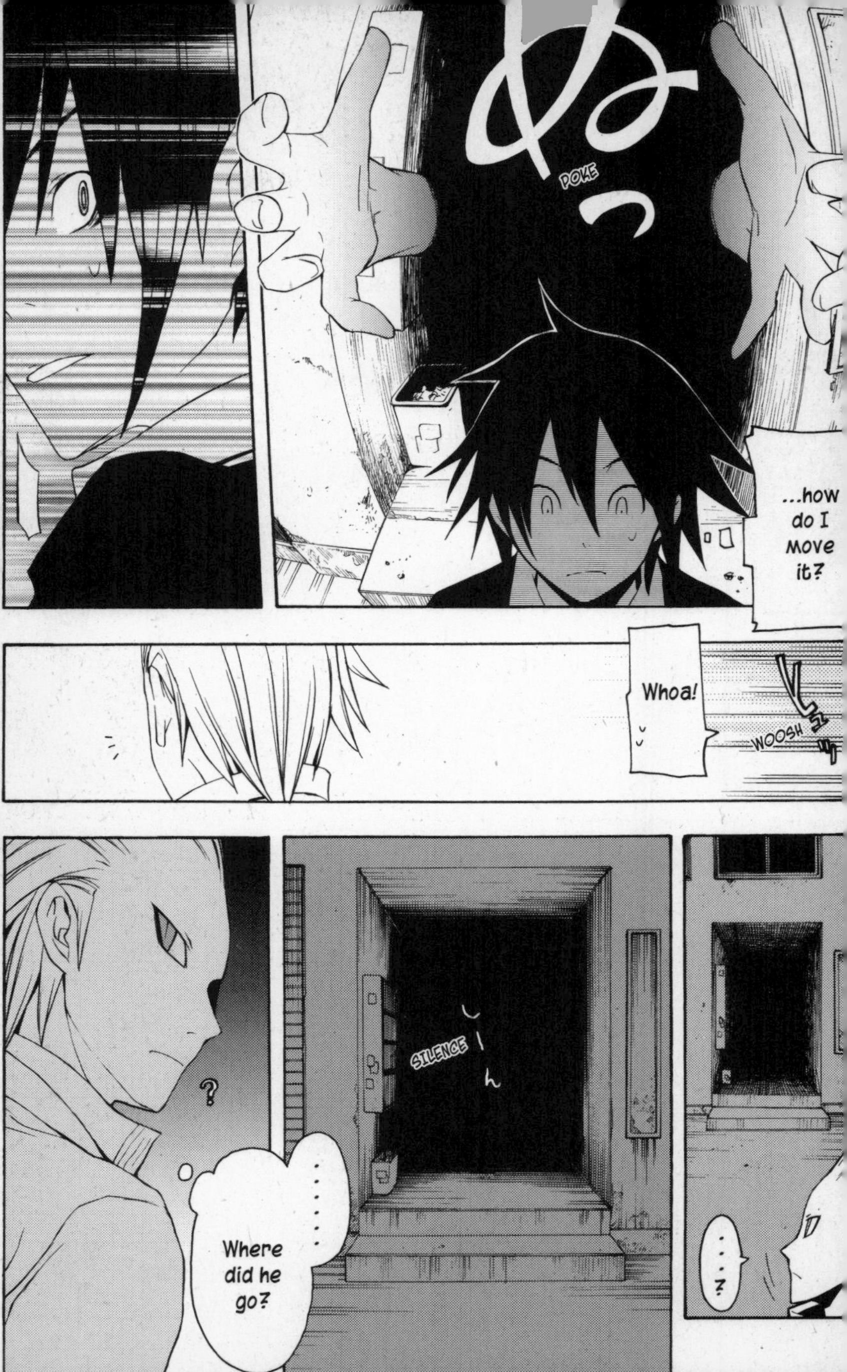

ぬっ
POKE
...how do I move it?
WOOSH
Whoa!
...?
しーん
SILENCE
......
Where did he go?

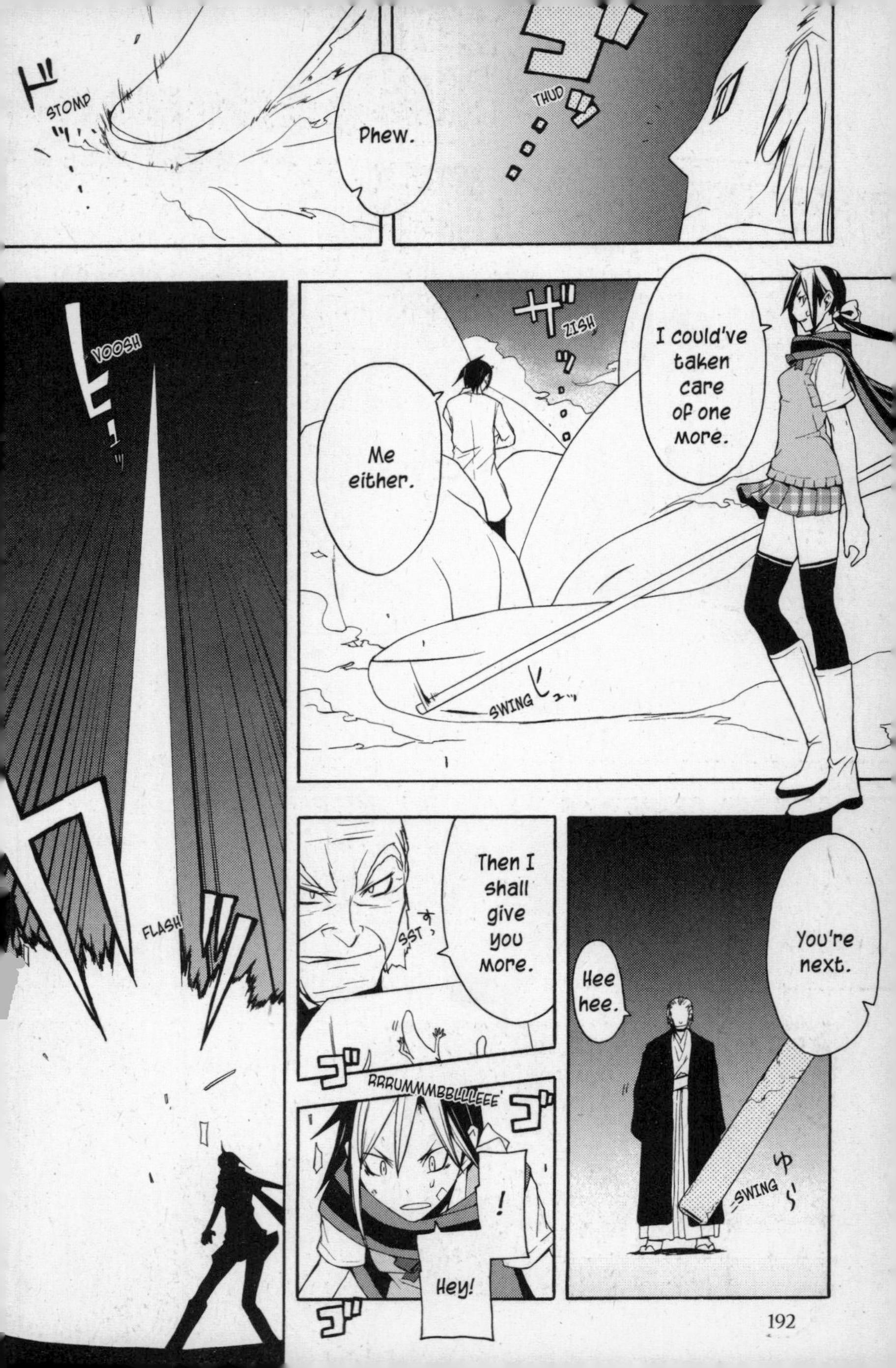

THUD
Phew.
STOMP
I could've taken care of one more.
Me either.
ZISH
SWING
You're next.
Hee hee.
SWING
Then I shall give you more.
SST
RRRUMMMBBLLLLEEE
!
Hey!
VOOSH
FLASH

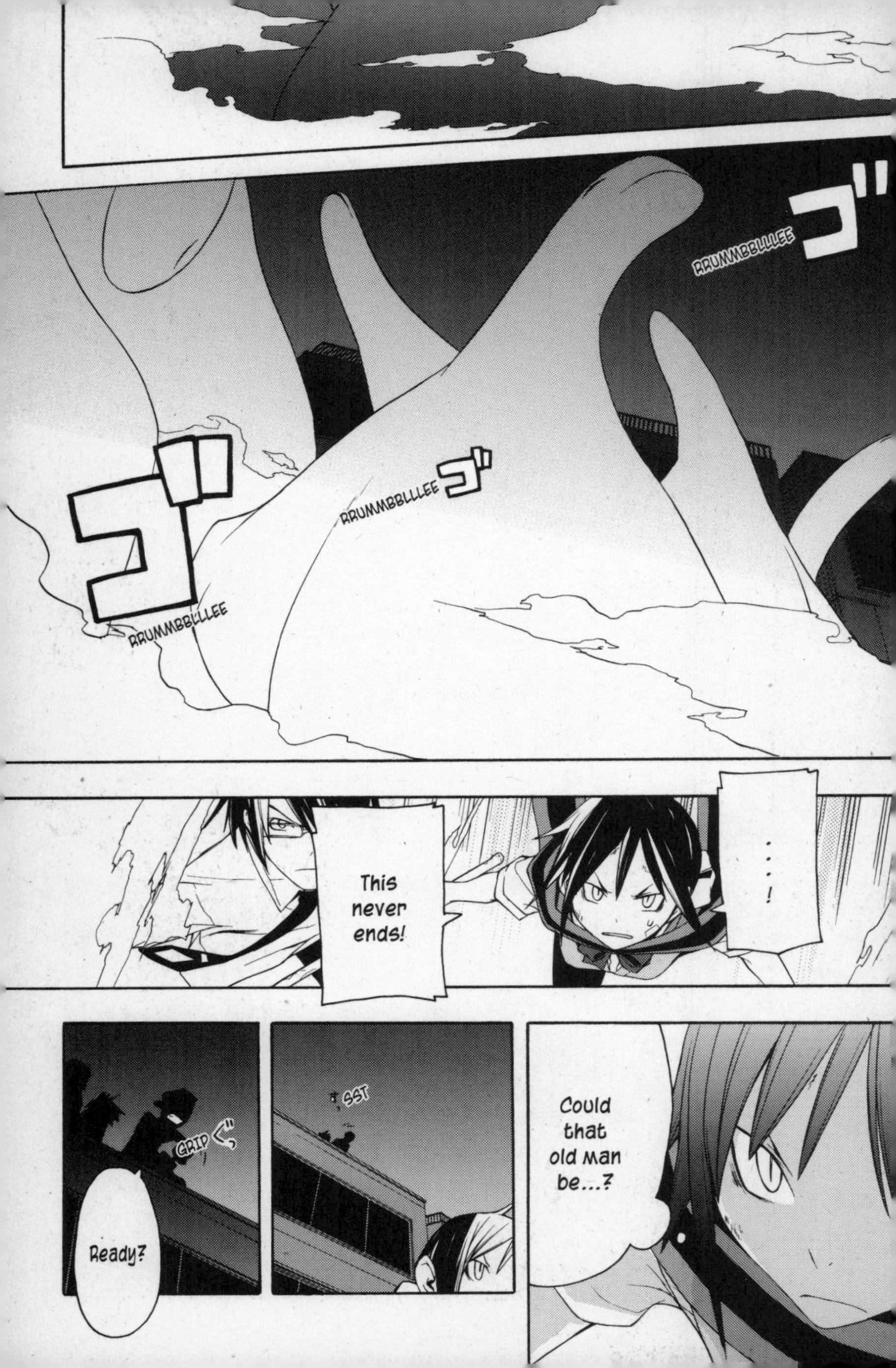
ゴ
RRUMMBBLLLEE
ゴ
RRUMMBBLLLEE
ゴ
RRUMMBBLLLEE
...!
This never ends!
Could that old man be...?
SST
GRIP
Ready?

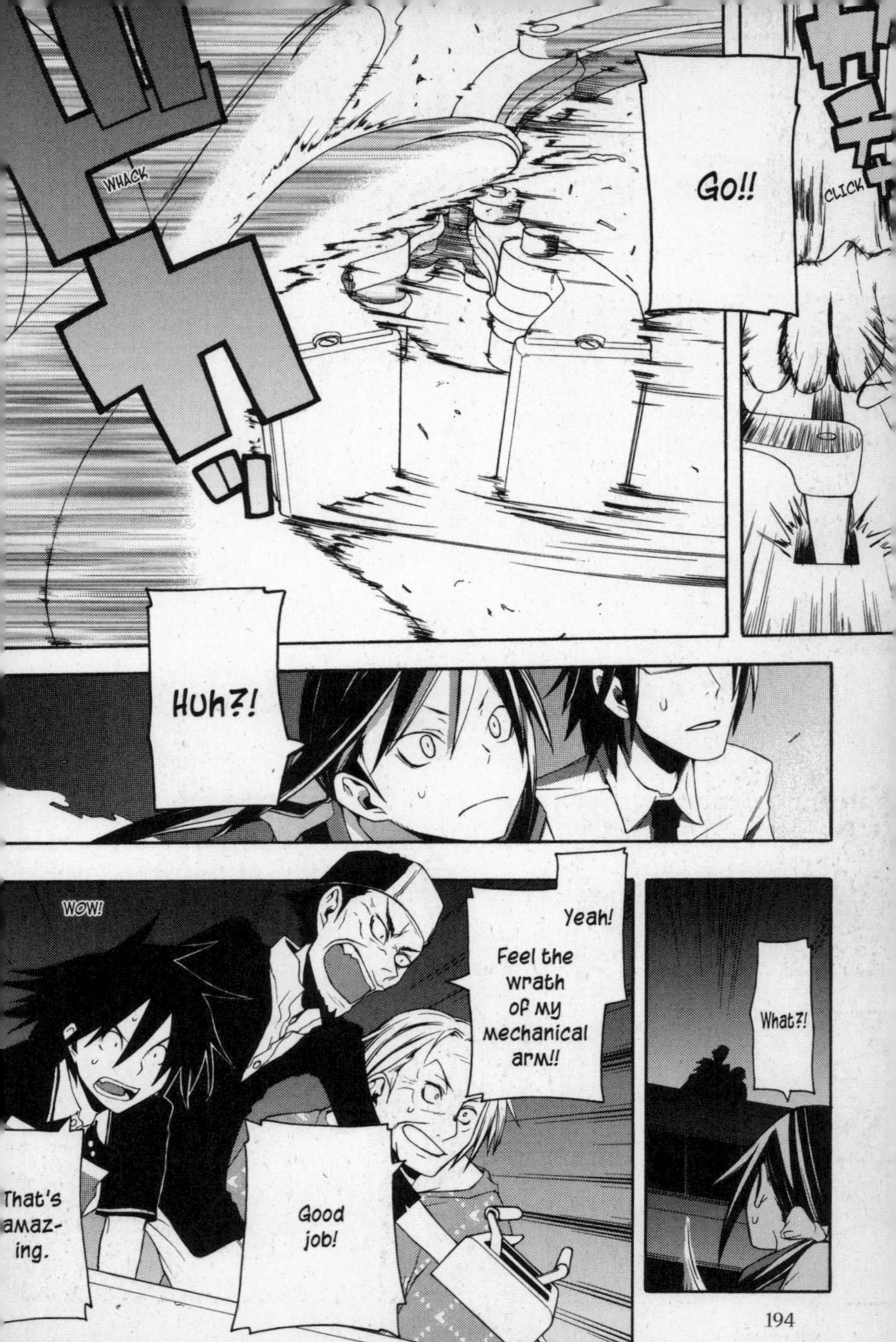
CLICK
GO!!
WHACK
Huh?!
What?!
Yeah!
Feel the wrath of my mechanical arm!!
WOW!
Good job!
That's amaz-ing.

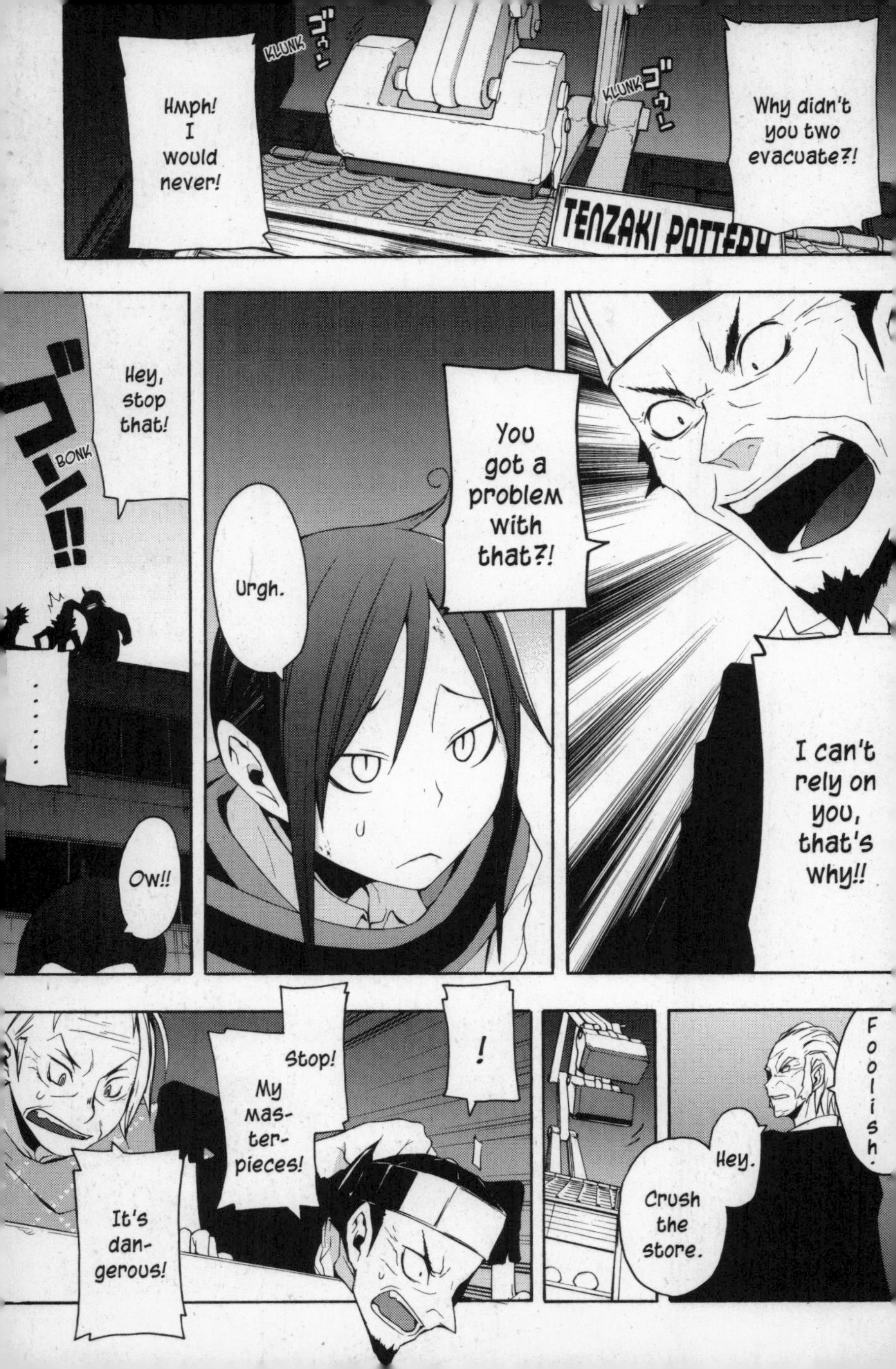
Why didn't you two evacuate?!
KLUNK
KLUNK
TENZAKI POTTERY
Hmph! I would never!
You got a problem with that?!
I can't rely on you, that's why!!
Urgh.
Hey, stop that!
BONK
......
Ow!!
Foolish.
Hey.
Crush the store.
!
Stop! My mas-ter-pieces!
It's dan-gerous!

GRIP

Er!

DASH

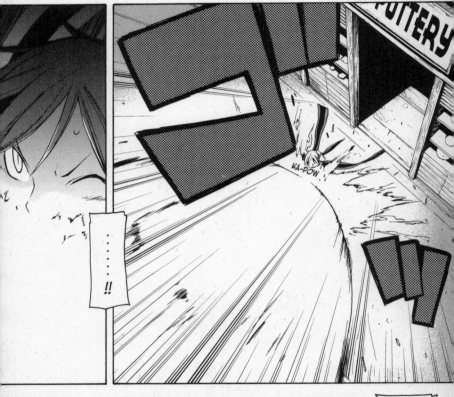

POTTERY

KA-POW

…………

!!

What are you doing? Hurry up and crush it!

Oh.

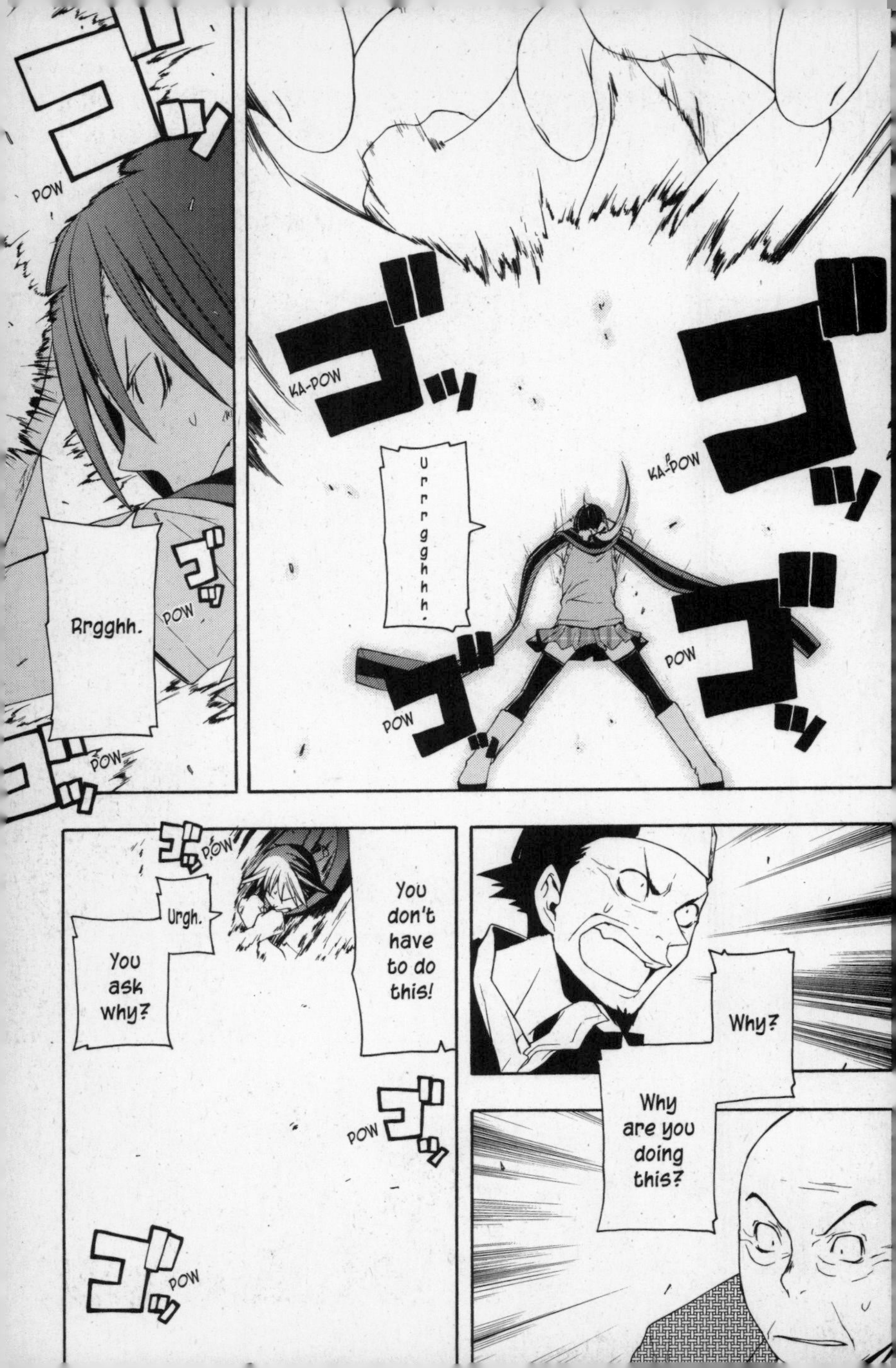
KA-POW
KA-POW
Urrrgghhh.
POW
POW
POW
POW
Rrgghh.
POW
Why?
Why are you doing this?
POW
You don't have to do this!
Urgh.
You ask why?
POW
POW

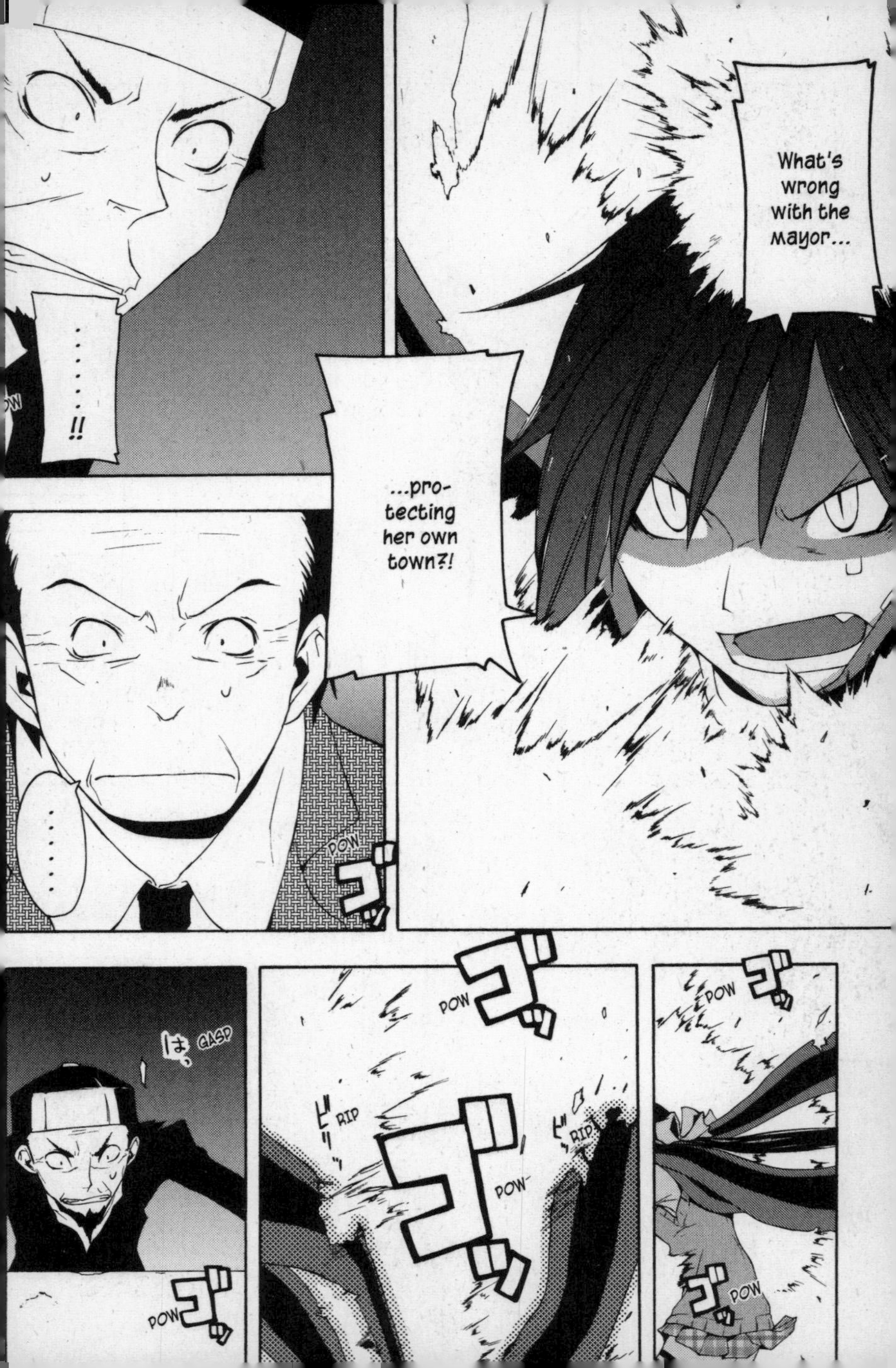

What's wrong with the mayor...
...pro-tecting her own town?!
......!!
POW ゴ
......
POW ゴッ
ゴッ POW
POW ゴッ
ビッ RIP
ゴッ POW
ビリ RIP
は、GASP
POW ゴッ

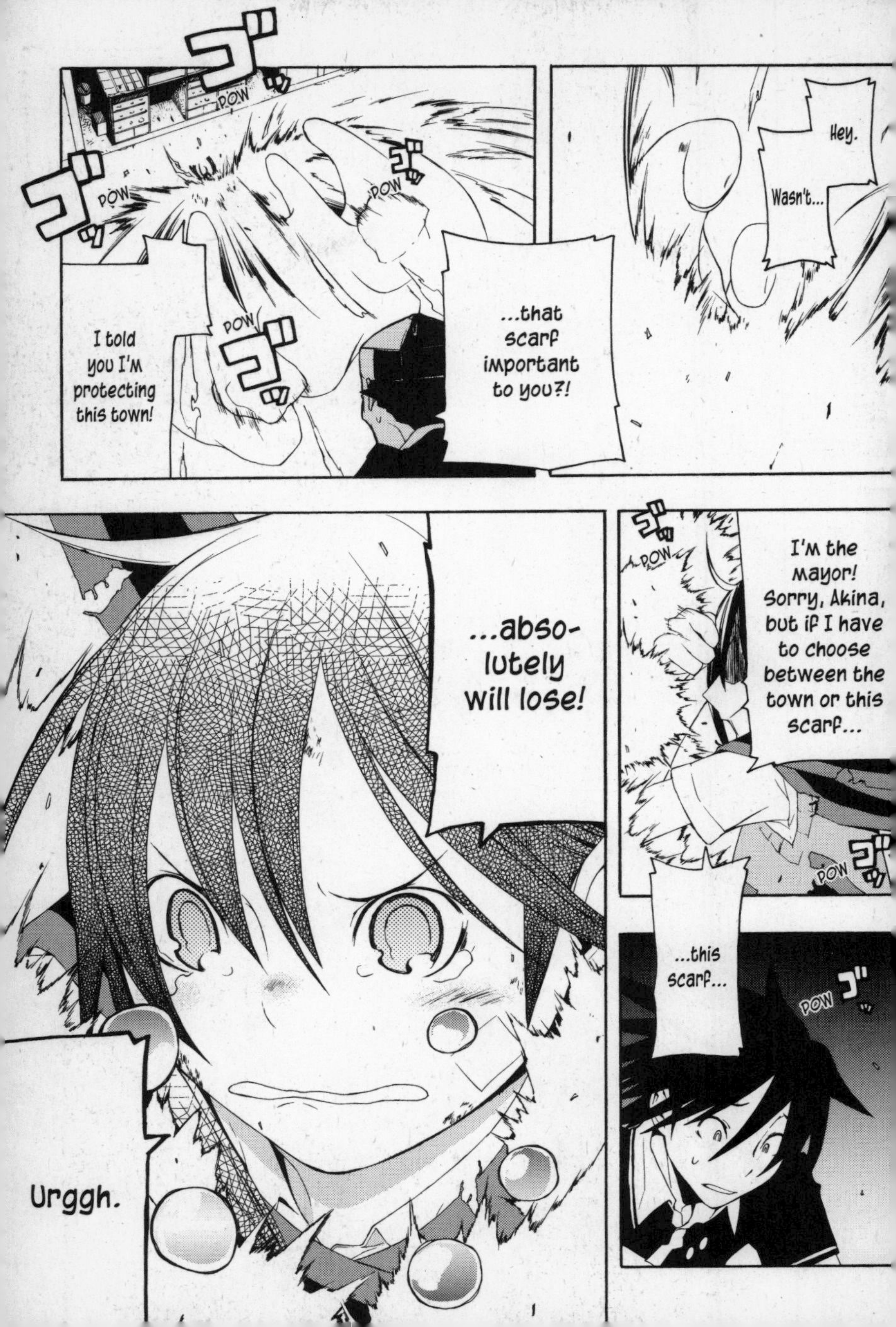
Hey.
Wasn't...
POW
POW
POW
...that scarf important to you?!
POW
I told you I'm protecting this town!
POW
I'm the mayor! Sorry, Akina, but if I have to choose between the town or this scarf...
POW
...this scarf...
POW
...abso-lutely will lose!
Urggh.

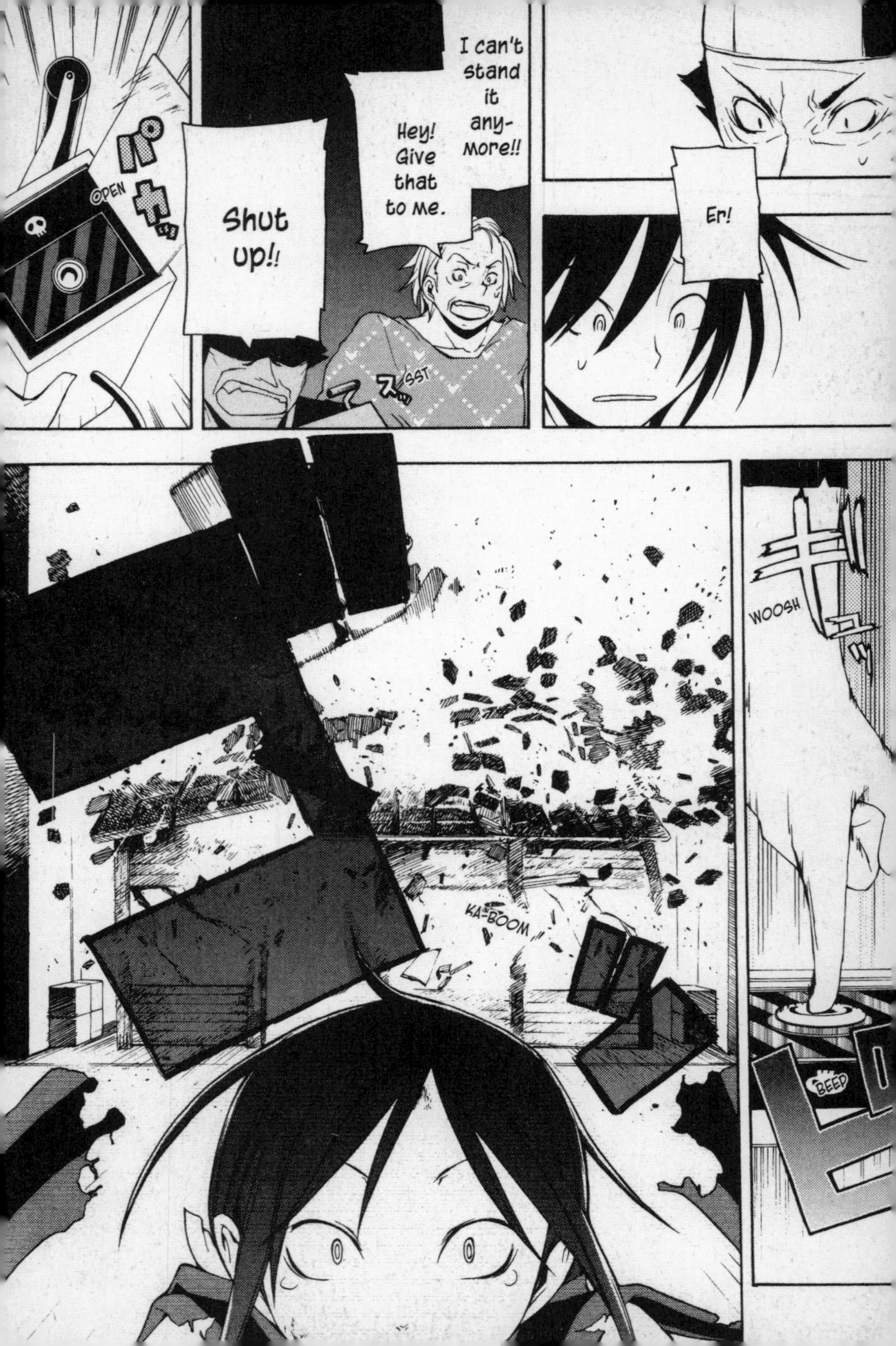
Er!
I can't stand it any-more!!
Hey! Give that to me.
Shut up!!
SST
OPEN
WOOSH
BEEP
KA-BOOM

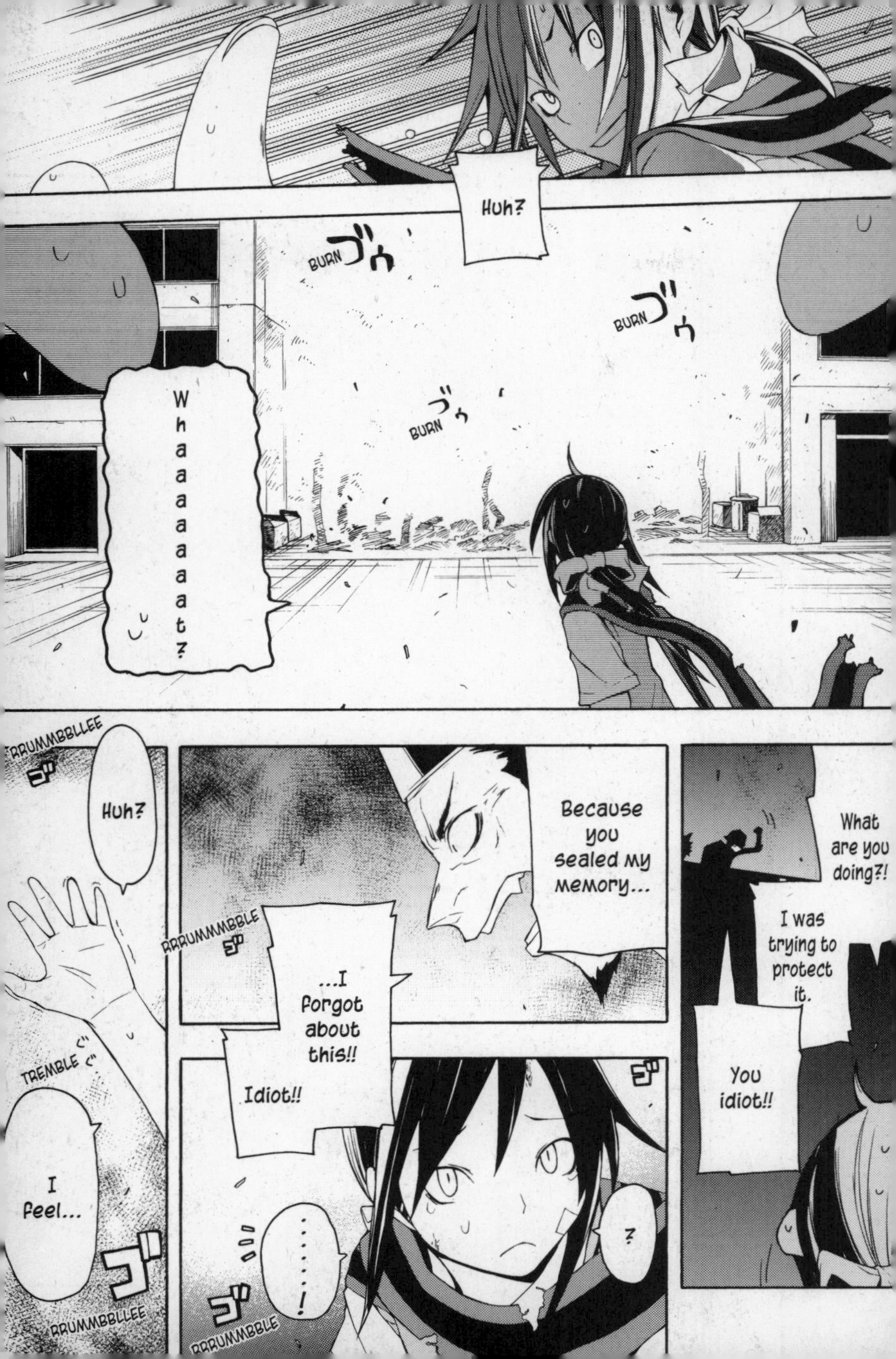

Huh?
BURN ゴゥ
BURN ゴゥ
BURN
Whaaaaaaaaat?
What are you doing?!
I was trying to protect it.
You idiot!!
Because you sealed my memory...
RRRUMMBBLE
...I forgot about this!!
Idiot!!
?
......!
RRRUMMBBLE
RRRUMMBBLLEE
Huh?
TREMBLE
I feel...
RRUMMBBLLEE

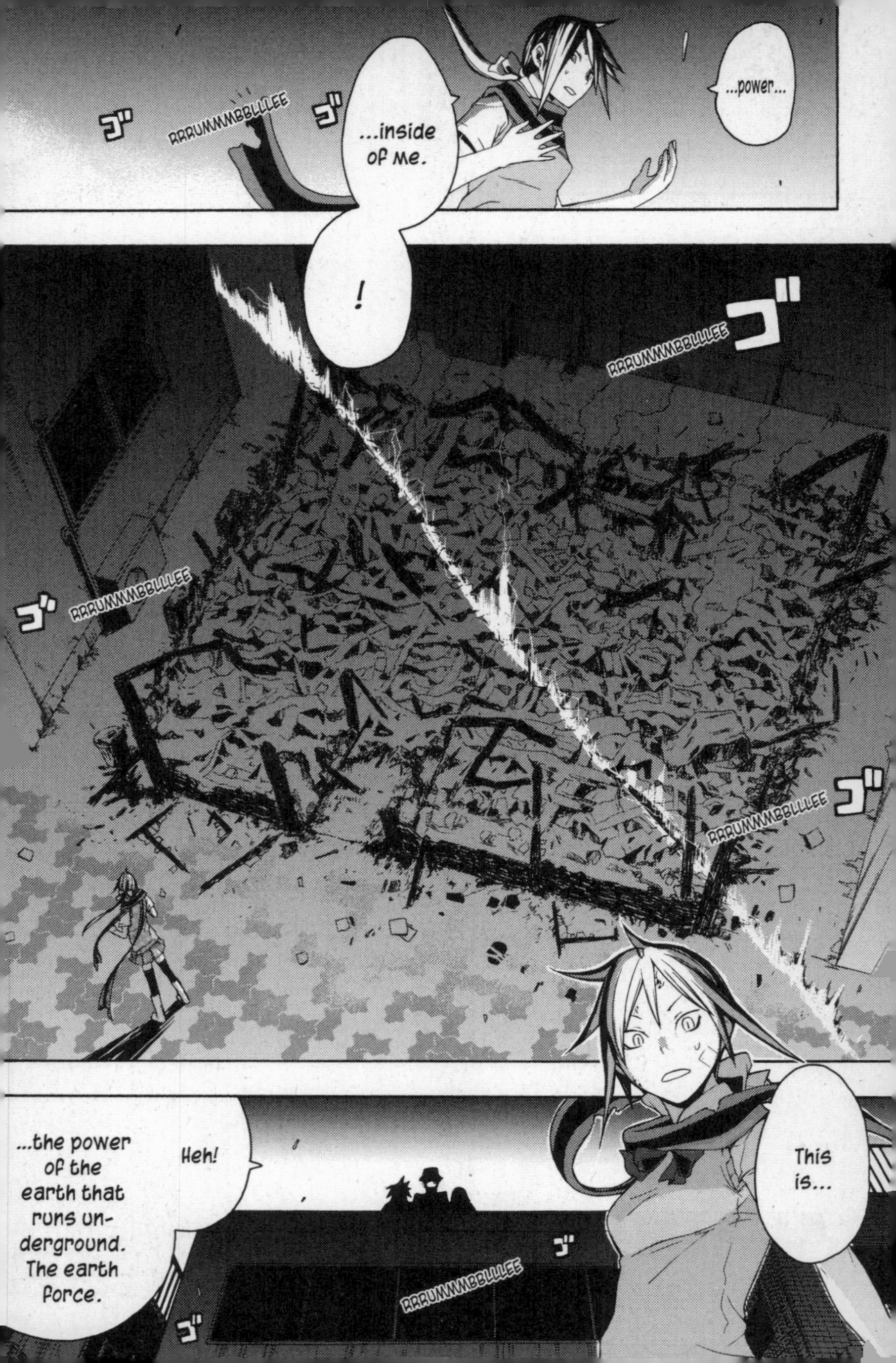

...power...
!
...inside of me.
!
ゴ
RRRUMMMBBLLLEE
ゴ
ゴ
RRRUMMMBBLLLEE
ゴ
RRRUMMMBBLLLEE
ゴ
RRRUMMMBBLLLEE
ゴ
This is...
Heh!
...the power of the earth that runs underground. The earth force.
ゴ
RRRUMMMBBLLLEE
ゴ

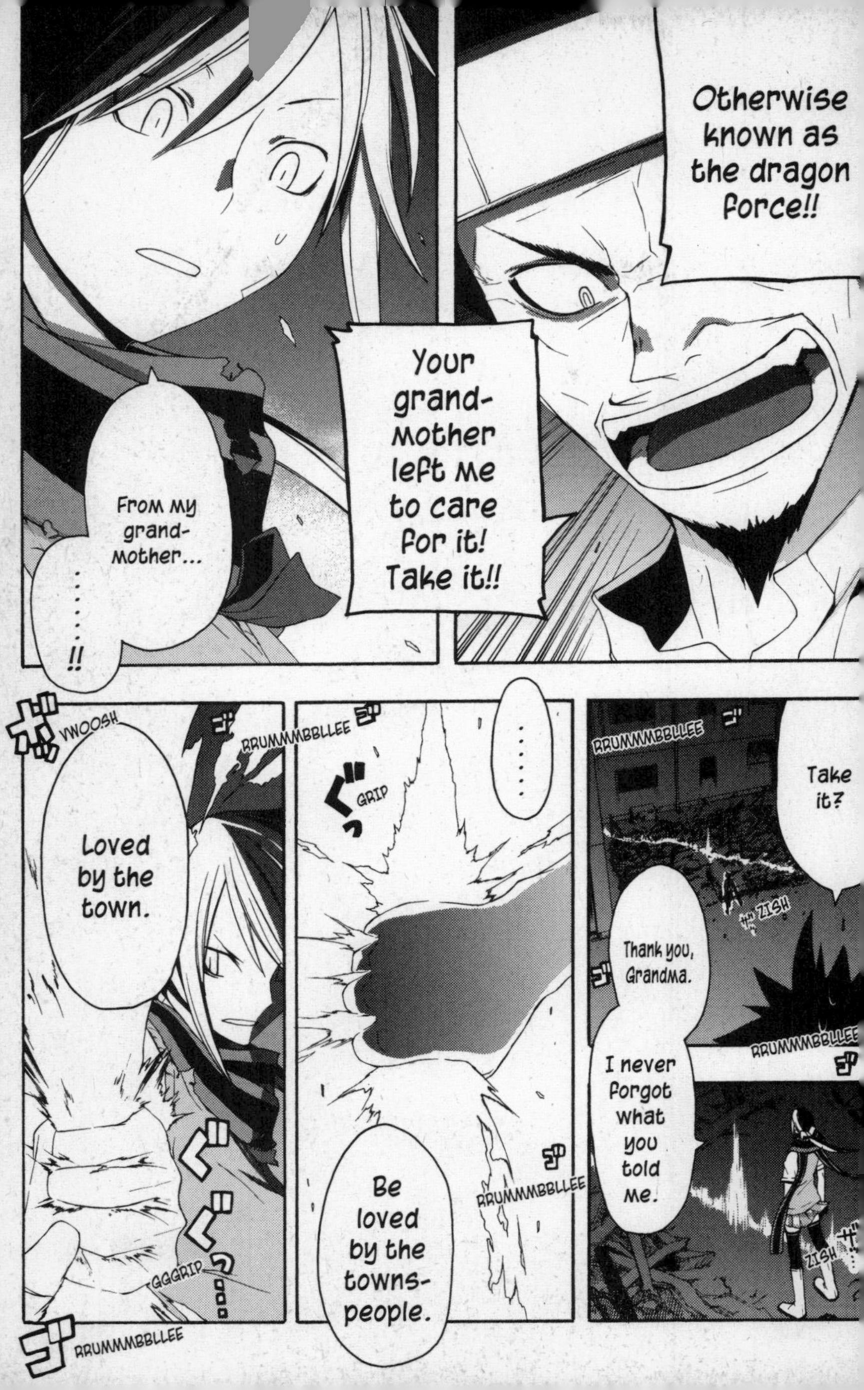

Otherwise known as the dragon force!!
Your grand-mother left me to care for it! Take it!!
From my grand-mother...
......!!
Take it?
BRRUMMMBBLLEE
ZISH
Thank you, Grandma.
BRRUMMMBBLLEE
I never forgot what you told me.
ZISH
......
GRIP
Be loved by the towns-people.
BRRUMMMBBLLEE
VWOOSH
BRRUMMMBBLLEE
Loved by the town.
GGGRIP
BRRUMMMBBLLEE

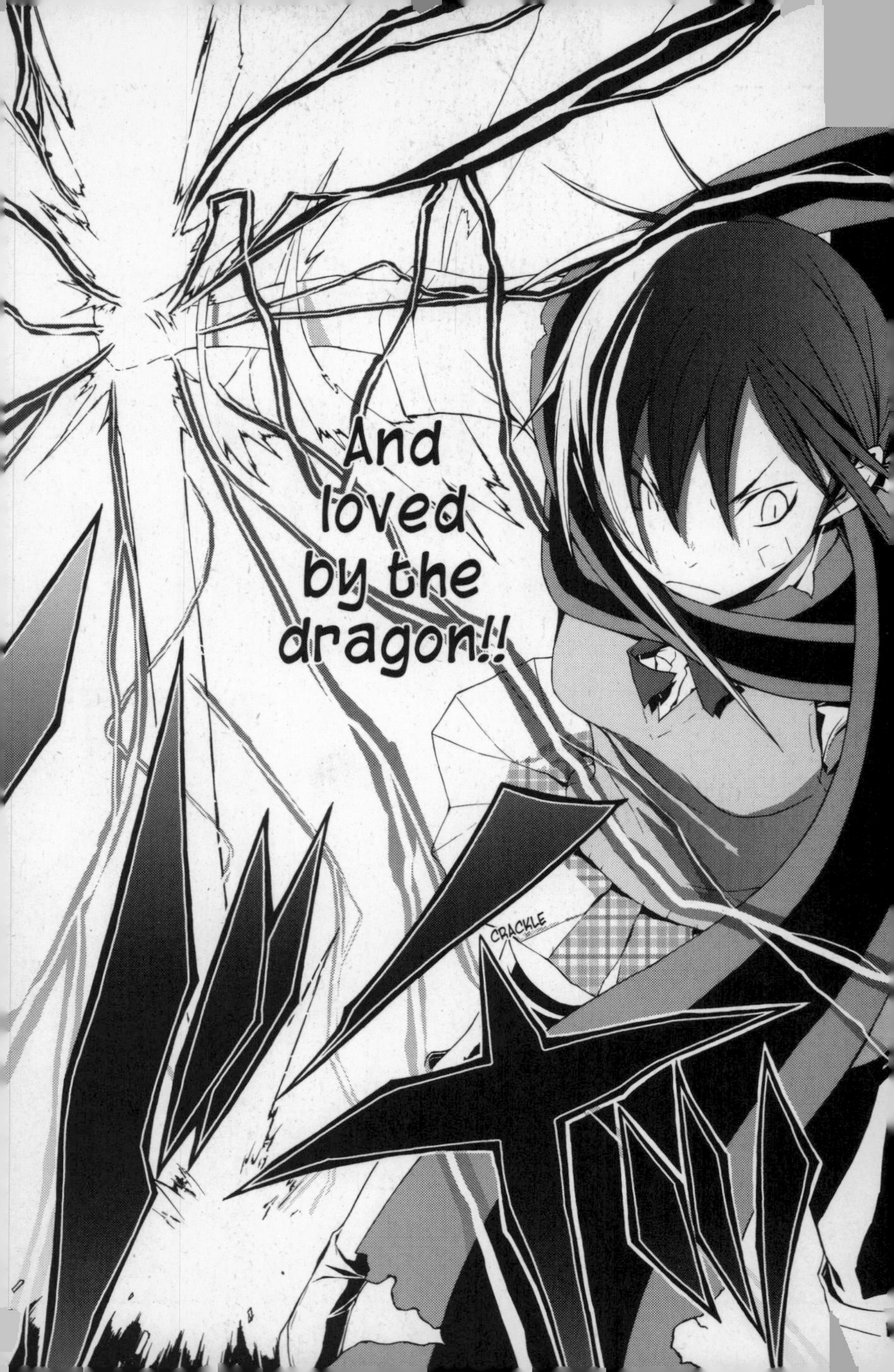
And loved by the dragon!!
CRACKLE

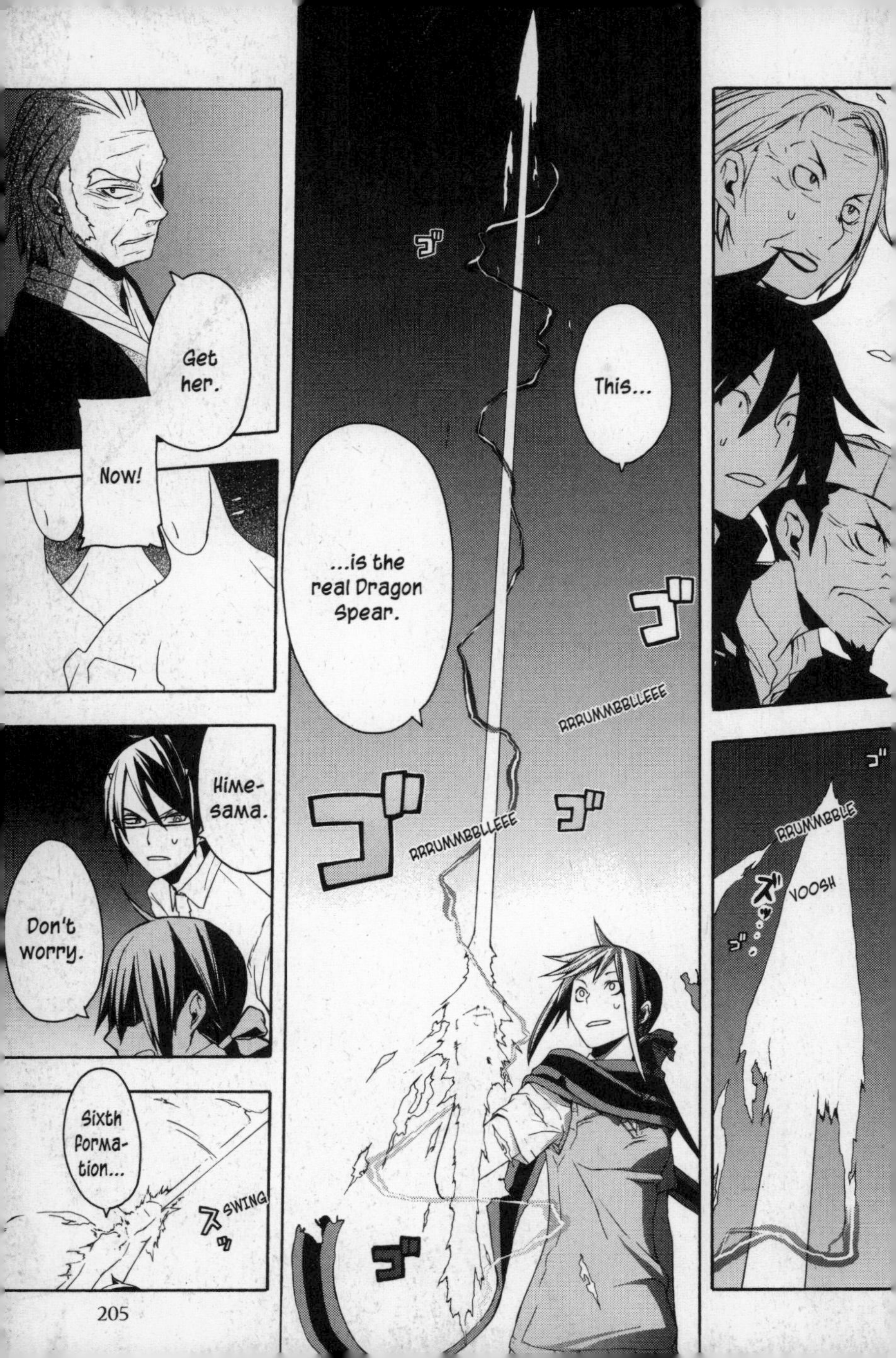
RRUMMBBLE
VOOSH
This...
...is the real Dragon Spear.
RRRUMMBBLLEEE
RRRUMMBBLLEEE
Get her.
Now!
Hime-sama.
Don't worry.
Sixth forma-tion...
SWING

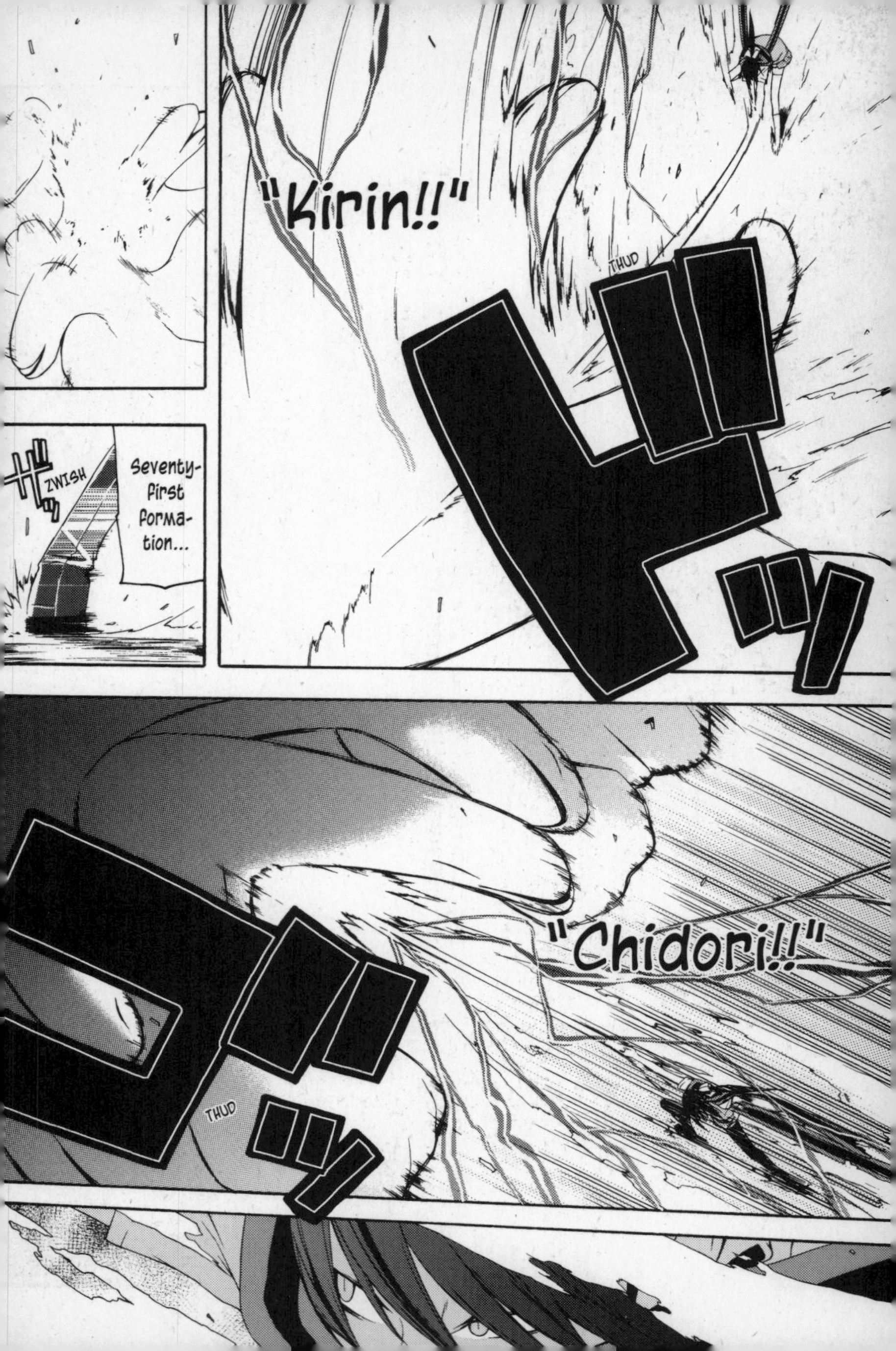
"Kirin!!"
THUD
Seventy-first formation...
ZWISH
"Chidori!!"
THUD

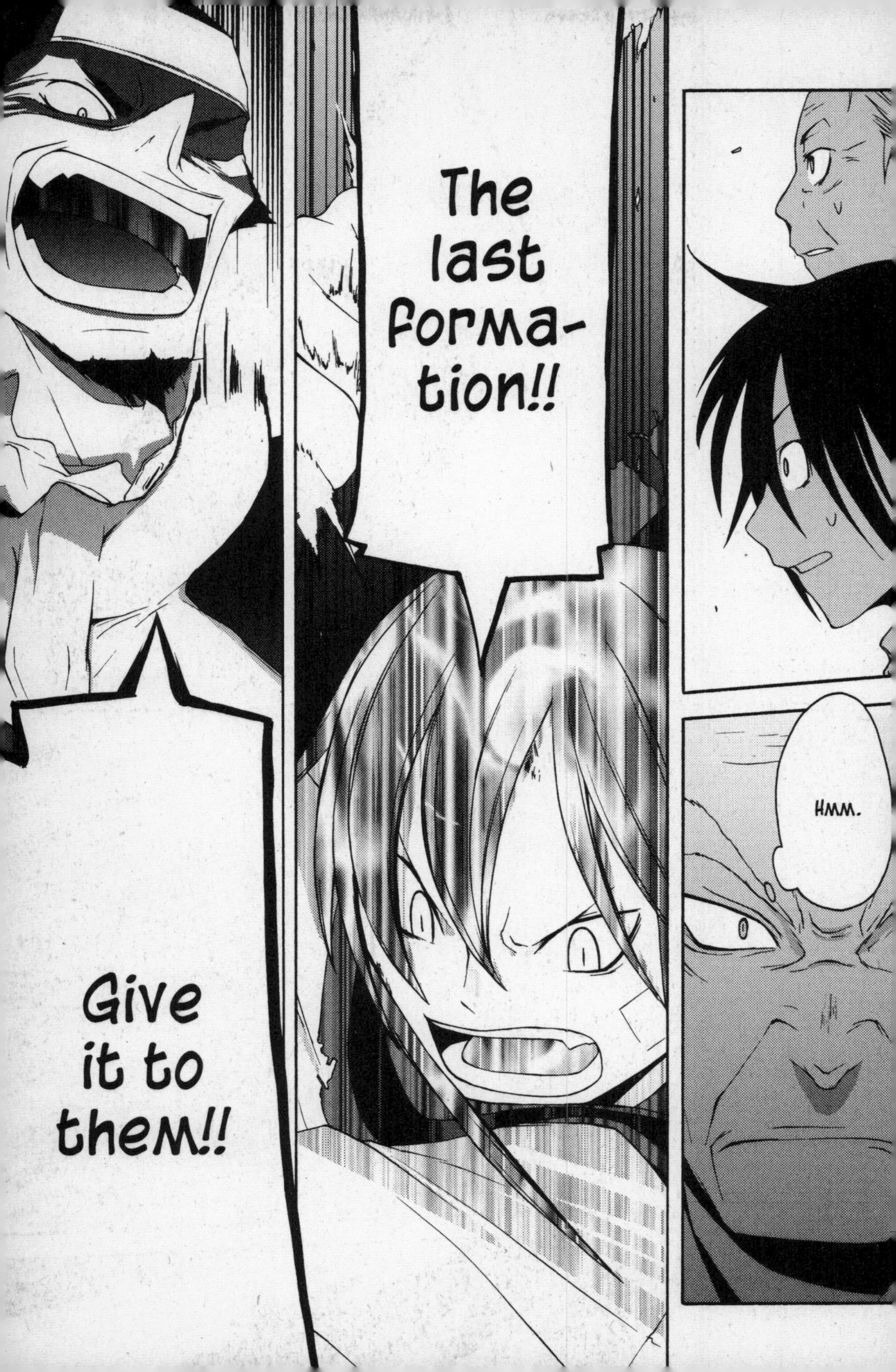
Hmm.
The last formation!!
Give it to them!!

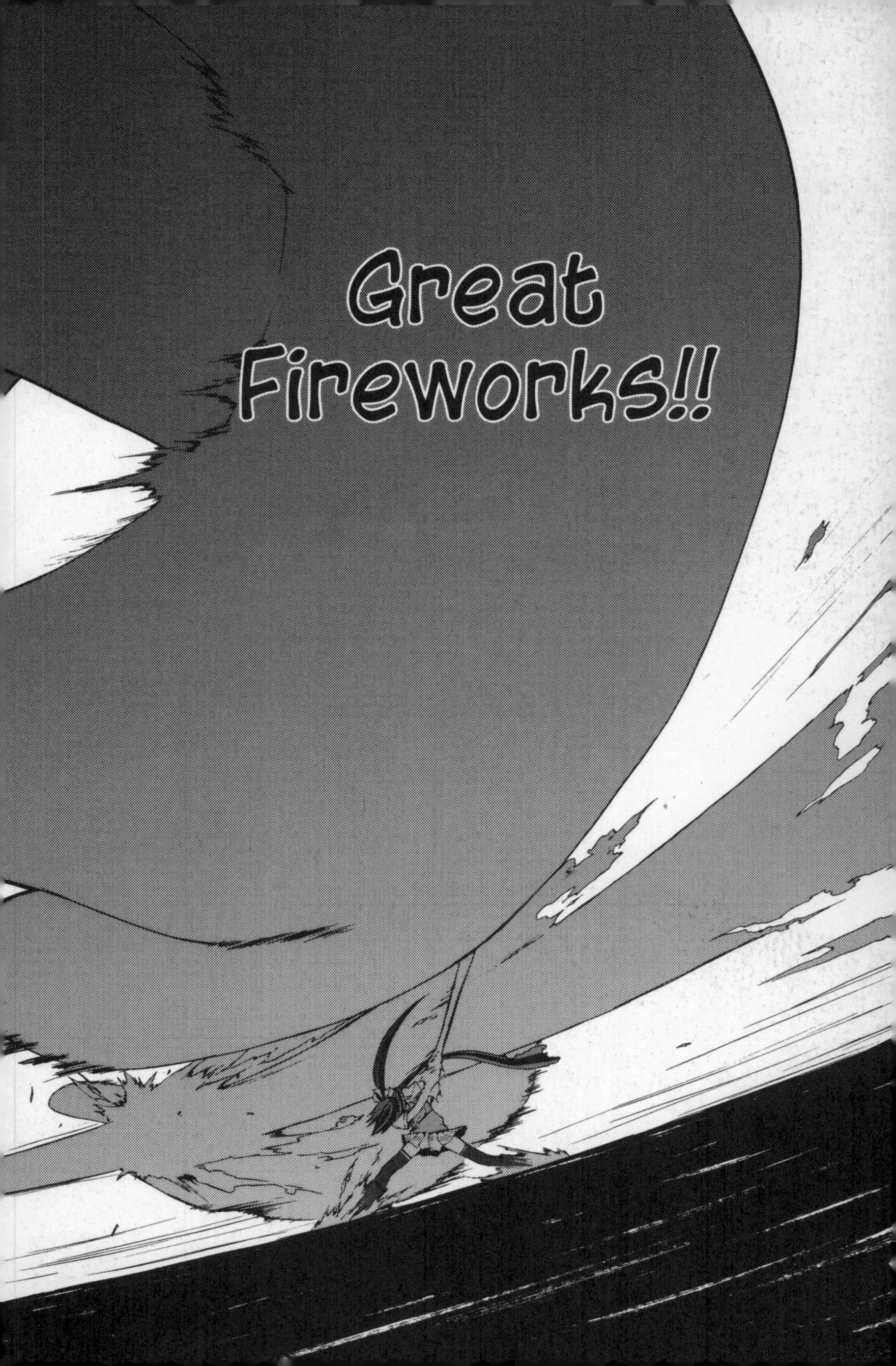
Great Fireworks!!

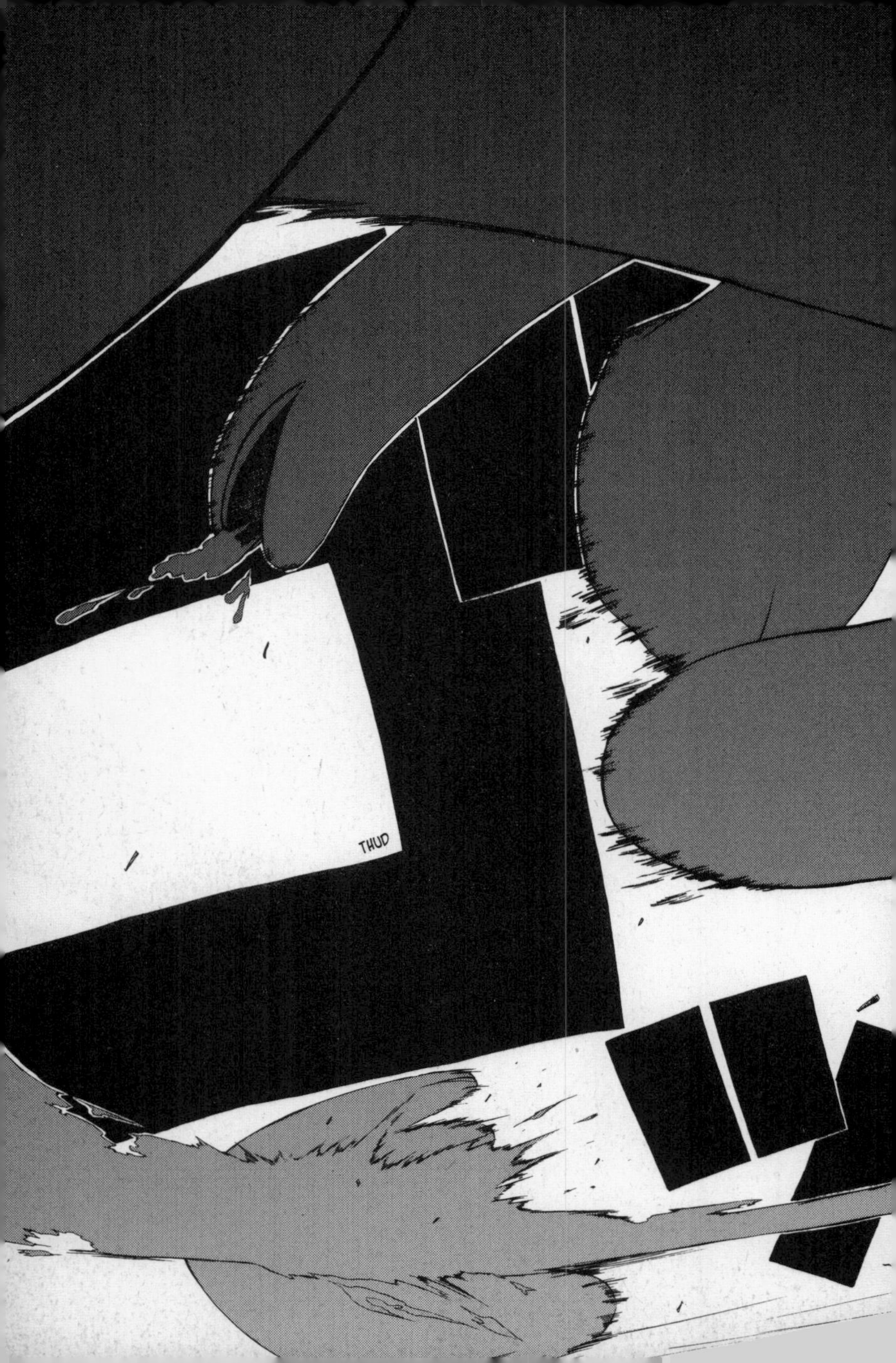
THUD

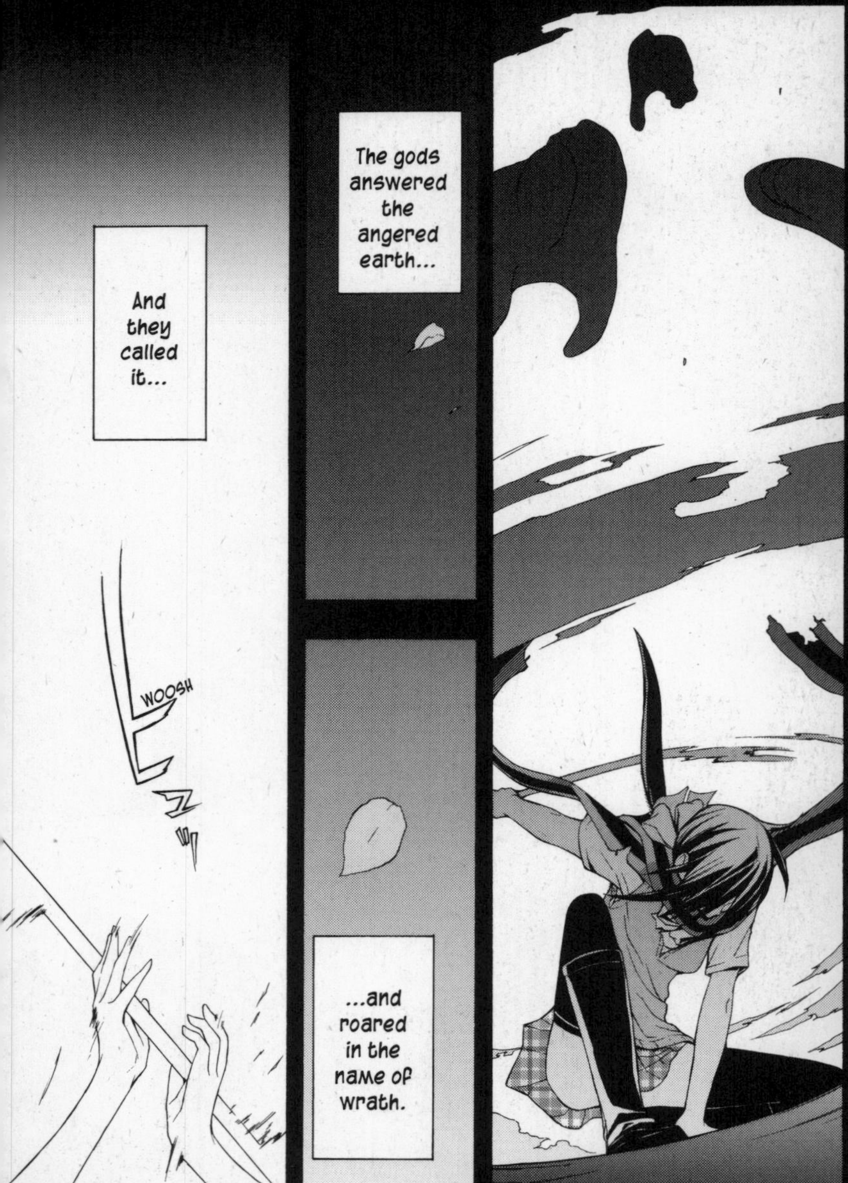
The gods answered the angered earth...
...and roared in the name of wrath.
And they called it...
WOOSH

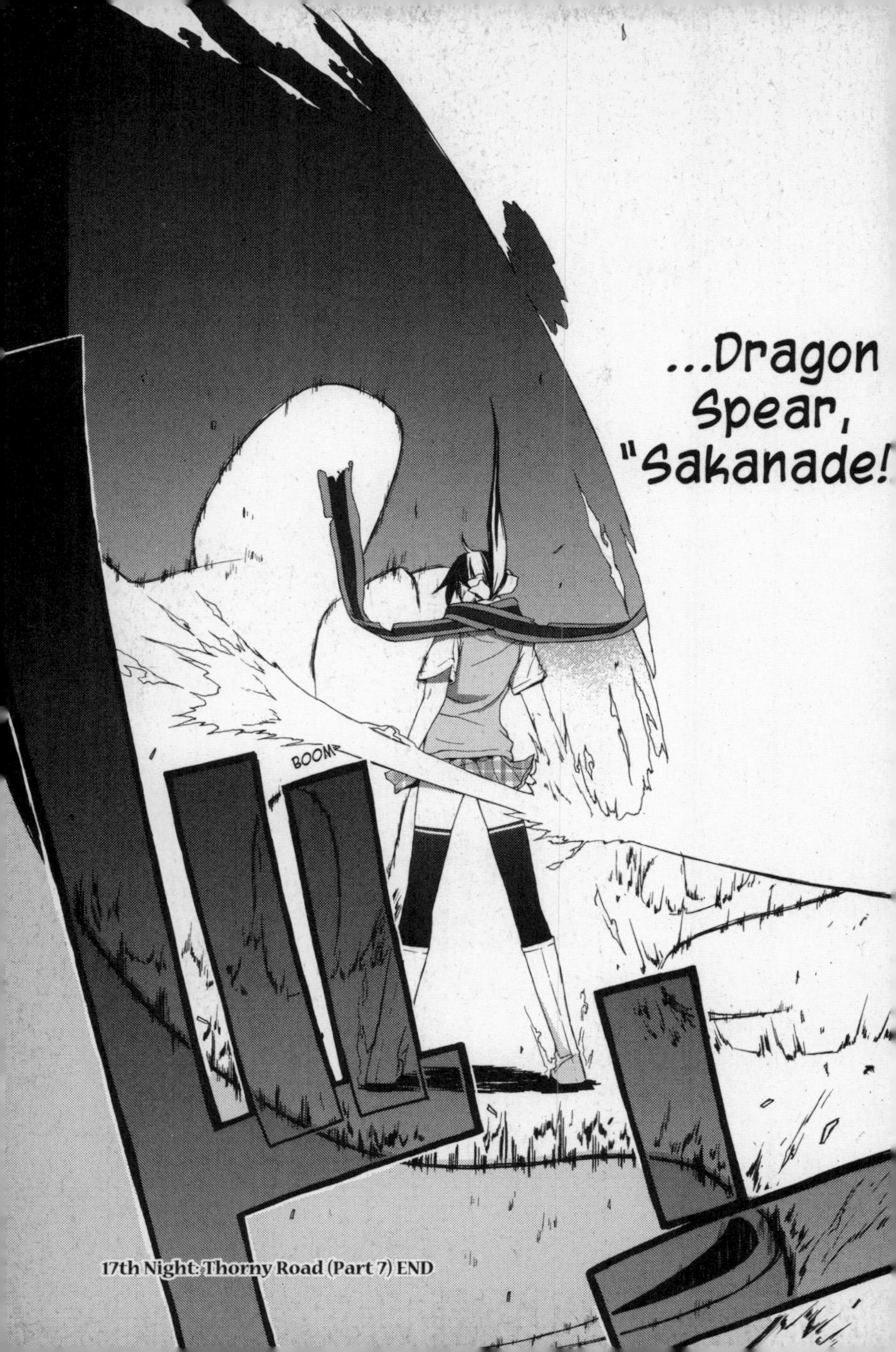
...Dragon Spear, "Sakanade!
BOOM

17th Night: Thorny Road (Part 7) END

Yozakura Quartet 3

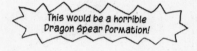

This would be a horrible Dragon Spear formation!
One hundred ninth formation... "Warai Meshi."
You don't even need the spear.

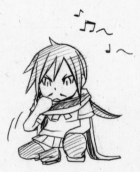

YozaQ!

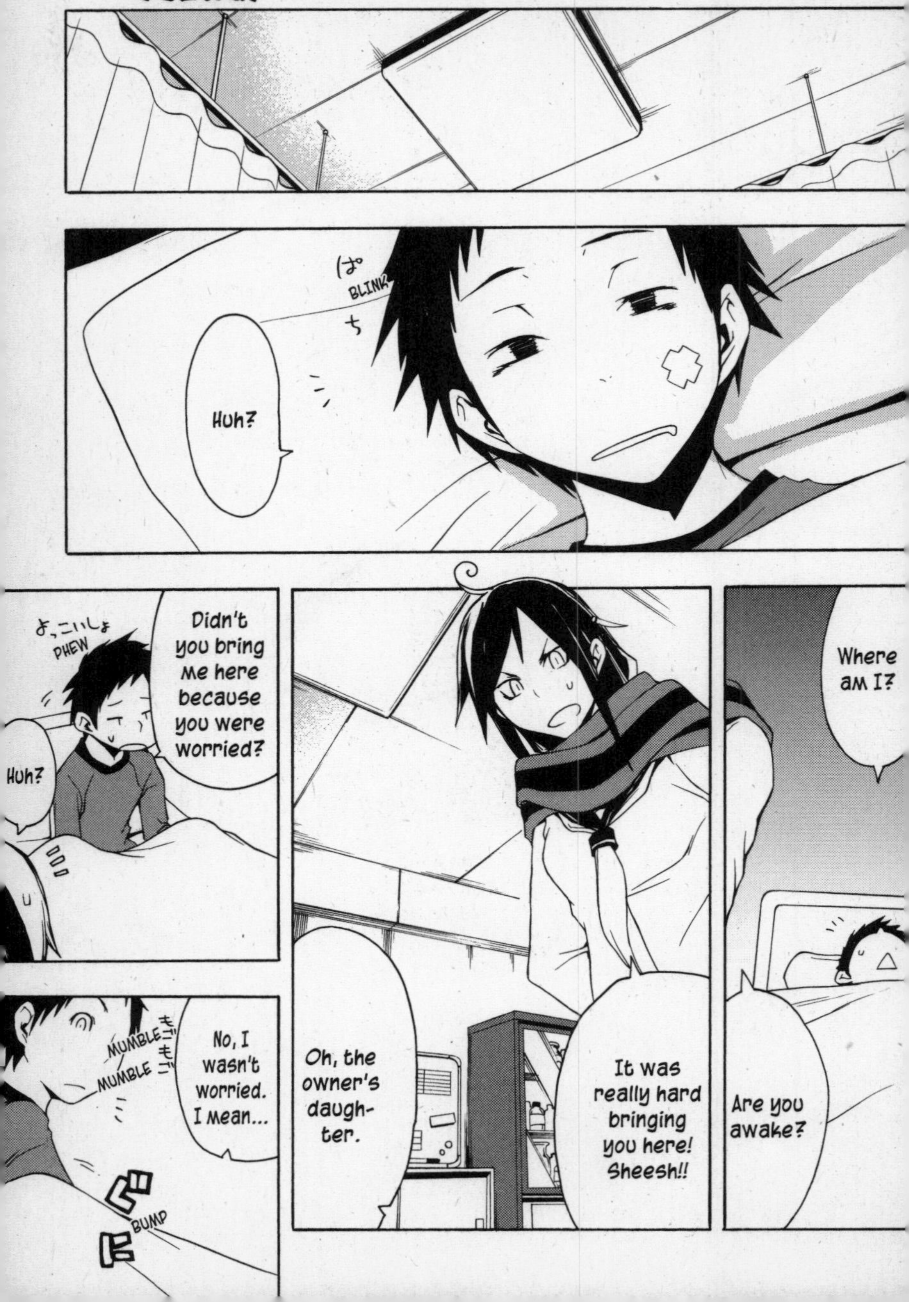
ぱち
BLINK
Huh?
Where am I?
Are you awake?
It was really hard bringing you here! Sheesh!!
Oh, the owner's daughter.
よっこいしょ
PHEW
Didn't you bring me here because you were worried?
Huh?
もごもご
MUMBLE MUMBLE
No, I wasn't worried. I mean...
BUMP

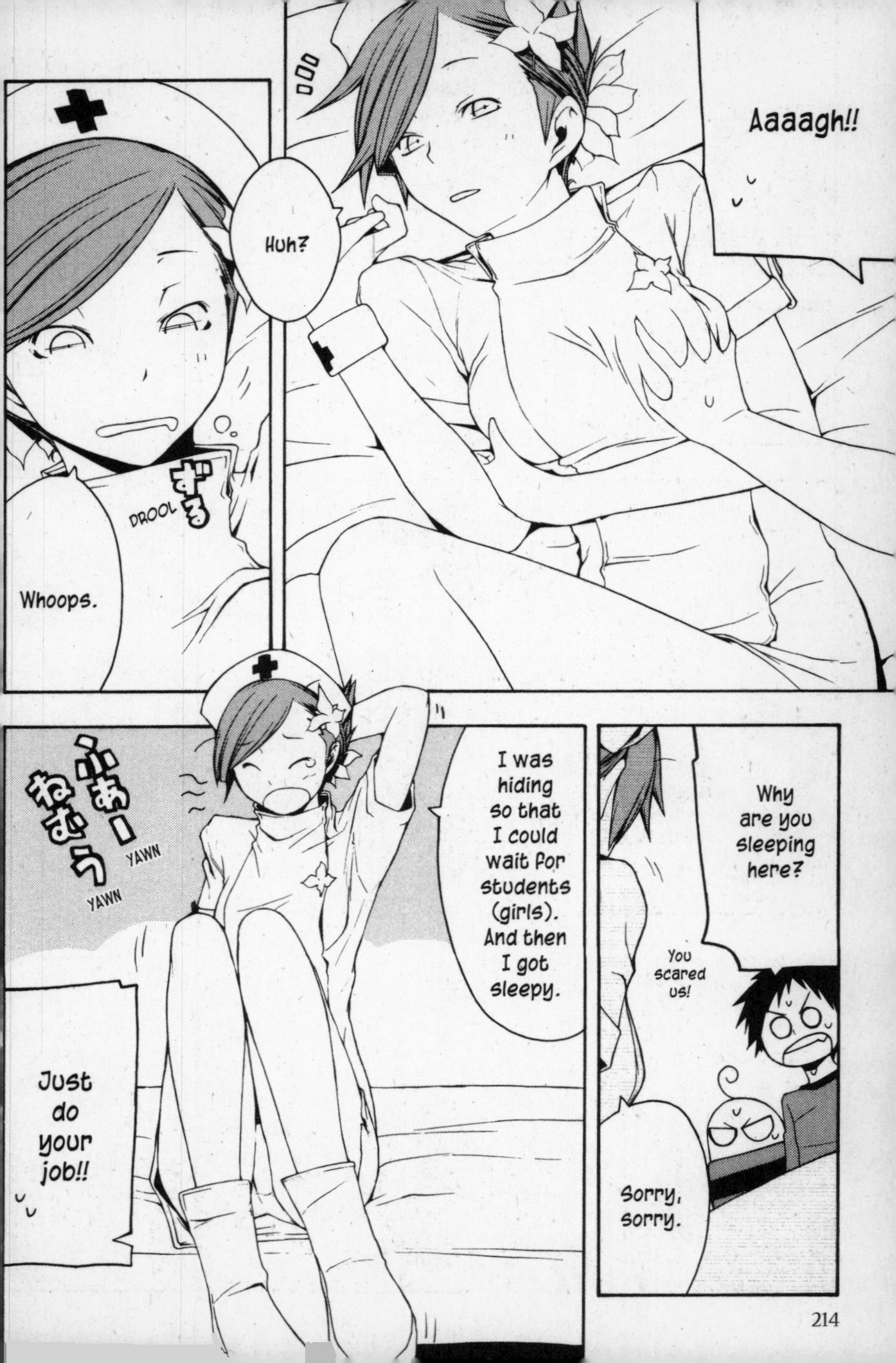
...
Aaaagh!!
Huh?
ずる
DROOL
Whoops.
Why are you sleeping here?
You scared us!
Sorry, sorry.
ふあー ねむう
YAWN
YAWN
I was hiding so that I could wait for students (girls). And then I got sleepy.
Just do your job!!

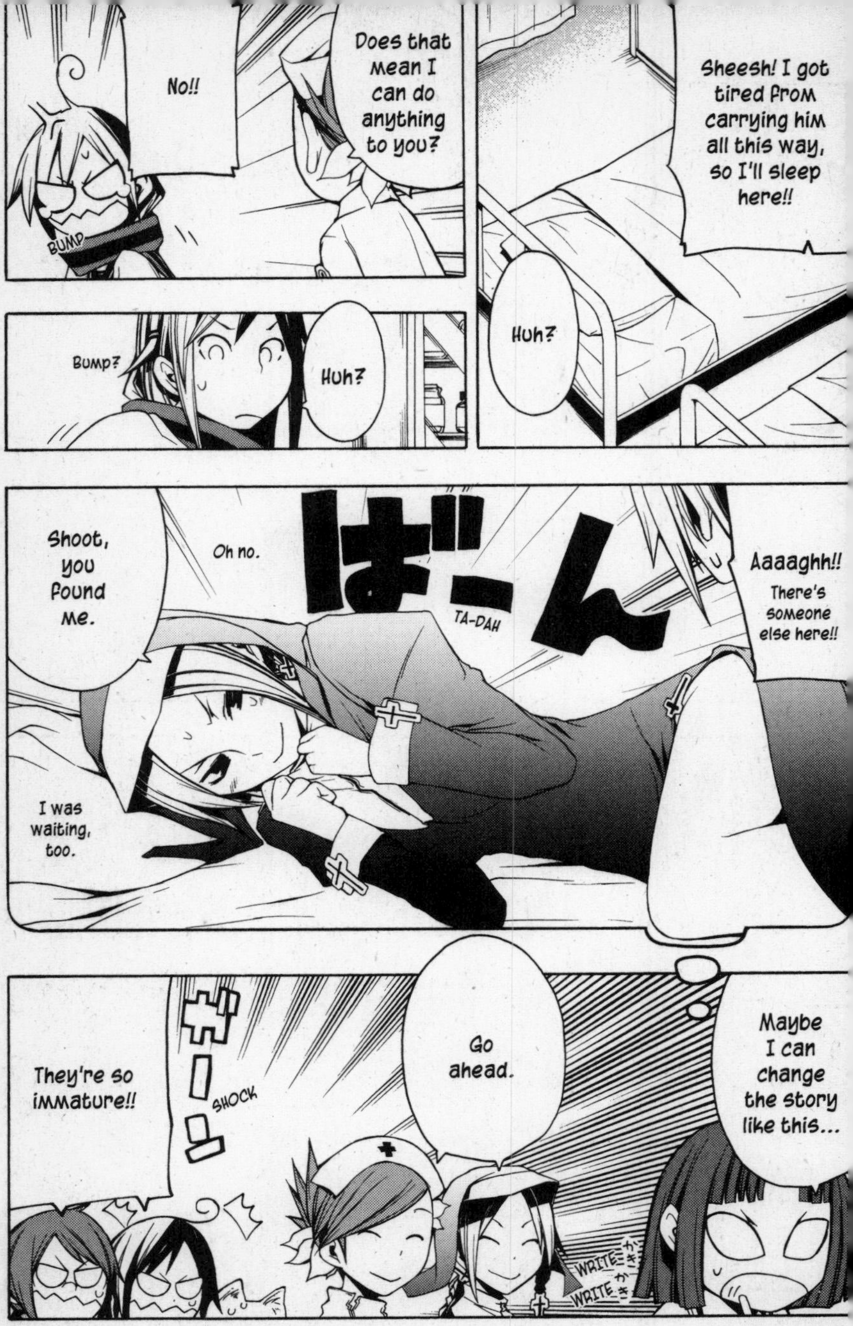
Sheesh! I got tired from carrying him all this way, so I'll sleep here!!
Huh?
Does that mean I can do anything to you?
No!!
BUMP
Huh?
Bump?
Aaaaghh!!
There's someone else here!!
ばーん
TA-DAH
Oh no.
Shoot, you found me.
I was waiting, too.
Maybe I can change the story like this...
WRITE かき
WRITE かき
Go ahead.
ガーン
SHOCK
They're so immature!!

Yozakura Quartet 3

1. Put hands in pocket.

Shortcut "micro-phone."

DING DONG

2. Use kotodama.

TA-DAH

3. Pull out the item with sound effects.

I was thinking of calling it "Fourth dimension kotodama."

Don't think so.

Cool!

First appearance: July 2007 Monthly Sirius
2nd Anniversary Celebration Bonus!
The title of this was "Roach."

Bonus Manga

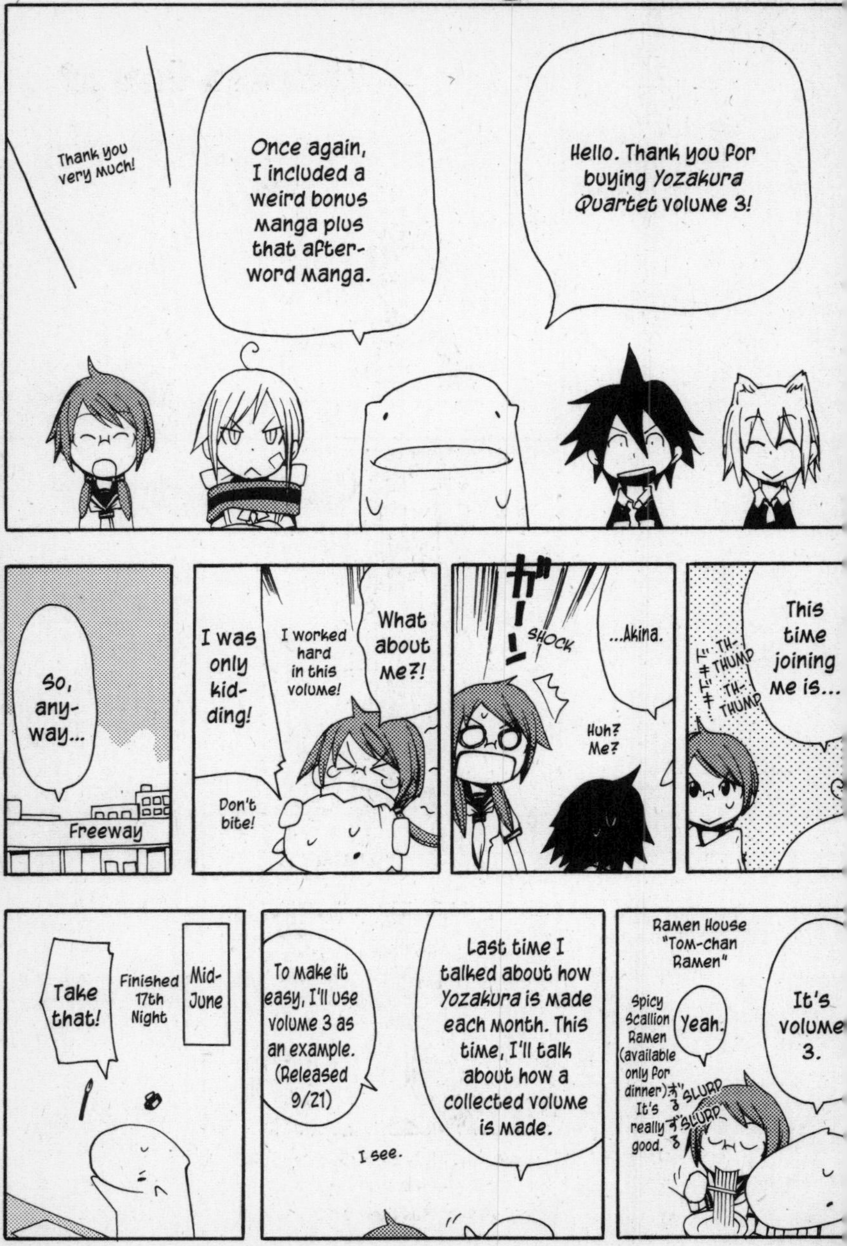
Hello. Thank you for buying Yozakura Quartet volume 3!
Once again, I included a weird bonus manga plus that afterword manga.
Thank you very much!
This time joining me is...
TH-THUMP TH-THUMP
...Akina.
SHOCK
Huh? Me?
What about me?!
I worked hard in this volume!
I was only kidding!
Don't bite!
So, anyway...
Freeway
Ramen House "Tom-chan Ramen"
It's volume 3.
Yeah.
Spicy Scallion Ramen (available only for dinner) It's really good.
SLURP SLURP
Last time I talked about how Yozakura is made each month. This time, I'll talk about how a collected volume is made.
To make it easy, I'll use volume 3 as an example. (Released 9/21)
I see.
Mid-June
Finished 17th Night
Take that!

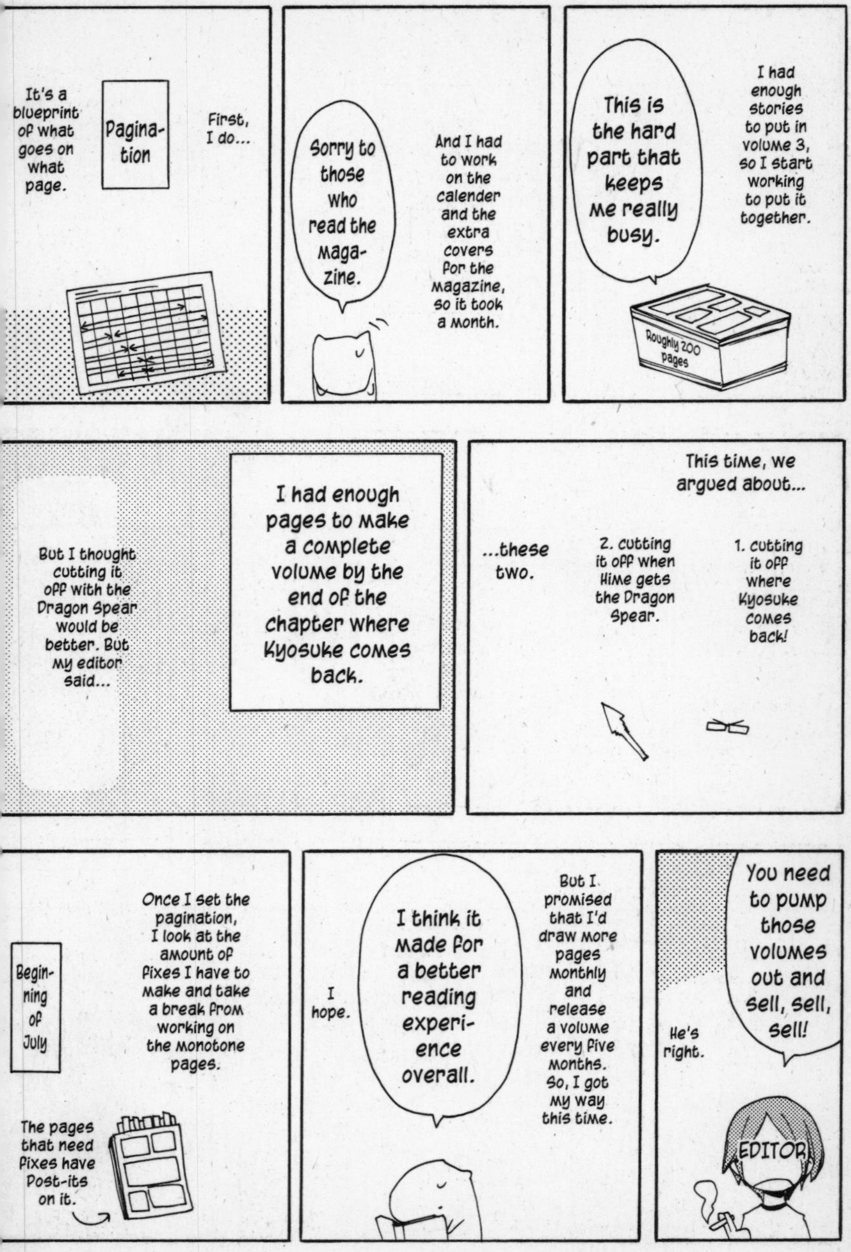
I had enough stories to put in volume 3, so I start working to put it together.
This is the hard part that keeps me really busy.
Roughly 200 pages
And I had to work on the calender and the extra covers for the magazine, so it took a month.
Sorry to those who read the maga-zine.
First, I do...
Pagina-tion
It's a blueprint of what goes on what page.
This time, we argued about...
1. cutting it off where Kyosuke comes back!
2. cutting it off when Hime gets the Dragon Spear.
...these two.
I had enough pages to make a complete volume by the end of the chapter where Kyosuke comes back.
But I thought cutting it off with the Dragon Spear would be better. But my editor said...
You need to pump those volumes out and sell, sell, sell!
He's right.
EDITOR
But I promised that I'd draw more pages monthly and release a volume every five months. So, I got my way this time.
I think it made for a better reading experience overall.
I hope.
Once I set the pagination, I look at the amount of fixes I have to make and take a break from working on the monotone pages.
Beginning of July
The pages that need fixes have Post-its on it.

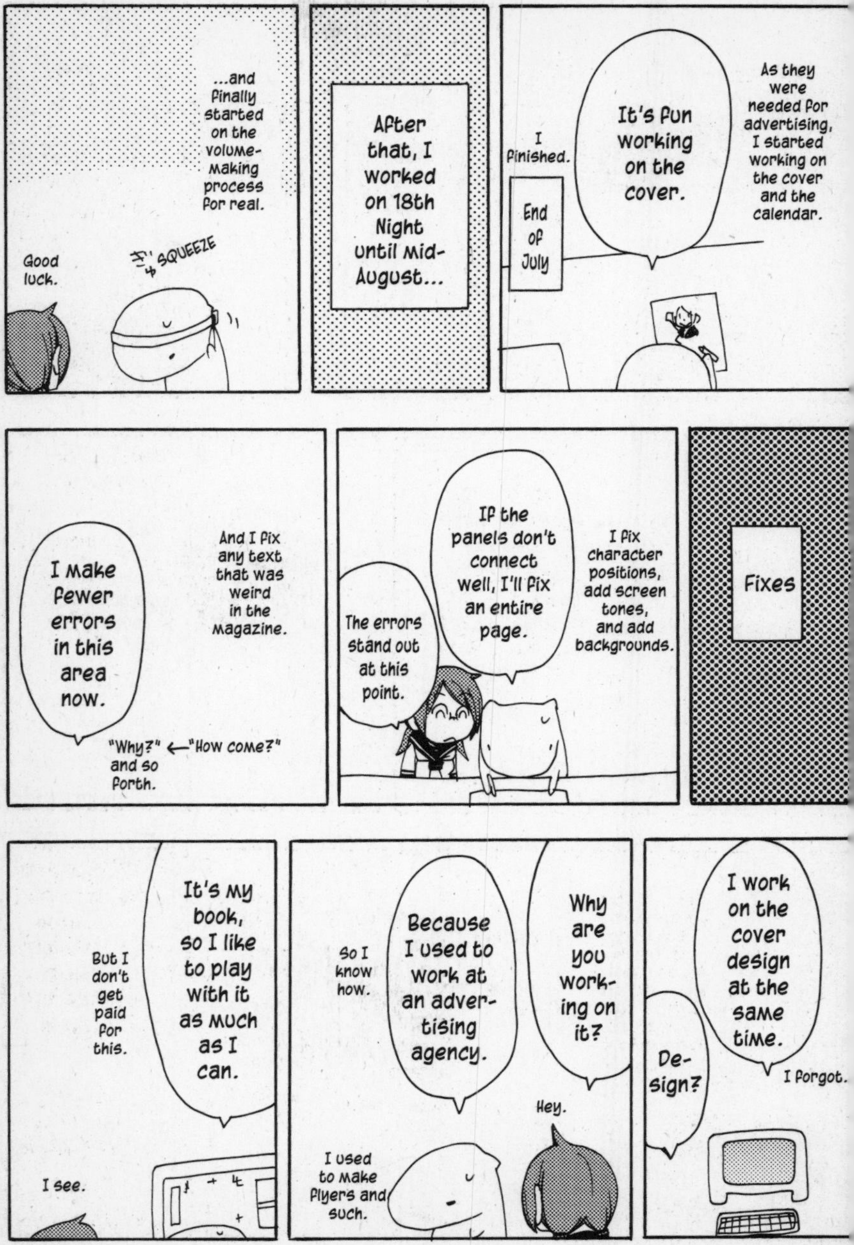
As they were needed for advertising, I started working on the cover and the calendar.
It's fun working on the cover.
I finished.
End of July
After that, I worked on 18th Night until mid-August...
...and finally started on the volume-making process for real.
SQUEEZE
Good luck.
Fixes
I fix character positions, add screen tones, and add backgrounds.
If the panels don't connect well, I'll fix an entire page.
The errors stand out at this point.
And I fix any text that was weird in the magazine.
I make fewer errors in this area now.
"Why?" ←"How come?" and so forth.
I work on the cover design at the same time.
I forgot.
De-sign?
Why are you work-ing on it?
Hey.
Because I used to work at an adver-tising agency.
So I know how.
I used to make flyers and such.
It's my book, so I like to play with it as much as I can.
But I don't get paid for this.
I see.

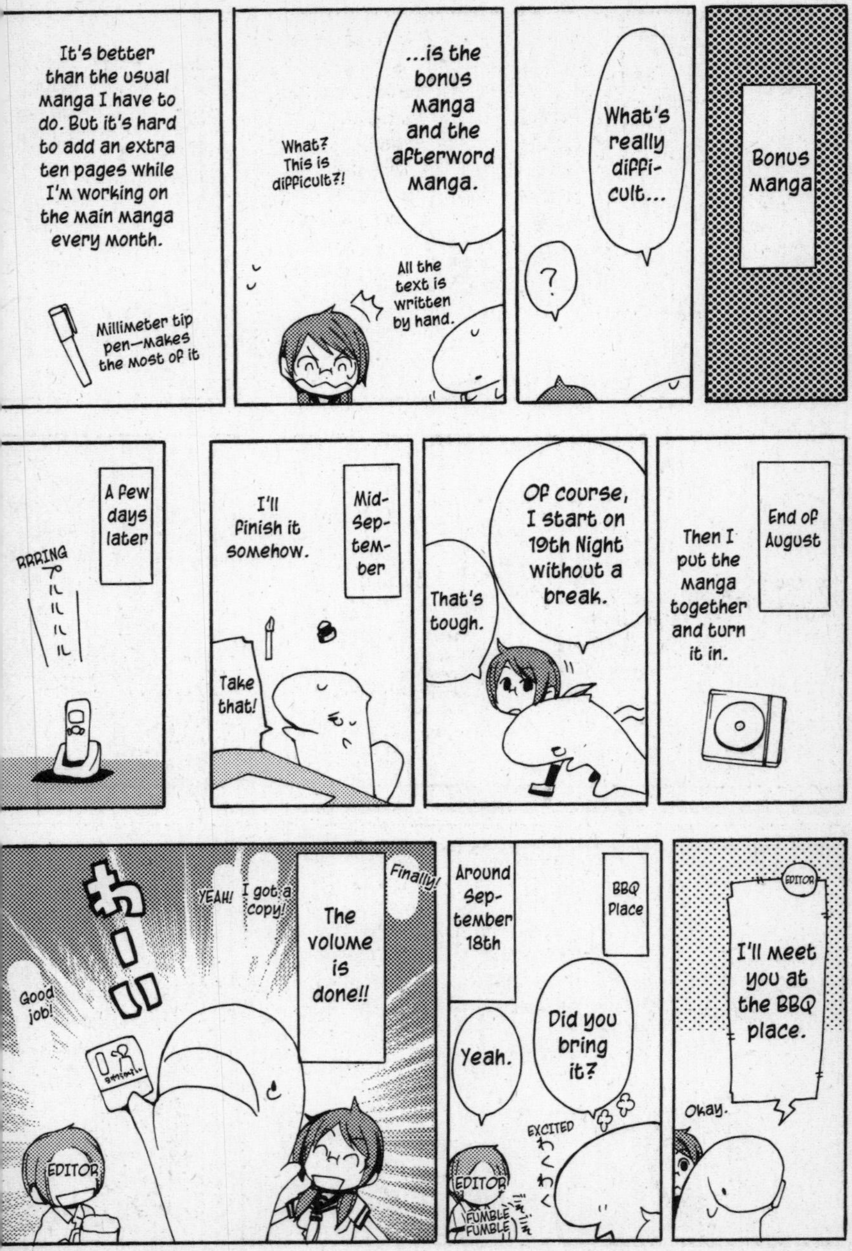

Bonus Manga
What's really diffi-cult...
?
...is the bonus manga and the afterword manga.
What? This is difficult?!
All the text is written by hand.
It's better than the usual manga I have to do. But it's hard to add an extra ten pages while I'm working on the main manga every month.
Millimeter tip pen—makes the most of it
End of August
Then I put the manga together and turn it in.
Of course, I start on 19th Night without a break.
That's tough.
Mid-September
I'll finish it somehow.
Take that!
A few days later
RRRING
EDITOR
I'll meet you at the BBQ place.
Okay.
Around September 18th
BBQ Place
Did you bring it?
Yeah.
EXCITED
わくわく
EDITOR
FUMBLE FUMBLE
The volume is done!!
Finally!
I got a copy!
YEAH!
Good job!
EDITOR

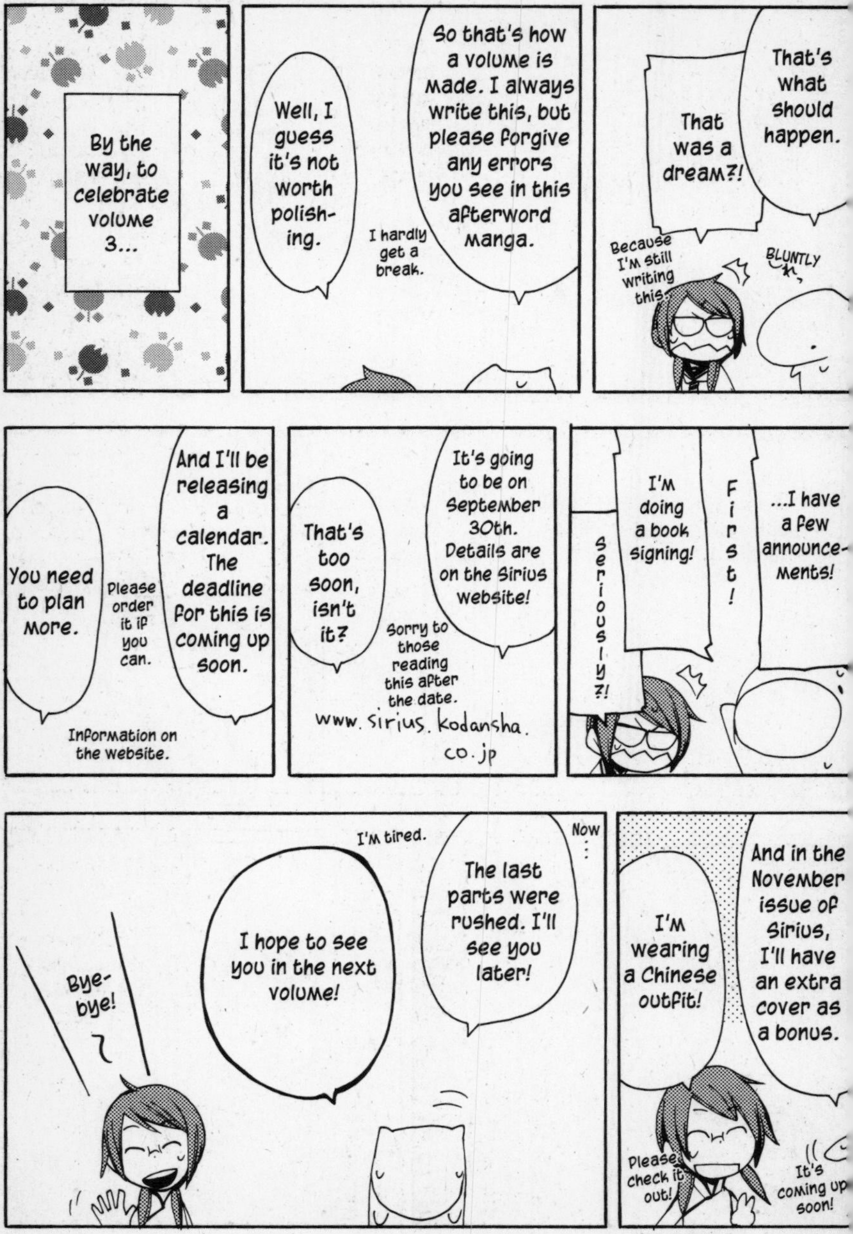
That's what should happen.
That was a dream?!
Because I'm still writing this.
BLUNTLY
So that's how a volume is made. I always write this, but please forgive any errors you see in this afterword manga.
Well, I guess it's not worth polishing.
I hardly get a break.
By the way, to celebrate volume 3...
...I have a few announcements!
First!
I'm doing a book signing!
Seriously?!
It's going to be on September 30th. Details are on the Sirius website!
That's too soon, isn't it?
Sorry to those reading this after the date.
www.sirius.kodansha.co.jp
And I'll be releasing a calendar. The deadline for this is coming up soon.
Please order it if you can.
You need to plan more.
Information on the website.
And in the November issue of Sirius, I'll have an extra cover as a bonus.
I'm wearing a Chinese outfit!
It's coming up soon!
Please check it out!
She changed!
Now...
The last parts were rushed. I'll see you later!
I'm tired.
I hope to see you in the next volume!
Bye-bye!

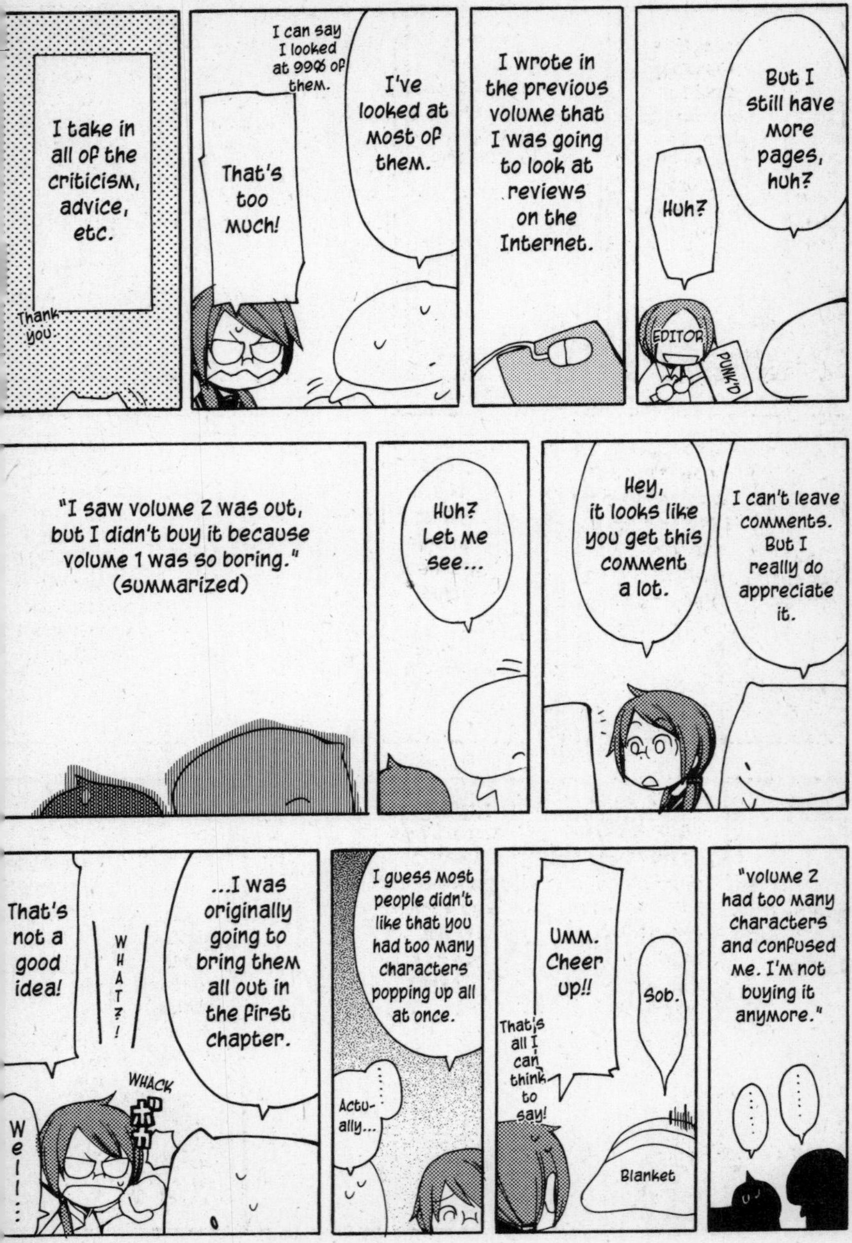

But I still have more pages, huh?
Huh?
EDITOR
PUNK'D
I wrote in the previous volume that I was going to look at reviews on the Internet.
I've looked at most of them.
I can say I looked at 99% of them.
That's too much!
I take in all of the criticism, advice, etc.
Thank you.
I can't leave comments. But I really do appreciate it.
Hey, it looks like you get this comment a lot.
Huh? Let me see...
"I saw volume 2 was out, but I didn't buy it because volume 1 was so boring." (summarized)
"volume 2 had too many characters and confused me. I'm not buying it anymore."
......
......
Sob.
Umm. Cheer up!!
That's all I can think to say!
Blanket
I guess most people didn't like that you had too many characters popping up all at once.
......
Actu-ally...
...I was originally going to bring them all out in the first chapter.
WHAT?!
That's not a good idea!
WHACK
Well...

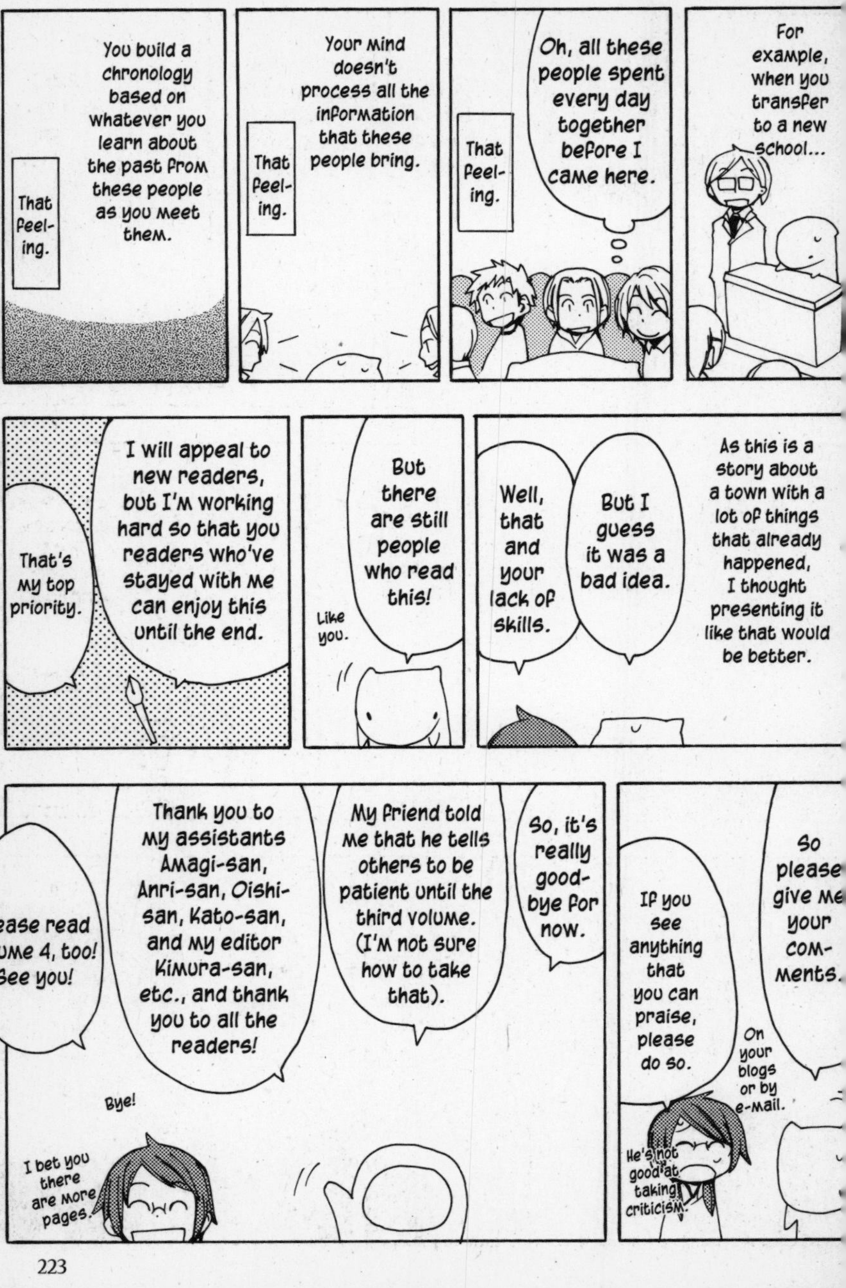
For example, when you transfer to a new school...
Oh, all these people spent every day together before I came here.
That feeling.
Your mind doesn't process all the information that these people bring.
That feeling.
You build a chronology based on whatever you learn about the past from these people as you meet them.
That feeling.
As this is a story about a town with a lot of things that already happened, I thought presenting it like that would be better.
But I guess it was a bad idea.
Well, that and your lack of skills.
But there are still people who read this!
Like you.
I will appeal to new readers, but I'm working hard so that you readers who've stayed with me can enjoy this until the end.
That's my top priority.
So please give me your comments.
If you see anything that you can praise, please do so.
On your blogs or by e-mail.
He's not good at taking criticism.
So, it's really good-bye for now.
My friend told me that he tells others to be patient until the third volume. (I'm not sure how to take that).
Thank you to my assistants Amagi-san, Anri-san, Oishi-san, Kato-san, and my editor Kimura-san, etc., and thank you to all the readers!
Please read volume 4, too! See you!
Bye!
I bet you there are more pages.

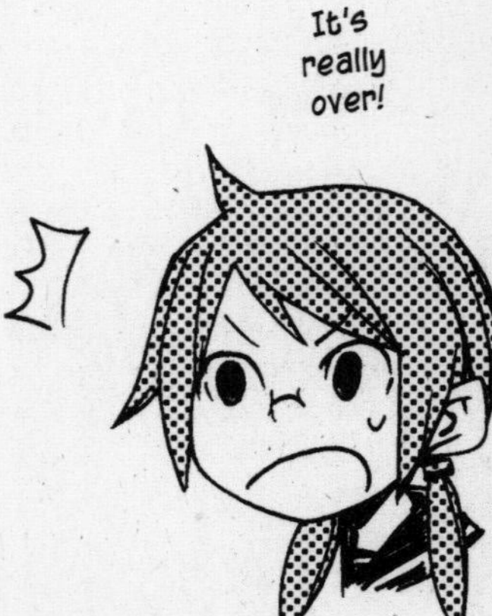
It's really over!

About the Author

Suzuhito Yasuda's cute and colorful character designs, sharp linework, and unique design talents have made him a popular artist in the fields of both manga and novel illustration. He has illustrated such Japanese novels as *Kamisama Kazoku*, *Scarlet Sword*, and *Maid Machinegun*. He has also worked on the manga series *Pinky:Comic* and *Ebony & Ivory*; *Yozakura Quartet* is his latest work.

His Preferred Tools:
PowerMAC G4 933Mhz
Apple studio display 17 TFT

PowerMAC G4 Cube
Apple Studio Display 17 CRT

Sony VAIO Notebook PCG542B

Translation Notes

Japanese is a tricky language for most Westerners, and translation is often more an art than a science. For your edification and reading pleasure, here are notes on some of the places where we could have gone in a different direction, or where a Japanese cultural reference is used.

Sakura

Sakura is the Japanese term for cherry blossoms. *Yozakura* in the title refers to *sakura* at night, or viewing *sakura* at night.

Kirin, page 36

Kirin is a comedic duo featuring Akira Kawashima and Hiroshi Tamura. Although their first impressions of each other weren't great, they eventually became good friends and formed their group.

Uchi-P, page 36

Uchi-P is an abbreviated term for *Uchimura Produce*, a TV show featuring comedians doing comedy sketches.

Azu-chan, page 36

Azu-chan is a gravure idol (a Japanese model who primarily poses in bikinis and other provocative clothing for magazine spreads). Her real name is Azusa Yamamoto, but she is known as Azu-chan.

Akiyuki Nosaka, page 66

Akiyuki Nosaka is a Japanese novelist, singer, and politician. He is a former member of the Diet. He also wrote the novel *The Grave of the Fireflies*, a story about a brother and sister trying to survive the war on their own.

Nasu Nakanishi, page 66

Nasu Nakanishi is a comedic duo comprised of Shigeki Nakanishi and Akiyuki Nasu. They are cousins.

Tet-chan, page 66

Tet-chan refers to Tetsuro Degawa, a Japanese comedian and actor. He is known more as a comedian but likes to call himself a "comedic actor." He has a husky voice that is very distinctive.

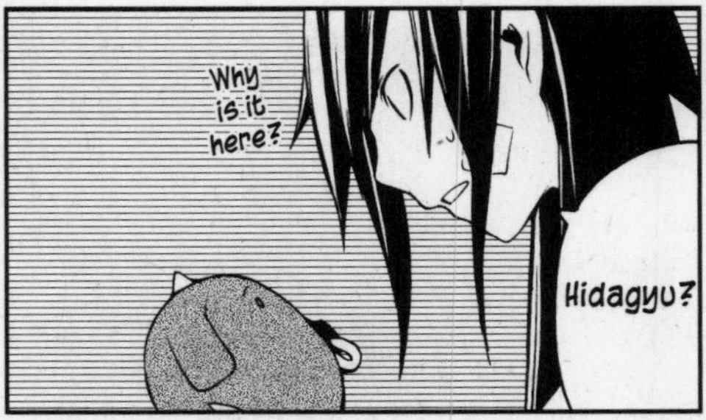
Hidagyu?
Why is it here?

Hidagyu, page 83

Hidagyu is clearly a fictional character in the world of *Yozakura Quartet*. The name Hidagyu refers to Japanese beef from cattle raised in Hida, a city in the Gifu prefecture. It's fatty and known to be expensive.

Kazuyoshi Nakamura, page 102

Kazuyoshi Nakamura is a musician. Originally inspired by Vincent van Gogh and Marc Chagall, he was pursuing a career in art until he turned fifteen years old. After that, he switched to music to express himself. His works didn't catch on right away, and he had been considering suicide if he didn't succeed.

Dayan, page 102

Dayan is a comedic duo featuring Yusuke Nishizawa and Atsuhiro Tsuda. They were classmates in junior high school. Their group name comes from their foreign English teacher.

Parachute Troop, page 102

Pepe Yano and Yuu Saito comprise the comedic duo Parachute Troop. Their participation in Uchi-P made them popular.

Kamaitachi, page 134

Kamaitachi is a comedic duo featuring Kenji Yamauchi and Ryuichi Hamaie. In their shorter routines, they would end each joke with Yamauchi hitting a gong.

Sekiya, page 134

Sekiya refers to Tsukasa Sekiya, one of the assistant directors on the show.

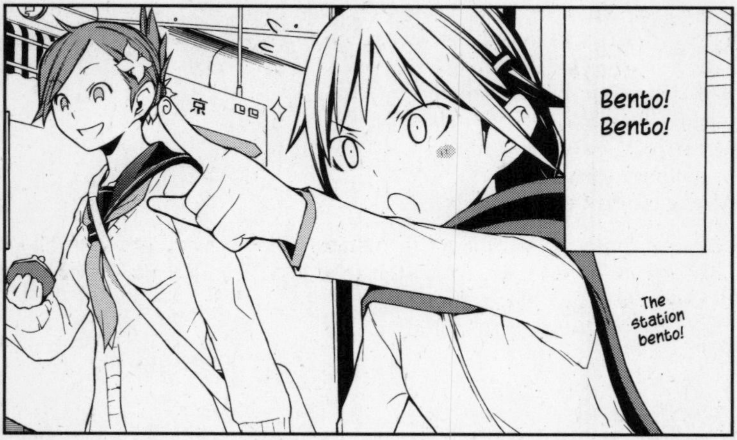
Bento!
Bento!
The station bento!

Bento, page 141

Bento means a boxed lunch. Part of the fun of riding a bullet train is eating a station *bento*. There are many kinds of *bento*, and some are available only in specific regions. You can buy them on the train (either in a specific car or a vendor will come by and sell them to you), but there's more variety at the station.

Sangen-jaya, page 153

Sangen-jaya is a town in Tokyo's Setagaya district. It's a popular place to live because of its convenient location.

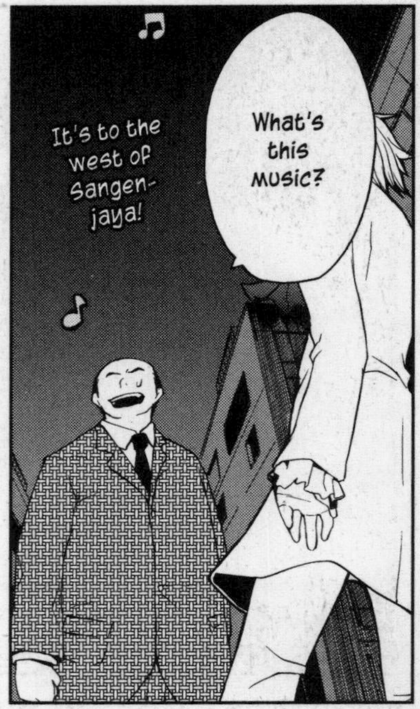
What's this music?
It's to the west of Sangen-jaya!

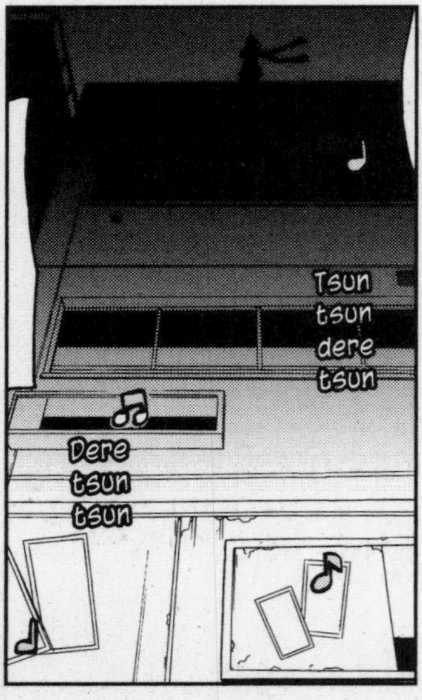
Tsun tsun dere tsun
Dere tsun tsun

***Tsundere*, page 153**

Hime is playing the town song "Tsundere," which she was teaching to the kids in volume 1. *Tsundere* is a term for a specific character trait, describing a person who is standoffish or aloof but can become loveable and adorable in different situations. This term first started in Japanese dating simulation games, then moved on to anime and manga, but is now widely used in mass media.

...Dragon Spear, "Sakanade!!"

Dragon Spear Formations, page 211

The Dragon Spear Formations introduced in this volume are mostly names of comedic duos introduced in the previous volumes. In *Warai Meshi*, one of the comedians has a mustache similar to the one Hime is putting on.

Weird Text and "Why," page 219

The change depicted here is between two different choices of character usage, both of which translate to "why." As this would not carry over in English, the closest comparison is between "how come" and "why." They have similar definitions and can be used interchangeably, but sometimes one sounds awkward and weird.

Papillon

BY MIWA UEDA

BUTTERFLY, SPREAD YOUR WINGS!

Ageha is a shy tomboy, but her twin sister Hana is the ultimate ultra-glam teen queen. Hana loves being the center of attention so much that she'll do anything to keep Ageha in her shadow. But Ageha has a plan that will change her life forever and no one, not even Hana, can hold her back. . . .

• From the creator of *Peach Girl*

Special extras in each volume! Read them all!

Psycho Busters

MANGA BY AKINARI NAO
STORY BY YUYA AOKI

PSYCHIC TEENS ON THE RUN!

Out of the blue, a beautiful girl asks Kakeru to run away with her. This could be any boy's dream come true, but there's something strange afoot.

It turns out that this girl is on the run from a shadowy government organization intent on using her psychic abilities for its own nefarious ends. But why does she need Kakeru's help? Could it be that he has secret powers, too?

• Story by Yuya Aoki, creator of *Get Backers*

Special extras in each volume! Read them all!

TOMARE!

止まれ

[STOP!]

FEB   2009

You're going the wrong way!

Manga is a completely different type of reading experience.

To start at the *beginning*, go to the *end*!

That's right! Authentic manga is read the traditional Japanese way—from right to left, exactly the *opposite* of how American books are read. It's easy to follow: Just go to the other end of the book, and read each page—and each panel—from right side to left side, starting at the top right. Now you're experiencing manga as it was meant to be!